WAR
IN HEAVEN
WAR
ON EARTH

*What Revelation Meant to the Original Readers
and what it Means for Us Today*

WAR
IN HEAVEN
WAR
ON EARTH

*What Revelation Meant to the Original Readers
and what it Means for Us Today*

BY BRADLEY S. COBB

Published in the United States of America by:
Cobb Publishing
704 E. Main St.
Charleston, AR 72933
www.CobbPublishing.com
CobbPublishing@gmail.com
479.747.8372

Paperback ISBN: 978-1-960858-27-6
Hardcover ISBN: 978-1-960858-29-0

A Prefatory Note

Revelation is a challenging book, both in reading and interpreting. It has been twisted to mean almost everything modern-day "scholars" or "pastors" want it to mean. But we aren't interested in them or their crazy interpretations. We are interested in what *the original readers* would have understood it to mean, because *it was written to them*. Their time, not ours. Their context, not ours.

Only when we find out what Revelation meant to the original readers can we make application of its lessons to ourselves.

You will find very few footnotes in this book. It's not a highfalutin "scholarly" treatise. I don't spend a lot of time quoting different commentaries and theologians. Why not? Because I'm more interested (and you should be too) in what God says than what man does.

This book is written for you, the person who wants to follow God, and who wants to get a better grasp on how the book of Revelation fits into all that. I have done my best to make this book easy to read and understand, but without dumbing it down (because regardless of what you might think, you aren't dumb).

I originally wrote this material several years ago as 48 sermons (they never asked me to do a sermon series again!), and had no plans to publish it at the time. But for the last 8 years, I have had requests from those who heard them, or who saw the outlines, or others (even some who disagree with me) who thought this material *needed* to be presented. So I spent the last year and a half revising, correcting, adding, clarifying, and completely reformatting it all to make it as useful as possible.

Thank you for taking the time to read it.

-Bradley S. Cobb
January 2022.

Special Thanks

To Jesse Cobb,
who patiently encouraged me during my 2,000 hours of work on
this material. I could not have done this without you. You are
amazing.

To Barbara Dowell, Linda Foshee, and Phyllis Campbell,
who all thought I was nuts when I started this series, but who with-
held judgment long enough to let me explain (and who decided I
wasn't so crazy after all).

To Alisa Beal,
who kindly asked me every six months since 2014 when my Revelation book would be ready. I hope the wait was worth it.

To Jimmie Beller,
who challenged me to rethink what I had always heard and believed about Revelation, with the words, "Are you sure about
that?" You were taken too soon.

To the church in Charleston, AR,
for the encouragement, questions, challenges, and patience as we
went over this material together. We love you all.
Even you, Grant.

CONTENTS

Study One:
An Introduction to the Views

The book of Revelation is a polarizing section of Scripture. It seems half the people with a Bible *only* talk about Revelation, and the other half avoids it completely! Some are certain they know *exactly* what it means, and others are certain *no one* can know what it means. If you were to take a survey of the religious world—even of just the church itself, you wouldn't even get agreement on the main idea of the book! If we can't even understand the main idea of the book, how can anyone expect to understand the details?

But here's the deal: we *can* know what the main idea of Revelation is. We *can* know which interpretations are wrong. We *can* know how the original readers would have understood it. After all, if *anyone* understood the book of Revelation, it was the original recipients (and we'll see that in a later lesson).

The main reason the book of Revelation is neglected is the crazy language and imagery—so different from what we're used to reading in the rest of the New Testament. *Beasts rising up from the sea, a dragon that waits to murder a newborn baby boy, locusts rising up out of a bottomless pit, a man on a white horse with a blood-splattered garment who is using his sword against his enemies.* This is just a sampling of the figures used in Revelation. That's very different from what we read in other New Testament books, with their focus on love, faith, obedience, and forgiveness.

Another reason Revelation gets neglected is the false and ridiculous interpretations promoted by the denominational world. Ask almost any denominational friend you have, and you are likely going to hear something about current events being foretold in Revelation ("The Coronavirus vaccine is the "Mark of the Beast!!!"). But people have been saying the same thing for years!!

I can't tell you how many world leaders in the past hundred years have been identified as "the antichrist" or "the beast"—and then those world leaders die, leaving modern-day guessers to find someone else to be their "antichrist."

With each passing generation, people are absolutely sure they—and they alone—understand the meaning of the book because of the events in their time. And with every passing generation, they are proven wrong.

With all this confusion, some think it presumptuous for anyone to claim "I know what the book of Revelation is talking about." Let me state from the outset, we can know—*without any doubt*—certain things about Revelation. But in order to do this, and in order to weed through all the junk and misinformation out there, we need to understand certain fundamental facts.

In this lesson, we will look at the main ways people interpret Revelation. We will also examine specific passages in this book that show the proper way to interpret it. And hopefully, by the end of this lesson, we will all be a little less leery of delving into this strange and wonderful section of the word of God!

THE FUTURIST METHOD

As the name suggests, the Futurist Method of interpreting the book of Revelation claims that most (if not all) of the book foretells something that has still not yet happened—still unfulfilled almost two thousand years after the book was written. Some believe *none* of the book of Revelation has been fulfilled. Others believe the letters to the seven churches in chapters 2 and 3 were written to actual first-century churches, but the rest of it is all future. And still others believe the seven letters refer to seven time periods (though there's disagreement on how that plays out), and the rest is still future to us.

To see just how much this method has pervaded our modern thinking, consider these:

The Battle of Armageddon.

Armageddon, as the phrase is generally used, denotes the absolute end of something. Usually, it's viewed as a battle at the end of time.

The Millennium, or the thousand-year reign.

Have you noticed that people tend to identify themselves religiously by their interpretation of one verse in Revelation? Pre-millennialists, post-millennialists, and a-millennialists? This idea is so ingrained that if you say something like, "There isn't going to be a thousand-year reign," their heads might just explode trying to comprehend the words.

Problems with the Futurist Method

First and foremost, in order to take this interpretation, you have to ignore the first and last chapters of the book.

> *Revelation 1:1—The Revelation of Jesus Christ...to show His servants **things which must shortly come to pass**.*

> *Revelation 1:3—Blessed is he that reads, and they that hear the words of this prophecy, and keep those things which are written therein, **for the time is at hand**.*

> *Revelation 22:6—...These sayings are faithful and true: and the Lord God of the holy prophets sent his angel to show to His servants the things **which must shortly be done**.*

> *Revelation 22:10—...Do not seal the sayings of the prophecy of this book: for **the time is at hand**.*

These statements are divinely-given evidence that the things written in Revelation would take place shortly after they were written. How shortly? We'll get into that in another lesson, but keep in mind that when Jesus said "repent, for the kingdom of heaven *is at hand"* (Matthew 4:17), the kingdom was a mere 3½ years away (Acts 2, Colossians 1:13, Revelation 1:9). The same word translated "shortly" (*tachos* in Greek) is translated "quickly" in Acts 22:18:

> *[I] saw him saying to me, "Make haste, and get* **quickly** *out of Jerusalem: for they will not receive your testimony concerning me."*

After reading that verse, what would you think is meant by that word? *Hundreds* of years? *Thousands* of years? No, you would, with plain common sense, know it is imminent and urgent!

Also, taking the everything-in-the-book-is-still-in-the-future position makes the book completely worthless to the first readers—and gives an impossible-to-obey command. What do I mean? Notice at the very beginning of the book, a blessing is pronounced on the ones who "*keep* [obey] those things which are written in it" (1:3). If none of it has happened yet, then it is impossible for any previous readers of Revelation to be blessed by reading it, since no one can *keep* the things written in the book yet.

The futurist view basically has John saying, "Things are about to happen…well, around 2,000 years or so from now, maybe…and if you read this book and keep the things written in it, you will be blessed… except you can't keep these things because you'll be dead and forgotten long before any of these things take place."

Taking this view makes our all-knowing God out to be a god of confusion. With each passing generation, the details in Revelation are given new applications to different countries and leaders, and with each generation, the applications are proven false over and over again.

Taking this view ignores that it was written to give instructions to real churches in the real first century. Jesus, in Revelation 2-3, spoke to real congregations about their real trials and troubles that they were enduring *back then!* Those who believe the entire book is set in the far future (from John's perspective) have to ignore these were real problems real churches were dealing with AT THE TIME IT WAS WRITTEN.

Commendable Points to the Futurist Method

Are there commendable points to the futurist position? Yes, but they still don't change that this method is opposed to John's own words.

- This view does attempt to make the book of Revelation relevant to each generation, but in doing so it renders it irrelevant to all preceding generations.
- This view does encourage people to look for God's workings in the affairs of mankind today.

It doesn't matter how many good points it may have, though; it contradicts Scripture, thus it cannot be correct.

This is the view taken by the majority of denominationalists including Baptists, Pentecostals, Methodists, Jehovah's Witnesses, Lutherans, Presbyterians, etc… They do not all interpret it the same way, but the majority of each of these groups place the bulk of the book in the far future from when it was written. Baptists and Pentecostals read Revelation with the idea of a thousand-year reign of Christ, a rapture, tribulation for seven years, etc… But some futurists don't hold to any of those things.

Suffice it to say that there are many different "flavors" to the futurist method, all of which contradict the clear statement that the things were "shortly come to pass."

THE HISTORICAL METHOD

This method of interpreting the book of Revelation became very popular during the Protestant Reformation (1500s) and the period thereafter.

Simply put, this view states the book of Revelation gives a prophetic overview of the entire future of the church from the first century through the final judgment. This view says Revelation foretells the apostasy of the Catholic Church, the rise of Islam, the split of the Greek and Roman churches, the attacks of the Huns, the Reformation Movement (some believing Martin Luther is under consideration in part), and some believe the American Restoration Movement (beginning around 1793) is foretold.

> *[T]he probable time for the beginning of the 1,260 years was A.D. 533. ... Gradually the church was corrupted until at the beginning of the 1,260 years the organization became the fully developed "man of sin" and the true church began its wilderness experience—lost to view as a visible organization.*[1]

Problems with the Historical Method

First off, it assumes God crafted an entire book to focus mostly on a group of people who aren't really the church (but instead, apostates), and the troubles this *imposter* church would go through. Do you believe God would pen a book, describing in advance a 1500+ year history of a false church?

Secondly, the overwhelming majority of the book is assigned to a time far distant from John's original audience. This makes the book have very little meaning to the original readers. It also, therefore, has a hard time dealing with the phrase "shortly come to pass."

Thirdly, it brings no comfort to first-century Christians undergoing persecution. "You're undergoing persecution now, but don't

---

[1] Hinds, John T., *The Gospel Advocate Commentary on Revelation*, notes on Revelation 12:14. The Restoration Movement (sometimes called the "Stone-Campbell Movement") is a name given to the work of many different men in many different places to leave denominational names, creeds, and doctrines behind in an effort to simply be "Christians" and follow nothing but the Bible. James O'Kelley (a Methodist) made efforts to this end around 1793. John T. Hinds, who wrote the above quote, identified with this movement, and hinted that it was foretold by God.

worry, eventually the church is going to go into nearly complete apostasy." Forgive me if I don't think the Christians in the first century would find that comforting at all.

Fourthly, most commentators who take this view have historical events lined up to match with almost the entire book (except for the judgment scene in chapters 20-21). You may say, *How is that a problem?* If their theories are all correct, and they've lined up Revelation with historical events, then there's nothing left to happen except for the final judgment. According to this general interpretation, there is nothing else scheduled to happen in/to the church, so the final judgment will be here any day now.

But what happens if there is another thousand years of life here on this earth? There's nothing in this method to account for any major events in the church, without backtracking and changing their applications.

Commendable Points to the Historical Method

This view encourages people to live in expectation of the final coming of Jesus, but that's something they should be doing anyway. It also encourages people to see the working of God in history.

THE SPIRITUAL METHOD

This view, taken by a growing number of people, basically states no historical events are under consideration in Revelation, but instead it is a series of symbolic visions designed to show the continual battle between good and evil—and ultimately Christ wins. There are no future events described, nor are there any past events described; just spiritual principles.

Problems with the Spiritual Method

- The inspired word says that the book of Revelation deals with actual events (1:1). This alone is enough reason to reject this interpretation.

- The inspired word says it deals with actual people (17:10—"Five kings have fallen, one is [presently reigning]").
- The inspired word says it (at least in part) deals with a specific city (11:8—The city wherein our Lord was crucified).

The proponents of this view say, "The battle between good and evil was about to come in full force, and that's why he says 'must shortly come to pass.'" The problem is the battle between good and evil has been going full-force since the beginning of time, continuing through the Old Testament, the time of Christ on earth, and during the ministry of the apostles—all before Revelation was written.

Commendable Points to the Spiritual Method
It does seek to make the book of Revelation relevant to every generation, because the battle between good and evil continues in each generation. But good intentions do not make up for ignoring clear statements from the book.

A Hybrid View
Many take a hybrid view of Revelation, taking chapters 2-3 as historical reality, making chapters 4-19 as spiritual warfare, and chapters 20-21 as the end of time.

THE PRETERIST METHOD

This method says the book of Revelation was written to comfort Christians during a time of persecution, to let them know God is in control, and the persecutors would be dealt with. More specifically, this method says most (some say all) the events described in Revelation were fulfilled, at the latest, during the days of the Roman Empire.

- Some believe it describes the overthrow of the Roman Empire (AD 487).[2]
- Others believe it describes the overthrow of Jerusalem and Judaism (AD 70).[3]

Most who interpret the book this way take a hybrid view, assigning the majority of it to the past, and some of it (chapters 20-21) to the future.[4]

Problems with the Preterist Method?

Some claim this view makes the book of no value today. Is that true? What about the books of the Old Testament, as well as the book of Acts—do they have no value today? After all, everything in most of *those* books has already happened, and has already been fulfilled. Just like with those already-been-fulfilled books, we can look at Revelation and see things God did, see His attitudes toward sin and evil, see what He expects of His people, and learn from it, making application to our own day and situation. This objection is not valid.

Some point to chapter 21, say "It's all about heaven after the second coming and the final judgment," then say, "So it can't *all* be in the past." This is something we will look at closer when we get to that point in our study. But just a preview here: the chapter doesn't describe heaven, but something that came "out of" heaven (Revelation 21:2, 10).

Some have leveled the charge: "This means you deny the second coming of Christ and a final judgment, and that you believe we are presently living in heaven." If that accusation seems crazy to you, then we're in the same boat. Those topics are clearly mentioned in

---

[2] This position can be found in commentaries by Homer Hailey, Jim McGuiggan, and others.

[3] This position can be found in commentaries by Foy E. Wallace Jr., Arthur Ogden, and others.

[4] See McGuiggan, Hailey, Arthur Ogden, and others.

other parts of the New Testament (Acts 17:31; Matthew 25:31-46; John 14:1-3; Hebrews 9:27; etc.). The question isn't whether the second coming and final judgment are real (they are), the question is whether Revelation discusses them. This accusation is clearly false.

Commendable Points to the Preterist Method

- It agrees with the inspired statements that the book is about things which must shortly come to pass.
- It makes the book have meaning and comfort to the people to whom it was written.
- It gives principles we can read and apply to our own lives (Stick with Jesus and you will win, God is in control, etc…), thus it has application to each generation of Christians.

This final view is the one we will use as we go through our study of Revelation (though the others will occasionally be referenced).

WHAT DOES THIS MEAN FOR US TODAY?

Now you may wonder, "Exactly how does this help me?"

- First, this introduction to the methods helps you understand where other people are coming from.
- Second, it helps you get a better understanding of the book so it isn't so mysterious (many people avoid the book, thinking it cannot be understood).
- Third, it helps you know which approaches *can't* be true (and when you eliminate those which cannot be true, you are better able to discover the true interpretation).

Do people misinterpret the Bible? Absolutely—and not just in Revelation! But the Bible *can* be understood if we look at the context, and compare it with what is said elsewhere in the Bible on the same topic.

STUDY TWO:
WHEN WAS REVELATION WRITTEN?

Historians can tell when something was written based on the things contained in it. If they find a letter written by Abraham Lincoln, and it mentions the effects of the Emancipation Proclamation, it is obviously written *after* that event. However, if they find a letter written by Lincoln mentioning it as something he is considering, then it is obviously written *before* that event.

The same thing is true of the Bible. The historical records of Samuel, Kings, Chronicles, Ezra, Nehemiah, and Esther were all written sometime *after* the events recorded in them had happened. That is the way historical books are written: *after* the events have occurred.

The prophetic books of the Bible were written *before* the events they prophesy took place. If the destruction of Jerusalem by Babylon in 586 BC is *prophesied*, then we know without any doubt it was written *before* 586 BC. If the Northern kingdom of Israel is mentioned as still existing, we know it was written *before* 721 BC when they were taken into captivity by Assyria.

You may wonder, *What does this have to do with the book of Revelation?*

The time period in which Revelation was written is a hotly debated subject throughout "Christendom."[1] You may wonder, *Does it really matter?* After all, some say, "So long as we agree it is inspired and it was written by the apostle John during his lifetime, does it really matter when it was written?"

The answer is: Yes, it actually matters.

---

[1] We will use this word to describe all groups that claim to be Christians, because it is much easier and shorter than saying, "the church, the denominations, and cults that claim to follow Jesus."

Why does it matter?

- Because some of the dates proposed for the book contradict Old Testament prophecies about the end of miracles and inspiration.
- Because the New Testament places the finalization of Scripture and the end of miracles at the same time.
- Because some of the dates proposed contradict information within the book of Revelation.
- Because the date in which it was written affects the interpretation of the book.

There are three main views as to the date in which Revelation was written:

- During the reign of Domitian (AD 81-96).
- During the reign of Vespasian (AD 69-79).
- During the reign of Nero (AD 54-68).

The goal in this lesson will be to look at the evidence and see which one of these is correct.

It should be noted from the outset that each of these views relies on different evidence. One view relies almost exclusively on *non-Biblical* evidence and *supposition*. One view relies almost exclusively on their interpretation of *one passage* within the book (and that interpretation is not held by anyone outside of this group). One view relies almost exclusively on the evidence *within* the Bible and *within* the book of Revelation.

Since the Bible is the inspired word of God, we will consider various forms of *Biblical* (therefore *inspired*) evidence to show when Revelation was written. Not supposition. Not unique interpretations. Just biblical evidence.[2]

---

[2] For those interested in uninspired evidence regarding the dating of Revelation, see Appendix A: External Evidence for the Early Date of Revelation.

1 CORINTHIANS 13:8-10
THE COMPLETION OF MIRACLES AND THE SCRIPTURES

Love never fails; but where there are prophecies, they will fail; where there are [miraculous] tongues, they will cease; where there is knowledge, it shall vanish away. Because we know in part, and we prophesy in part. But when that which is complete has come, then that which is in part shall be done away (1 Corinthians 13:8-10).

Miracles are supernatural things, done by humans, through the power of God. This includes prophecies, tongues, and knowledge (supernatural knowledge, like Christ promised the apostles in Luke 12:11-12). All of these, according to Paul, would "fail," "cease," and "vanish away." All of these miracles were called "in part" or "partial." They're contrasted with something "complete" or "perfect." When "that which is complete has come, then that which is in part [miracles] shall be done away."

"That which is complete" refers to the completely revealed will of God. It is called "that good, and acceptable, and *perfect* (or complete) *will of God*" (Romans 12:2). It is called "the *perfect* (or complete) *law of liberty*" (James 1:25). Both of these passages use the same word and describe the New Testament, the word of God—in other words, *the Scriptures*.

This is the conclusion: according to 1 Corinthians 13:8-10, when the final book of the New Testament was written, miracles would come to an end.

Why is this important? Because if we know for certain when miracles ended, then by this Biblical statement, we can know for certain when the New Testament was completed.

So the question to ask is: *Can we know when miracles ended?*

ZECHARIAH 13:2
THE PASSING OF PROPHECY

*And it shall come to pass in that day, says the LORD
of hosts, that I will cut off the names of the idols out
of the land, and they shall be remembered no more:
and also I will cause the prophets and the unclean
spirit to pass out of the land (Zechariah 13:2).*

Look at the context of this statement. Just a handful of verses
earlier, Zechariah gives a prophecy of the death of Jesus Christ:
"They shall look upon me whom they have pierced" (Zechariah
12:10; quoted in John 19:34-37). In 13:1, he gives a prophecy of
spiritual cleansing opened to the inhabitants of Jerusalem (see Acts
2). In 13:7, he gives a prophecy of the apostles abandoning Jesus:
"smite the shepherd and the sheep shall be scattered" (quoted and
fulfilled in Matthew 26:31). Then, at the beginning of the next chapter, Zechariah gives a prophecy of God Himself leading the nations
against Jerusalem, destroying the city (Zechariah 14:1-2—the same
thing Jesus foretold in Luke 21:20-22).

In the midst of these prophecies, Zechariah records God saying,
"I will cause the *prophets* and the unclean spirits *to pass out of the
land*" (Zechariah 13:2).

So, sometime between the death of Christ and the destruction of
Jerusalem by foreign nations (led by God), God would cause prophecy to cease. When you put this with 1 Corinthians 13:8-10, which
showed prophecy would end when the Word (the New Testament)
was completed, you now have a time marker for the completion of
the New Testament—sometime between the death of Jesus and the
destruction of Jerusalem by foreign nations, led by God.

The Roman Empire destroyed Jerusalem in AD 70, which was
an event prophesied and orchestrated by God Himself. But there's
more…

MICAH 7:15
MARVELOUS THINGS

According to the days of your coming out of the land of Egypt will I show to him marvelous things (Micah 7:15).

To make sure this passage is understood in context, look at the time period under consideration. Micah 7:18-19 speaks of a time when God would forgive the sins of the Jews ("*our* iniquities") and the Gentiles ("*their* sins"). This could only refer to the time of the gospel, which is "the power of God to salvation…to the Jew first, and also to the Greek [or Gentile]" (Romans 1:16). Micah 7:20 speaks of the time when God would fulfill His promise to Abraham and Jacob. What promise, you ask?

"In your seed, all nations of the earth will be blessed" (to Abraham—Genesis 22:18; to Jacob— Genesis 28:14).

Galatians 3:14-16, 26-29 says this is fulfilled to both the Jews and Gentiles *in Christ Jesus*:

*That the **blessing of Abraham** might come on the Gentiles through Jesus Christ; that we might receive the **promise** of the Spirit through faith... Now to Abraham and his seed were the promises made. He did not say," And to seeds," as of many; but as of one, "And to your seed," which is Christ.*

You are all the children of God by the faith, in Christ Jesus, because as many of you as have been baptized into Christ have put on Christ. There is neither Jew nor Greek, there is neither bond nor free, there is neither male nor female: for you are all one in Christ

*Jesus. And **if you are Christ's**, then **you are Abraham's seed**, and heirs **according to the promise.***

Therefore, the time period under consideration in Micah 7 is the time of the church. Keep that in mind as we consider verse 15.

This verse says God will do "marvelous things" "according to the days of the coming out of Egypt." What marvelous things did God do when they were coming out of Egypt?

- The Ten Plagues (miracles)
- Crossing the Red Sea (miracle)
- Water from a rock (miracle)
- Etc...

How long were they coming out of Egypt? They were considered to be "coming out of Egypt" until they entered the Promised Land, 40 years later (see Hebrews 3:9-10). In fact, Micah 7:15 has often been offered as proof miracles in the church would last 40 years.[3]

This passage *by itself* might not be conclusive, considering it is possible God is saying it is "like the days when you were coming out of Egypt" instead of "according to the time period…" But it is quite interesting that the church began on the Day of Pentecost, AD 30—and if you add 40 years, you wind up at AD 70. The exact same timeframe given by Zechariah.

Crossing Red Sea (1440 BC)	"coming out of Egypt"	Entering Promised Land (1400 BC)[4]
	← 40 Years →	
Church established (AD 30)	Miracles in the Church	Jerusalem Destroyed (AD 70)

---

[3] Guy N. Woods, in the Woods-Franklin Debate, used this passage in this way, as did Ben Bogard (a famous Baptist debater of the 20th century) in his debate with Aimee Macpherson (pages 42-43).

[4] The dates here are estimates, but the 40-year span is confirmed repeatedly in Scripture.

JOEL 2:28-32/ACTS 2:16-21
IN THE LAST DAYS,
I WILL POUR OUT FROM MY SPIRIT...

As with the other passages, context is important. Chapter 1 of Joel describes a locust plague God sent against Judah, accompanied with famine, drought, and fires (1:11-12, 19-20). The priests were told to call the people to the house of Jehovah (the temple in Jerusalem) to cry to God (1:14).

Joel 2:1-11 describes the destruction of Jerusalem and Judah. It is called *a day of darkness and gloominess* (2:2), and Joel uses apocalyptic, prophetic language to describe the overthrow of their nation (2:10).

- The earth shall quake.
- The heavens shall tremble.
- The sun and moon will be dark.
- The stars will not shine.

The main topic of the book of Joel is punishment and destruction against Judah and Jerusalem—sent by God. Keep that in mind as you look at the passage under consideration.

The New Testament Application of this Prophecy

Joel 2:28-32 is a prophecy of events *in the first century*. Peter quoted it and said it applied to what happened beginning at Pentecost.

> ***This is that*** *which was spoken by the prophet Joel; [when he said]* *"And it shall come to pass in the last days,"* *says God,* *"I will pour out from my Spirit on all flesh: and your sons and your daughters shall prophesy, and your young men shall see visions, and*

> *your old men shall dream dreams. And on my serv-
> ants and on my handmaidens I will pour out from my
> Spirit in those days; and they shall prophesy. And I
> will show wonders in heaven above, and signs in the
> earth beneath; blood, and fire, and vapor of smoke;
> the sun shall be turned into darkness, and the moon
> into blood, before that great and terrible day of the
> Lord comes. And it shall come to pass, that whoever
> shall call on the name of the Lord shall be saved"
> (Acts 2:16-21).*

After the Jews heard the apostles speaking in tongues (a miracle), Peter said, "*this is that* which was spoken by the prophet Joel,"
and then he quotes Joel 2:28-32.

This prophecy begins with "it shall come to pass in the last
days…" The book of Joel deals with judgment upon Judah and Jerusalem up to Joel 3:2. "The last days" in this passage *does not refer
to "the gospel age," or "the Christian dispensation."* "The last
days," using the context of the book of Joel (and as we will see in a
minute, the context of Peter's sermon), is a reference to the last days
of the Jewish nation and Judaism.

Miracles (prophesy… visions… dreams—Acts 2:17-19), according to Joel's prophecy, would take place *in the last days of Judah and Jerusalem.*

The "Last Days" of Judah and Jerusalem

Now, some might object to this, but this usage of the term "the
last days," to refer to the end of Judah and Jerusalem, is common in
the Old Testament.

> *The word that Isaiah the son of Amoz saw **concern-
> ing Judah and Jerusalem.** And it shall come to pass
> **in the last days**, that the mountain of the LORD'S
> house shall be established in the top of the moun-
> tains, and shall be exalted above the hills; and all*

nations shall flow into it (Isaiah 2:1-2).

The last days of what, Isaiah? *The last days of Judah and Jerusalem!* If the prophecy is about Judah and Jerusalem (which Isaiah said it was), then the "last days" must be the last days of Judah and Jerusalem.

> *Therefore shall Zion for your sake be plowed as a field, and **Jerusalem shall become ruins**, and the mountain of the house [the temple mount] as the high places of the forest. **But in the last days** it shall come to pass, that the mountain of the house of the LORD shall be established in the top of the mountains, and it shall be exalted above the hills; and people shall flow into it (Micah 3:12-4:1).*

"Jerusalem is going to be destroyed, but in the last days..." The last days of what, Micah? *The last days of Jerusalem!* We must pay attention to context!

Since Joel prophesied miracles would take place in "the last days" of Judah and Jerusalem, when do you suppose they would end? But let's get back to what else Joel says about these "last days."

Apocalyptic Imagery

The prophecy goes on to give prophetic descriptions that describe the overthrow of a nation (Acts 2:19-20).

- Wonders in heaven
- Blood, fire, vapor of smoke
- Sun to darkness
- Moon to blood.

These phrases, and others very similar, are used throughout the Old Testament to describe God's punishment on a nation. In fact, God inspired Joel to use some of this very same language to describe judgment on Jerusalem earlier in the very same chapter!

Therefore, the prophecy of miracles in the last days of the Jewish system is connected with, and ends with, the overthrow of a nation. But what nation? Remember the context! The only nation whose overthrow is described in Joel is Jerusalem/Judah. When Peter quoted this passage, the only nation whose overthrow was anywhere in the near future—the only nation whose overthrow was of any concern to the Jews—was Judah.

The Day of the Lord

The prophecy of Joel speaks of the "great and terrible day of the Lord" (Acts 2:20). In the Old Testament, the phrase "the day of the Lord" always, 100% of the time, refers to a day of judgment against someone—most frequently, it describes judgment against God's chosen people, the Israelites.

As we saw with the apocalyptic phrases used by Joel, this day of judgment is connected with the overthrow of a nation. And the *context* of Joel shows this day of judgment is against the *Jewish nation*.

Salvation from Destruction

Joel's prophecy, after describing the overthrow of a nation, and God's judgment coming in the last days of Judah/Jerusalem, says, "It shall come to pass, that whoever shall call on the name of the Lord shall be saved" (Acts 2:21).

If you had just been told the prophecy about the final days of your nation was about to be fulfilled, and your nation was going to be overthrown, and God was going to bring judgment upon it—what would you think when the next words are "whoever shall call on the name of the Lord shall be saved"?

Saved from what? Well, the context of the prophecy would certainly make you think it meant being saved from the coming destruction of the Jewish nation. There was a time element to this prophecy. The Jewish nation was destroyed in AD 70. God, through Joel, promised miracles would take place *in this time period*:

- The last days of Judah and Jerusalem.

- Before the day of judgment brought upon Jerusalem and Judah by God.

But just so we can make it a little more clear, let's go to the end of Peter's sermon.

> *"With many other words did he testify and exhort, saying "save yourselves from **this** wicked **generation**." (Acts 2:40).*

Notice what Peter said: "*This* wicked generation." Speaking of the destruction of Jerusalem, Jesus said that "*this* generation" would not pass until all the things He prophesied about their destruction were fulfilled (Matthew 24:1-34, especially verse 34). In Matthew 23:34-36, Jesus said that Jerusalem would be held accountable for the blood of the apostles and prophets, and that "all these things shall come upon *this* generation."

It was THAT generation, which Jesus and Peter both spoke about, that would be destroyed. And the only way to save themselves was to turn to Jesus as the Savior. "Whoever shall call on the name of the Lord shall be saved." Saved from sins, yes, but also saved from the destruction of the city and nation of the Jews.

The context of Joel, and Peter's words, show that miracles would take place during the last days of Judah/Jerusalem—and those last days ended in AD 70.

SUMMARIZING THE OLD TESTAMENT EVIDENCE

Zechariah says miracles would pass from the land sometime between the death of Christ and the destruction of Jerusalem. Micah appears to limit miracles in the church to 40 years (conveniently enough, covering the same time period as Zechariah). Joel says miracles would take place in the last days of Judah and Jerusalem before God judges and overthrows them (again, the exact same time period).

Taking these things into consideration, we have conclusive Old Testament evidence that miracles would cease by the time of the destruction of Jerusalem.

Since this is true, we can know *for certain* that no book of the Bible was written after that time, because 1 Corinthians 13:8-10 said miracles would end *after* the Scriptures were completed. If miracles ended by AD 70, the Scriptures (including Revelation) were completed *before* that point.

But let's now look at evidence within Revelation itself.

REVELATION 1:1, 3; 22:6, 10
THINGS WHICH MUST SHORTLY COME TO PASS

As I mentioned in the previous lesson, the book of Revelation clearly states the events contained within its 22 chapters were going to happen very soon. John was inspired to write "The time is at hand," which means it was very near.

We saw that when the word translated "shortly" is used elsewhere in the New Testament, it means something *imminent*, not something generations away. Remember, Paul was told to get "*quickly*" [same word in Greek] out of Jerusalem (Acts 22:18). Paul told Timothy he knew he was about to die, and therefore to "*come shortly*" [same word in Greek] to him with his cloak and parchments (2 Timothy 4:6-9).

So, since the book of Revelation says the things contained in it were "at hand," and "shortly come to pass," then the things described in it were *about to happen*.

So how does this help us prove when it was written?

REVELATION 11:8
"WHERE OUR LORD WAS CRUCIFIED."

Right now, we won't get in to the events which take place in chapter 11, but John is very clear to say some of them would take place *in the city where our Lord was crucified.*

> *And their dead bodies shall lie in the street of <u>the great city</u>, which spiritually is called Sodom and Egypt, <u>where also our Lord was crucified</u>.*

It ought to be simple enough to determine what city is under consideration. Luke 13:33—Jesus says, "I must walk today, and to-morrow, and the day following, for *it cannot be that a prophet perish out of Jerusalem.*" Jesus was tried and condemned and murdered *in the city of Jerusalem.*

Regardless of how we want to interpret the events, John is very clear to tell us some events in Revelation (events which were *about to happen*) would take place in the city of Jerusalem.

This proves beyond any reasonable doubt *Jerusalem was still in existence when the book was written.* You can't have events take place in "the great city" when the "great city" doesn't exist anymore.

WHAT DOES THIS MEAN FOR US TODAY?

There are other passages in Revelation we could look at which would also prove it was written prior to the destruction of Jerusalem, but we will save that for the next lesson when we look at the *purpose* of the book.

The Bible shows when it was completed.
The Old Testament prophesied miracles would cease prior to the destruction of Jerusalem. The apostle Paul said the New Testament writings would be completed before miracles ceased. Therefore, the

Bible teaches that the New Testament writings were all finished prior to AD 70. *This includes the book of Revelation.*

Therefore, this book could not have been written during the reign of Domitian (AD 81-96). This book could not have been written during the reign of Vespasian (AD 69-79). This book was written during the reign of Nero (AD 54-68).

Discussion of biblical topics needs to be centered around the Bible.

We have proven—*from the Bible*—when the book of Revelation was written. We have not looked at any uninspired evidence, because when the Bible says something, it doesn't matter what uninspired men say or think to the contrary. Most commentaries on Revelation will quote church fathers, church traditions and stories, and opinions of other so-called "scholars" in an effort to prove that the book of Revelation was written near the end of the first century (AD 95-96), but they offer no actual proof from the biblical text itself.

When you discuss a Bible topic, do not *ever* settle for "well I think" or "my opinion is this…" Go with a "thus saith the Lord!"

Miracles ended when Jerusalem was destroyed.

Remember, miracles are *supernatural things, done by humans, by the power of God.* Scriptures foretold those would cease. And though the purpose of this lesson was to show when the Bible (and thus Revelation) was completed, it also shows when miracles ceased.

Any group claiming to do miracles (speak in tongues, do miraculous healings, etc.) today is lying. They are claiming power that God said ceased nearly 2,000 years ago.

STUDY THREE:
WHAT ON EARTH
IS REVELATION ABOUT?

If you're like me, you aren't likely to go see a movie without at least first knowing something about it. Is it a comedy? Action? Drama? Chick-flick? Is it animated? Live action? What is it rated? Why is it rated that way? What is it about? Perhaps tops on the list of whether or not I want to see it is if my sister recommends it—If she does, I probably won't like it.

When you want to study a book of the Bible, doesn't it make sense that you'd kind of want to know what it's about before you get into reading it? Sure, you could just read through one of the 66 books in it, but it makes much more sense if you first have an idea what the book is talking about ahead of time.

For example: read through 1 Thessalonians, and you will be able to gain some helpful knowledge. But if you understand Paul planted the church there, that Jews persecuted the church with a mob of thugs, and that after just three weeks the disciples helped Paul escape the city—then many parts of the book become more meaningful, like how worried Paul was that they would give in to the pressure from the Jews.

Knowing something about the book and its meaning is much more important when you're talking about Revelation.

In this lesson, we will go through parts of the book to show what Revelation is all about. Don't worry, we will actually start digging into the text starting in the next lesson.

> "The book of Revelation is the greatest piece of literature ever penned. It is a masterpiece presentation. It challenges our...power to reason, judge, comprehend and understand. It challenges our imagination... It challenges our observation... It challenges

our overall knowledge of the Bible and our will to learn, because so much study must go into learning, even generally, what is revealed in this book. It tries our patience…to keep on studying when we have just learned that we were wrong about previous conclusions, and it challenges our endurance… It is indeed a masterpiece in literature. It brings together Old Testament prophecies, both of victory and desolation, and shows their impending fulfillment as things 'shortly come to pass…'"[1]

REVELATION IS A REVEALING!

First, it *must* be understood that the book of Revelation is exactly what it claims to be: a book which *reveals* (1:1). The word translated "revelation" is *apokalupsis* (from which we get our word *Apocalypse*), and it means an unveiling, an uncovering, or a revealing. So, according to the very first verse, this book was written to *reveal* something, not to *conceal* it. But what was it supposed to reveal?

It was the revelation of Jesus Christ.

It was *given* by Jesus (through His messenger), *concerning* Jesus, about something Jesus *was going to do*.

This revealing was "of things which MUST shortly come to pass."

This gives us our first big clue to what the book of Revelation is all about. In the last lesson, we saw *from Scripture* that all books of the Bible were completed prior to the destruction of Jerusalem (AD 70). The book of Revelation was written sometime in the early to mid-60's.

Because of John's statement at the beginning of the book, we can know the things in the book were fulfilled *shortly* after the book

---

[1] Ogden, Arthur, *The Avenging of the Apostles and Prophets* (Pinson, AL: Ogden Publications, 1985), p. 1.

was written. The events were "at hand" (1:3). What does "at hand" mean? John the Baptist said the kingdom was "at hand" about 3½ years before the kingdom came into existence on Pentecost.

So let's be generous and stretch "at hand" to mean 10 years. No, let us stretch it even more, and be liberal, saying "at hand" can mean 20 years. Even with this liberal use of the phrase, the latest the events in Revelation would take place is by 85 AD. We will narrow this down considerably in a moment.

COMING WITH CLOUDS

Revelation describes a "coming with clouds" (1:7). This isn't the first time in the Bible this imagery is used. Isaiah 19:1-4 describes God coming, *riding on a cloud*, and it is a scene of judgment against the nation of Egypt, whom God will overthrow.

Since most of the imagery in Revelation comes from the Old Testament, we need to look there to understand what different symbols mean. If *coming with clouds* in the Old Testament described God coming in judgment, then we should assume (and if we read through the book, it becomes clear) when it is used in Revelation, it means the same thing. Jesus used this phrase the same way, describing His coming in judgment on Jerusalem as a "coming in the clouds" (Matthew 24:30).

So, using the information we already know from the Bible, we can know *for certain* that the Book of Revelation describes a coming in judgment which took place between AD 64 and 85.

THE TRIBES OF THE EARTH SHALL MOURN

Revelation 1:7 says: "All kindreds of the earth shall wail" (KJV). This *exact* wording (in Greek) is used by Jesus in Matthew 24:30, but there (in the KJV) it is translated, "all tribes of the earth shall mourn." Jesus stated this in context of the destruction of Jerusalem (Matthew 24:1-34). The tribes under consideration in Matthew were the literal tribes of Israel—after all, the Jews were the only ones who mourned or wailed over Jerusalem's destruction—the Romans sure didn't, they celebrated! Since Revelation 1:7 uses the exact same words, it seems logical to suggest the same people are under consideration.

Therefore, Revelation describes a coming in judgment which took place between AD 64 and 85, which caused the physical Israelites to mourn.

THE HARLOT IDENTIFIED

The book of Revelation describes a judgment that would cause the Israelites to mourn, but in Revelation 17, we find out this judgment is on a *city*. Revelation 17:1—the judgment is upon the great harlot called Babylon. But God doesn't leave the identity of this harlot to the imagination. In verse 18, the harlot is called "the great city" which rules over the kings of the earth. We're introduced to "the great city" back in 11:8—"the great city, which spiritually is called Sodom and Egypt, where also our Lord was crucified."

- Jesus was only crucified in one city: Jerusalem.
- Jerusalem was called "Sodom" in the Old Testament (Isaiah 1:9, Jeremiah 23:14, Ezekiel 16:46-56).
- Jerusalem was called the faithful city which had become a harlot (Isaiah 1:20).
- Jerusalem is frequently viewed as a harlot in the Old Testament.

"BUT," the argument comes, "Jerusalem didn't rule over the kings of the earth!" Is that a valid argument? The word "earth," in Greek, is *ge* (as in *ge*ology), and is often translated "land" (as in the Promised Land). The apostles specifically said who the "kings of the earth [*ge*]" were in Acts 4:26-27: Herod and Pontius Pilate. These men were only in one land: the land of Israel. And the capital city of Israel was...?

Therefore, the Book of Revelation describes a coming in judgment *against a city,* which took place between AD 64 and 85, which would cause the physical Israelites to mourn. By now, perhaps you have an idea of which city is under consideration, but let us continue.

THE CAUSE OF THE JUDGMENT

Revelation 18:20-19:2 describes the reasons for this judgment. The judgment on the city called Babylon was so God could avenge the blood of the apostles and prophets (18:20). Because of this, the judgment on the city would be violent (18:21). This city was guilty of the blood of prophets, of saints, and of ALL that were slain on the earth [*ge*] (18:24).

Now, let us compare this with something Jesus said while He was here on earth (Matthew 23:34-39). To the city of Jerusalem, Jesus says:

> *"I send to you prophets, and wise men, and scribes: and some of them you shall kill and crucify, and some of them you shall scourge in your synagogues, and persecute them from city to city, that* **upon you** *may come* **all the righteous blood shed upon the earth**, *from the blood of righteous Abel to the blood of Zechariah, the son of Berechiah, whom you slew between the temple and the altar. Truly I say to you, all these things shall come upon this generation.* **O Jerusalem, Jerusalem**, *you that kill the prophets and stone them which are sent[2] to you..."*

---

[2] The Greek word for "them which are sent" is the same word as "apostles."

The judgment on "Babylon" was *to avenge the blood of the apostles and prophets* (Revelation 18:20). Jesus said that the blood of the apostles and prophets was going to be avenged *on Jerusalem*.

The judgment upon "Babylon" was *because they were guilty of the blood of the saints* (Revelation 18:24). Jesus said that the blood of *ALL the righteous* (in other words, saints) would be avenged *on Jerusalem*.

According to Jesus, God would avenge the blood of the apostles, prophets, and all the righteous by destroying Jerusalem. *According to Revelation*, God destroyed "Babylon" in order to avenge the blood of the apostles, prophets and all the righteous.

Only two options exist at this point:

1. *Babylon is Jerusalem*, and Matthew 23:34-39 is describing the same events as Revelation 18:20-19:2.
2. Or *God somehow messed up* and didn't actually avenge the blood of the apostles, prophets, and saints when He destroyed Jerusalem and had to find another city to destroy to finish the avenging.

God is not a failure, so we can eliminate the second option.

Taking what we've shown straight from the Bible, we can know Revelation describes a coming of Jesus Christ in judgment upon the city of Jerusalem in AD 70, which caused the physical Israelites to mourn and wail.

WHY THIS?

What purpose does it serve to have a book about this event? Revelation was written about the destruction of Jerusalem, the once faithful city that had turned (spiritually) into a harlot, and was guilty of the blood of Jesus, the apostles, the prophets, and all the other righteous. But the question still remains: why would God give us a book about it?

It shows the fulfillment of Old Testament prophecy.

The destruction of Jerusalem was mentioned in Zechariah 14:1-2, Isaiah 2:1-4, Micah 3:12-4:2, Joel 2:28-32; also throughout Deuteronomy.

It shows the visible end of the Old Testament system.

Jeremiah spoke of the new covenant God would make with His people (Jeremiah 31:31). This new covenant was instituted on the Day of Pentecost after the death and resurrection of Christ (Acts 2). But the Old Testament system, the Law of Moses, was still being practiced by the majority of the Jews. The fact they could still *practice* the Old Law caused many Jews to think Christianity couldn't be the New Covenant. With the destruction of Jerusalem, of the temple, of the altar, and of the genealogical records, it became physically impossible to follow the Law of Moses properly—in fact, *God made it physically impossible for anyone to do the things required for forgiveness under the Old Testament.*

- There has been no altar for sacrifices since AD 70.
- There has been no temple in which the High Priest could enter with the Day of Atonement sacrifice for the people since AD 70.
- There have been no records of lineage proving descent from Aaron for someone to be a High Priest since AD 70 (there have been no high priests since that time).

Physical Jerusalem was destroyed so the New Jerusalem could shine forth.

After the judgment scene in Revelation 20, the New Jerusalem descends out of heaven and is described as glorious. Before Jerusalem's destruction, Christianity was viewed as a "sect" of Judaism (Acts 24:5, 28:22). It has been accurately stated that Christianity grew up under the umbrella of Judaism.

Some might (and some have) argue the destruction was irrelevant to the church except that the persecutors (the Jews) were silenced. However, let me ask you a question: In the Old Testament, when did Israel become a nation? It was when they crossed the Red Sea and were freed from Egyptian bondage (God called them a "nation" shortly thereafter when He gave the Law to Moses). However, even though they were a nation with laws from God, there was a way in which they hadn't fully arrived as a nation until they entered the Promised Land 40 years later.

The church was God's new nation beginning from Pentecost, but there was a sense in which the church wasn't completely revealed until the Old Jerusalem was done away with, 40 years later. After the destruction of Jerusalem, the church shone clearly in its full glory as the New Jerusalem, the dwelling-place of God (see Revelation 21).

CONCLUSION:

Though many of the symbols in Revelation may seem confusing, we can know the overall picture of the book, and as such, we can have a better understanding of the details: The book of Revelation paints a vivid picture of the destruction of the city of Jerusalem and all it stood for, the complete abolishment of the Old Testament system, the avenging of the blood of all of God's servants, and the status of the church of Jesus Christ as the only way to have access to God.

In the next lesson, we start digging into the text of Revelation.

STUDY FOUR
LESSONS FROM REVELATION 1:1

There's a joke I remember telling when I was in third grade. It goes like this:

> *You are a bus driver. You have 82 passengers. At your first stop, 20 passengers get off, and 10 get on. At your second stop, 39 passengers get off, and 2 get on. At your third stop, 2 passengers get off, and 33 get on. At your final stop, all the passengers get off.*
>
> *How old is the bus driver?*

Without exception, the answer was always, "I don't know." So I would repeat the first line of the joke, *You are a bus driver*. At that point, they get it. They hadn't paid attention to what was said at the very beginning—which ended up being the key to the whole joke.

Some people misinterpret the book of Revelation for the same reason. They read the first verse, gloss over it, forget about it, and go on. The first verse tells us more than most people realize, and that is what we will focus on here: lessons we can learn from the first verse of Revelation.

THINGS WHICH MUST SHORTLY COME TO PASS

Jesus is not the focus of the book of Revelation. Don't get me wrong, there are a lot of things in the book of Revelation about Jesus, His nature, and His workings, such as:

- Jesus' birth and ascension (12:1-5).
- Jesus as the sacrificial Lamb of God which takes away the sins of the world (chapter 4).
- Jesus who is still "like unto the Son of man," showing He retained His humanity after the ascension (1:13).

- Jesus as the leader of His armies (19:11-13).
- Jesus as the High Priest (1:12-13).
- Jesus' coming in judgment against Jerusalem (1:7, chap. 18).

But each one of these simply repeats something that had already been revealed in the New Testament. *It was nothing new.*

The focus is on "things" or "events"

The phrase "the Revelation of Jesus Christ" is followed by the words *"which God gave to Him."* The Revelation is something that originated with the Father, was given to the Son, and then the Son sent it (via symbols given by an angel to John) to His servants.

The Revelation of Jesus Christ is the Revelation that *belongs* to Him. Yes, it contains things about Him, but the revelation (the thing revealed) is not *about* Jesus specifically. It is about something else. The book of Revelation is about "things which must shortly come to pass." *This* is what is being revealed. This is something not fully known or fully understood previously, but was being revealed in this book.

You may say, "Wait a minute! Didn't Jesus prophesy about the destruction of Jerusalem?" Yes He did, but no one knew when it was going to come. He gave them signs to look for in Matthew 24, but those signs hadn't happened yet. Now, Jesus reveals to them: *It is time!* Jesus gives them more detail this time as well, details they didn't have before.

The focus of the book is this: *The Revelation of Jesus Christ of things which must shortly come to pass.* A series of events which would soon be seen by those first century Christians.

"Must"

The word "must" means it is a moral necessity. It was morally necessary that this judgment happen, and happen very soon. God's justice demanded that these events had to take place quickly (See also Luke 24:46).

Never, ever, ever, ever forget this when you read through Revelation. When you are wondering, "What does this verse mean?" remember that the book is about things which must shortly come to pass. When you are wondering, "Could this part really be talking about the overthrow of Jerusalem?" Remember when it was written, and that this book was about things which had to shortly come to pass—and this was from *the original readers' perspective,* not ours some 1950 years later. God said it at the beginning (1:1) and the end (22:6).

We must interpret this book in light of what it says about itself. If someone ever asks you, "What is the book of Revelation about?" then you just point them to the very first verse and show them it is about "things which must shortly come to pass" in the first century.

Shortly come to pass = 2,000 years?!?!?

Those of the futurist persuasion try to twist the words beyond all recognition, if they deal with them at all. John Walvoord (whose commentary on Revelation has sold over 100,000 copies) said,

> "'...quickly or suddenly coming to pass,' indicating rapidity of execution after the beginning takes place. The idea is not that the event may occur soon, but that when it does, it will be sudden."

Herbert W. Armstrong (Worldwide Church of God) proudly proclaimed in 1959 that the events in Revelation were describing "this very hour in which we live—it draws back the curtain on the FUTURE!" He soon after quotes verses 1-3, but says nothing about the phrase "shortly come to pass."

Timothy LaHaye (co-author of the "Left Behind" series) says,

> "Further on in the verse, we find that this is the Revelation of Jesus Christ 'to show unto his servants things which must shortly come to pass.' Again we see that the emphasis of the book is on future events."

Others say "shortly come to pass" means it is about to happen, but something that is quick for God may be thousands of years for us, so it could be centuries or millennia away. Pardon my frankness, but that's stupid. Apparently some people think God is unable to adequately explain time to us, or else He just plain doesn't know *how* to tell time.

But isn't God the one who gave Jonah the message: "Yet 40 days and Nineveh shall be overthrown"? (Jonah 3:4-7). Didn't God relay to Daniel that he was to seal up a vision because it was "many days" away (400 years away)? (Daniel 8:26). God knows how to tell time, and He knows how to adequately get timeframes across to mankind in language they can understand. If God says something is about to happen, then it is about to happen. And that was His message to the original readers of Revelation.

A BOOK OF SYMBOLS

The Book of Revelation is revealed in symbolic language. The first verse says Jesus sent and *signified* this Revelation. The word "signify" means *sign*-ify, or told in signs/symbols or in figurative language. Thayer's definition is "to give a sign."

Anyone who reads through the book of Revelation can easily see the book is written in signs and symbols. Some of these symbols are defined for us (1:20, for example). Other symbols aren't (the description of Jesus in 1:13-16).

But believe it or not, there are those who actually DENY that the book was written in symbols and signs.

LaHaye says,

> *"True, there are some symbols in the book, and God calls them symbols…However, it is wrong to classify the entire book as a book of signs and symbols, suggesting that they cannot be taken literally… There is*

far more in the book of Revelation that should be accepted literally than should be spiritualized."

I don't know that a person can be more disrespectful to God's word than to say it means the exact opposite of what God actually said (like LaHaye does here, and like most denominations do with every passage which discusses baptism's relationship to salvation... but I digress).

The general rule when interpreting the Bible is to take it literally unless it is impossible to do so. Is Jesus literally a piece of wood with a knob and hinges? No! Then we know that he was not literally a door.[1] Did Herod have four legs and a long, bushy tail? No! Then we know he wasn't literally a fox.[2]

The rule when interpreting Revelation is to understand that while there are some literal things, the majority of the book is figurative. Is there a literal 144,000 people in heaven? If so, they are all male, Jewish virgins—it would mean no women will be in heaven. Is there a literal thousand-year reign of Jesus? Then the Bible contradicts itself saying Jesus is now (and has been for 2,000 years) the King of kings (1 Timothy 6:15). Not only that, but if it is literal, then the only people who will reign with Him are those who literally were beheaded (Revelation 20:4). So much for Paul saying that all Christians will live and reign with Him (2 Timothy 2:12)!

So, if you ever wonder what something means in Revelation, remember that (1) the book is to show things which must shortly come to pass, and (2) it is told in symbolic language: most of it is NOT to be taken literally.

WRITTEN TO BE UNDERSTOOD

People often wonder how it is that we got the Bible, and the first

---

[1] John 10:9
[2] Luke 13:31-32

verse of Revelation gives us much of the answer.

"The Revelation of Jesus Christ, which God gave to Him…"

The Father is the originator of the Bible and of all inspired words recorded in it. Jesus Christ Himself, while on earth, made it abundantly clear that He did not speak His own words, but He spoke and did whatever the Father told Him to speak (John 7:16; 12:49; 14:10, 31; Compare this with what Paul said in Ephesians 3:2-5).

"Which He sent…to His servant John"

The New Testament scriptures originated with the Father, but were delivered by Jesus Christ to His servants (the apostles and other inspired writers). But since Jesus is sitting at the right hand of God (Acts 2:32-33), how did He get this message delivered to the inspired writers? Jesus explains this in John 16:12-14, by saying He would send the Holy Spirit (which was promised to Him—Acts 2:32-33) and the Holy Spirit would guide the apostles into all truth, including "things to come" (John 16:14). Keep this in mind when we look at Revelation 1:10—John was "in the Spirit on the Lord's Day" when he received the revelation. Peter said the Scriptures didn't originate with man, but "holy men of God spoke as they were moved by the Holy Spirit" (2 Peter 1:21).

The Scriptures originated with the Father, were given to the Son to deliver to His inspired servants, through of the Holy Spirit.

In Revelation, Jesus used an angel (literally, a *messenger*). John was "in the Spirit" when the vision was given to him, and in the vision, an angel showed him the events that are recorded. This also occurs in Daniel, where Gabriel comes and shows a vision to Daniel and helps explain it to him. The use of an angel in bringing about inspired writings is rare, and only used in specific instances.

"To show to His servants"

Inspiration has a purpose. It's not to make the Father feel good about originating it. It's not about Jesus' delivering it. It's not about the Holy Spirit bringing it to the mind of an inspired servant of Jesus.

It's not about the servant himself. *The purpose of inspiration is to deliver God's message to His people so they can understand it.*

The purpose of this Revelation was specifically "to show to His servants" the things recorded in it. This matches perfectly with Paul's statement in Ephesians 3:3-4, "by revelation he made known to me the mystery…whereby, when you read, *you may understand* my knowledge in the mystery of Christ."

The purpose of inspired writings is to inform, encourage, and equip God's people to understand His will and live for Him.

WHAT DOES THIS MEAN FOR US TODAY?

Scriptures can be understood

Consider something for a moment: All inspired Scriptures (including Revelation) were written for you (not *to* you, but *for* you). They contain knowledge of who God is. They contain knowledge of our sinful condition and the punishment we deserve for those sins. The Scriptures also contain all the information we need in order to receive showers of blessings and the escape the punishment of sins. They contain God's one and only plan of salvation for mankind—and it is understandable (See Acts 2:22-38).

Yes, there are "some things hard to understand" (2 Peter 3:16), but the answer to "What must I do to be saved" is not one of those hard-to-understand-things. If you're interested in knowing what the Bible says about that, check out Appendix B: Are You Saved?

STUDY FIVE
THE BLESSING (REVELATION 1:1-3)

Quite frequently, I'll hear a song for the first time, and it will remind me of some other song. Many songs have the same notes, similar melody, similar guitar riffs, etc...

Many times I read through the Bible, and run across a passage that reminds me of other passages. This is especially true when going through Revelation, because so much of the book uses imagery from the Old Testament and some of Jesus' teachings. "Blessed are the poor in spirit," "blessed are the meek," "blessed are those who hunger and thirst after righteousness," "blessed are the peacemakers." These should be very familiar to all of us, as they are part of the beatitudes from the Sermon on the Mount in Matthew 5. But that is not the only section of Scripture with beatitudes in it. Revelation actually has seven beatitudes scattered through it (1:3, 14:13, 16:15, 19:9, 20:6, 22:7, 14).

In this lesson, we will look at the first one, found in Revelation 1:3, to see what it meant for the original readers, and what it means for us today. But before we get there, let's recap.

A RECAP THUS FAR:

The book of Revelation is a prophecy of events which were about to happen (1:1, 3, 22:6, 10). As such, we must look for its fulfillment *close to the time the book was written.* Any interpretation which places all (or even most) of the book in a time far removed from when John wrote is false, because it contradicts what the book says about itself—the time was then at hand!

When something in the book doesn't make sense, remember that the book dealt with things that the first-century Christians would recognize/see/experience. The book of Revelation was written prior to the destruction of Jerusalem in AD 70. Jerusalem still exists when the book was written, and at least some of the events recorded in the book would take place there (11:8). The book dealt with things that—around 64 AD—were about to happen. When something in the book is confusing, remember it was about things which were about to happen when John wrote it down.

Revelation is written in figurative language (1:1). This book cannot be read and applied as though all the contents are literal. When something doesn't seem clear, remember that it is written in figurative language.

The book of Revelation was written to be understood (1:1). It was delivered from the Father to the Son to John so Christians could understand it. It is called a "revelation" or a revealing, not a concealing. As we will see in this study, Jesus fully expected this book to make sense to the original recipients.

Some say the original readers understood it, but the key to understanding it has disappeared. That says God has made it impossible for anyone today to understand one of the biggest books in the New Testament. Would God really have made it impossible for part of His word to be understood?

THE PENMAN OF REVELATION

"...which He gave to His servant, John, who bore witness of the word of God, and of the testimony of Jesus Christ, and of all things that he saw."

Who actually wrote down the Revelation? Believe it or not, this topic is actually argued and debated in the religious world, especially among those who consider themselves to be "scholarly."

Which John?

We know from verse 1 that the Revelation was revealed to a man named John who was a servant of Jesus Christ. But which John was it? Since I know you're smart, I will make this brief. This John was one who "bore witness of the word of God, and of the testimony of

Jesus Christ, and of all things that he saw" (Revelation 1:2). The phrase "bore witness" (one word in Greek) is the word "martyr," which literally means "to give testimony" or "to give witness." It is spoken in past tense, showing it happened in the past *and was finished*. Some translations (I'm looking at you, NIV) use present tense, but that isn't what the original says.

What John can you think of who had already given his testimony concerning the word of God, the things which Jesus said, and all the things which he saw Jesus do?

I'll give you a hint: John 1 says "In the beginning was the Word, and the Word was with God, and the Word was God...the Word became flesh and dwelt among us, and we beheld His glory as of the only-begotten Son of the Father." (John 1:1, 14). John 21:24-25 says the writer gave his "testimony" or "witness" about the things he saw Jesus do and teach. According to John 13, this John (who calls himself "the disciple whom Jesus loved") was at the last supper—and only the 12 apostles were there with Jesus (Matthew 26:20; Mark 14:16-18).

Some might argue against this being a reference to John's gospel, and say, "This could refer to John's preaching." Not so, because the thing described in verse 2 is something in the *past tense*, something completed, something that John is *not doing anymore*. Unless they want to argue that John decided to never preach again, this argument falls flat.

The apostle John is the writer of Revelation.

BLESSING ON THE READER

"Blessed is he that reads...the words of this prophecy" (1:3).

In the synagogues and in the early church, it was common for someone to go before the rest of the congregation and read from the Scriptures. Jesus did this in the synagogue at Nazareth in Luke 4:16-

20. Paul commanded his letters be read to the congregation (Colossians 4:16). Not everyone was literate in those days, so those who were able to read (and read well) were expected to help the others by reading aloud so they could hear and understand them as well. Imagine what would happen if the few people in a congregation who *could* read refused to tell the rest of the Christians what had been written to them!

Why is the one reading the Scripture blessed?

First, because he is reading God's word. Regardless of which section of Scripture we are reading, we are always blessed in reading God's word.

Second, because it is more blessed to give than to receive (Acts 20:35). In reading it, he gives of himself to the other members. In reading it, he shows compassion and concern for others, and shows himself to be a servant. In reading it, he helps other members understand what has been written.

Third (and perhaps this should have been first), God's word says the one reading this book will be blessed in his reading because "the time is at hand" (1:3). By reading this book, the original readers prepared themselves for what was about to happen. It would encourage and strengthen them to endure, knowing what would "shortly come to pass."

What makes it a blessing?

It is a blessing specifically because "the time is at hand" when John wrote. Yes, we can be blessed by a study of Revelation, but not like the original readers. We are blessed by reading Revelation in the same way we are blessed by studying books of the Old Testament whose events have been fulfilled.

The original readers were blessed by being prepared for the events which were about to take place. For us, the blessing is we see God's promises fulfilled, and learn principles about staying faithful in all situations (good or bad), because victory only comes in Jesus.

We are blessed when we read *all* of God's word (not just Revelation). We can learn about Jesus Christ and the hope he offers by means of His death on the cross. We can learn about the spiritual blessings that come from following Him (Ephesians 1:3). We can learn the answer to "what must I do to be saved?" (Acts 2:37-38). We can learn how to prepare ourselves for battle against the temptations of Satan (Ephesians 6:10-17).

But the blessing in Revelation isn't only on the one reading...

BLESSING ON THE HEARERS

Blessed...[are] they that hear the words of this prophecy (1:3).

The blessing is not just on the one reading it in the congregation, but also to those hearing it. This doesn't mean someone just hearing *sounds*, but someone who is actually *listening*. So often, people will sit through a Bible class or a sermon—and though they hear the words, it goes in one ear and right out the other. This blessing is upon those who *pay attention* to the reading of God's word.

Why is it a blessing for the hearers?

Why was it important for the original readers to pay attention to what was said in Revelation? Because for them, "the time is at hand"! For them, it was something they were about to experience and they needed to be aware of what was going on.

There is always a blessing when we honestly listen to God's word. We have a better knowledge of what God has promised for those who obey Him. We have a better understanding of what God expects from us. We are built up and encouraged if we are doing right. We are humbled and corrected if we are doing wrong. On the Day of Pentecost, 3,000 were blessed because they honestly heard what Peter taught them (Acts 2:21-22, 38, 41).

But reading and hearing God's word is not enough...

BLESSING ON THE DOERS

Blessed [are]...they that...keep the things which are written in it.

To "keep" something is to obey it. "If you love me, keep my commandments" (John 14:15). What does "keep my commandments" mean? To obey them! Hearing alone isn't enough (James 1:22). For those who originally received the book of Revelation, this would get their attention—a blessing is pronounced upon those who obey what is written in the book!

Why are doers blessed?

But why should they obey what is in the book? Because "the time is at hand!" The Christians had been persecuted heavily, but things were going to intensify even more (starting in AD 64 as Romans and Jews both ramped up their persecution against the Christians). Many Christians were put to death; many more would be tortured in an attempt to get them to renounce Jesus Christ. Today, many Christians get lazy and act as though they've got plenty of time to make things right with God; this was not the case for those who first received this letter. Wishy-washy Christians were basically told, "You'd better straighten up now, because you might not make it through these upcoming events." The faithful were told to hold on, because the horrible persecution would not last forever (see Revelation 2:10).

What kind of commands were they supposed to keep? "Remember where you've fallen from and repent and do the first works" (2:5). "Be faithful to death" (2:10). "Repent" (2:16). "Hold fast till I come" (2:25). "Be watchful, and strengthen the things which remain, that are ready to die...Remember how you received and heard, and hold fast, and repent" (3:2-3). "Hold fast what you have" (3:11). "Be zealous...and repent" (3:19). And those are just with the first few chapters. They were supposed to keep these commands because "the time is at hand."

What about keeping the commandments today? "You be doers of the word, and not hearers only" (James 1:22). A person who reads the Bible, but makes no application to himself, is lost. A person who hears the Bible read and explained, but doesn't ever live by it, is lost. It is only when someone "keeps" the things in the Bible that he is blessed.

WHAT DOES THIS MEAN FOR US TODAY?

Do you have time?

Is it really all that important that we keep the commandments of God *now*, or can we wait until later? Most people seem to think they've got all the time in the world. My cousin was a teenager who went to church his whole life. He could quote the plan of salvation for the teacher on Sunday morning. But he had never obeyed the gospel. He told his parents that he'd make sure to do it sometime, but he wasn't ready to do it yet. One day back in 2016 I got a call that he was killed in an automobile accident.

A man named Jim was an elder in the church. His wife decided to run off with another man, and Jim was devastated. He stopped coming to worship altogether. When someone would talk to him about it, he would tell them, "I know I should start going back, and I plan on it." But he never did, and just a few weeks ago, this man died.

Both of these people had read the Bible, heard many sermons from its pages, but didn't obey the commands of God.

Here's what most people don't seem to understand: the time is at hand for each of us! Let me ask you a question, "Are you going to die today?" Not a one of you can answer with a "no" and know that for certain. Do you realize today could be your last day alive? Can you tell me for certain Jesus will not return to judge the earth tomorrow? Of course you can't. It is no wonder the apostle Paul impressed on people the seriousness of making their lives right *now* instead of waiting. "*Now* is the acceptable time, behold *now* is the day of salvation!" (2 Corinthians 6:2). The Philippian jailor was baptized at midnight because it is too important to put off even for a few hours! (Acts 16:25-34). When should you obey God's word?

Now!

Don't put it off any longer!

STUDY SIX:
WHO IS THIS JESUS?
(REVELATION 1:4-6, 8)

Ask someone to describe Jesus, and you'll likely hear the following answers: Born of a virgin; Lived a perfect life; A good teacher; Died on a cross; Raised from the dead. And of course, all these are true. But when you read Revelation, you will find things about Him you might not have thought about.

In this lesson, we will be taking a look at some of those things found in Revelation 1:4-6. We will especially concentrate on the things said about Jesus. But let's make sure we cover all the bases.

"JOHN..."

As we saw in the last lesson, this is John the apostle. He is the only "John" then living whose writings would have been immediately accepted as inspired. This is important to remember, because this entire book has a sense of urgency to it—"the time is at hand"!

"TO THE SEVEN CHURCHES WHICH ARE IN ASIA."

These were seven literal congregations which existed in the Roman province called "Asia." This is not the continent of Asia, but the western edge of Asia Minor, across from Greece and Achaia.

Why seven churches?
The number seven occurs very frequently throughout Revelation, and carries the idea of completeness. We will see it again later on in this very same verse. The number seven appears 54 times in Revelation.

Since "seven" carries the idea of completeness, being addressed to "seven churches" shows its message was also for all the churches at that time. This is seen in the repeated statement "he that has an ear, let him hear what the Spirit says to the churches" (2:7, 11, 17, 29, 3:6, 13, 22). These seven congregations were representative of congregations everywhere.

Why write to Asia if it is about Jerusalem's destruction?

One of the biggest objections to the book being about the destruction of Jerusalem is: *"Why would a book describing the destruction of Jerusalem be written to congregations in Asia (over 1000 miles away)?"* I will level with you, this is the question I struggled with the most. But let's look at the evidence.

1. Most of the Christians in this area were Jews.

1 Peter was written to the "diaspora" (scattered ones) (1 Peter 1:1). This word "diaspora" appears three times in the New Testament, and refers to Jews who lived outside of the Promised Land (see John 7:35). Specifically, Peter wrote to the Jews *in Asia* and some of the surrounding areas who had become Christians.

Some people object, saying the Christians in that area were mostly Gentile. But the Bible points the other way. Peter was an apostle to the circumcision (Jews) (Galatians 2:7-10). It would be strange indeed for the apostle to the Jews to write a letter addressed almost exclusively to Gentiles.

Being Jews, they would have been interested to say the least.

2. Many Jewish Christians were considering going back.

Many Jewish Christians (and this would include some of the Christians in Asia) were giving serious thought to going back into Judaism (the entire book of Hebrews was written to fight this mass exodus). Some were scoffing because Christ had not returned in judgment on Jerusalem like He had promised in Matthew 24, and everything was continuing as normal. Revelation lets them know Judaism was about to be overthrown and Christians were God's *only* people.

3. Don't go to Jerusalem!

At least some Jewish Christians still made trips to Jerusalem for the annual feasts (Acts 20:16 shows Paul desiring to return to Jerusalem for Pentecost). This was a warning to not go anymore.

4. Jewish Christians were suffering greatly

The Jewish persecution against the Christians was very heavy in these areas (see Revelation 2:9, 3:9). Christians in Asia were undergoing "manifold temptations" (1 Peter 1:6), and were about to undergo a "fiery trial" (1 Peter 4:12). The rest of their brethren were undergoing the same sufferings (1 Peter 5:9). Nero had given his blessing to the Jews in AD 64 for them to do whatever they wanted to the Christians. The overthrow of Jerusalem was a promise that the persecutions would soon diminish—if not altogether cease—from the Jews.

The Roman Empire (under Nero) began a heavy persecution of Christians within Rome (64-68 AD), and the rulers of the Provinces likely followed suit. Christians in Asia needed reassurance and encouragement. During the Jewish/Roman War of 66-70 AD, most Roman soldiers did not make a distinction between religious Jews and Jewish *Christians*. Many Christians in Asia were killed during this war. They needed encouragement during this time of fiery trial. If you were a Jew (regardless of whether you were a Christian), you were considered Rome's enemy.

5. God did the same thing in the Old Testament.

When Jerusalem was about to be destroyed by Babylon in 586 BC, God had Ezekiel prophesy about it—and his message was delivered to the Jews in the area of Babylon, *not anywhere near Jerusalem* (over 400 miles). So there is biblical precedent for addressing a book about the destruction of Jerusalem to God's people outside of Jerusalem.

6. The Christians in Asia were the closest—and needed to hear the same message.

John being in Patmos (Revelation 1:9), the congregations in Asia would have been the closest to him. If you want to get a message out to *all* the Christians, your best bet is to spread the message close to where you are and then let it spread from there. Uninspired tradition says John spent much time in this area prior to Jerusalem's destruction, so he might have been familiar with these congregations as well.

7. Addressed to the churches in Asia, but not ONLY for them.

Since this is a book of symbols, these congregations are also symbolic of the entire church everywhere. Almost every book of the New Testament was addressed to a specific person of group of people, yet *every* book was intended for *all* Christians and congregations to read and apply to themselves. Why would Luke write his two works (Luke and Acts) to Theophilus? Why not to the church as a whole? Why didn't Paul write his letters just to "the church, wherever it happens to be"? It's because there were people that got the message first, who needed to hear it first, but it was never intended that they be the *only* recipients of the letters.

As soon as an inspired letter arrived, the congregation was expected to copy it and send it on to the next congregation (see Colossians 4:16). Revelation was *never* meant to be a letter *only* for the seven churches in Asia. They were just the first ones to receive the letter

So, just because it was initially addressed to the seven churches in Asia (which were the closest to where John was), it was expected that they would immediately copy it and send it to other congregations so it would spread quickly. And the quicker it gets to a congregation, the quicker another copy is made and the quicker it spreads.

8. The Jerusalem Christians had been warned already.

The Jewish Christians in Jerusalem had the book of Matthew (which includes the signs to look for in chapter 24), as well as possibly having at least some of the apostles and James, the brother of Jesus, still living there. So though the book of Revelation intimately concerned them, it isn't like there were unaware of the destruction Jesus had prophesied.

So in a nutshell…

The Christians in Asia were primarily Jewish, undergoing Jewish persecution (with the blessing of Rome), and about to undergo Roman persecution as well (being a Jewish Christian gave you a double-whammy). These Jewish Christians were likely wondering when Jesus was going to fulfill His word, having doubts about Christianity, and contemplating a return to Judaism in the face of all this persecution. The congregations in Asia were typical of all congregations both then and now. The quickest way to get the word spread about the contents of the book was for John to send it to the closest congregations and let them spread it; but the book was never intended solely for the churches in Asia.

If there is any other question as to why this would have been written to the seven churches in Asia, we will have to just say: *Jesus said to write it to them* (1:11).

GREETINGS FROM THE GODHEAD (1:4-5)

> *John to the seven churches which are in Asia: Grace to you, and peace, from him who is, and who was, and who is to come; and from the seven Spirits which are before his throne; and from Jesus Christ, who is the faithful witness, and the firstborn from the dead, and the prince of the kings of the earth.*

"Grace and peace…"

These were the common Greek and Hebrew greetings: *Grace* means "favor" and *Peace* is a reference to inner peace, tranquility. *Peace* is the same as the Hebrew word *Shalom*—as in Jeru-shalom (Jerusalem), and in Ab-Shalom (Absalom) and Shalom-on (Solomon).

We often wish people blessings when we greet them, perhaps without even realizing it: "Good morning," "good evening," "have a nice day," etc. But these blessings wished upon the churches by

John could only come from one source: the Godhead.

"From the one who is, who was, and who is to come."

There can be no doubt this is speaking of God the Father. This one is described as being ever existing (the meaning of the name Jehovah). He is also the one who sits on the throne—and is distinguished from the Lamb (Revelation 5:6-7). Most of chapter 4 describes God the Father on His throne.

> *6:16—"Hide us from the one who sits on the throne...and from the Lamb."*

> *7:10—"Salvation to the one who sits on the throne...and to the Lamb."*

This description of eternality, however, is also used of Jesus Christ (as we will see momentarily).

Do you want grace? Do you want peace? These can only be found in God.

"From the seven Spirits before His throne."

Some believe these are seven individual spirit messengers (angels) which do God's bidding. Let me just say, "No way." Exactly how does grace or peace come from angelic beings? It doesn't. Grace comes from God.

Since seven is a number which symbolizes completion or perfection, this is a reference to the Holy Spirit. This is the only view that makes sense. Let's look at the evidence:

The "seven spirits" were upon the Lamb, Jesus Christ (Revelation 5:6). Jesus, quoting Isaiah, said the Spirit of the Lord was upon Him (Luke 4:18). The Holy Spirit descended upon Jesus at His baptism (Matthew 3:16). Jesus had the Holy Spirit without measure (John 3:34). Jesus received the promise of the Holy Spirit after His ascension (Acts 2:33).

If anyone had doubts about the reality of the Holy Spirit in the Godhead, this should eliminate it, because no other being or group of beings could be given equal standing with the Father and the Son.

"AND FROM JESUS CHRIST..." (1:5-6)

...Jesus Christ, who is the faithful witness, and the firstborn from the dead, and the prince of the kings of the earth. To him who loved us, and washed us from our sins in his own blood, and has made us kings and priests to God his Father; to him be glory and dominion forever and ever. Amen.

There are many things said about Jesus in these verses.

He is the faithful witness (martyr).

This means His testimony (in His teaching, His life, His death, and through the Apostles) is trustworthy, is completely accurate in portraying what God the Father wanted taught (See John 8:14). We can see this as a description of Christ's earthly ministry.

He is the first begotten of the dead ones

The word "dead" is plural in Greek. So He is the preeminent one, the first and foremost of all those who have been or ever will be raised from the dead. But more than that, He is the first one to be reborn from the dead, a new existence—never to die again. Others had been raised from the dead, but they were simply brought back the way they were, and would die again. Jesus was reborn, and had taken on immortality—He could never again die. This is a description of the resurrection of Christ.

He is the prince of the kings of the earth.

The word "prince" means the chief ruler, the highest ruler (See Acts 5:31). He is the king of Israel (John 1:49, 12:13). He is the king of the Jews (Matthew 27:11, 37). He is the King of kings (1 Timothy 6:15).

The phrase "kings of the earth" could have one of two meanings here, both of which are accurate. It could mean Jesus' role as ruler places Him above all other kings in the entire world, which is absolutely true (Daniel 7:13-14). It could also be a reference to the rulers of the Land (Israel, the Promised Land), as the inspired apostles used the phrase in Acts 4:25-29. If this is the case, then it means the leaders of the Jews (who were behind His crucifixion) would have to answer to Him. Though both are true, this second interpretation fits better with the events described in the book (the destruction of Jerusalem and Judaism).

Regardless of which view is taken, this describes Jesus in His ascended state.

He is the one who loved us.

Even when He was completely abandoned by His closest friends, Jesus showed love by dying for them (and for us). Even when the Jewish mob was hurling insults at Him while He hung on the cross, Jesus showed love for them in His words, "Father, forgive them, for they know not what they do" (Luke 23:34).

He is the one who washed us in His own blood.

This is written to Jesus' blood-bought servants (1:1), and the only ones who can receive the blessings of Jesus' love are those who have taken advantage of what He did. It is universally agreed this is a reference to being washed from our sins in the blood of Christ. Don't you find it interesting that the only other verse which talks about washing away your sins says it is done in baptism? (Acts 22:16). The only ones who have been washed in the blood of Christ are those who have submitted to Him in baptism.

Some translations have the word "released" (NASB) or "freed" (NIV) instead of "washed," because some Greek manuscripts accidentally left out a letter: *lousanti* vs. *lusanti*. Ultimately, both words express truth, so I see no reason to dwell on it.

He is the one who made us kings

Some say, "How are Christians kings?" This isn't to say we are actively ruling over other people. It means we have become part of the royal family. Jesus is the King of kings, and we—being made children of the heavenly Father through Christ—are now part of that royal family, granted access to all the privileges that come with it.

Doesn't the king give preference to His family? As part of the royal family, we have the right and privilege of approaching the Father with our requests.

He is the one who made us priests to God the Father.

Priests can approach God in prayer and seek forgiveness. Under the Old Testament, if you wanted forgiveness of your sins, you had to go to the priest so he could offer a sacrifice on your behalf. The High Priest offered a sacrifice once a year for unknown sins of the people (Hebrews 9:7). But since Jesus has made *us* to be priests, we can go to the Father directly, seeking forgiveness for ourselves—we don't need an earthly priest to do it for us!

Christians are a chosen generation, a royal (kingly) priesthood (1 Peter 2:9)—and this is done through Christ!

His dominion (rule) is forever and ever.

This idea is also found in Isaiah 9:6-7 and Daniel 7:13-14. There will never be another kingdom of God other than what presently exists: Christ's rule over His people—the church. This reign was a present reality in the first century. So how is it some claim Christ isn't reigning and won't be until He comes back?

(Because of the importance of verse 7, we will deal with it exclusively in the next lesson.)

THE MYSTERY OF VERSE 8

> "I am Alpha and Omega, the beginning and the ending," says the Lord, "who is, and who was, and who is to come, the Almighty."

Should verse 8 apply to the Father (since part of what is said matches the description of the Father from verse 4)? Or should it apply to the Son (since part of what is said matches with the description of the Son from verse 11)?

It is clear whoever is speaking the words in verse 8 is speaking all of them about Himself. It seems the best way to interpret this is as a description of both the Father and the Son, showing their equality as deity.

John applied Old Testament prophecies about Jehovah on His throne to Jesus (see John 12:37-41, quoting Isaiah 6). So it shouldn't be any surprise if here John were to write in a way that equates the Father and the Son in their eternality. It is a connecting, or transition verse which connects the eternality of the Father to that of the Son.

He is the "Alpha and the Omega."

This is the first letter and last letter of the Greek alphabet. This phrase doesn't just mean he is the A and the Z, but it implies everything in between as well. God (Father and Son) is at the beginning, and will still be there at the end.

He is "the beginning and the End."

The creation of all things physical is attributed to God the Father (Genesis 1) and God the Son (John 1). The end of all things physical is an event in which the Father and the Son will be involved as well.

He is eternal.

He is the one who is, who was, and who is to come. Jesus (as part of the Godhead) has always existed, and will always exist.

WHAT DOES THIS MEAN FOR US TODAY?

Jesus is God

Jesus is God, just as John 1:1 says He is. Otherwise John was blasphemous in equating the eternality of the Father and the Son. Let us take care not to minimize the glory, grandeur, and power of Jesus—God the Son.

Grace and peace comes through obedience to God.

Grace and peace only come by means of the Father, Son, and Holy Spirit. The Father originated the plan of redeeming man. The Son carried out the plan through His perfect life and His death on the cross as the perfect sacrifice for our sins. The Holy Spirit proved these things to be so through miraculous works and in recording these things for us to read, know, hear, and obey.

There is no grace outside of obedience to the inspired Scriptures. There is no grace outside of the blood-bought church of Jesus Christ. There is no grace outside of Christ.

STUDY SEVEN:
COMING IN THE CLOUDS
(REVELATION 1:7)

Jesus is coming soon! How many times have you heard that? People are confused about *when* Jesus is going to come, *how* He is going to come, and what He's going to do when He finally does come. So when they look in the Scriptures, and see descriptions of a "coming" of Jesus Christ, they automatically assume it is a description of the final coming of Christ.

That isn't always the case.

So, what do we do with Revelation 1:7? Is it speaking about the final coming of Jesus Christ? Is it talking about His coming in judgment upon Jerusalem? Is it talking about His coming in judgment upon the Roman Empire? Is it talking about coming in judgment against a specific congregation or group of congregations? Is there any way we can know for sure???

If we look back over the things we've covered thus far, along with other passages in the Bible which describe similar things, the meaning of Revelation 1:7 becomes clear.

What is this book about?

Remember that this book was written about things which "must shortly come to pass" (1:1, 22:6), and things which were "at hand" (1:3, 22:10). It was written before the fall of Jerusalem, because some of the events which were "at hand" were to take place in that city (11:8). Knowing the book was written about things which were about to happen, and that its spread was urgent (the time is at hand!), should we assume this verse refers to something at least 2,000 years away?

Remember the book describes the overthrow of Jerusalem. Matthew 23:34-39 explains why it was necessary.

- Jerusalem was guilty of the blood of ALL the righteous.

- Jerusalem had killed the apostles and prophets.
- Jerusalem would be destroyed to avenge all this blood.

Revelation 18:20-19:2 gives the reasons for the overthrow of the city called "Babylon."

- Babylon was guilty of the blood of ALL the righteous.
- Babylon had killed the apostles and prophets.
- Babylon's destruction was to avenge all this blood.

Therefore: Jerusalem is Babylon.

Remember Revelation is written primarily in figurative language. Though not every part is figurative, we should interpret it as figurative speech more often than not. So, keep that in mind as we look at this verse.

> *Behold, he is coming with clouds; and every eye shall see him, even those who pierced him: and all tribes of the earth shall wail because of him. Even so, Amen.*

"BEHOLD, HE IS COMING WITH CLOUDS."

There is more than one kind of "coming" of Jesus Christ. Jesus promised to come in judgment against Jerusalem (Matthew 24:27, 30). Jesus threatened to come in judgment against individual congregations (Revelation 2:5, 16, 3:3). Jesus is coming to judge the world on the final day (Matthew 25:31-33).

John says Jesus "cometh" (KJV) or, more literally, "is coming." This is in present tense, and indicates this coming has already begun (hence the urgency of the letter). The events foretold in Revelation had already been set into motion. The judgment was shortly to take place!

Coming with clouds or *coming in the clouds* is an idea from the Old Testament. If we understand what it meant in *those* passages, we can understand what it means in Revelation 1:7.

Jeremiah 4:12b-14

> *Now I will also speak judgment against them, Be-*
> *hold, he shall **come up like clouds**, and his chariots*
> *like a whirlwind, His horses are swifter than eagles,*
> *Woe to us, for we are plundered! O Jerusalem, wash*
> *your heart from wickedness that you may be saved,*
> *How long shall your evil thoughts lodge within you?*

This speaks of *coming like clouds*, and is a description of God's coming in judgment against Jerusalem/Judah for their sins. This was fulfilled when Babylon took Israel captive and destroyed the city of Jerusalem in 586 BC.

From this passage, you can see that a coming of God with clouds doesn't necessarily mean the final judgment—sometimes it describes judgment against a city or a nation. One writer said coming with clouds means a day of gloominess, for they were about to be punished. With that in mind…

Ezekiel 34:12

> *As a shepherd seeks out his flock on the day he is*
> *among his scattered sheep, so will I seek out My*
> *sheep and deliver them from all the places where*
> *they were scattered **on a cloudy and dark day**.*

God describes the day Israel was scattered as a "cloudy" day. This cloudy day was the same one Jeremiah described above, when God would come like clouds—the day of judgment against them, carried out by Babylon.

Ezekiel 30:3-4, 18

> *For the day is near, even the day of the LORD is*
> *near, **a cloudy day**; it shall be the time of the heathen.*
> *And the sword shall come upon Egypt, and great pain*

shall be in Ethiopia, when the slain shall fall in Egypt, and they shall take away her multitude, and her foundations shall be broken down.

This day of the Lord (which includes much bloodshed and violence) was called a "cloudy day." Verse 18 of the same chapter says

*At Tehaphnehes also the day shall be darkened, when I shall break there the yokes of Egypt: and the pomp of her strength shall cease in her; as for her, **a cloud shall cover her**, and her daughters shall go into captivity.*

Ezekiel 32:7

*And when I shall put you out, I will cover the heaven, and make the stars thereof dark; I will cover the sun **with a cloud**, and the moon shall not give her light.*

Joel 2:1-2

*You all blow the trumpet in Zion, and sound an alarm in my holy mountain: let all the inhabitants of the land tremble: for the day of the LORD comes, for it is near at hand; A day of darkness and of gloominess, **a day of clouds** and of thick darkness, as the morning spread upon the mountains: a great and strong people; there has not been ever the like, neither shall be any more after it, even to the years of many generations.*

The day of the Lord against Jerusalem (Zion) is described as a day of clouds. This is a warning of judgment against His people.

Zephaniah 1:14-17

The great day of the LORD is near, it is near, and hurries greatly, even the voice of the day of the LORD: the mighty man shall cry there bitterly. That

day is a day of wrath, a day of trouble and distress,
a day of wasteness and desolation, a day of darkness
*and gloominess, **a day of clouds** and thick darkness,*
A day of the trumpet and alarm against the fenced
cities, and against the high towers. And I will bring
distress upon men, that they shall walk like blind
men, because they have sinned against the LORD:
and their blood shall be poured out as dust, and they
flesh as the dung.

"The day of the Lord," a phrase which in the Old Testament *always* refers to judgment upon a nation, people, or city, is called "a day of clouds."

Isaiah 19:1-4

*The burden of Egypt. Behold the LORD **rides upon a***
***swift cloud**, and shall come into Egypt: and the idols*
of Egypt shall be moved at His presence, and the
heart of Egypt shall melt in the midst of it...And the
Egyptians will I give over into the hand of a cruel
lord; and a fierce king shall rule over them, says the
Lord, the LORD of hosts.

God will come (it is a *coming*) into Egypt upon a cloud. This coming on a cloud is to overthrow Egypt.

Psalm 104:1, 3

Bless the LORD, O my soul. O LORD my God, you
are very great; you are clothed with honor and maj-
esty...Who lays the beams of his chambers in the wa-
*ters: who **makes the clouds his chariot**: who walks*
upon the wings of the wind...

The clouds are God's chariot. A chariot is an instrument of war. If God is coming in the clouds/chariot, He is coming to wage war or bring judgment.

Matthew 24:30

> *And then shall appear the sign of the Son of man in heaven: and then shall all the tribes of the earth mourn, and they shall see the Son of man **coming in the clouds of heaven with power and glory**.*

Note what Jesus says just four verses later: "Truly I say to you, *This generation shall not pass till all these things be fulfilled*" (24:34). This coming of Jesus in the clouds of heaven would happen in the lifetime of that generation in which Jesus lived.

Matthew 26:64

> *Jesus says to him, "You have said it. Nevertheless, I say to you, Hereafter shall you see the Son of man sitting on the right hand of power, and **coming in the clouds of heaven**."*

Jesus spoke this to the high priest, Caiaphas, in front of the scribes and elders (26:57). Jesus was speaking *to them*, and said to them, *you* will see the Son of man coming in the clouds of heaven. The most logical way to understand this passage is that Jesus was saying some of them would live to see it happen (especially when you put it with Matthew 24:30, 34).

Before we continue…

Each of the passages we have looked at describe divine *judgment* on a city, nation, or people—and each one describes it as "cloudy," "with clouds," or "on the clouds." Not one of these passages describe the final coming of Jesus at the end of time. When the original readers of Revelation heard verse 7, *these passages* would have been the backdrop for their understanding of "coming with clouds."

With this in mind, let's look at our verse.

Revelation 1:7

Based on the usage of comings and clouds in the Old Testament, and in Jesus' own words, and also remembering the context of Revelation ("shortly come to pass" and "at hand"), we should not assume this is talking about Jesus' final coming to judge the world. That event was not "shortly come to pass" or "at hand." This verse should not be taken as Jesus literally descending in literal clouds to the literal earth. This is a description of Jesus' imminent coming in judgment against Jerusalem.

Homer Hailey, who applies the book to the destruction of Rome, some 400 years after Revelation was written (thus doesn't agree with us on the dating or application of this verse), had this to say about verse 7:

> ...this passage...includes the idea of His coming on clouds in all judgments before that great event... Jesus promised that He would come "on the clouds of heaven" in judgment against Jerusalem. (Commentary on Revelation, pg. 102)

Jim McGuiggan, who also applies the book to Rome instead of Jerusalem, had this to say:

> The "2nd" (final) coming of Jesus? Perhaps so, but before you draw your conclusion, remember 1:1, 3, 22:6, 7, 10. Remember you're in an apocalyptic book, and while that doesn't mean every jot and tittle is figurative, it does mean you lean first in the figurative direction.
>
> Check the word "coming" in the Bible. See for example the "comings" in the seven letters in the next two chapters. Go ahead, read the letters now. Tell me what you think of those "comings." Ask yourself about Isaiah 19:1, James 5:8 [Be ye also patient; stablish your hearts: for the coming of the Lord draweth nigh.] and a host of others...And while you're look-

ing, read Matthew 24:30, 34. Note that similar language is used in this text, but that verse 34 claims it was fulfilled in the generation in which Jesus lived" (Revelation, pgs. 36-37).

The "coming with clouds" is not the final coming of Jesus. Instead, the context of Revelation, and the previous use of "clouds" imagery in the Bible, demands we interpret it to be a coming in judgment—on Jerusalem.

Oh, but what about the next phrase, "every eye shall see him"?

"EVERY EYE SHALL SEE HIM, AND THEY ALSO WHICH PIERCED HIM."

Are we to take this phrase literally, as in every literal eyeball which has ever existed will literally see the literal Jesus in His literal coming to literal earth in literal clouds? This is the way most people seem to view this verse. But that goes against the idea of this being something which was "shortly come to pass" and "*sign*ified" (told in symbols).

Let's examine some things which will help us to understand this part of the passage.

The word translated "see" means to gaze upon or to stare at. It is the same word used in John 19:37—"they shall *look* upon him whom they have pierced." This is a quote from Zechariah 12:10. Let's read in its context.

> *And I will pour on the house of David, and on the inhabitants of Jerusalem, the spirit of grace and of supplications:* **and they shall look upon me whom they have pierced**, *and they shall mourn for him, as one mourns for his only son, and shall be in bitterness for him, as one that is in bitterness for his firstborn. In that day shall there be a great mourning*

> *in Jerusalem, and the mourning of Hadadrimmon in*
> *the valley of Megiddon [Armageddon, Revelation*
> *16:16]. And the land shall mourn, every family*
> *apart; the family of the house of David apart, and*
> *their wives apart; and the family of the house of Na-*
> *than apart, and their wives apart; The family of the*
> *house of Levi apart, and their wives apart; the family*
> *of Shimei apart, and their wives apart; All the fami-*
> *lies that remain, every family apart, and their wives*
> *apart (Zechariah 12:10-14).*

Zechariah says the pierced one will be gazed upon (same word as in Revelation 1:7) by those who pierced Him. The result would be mourning in Jerusalem, as in the days of the battle of Armageddon (which was a past event—2 Kings 23:29) when King Josiah was killed. All of the land (same word as "earth" in Revelation 1:7) would mourn, all the different families of the land would be in mourning.

This points to destruction, brought by God, which would bring mourning to the people of Jerusalem.

Oh, I see!

When we say, "Oh, I see," often what we mean is, "I understand." The Bible uses it that way as well.

Galatians 3:1

> *O foolish Galatians, who hath bewitched you, that*
> *you should not obey the truth, **before whose eyes** Je-*
> *sus Christ has been evidently set forth, crucified*
> *among you?*

Jesus didn't go to Galatia, nor was He crucified there. But Paul could say they saw the truth about Jesus—meaning they *understood* it.

Ephesians 1:18

The eyes of your understanding being enlightened...

Again, "eyes" here is not a reference to the physical eyeball, but to understanding.

It was "seen" or understood.

Even heathen Gentiles understood Jerusalem was destroyed because of what they did to Jesus.

Mara bon Sarpion, a Gentile in prison, wrote to his son in AD 73, and included the following words:

> What advantage did the Jews gain from executing their wise king? It was just after that that their kingdom was abolished. God justly avenged these three wise men: the Athenians died of hunger; the Samians were overwhelmed by the sea; the Jews, ruined and driven from their land, live in complete dispersion.

Arthur Ogden (in *Avenging of the Apostles and Prophets*) said:

> "Neither Jesus nor John meant that He would be seen with the human eye. The expression is used metaphorically. The thought is that mankind would see God's hand in the events transpiring in the desolation of Israel and the destruction of Jerusalem. Even the rulers of the Jews who were responsible for Jesus' death would likewise perceive His involvement in this destruction for they which pierced him would also see him (Matthew 26:64)." (pgs. 105-106)

Foy E. Wallace (in *The Book of Revelation*) said:

> "Both the impact and the import of the occurring events would be of universal knowledge. The siege and fall of Jerusalem would be known to the entire

population of the Roman empire, both Jewish and pagan." (pg. 71)

WHO ARE THE ONES WHO PIERCED JESUS?

According to Zechariah 12:10-14, it is the Jews. According to Matthew 27:24-25, it is the Jews. According to Acts 2:23, 36, it is the Jews.

There was only one man who literally pierced Jesus, the Roman soldier in John 19:34. However, Revelation 1:7 cannot refer to him, because John says *they* which pierced Him. The word "they" is plural, showing that a specific *group of people*, not a specific person, is under consideration.

The ESV (and other translations as well) reads "and every eye shall see Him, *even* those who pierced him." When the Greek word *kai* is translated "*even*," it can have the sense of repeating or specifying something. 1 Corinthians 15:24—"when he shall have delivered up the kingdom to God, *even* the Father..." 2 Corinthians 1:3— "Blessed be God, *even* the Father..." 1 Thessalonians 3:13—"before God, *even* our Father..." 2 Thessalonians 2:16 reads similarly. Which God? God the Father (as opposed to the Son or the Holy Spirit).

Similarly, in Revelation 1:7, we see something being repeated and specified: every eye shall see Him—whose eyes? The ones who pierced Him—*The Jews*.

ALL KINDREDS OF THE EARTH SHALL WAIL BECAUSE OF HIM

As we mentioned a few lessons ago, the phrase "all kindreds of the earth shall wail" (KJV) is the same (in Greek) as the phrase translated "all tribes of the earth shall mourn" in Matthew 24:30. The kindreds are the tribes.

In Matthew 24:30, the tribes of the earth would mourn because of Jesus' coming in judgment upon Jerusalem in that generation (see 24:34). The exact same group of people is under consideration in Revelation 1:7, and they would mourn for the exact same reason: *Jesus is coming with the clouds in judgment upon Jerusalem.*

What tribes would mourn when Jesus comes in judgment upon Jerusalem? The tribes of Israel—the Jews.

As we showed in an earlier lesson, the word "earth" (*ge*) is the word also translated "land" (as in the Promised Land), and matches perfectly with what Zechariah said in 12:10-12.

- 12:10—"they shall mourn." Who? The Jews.
- 12:11—"A great mourning in Jerusalem."
- 12:12—"And the land [same word as in Revelation 1:7] shall mourn."

When you see the phrase, "the earth," in Revelation, it usually normally refers to the land—the Promised Land of Judea.

Why would the tribes of Judea wail or mourn?

Because Jesus is coming in judgment against them (just like He said He would in Matthew 24). Because the one city that was central to their entire lives—physically, nationally, spiritually, economically, religiously—was about to be destroyed. Because many of their friends and relatives (and perhaps even their own lives) would be destroyed. Because they would realize they brought it upon themselves.

WHAT DOES THIS MEAN FOR US TODAY?

Are you in the same situation?

The "coming with clouds" was a description of coming in judgment. This "coming with clouds" was "shortly come to pass" and "at hand" (1:1, 3). The "coming with clouds" would cause the Jews to mourn. This "coming with clouds" would take place during the days of the generation Jesus spoke to (Matthew 24:30, 34). This "coming with clouds" is a description of Jesus' coming in judgment against the Jewish nation.

Why was Jesus going to come in judgment upon the Jews? Because they had rejected Him, and obeyed not the gospel.

> *Jesus Christ will come "in flaming fire, taking vengeance on those who know not God and who obey not the gospel of our Lord Jesus Christ" (2 Thessalonians 1:7-8).*

Here's the question for each of you now: Spiritually speaking, are you in any better shape than the Jews were? Have you continued to reject Christ's invitation? Have you put off obeying the gospel?

Jesus said the destruction of Jerusalem would be violent and bloody, a "great tribulation such as was not since the beginning of the world to this time, no, nor ever shall be." If you aren't a Christian, you are in the same spiritual condition as the people who deserved that destruction. Please give that some serious thought.

Study Eight:
The Vision of Jesus

On a lonely, rocky, wind-swept island in the Aegean Sea, an island known for fishing villages and exiled Roman prisoners, a man stood. He was in his mid-60s, and didn't get around as easily as he once did. Why was he on this island? Some think he was a prisoner there, others think he went there to preach, and still others think he went there for a different purpose. This man was the apostle John. And this is the setting for what we are about to read.

JOHN'S SITUATION (1:9)

I John, who am also your brother, and companion in tribulation, and in the kingdom and patience of Jesus Christ, was in the isle called Patmos, for the word of God, and for the testimony of Jesus Christ.

As John wrote to the churches, he offered them hope. John could honestly say, "I understand what you're going through; I feel your pain," because he was enduring the same things they were. He said, "I am your brother and companion in tribulation, and in the kingdom, and patience of Jesus Christ."

He was their brother in Jesus Christ.
All Christians are brethren, siblings, in Jesus Christ, born again as children of the Father in heaven. This happens when one is baptized (John 3:3-5, Galatians 3:26-27).

He was their companion in tribulation.
The persecution of Christians during AD 64-70 was fierce. The Jews persecuted Christians heavily, and Rome joined in. Then the Roman-Jewish war broke out, and Christians got targeted in that as well (because Christianity was viewed as a sect of Judaism, and many of the Christians were Jews). This persecution stretched across

the entire Roman Empire.

The word "tribulation" is used by Jesus to describe the time leading up to the destruction of Jerusalem (Matthew 24:21). Christians were to flee from Judea when they saw the armies of Rome surround the city, because shortly after that, there would be great tribulation, such as had never happened before and would never happen again. And immediately after that tribulation, Jerusalem would be destroyed (Matthew 24:29-30). "Tribulation" in Revelation 1:9 is speaking of the same troubles, which would affect most Christians alive at that time.

John was indeed suffering in the persecution just as badly as the Christians to whom he wrote.

He was their companion in the kingdom of Jesus Christ.

When Jesus comes back to earth, He will set up His kingdom, and reign on earth from Jerusalem for a thousand years! You've heard that before, right? The problem with that theory is it completely ignores what John wrote back in the first century—the kingdom of Jesus Christ was already a present reality. *You can't be in a kingdom that doesn't exist!* Jesus Christ has been reigning in His kingdom for almost 2,000 years already! (You might also want to read Colossians 1:13.)

John wrote this to suffering Christians to remind them: we are in the kingdom! Though things might look bleak, and in fact were going to get worse before they got better, they needed to remember the kingdom was real. They needed to remember that even if they were put to death, they were in the kingdom of Jesus Christ, and they were saved! John isn't just stating "Oh by the way, remember the kingdom exists," but instead reminds them of their hope, and helps build their confidence in the face of the severe persecution. It is as though he is saying, "My friends, let us face this persecution with confidence, and let's face it together!"

John was their companion in the patience [perseverance] of Jesus Christ.

This patience can be found in Jesus Christ. This patience, or *perseverance*, comes from the knowledge that Jesus is who the Bible claims He is, and the confidence that staying faithful to Him will result in eternal life. When you have that confidence, it makes persevering much easier. John basically says, "we're in this together; we're being persecuted; but we're in the kingdom of Jesus Christ, so we can overcome these persecutions!" It is a message of great hope!

John was on the isle of Patmos.

This island was a place political prisoners were exiled. The Old Syriac translation (second century) titles the final book of the Bible: "The Revelation, which was made by God to John the Evangelist, in the island of Patmos, to which he was banished by Nero."

John was on this island "for the word of God, and for the testimony of Jesus Christ." John nowhere explicitly states he was on Patmos as a prisoner, or that he had been exiled there. It is possible John was (in fulfilling his apostolic duties) acting as a missionary to some of the villages that existed on the island.

Some believe John went to Patmos for the singular purpose of receiving the Revelation…but that's not very likely. After all, isn't God powerful enough to give John this vision wherever he happened to be?

It is most likely that John was on Patmos as a result of his preaching the gospel (perhaps even as a direct result of his publishing and distributing his gospel account—see the same wording in 1:2).

THE VOICE! (1:10-11)

I was in the Spirit on the Lord's day, and heard behind me a great voice, like a trumpet, Saying, "I am

Alpha and Omega, the first and the last," and, "What you see, write in a book, and send it to the seven churches which are in Asia;nto Ephesus, and to Smyrna, and to Pergamos, and to Thyatira, and to Sardis, and to Philadelphia, and to Laodicea."

John was in the spirit.

There are different interpretations as to what this phrase means. Some say it means he was worshiping "in spirit" (no "the" in Greek here). Some say it means he was sitting there in a state of spiritual ecstasy (??). Some say it means he was thinking of spiritual things. What we can know is John was no longer speaking of physical things, but of the vision.

The vision started with the point that he was "in the spirit." It is similar to Paul's "non-body" experience where he was caught up to heaven and saw things (2 Corinthians 12:2-3). It is because John was "in the spirit" that he was able to see the vision. John was now on a spiritual plane.

On the Lord's Day.

Some say this means "day of the Lord," and as such refers to a day of judgment upon someone (most likely Jerusalem). But John received the vision "on the Lord's day." Then he would have to write it down. Then he would have to send it. Then it would have to get distributed to the seven churches in Asia, and eventually make its way to Jerusalem. If this phrase refers to the destruction of Jerusalem, then that destruction was going on when he was writing, and the warnings would be far too late to be of any good.

The Greek word used here for "Lord's" (*kuriakos*) is only used twice in the entirety of the Bible—here, and in 1 Corinthians 11 when describing the "Lord's Supper." It means "belonging to the Lord." The phrase "day of the Lord" appears in the New Testament, but never using this word (see Acts 2:16-22). The early Christians (first and second century) universally referred to the first day of the week as "the Lord's Day." This is the day wherein our Lord was raised from the dead. This is the day we celebrate His death in the Lord's Supper. It is the day the early church met (Acts 20:7, 1 Corinthians 16:1-2).

Therefore, John's vision was given to Him on a Sunday. And really, don't you think that's appropriate? The day of the week in which Christ overcame death is the day of the week in which Christ gives the message to others that they can overcome as well!

Then John heard a great voice, like a trumpet.

Trumpets are loud, and when used by those who can play them, they are clear and unmistakable. Trumpets were used (and are still used) to call attention to something. Trumpets were also used (and sometimes still are) in battle.

This great voice immediately got John's attention.

The Voice said: I am the Alpha and Omega, the first and the last (v. 11).

This is Jesus Christ speaking. We know this because John sees "one like to the Son of man" (v. 13). We know this because he also says, "I am he that lives and was dead" (v. 18).

The Voice then said, "What you see, write in a scroll"

This is the divine commission to write down the contents of the vision. What John was about to see revealed was of extreme importance, for God wanted the record of it kept.

"...and send it to the seven churches that are in Asia; to Ephesus, Smyrna, Pergamos, Thyatira, Sardis, Philadelphia, and Laodicea" (v. 11).

This vision was not just for John's benefit, but he was commanded to write it down and start sending it to the churches. These seven churches are given in the order in which the letter would travel once it left Patmos, traveling along the main roadways in that area. We will deal with the individual cities as we get into chapters 2 and 3.

WHAT JOHN SAW (1:12-16)

And I turned to see the voice that spoke with me. And having turned, I saw seven golden candlesticks. And in the midst of the seven candlesticks one like the Son of man, clothed with a garment down to the foot, and clothed about the chest with a golden sash.

His head and his hairs were white like wool, as white as snow; and his eyes were like a flame of fire; and his feet like fine brass, as if they burned in a furnace; and his voice like the sound of many waters.

In his right hand, he held seven stars: and out of his mouth went a sharp two-edged sword: and his countenance shone like the sun in its strength.

Since John was given the command to write what he *saw*, he turned to look and see the One who spoke to him (v. 12). At this point, he hadn't seen anything to write down yet.

When he turned, he saw seven golden candlesticks.

Most translations say "golden lampstands." In the temple of the Old Testament, there was a golden lampstand which had seven arms to it. In John's vision, there are seven *individual* lampstands. Jesus explains that the golden lampstands are representative of the seven churches (v. 20).

Since seven is a number used throughout Revelation to symbolize completeness or perfection, the seven candlesticks/lampstands represent all the individual congregations of the Lord's church. The church isn't the light, but they hold up the light for others to see.

He was clothed with a garment down to the foot.

In the midst of the golden lampstands was Jesus Christ Himself—but not the way John remembered Him!

Josephus says the garments of the high priest went down to the foot (*Wars*, 5.5.7). Royalty often wore garments which went to the foot, and some have suggested perhaps this is a symbol of Jesus' role as King. Given that He is among the lampstands (reminiscent of the priest in the temple), it seems more likely this is a symbol describing Jesus as the High Priest.

He wore a golden sash around his chest.

This is similar to what the high priest of Israel wore (Leviticus 8:7, Josephus *Wars* 5.5.7). This sash or belt being gold shows the preciousness and value of Jesus' role as our High Priest.

His head and hairs were white as wool, as white as snow.

Some see in this a symbol of absolute purity (which certainly would describe Jesus). The hair white as snow shows age, and implies wisdom. This is a way of describing Jesus as eternal (the age), with unlimited wisdom. It is important to note this is how Daniel described the Ancient of Days—God the Father—in Daniel 7:9. This description of Jesus Christ shows that He is indeed God.

His eyes were as a flame of fire.

The eyes are what we see, know, and understand things with. All things are visible to Jesus, He needs no external light to see, for His eyes have their own light. Hebrews 4:13—"all things are naked and opened to the eyes of him with whom we have to do."

This is similar to Daniel 10:5-6. The vision Daniel saw described the things that would happen to his people (the Jews) in the "latter days" (Daniel 10:14). That vision begins in chapter 11, and goes through the end of the book (chapter 12). In 12:1, Daniel is told, "there shall be a time of trouble, such as never was since there was a nation even to that same time." This is the same thing Jesus said with regards to the destruction of Jerusalem (Matthew 24:21). It is very likely some of the imagery here is designed to bring Daniel's vision to mind, and let the people know the end of the Jews is near.

His feet were like fine brass, as if they burned in a furnace.

Again, this is similar to Daniel 10:5-6. Consider Micah 4:13—

God promised to give his people feet of brass so that they could beat in pieces many people (NASB—pulverize many peoples). Jesus with feet of burning brass shows His ability to "tread down the wicked" and make them "ashes under the soles of [His] feet" (Malachi 4:3). This shows Jesus' power to easily destroy His enemies – nothing can stand in His way.

His voice was as the sound of many waters.

We've already read that His voice was like a trumpet—loud and clear. Now it is described as "the sound of many waters." You can hear a river long before you can actually see it; it is loud and its sound carries; it is "powerful and majestic."[1] Another possibility is that later on in Revelation, "many waters" has a reference to "many peoples" (17:1, 15), and perhaps means Jesus "speaks through the instrumentality of men."[2]

In His right hand, there were seven stars.

The right hand is the hand of power. Jesus is on the right hand of God (Acts 2:33). The apostles offered Paul and Barnabas the right-hand of fellowship (Galatians 2:9). Most people are right-handed, and it is the hand they wield their weapons with. The point is these stars are within His power, and were being used for His purposes.

Imagine a being powerful enough to hold one star, let alone seven in His hand. They are millions of degrees hot, yet Christ has no problem holding them. This is power.

Out of His mouth went a two-edged sword.

A single-edged sword was only good for cutting one way, and not as effective in battle. A double-edged blade meant you could kill someone coming or going. The word here refers to a big, heavy, Thracian battle-sword, as opposed to the smaller Roman blade. So,

---

[1] David L. Roper, *Revelation, Vol. 1* (Searcy, AR: Resource Publications, 2002), p. 87.

[2] Ogden, *Avenging of the Apostles and Prophets*, p. 115

Jesus is pictured as having destructive power by His mere words. By the word of His mouth, His enemies will be destroyed.

The sword of the Spirit is the word of God (Ephesians 6:17). The Word of God is sharper than any two-edged sword…and is a discerner of the thoughts and intents of the heart.—Hebrews 4:12.

Not only is it through the word of Jesus' mouth that the enemies would be destroyed, but it is also based on the Word of God—the Scriptures. God's word determines the friends and the enemies.

His countenance (face) shone like the sun in its strength.

Just as during the transfiguration, Jesus' face shone bright as the sun (Matthew 17:2). At that event, God spoke from heaven and said, "This is my beloved Son, in whom I am well pleased. You listen to Him" (Matthew 17:5). Jesus is the "brightness of His glory, and the express image of His person" (Hebrews 1:3). This again shows that Jesus is Deity. It is a symbol of great power and majesty.

DON'T BE AFRAID (1:17-18)

And when I saw him, I fell at his feet as dead. And he laid his right hand on me, saying to me, "Don't be afraid; I am the first and the last. I am the one who lives, and was dead; and, behold, I am alive forevermore, Amen; and I have the keys of hell and of death."

In the face of this awesome and frightful sight, John fell down at Jesus' feet as though he was dead (v. 17). Though John had known Jesus, been friends with Him, and even been called "the disciple whom Jesus loved," this vision of Jesus overwhelmed him. How would you react to seeing this vision?

Jesus placed His right hand on John and said, "Fear not" or "Don't be afraid." Isn't it amazing that the Jesus who was just pictured as all-powerful, ready to destroy His enemies, has compassion and concern for His people? He reached down and said, "Don't be afraid." When we obey God's will, we have nothing to fear! But when we disobey God and place ourselves among His enemies, we are put ourselves in the target of Jesus' destructive power.

The Christians to whom John wrote would find comfort in this as well, because Jesus says, "Fear not…I am the one who lives and was dead, and behold, I am alive forevermore… and *I have the keys of hell and death.*" Christians undergoing persecution, even to the point of death, have the assurance of Jesus Christ: "I died too, but I am now alive forevermore."

They have the assurance of Jesus Christ when He says, "I have the keys of hell [Hades] and death." When you die, Jesus has the keys to take you from the realm of death and give you eternal life. No longer should death be something to fear. "To die is gain," said the apostle Paul.

THE REPEATED COMMISSION AND EXPLANATION (V. 19-20)

Write the things which you have seen, and the things which are, and the things which shall be afterwards.

Here is the mystery of the seven stars which you saw in my right hand, and the seven golden candlesticks. The seven stars are the angels of the seven churches: and the seven candlesticks which you saw are the seven churches.

Write what you have seen.
After reassuring John, Jesus tells him to *write what he has seen.* This is a reference to the vision of Christ John had just witnessed. Then Jesus tells John to write "the things which *are* [present tense] and the things which *shall be* [future tense] afterwards." That is, John is to write down the things he will see throughout the vision.

According to Jesus, part of Revelation deals with things that were present realities when John wrote (such as the condition of the churches in chapters 2-3). And part of Revelation deals with things that had not yet happened, but they were "at hand" (1:1). When John wrote, some of the events were already set into motion (the Jewish persecution of Christians, for example), but there were still things in Revelation that would happen later (like the destruction of Jerusalem). The NASB reads, "the things which are, and the things which shall take place after these things."

In case it was unclear what the stars and the candlesticks meant, Jesus explains it for John (and us).

The seven stars are the messengers of the seven churches.

The word "angel" means "messenger"; the context must determine if that messenger is a heavenly one or an earthly one.

Who are these angels/messengers? They can't be literal heavenly angels, because that would mean Jesus had to send an angel (1:1) to tell John to write a letter so heavenly angels could get the message from Christ. Does anyone really think Jesus needs John's help to get a message to angels? Also, nowhere in Scripture is there even the hint of angels being over congregations of God's people.

Some have suggested the messenger is the preacher. Others suggest the messenger is the one reading the letter to the congregation (see 1:3). Others suggest the messenger is a description of the eldership as a whole.

The messengers are the ones who take the message written by John and deliver it to the congregation. The message is not for the messenger himself, but for the congregation—"he that has ears to hear, let him hear what the Spirit says to the churches." In some places, this might be the regular reader. In some places, this might be the preacher. In some places, this might be one of the elders, or the eldership as a whole. The point is that this is a message to be delivered by the messengers *to the congregations*.

The seven candlesticks/lampstands are the seven churches.

The vision shows Jesus can only be found among the churches.

You cannot have Jesus outside of the church, for Jesus' mission and work as High Priest is only among the churches.

WHAT DOES THIS MEAN FOR US TODAY?

Do you want to be on the side of the loving, compassionate Christ who will slaughter and pulverize His enemies?

Let's recap this vision. Jesus is seen as the High Priest among the golden lampstands/candlesticks. He is eternal, all-knowing, all-seeing. He cannot be defeated; no enemy can stand in His way. He needs only speak the word, and the battle is His—the enemies are defeated. This is a vision of Jesus Christ in all His power and glory as the King of kings and Lord of lords.

Doesn't this vision of the all-powerful Christ make you want to re-examine your life and make sure you are truly on His side?

STUDY NINE:
JESUS' LETTER TO EPHESUS
(REVELATION 2:1-7)

In the Gospel accounts, we have recorded things Jesus *spoke*, but we have nothing He actually *wrote*. The closest thing we have to Jesus' writing is when He knelt down and wrote in the dirt when the scribes and Pharisees brought the woman caught in the act of adultery (John 8:6-8). Many sermons have been preached, and articles written, and speculations given on what Jesus actually wrote in the dirt. But all of them are just that: speculations.

One person lamented that the greatest teacher in the world never wrote down His teachings for us: they only live through what others *said* Jesus said. That ignores that the Gospel records are *inspired* accounts, given by Christ through the Holy Spirit (John 16:12-15).

In the book of Revelation, chapters 2 and 3, we have letters written (or at least dictated) by Jesus Christ Himself to the churches of Asia.

It is important to remember, before we get into these letters, these were *actual* congregations in existence when John wrote. John was on the isle of Patmos when he wrote (Revelation 1:9), and he wrote to the seven congregations that were nearest to him, seven literal churches of Asia (Revelation 1:4, 11).

This study covers the first of the seven letters: the Letter of Jesus Christ to the church at Ephesus.

THE HISTORICAL BACKGROUND OF EPHESUS

In order to fully understand the letters to the seven churches, you must know about the cities themselves. With Ephesus, we have both *historical* and *biblical* evidence to consider, so the introduction to this city will take a bit longer than the others.

Ephesus was the major city and capital of the province of Asia.

It is estimated that this walled city was home to 400,000-500,000 people near the end of the first century. It was (at that time) the main seaport for the province. It is said that Ephesus was second only to Rome in grandeur and power in the Empire. The Cayster River ran through the city, and at the time was a wide river on which ships could travel. It was the quickest way to take goods from the sea to Smyrna. Today the river is much smaller, and the silt it carried to the harbor has built up over the last 2,000 years—and today Ephesus is around six miles from the sea.

It was *the* major thoroughfare for anyone wanting to enter Asia Minor. Almost all merchandise shipped to or from Asia went through Ephesus. Anyone wanting to go to a city of Asia (unless it was another harbor town) went through Ephesus to get there. The major roadways of Asia Minor went through Ephesus. One went north/south, and another went eastward, crossing at Ephesus.

This city had existed for hundreds of years before New Testament times. Some archaeologists place the founding of Ephesus around 1000 BC. The temple of Artemis ('Diana' in Acts 19) was built in Ephesus around 350 BC.

This city was very modern for its time. It had lighted streets, paved roads (some paved with marble), sidewalks which were mosaics, an enormous amphitheater which sat 25,000 people, and even large public restrooms. Some of its streets were lined with marble columns which possibly were used for an elaborate roof overhead to keep people dry as they walked about. The amphitheater was built into the side of a mountain, and it is said that when someone on the stage dropped a coin on the marble stage, the people in the uppermost row could hear it clearly. It was used for drama performances, but also for gladiatorial combat (a large gladiator graveyard was discovered there in 2007). You can still visit the amphitheater today.

This city had a religious importance as well. The temple of Diana (one of the Seven Wonders of the World) received frequent visitors from all over the Roman Empire. It was a center of pagan worship, and many came for that reason. Many in Ephesus gave credit to Artemis (Diana) for the city's growth and power. This temple was also an architectural wonder. It was the largest building in the world at the time, being 361 feet long. Some ancient writers placed this temple ahead of the pyramids in impressiveness. The Parthenon in Athens is an impressive building, but the temple of Diana was twice as tall (almost 100 feet), and had 127 marble columns with seven-foot wide bases—all covered in pure gold. In addition to being a museum (housing paintings and statues from around the world), it was also known as the most secure bank in the world.

Ephesus was also home to emperor worship. Very early on, the emperor was worshiped as a god in places like Ephesus. There still exists a temple there, built to the honor of Domitian. Part of the statue of Domitian still exists. The forearm alone is six feet long, to give you an idea of how big the statue itself was. Ephesus was also home to many of the "mystery" religions. So, regardless of your religious persuasion, you could find a home for it in Ephesus.

As you consider the history of Ephesus as a city, remember these things:

- It was known for its acceptance of practically anything and everything in the name of religion.
- As such, it was a city of competing religious groups, many of whom had a "we are right, you are wrong" attitude.

THE BIBLICAL BACKGROUND
OF THE CHURCH AT EPHESUS

After spending 18 months in Corinth, Paul sailed to Ephesus with Aquila and Priscilla and taught for a short time in the synagogue there (Acts 18:18-20). Paul left Aquila and Priscilla there while he returned to Jerusalem. Sometime later, Apollos came to

Ephesus and began preaching boldly in the synagogue (Acts 18:24). Aquila and Priscilla took him aside and taught him the way of the Lord more perfectly (18:26). The church in Ephesus existed at this point, as they sent a letter to Achaia asking the brethren there to receive Apollos, who decided to go there and preach (18:27).

Paul later returned to Ephesus and worked with them for three years (Acts 20:31). He met twelve disciples who didn't know of baptism into Christ (19:1-7). He spent three months teaching in the synagogues (19:8) until the hard-hearted Jews began to speak evil of him and the Christians (19:9), at which point the Christians separated themselves from the synagogue and Paul began to teach daily in the school of Tyrannus for two years (19:9-10).

The evangelism efforts of Paul and the church in Ephesus were making a noticeable dent in the worship of Diana/Artemis (19:23-41). Those who made their living from selling shrines or miniature statues of Diana were losing money. This is a city of at least a quarter million people (some say as many as half a million), and there were literally millions of visitors who passed through the city each year, many of them headed to the temple of Diana. The Lord's church in Ephesus was larger than you might think—it was so influential that it made a noticeable impact on the worship of Diana. The entire city was set in an uproar, and the disciples feared for Paul's life.

Paul left Timothy in Ephesus (1 Timothy 1:3) after leaving to go to Macedonia (Acts 20:1-2). Timothy was warned about things going on in the congregation there. Some were trying to change the doctrine of Christ (Ephesians 1:3). Some had made shipwreck of the faith of others (1:19-20). Some women had apparently been attempting to take a leadership role, prompting Paul's instructions on the matter (2:9-15). The congregation was large enough that more elders and deacons wasn't just a possibility, it apparently was a necessity, for Paul gave the qualifications to Timothy just mere months after leaving Ephesus (3:1-13). There were other false doctrines on the horizon that would be introduced (4:1-3). Accusations were being made (or would be made) against some in the eldership by some of the members (5:19). Some were trying to schmooze with Timothy to get him to install them as elders when they weren't really qualified (5:21-22). The problems in the church at Ephesus and the worries that Timothy had over them caused him stomach infirmities (some believe this is a reference to ulcers) (5:23). There were issues in the congregation regarding slaves and their masters (6:1-2). There were others who were teaching money proves you're righteous— just like modern-day "prosperity gospel" preachers (6:5).

Timothy left Ephesus before Paul sailed for Troas (Acts 20:3). On his way back to Jerusalem, Paul met with the Ephesian elders (20:16-38). He gave them instructions about being on the lookout for wolves who would enter in among them, even in the eldership, and who would try to draw away people after themselves.

After being put into prison in Rome, Paul wrote a letter to the Ephesians. Judaizing teachers[1] had entered Ephesus, prompting Paul's words in Ephesians 2:11-18. Paul reminded the Ephesian Christians *they* were the real temple (2:21). Paul emphasizes the importance of the church repeatedly in the book, implying some in Ephesus were teaching the church wasn't all that important. Unity was an issue (no surprise, considering all these other issues), prompting Paul's words about the seven ones in 4:1-6. It seems clear that some in the congregation were having a difficult time leaving their past lives behind (4:22-32).

It is a few years after this that Jesus dictates the letter to Ephesus in Revelation 2:1-7.

There are some important points to remember from the biblical history of Ephesus and the church there:

---

[1] Jews who insisted non-Jews couldn't be saved, couldn't be part of the church, unless they were circumcised first.

- *Ephesus was a city of people heavily dedicated to their religion of choice.* Remember the uproar when it was suggested Paul was speaking against Artemis. Remember that Paul was *disputing* in the school of Tyrannus for two years…he had to be disputing with someone.
- The congregation there was quite large, and growing due to the church's evangelistic efforts—it wasn't all Paul's doing.
- They had been warned about false teachers and false doctrines and the need to be on the lookout for them.

JESUS DESCRIBES HIMSELF (2:1-2)

To the messenger of the church of Ephesus write; "These things says the one who holds the seven stars in his right hand, who walks in the midst of the seven golden candlesticks: 'I know your works…'"

He is the one who holds the seven stars in His right hand.
Jesus is the one in control, and the church needed to know that. They are under His authority, so they needed to listen.

He is the one who walks among the seven golden candlesticks.
Jesus is ever among the churches, watching over them; He knows them and has authority over them.

He is the one who knows their works.
Jesus, being ever in the midst of the churches, sees everything they are doing. When Jesus says, "I know," it can be a good thing or a bad thing, depending on what that church is doing. When we are doing what is right, it's a comfort to know Jesus sees us. When we aren't doing right, it's a frightening thing. There will never be any way of arguing, Jesus sees all and knows all perfectly.

JESUS COMMENDS THEM (2:2-3, 6)

*"I know your works, and your labor, and your pa-
tience, and how you can't bear those who are evil.
You have tested them who say they are apostles, and
are not, and have found them to be liars. And have
endured, and had patience, and for my name's sake
labored, and have not fainted."*

*"But this you have, that you hate the deeds of the Ni-
colaitans, which I also hate."*

Works, labor, and patience

Jesus knows their *works*, *labor*, and *patience*. These Christians
were doing good works, helping each other, supporting each other,
and perhaps other things as well.

They were laboring, which is the idea of tiring work, toiling,
hard work—not necessarily physical labor, but more of an untiring
dedication to staying doctrinally pure. This will become evident in
a moment.

They had patience. They were enduring, and did not let persecution dissuade them from following Jesus. This is the "patience of
Jesus Christ" mentioned in 1:9.

They would not tolerate evil.

This refers to false teachers, the wolves that Paul mentioned
back in Acts 20. They took Paul's warnings seriously and would not
tolerate any false doctrines or false teachers. Some claimed to be
apostles, and the church at Ephesus tried/tested them and exposed
them to be liars (2:3). They hated the deeds of the Nicolaitanes,
which Jesus also hated (2:6). The Nicolaitanes were those who held
the doctrine of Balaam, specifically promoting the eating of meat
sacrificed to idols and promoting adultery. Eating meat sacrificed to
idols was a massive issue between the Jewish and Gentile Christians
as early as AD 51 (Acts 15). 2 Peter and Jude both deal with those

who were promoting adultery (physical or spiritual could be under consideration—or both).

Just a note for consideration—Jesus commended the church at Ephesus for hating the same thing He hated. We are encouraged to *hate* sin.

They had labored for the name of Christ.

They had endured (borne, KJV), persisted, and had not fainted. They showed no signs of backing down from doing these works or staying doctrinally pure. This is the epitome of a "sound" congregation.

However…

JESUS REPRIMANDS THEM (2:4-5)

"Nevertheless I have something against you, because you have left your first love."

The church at Ephesus had left their first love.

What is this "first love" they had left? It obviously isn't sound doctrine, because they held firm to that. They were as doctrinally pure as one could get.

Had they left the love of Christ behind? It seems possible they had turned into a congregation staying faithful out of pride—*look at us, we're so faithful!* It could be they were going through all the right motions, holding all the right doctrines, but not doing it in love. Paul said the best works, without love, are meaningless (1 Corinthians 13:1-3). It could be their Christian life had become one of "I have to" instead of "I want to."

Had they left the love of souls behind? Remember this church had grown exponentially because of evangelism and love of lost souls. Had the results of evangelism slowed down to the point where they gave in to discouragement? Had they stopped bringing the lost to Jesus and shifted their focus to simply maintain the status quo? If we are honest, we could see many (not all, but many) "sound congregations" are the spittin' image of Ephesus: a doctrinally sound congregation that has lost the love for bringing souls to Christ.

Had they left the love of each other behind? Could it be even though they were in agreement doctrinally, they were biting at each other?

Whichever of these it is, it shows something none of us should ever forget: Being "sound" is worthless if we do not have love for Christ, for brethren, and for lost souls.

JESUS WARNS THEM (2:5)

"Therefore, remember where you have fallen from, and repent, and do the first works; or else I will come to you quickly and remove your candlestick from its place—unless you repent."

Repent, Remember, Repeat

The church at Ephesus—doctrinally pure—was told to repent, remember the way they used to be, and to start doing their first works again. Repent, Remember, Repeat.

When a congregation first begins, there is often a sense of enjoyment and excitement, a desire to share the good news with others. After a while, the congregation often loses that enthusiasm. This shows a lack of love for the Lord, and a lack of love for lost souls.

If they did not repent, their candlestick would be removed.

In order to understand what Jesus is saying, we need to remember the vision from chapter one. Jesus was visualized as the ultimate High Priest, standing in the spiritual temple—the church—among the individual congregations (the seven candlesticks). To have the candlestick removed means that congregation would no longer be considered part of Christ's church, no longer part of Christ's temple. To have their candlestick removed means salvation was lost.

Remember, they were teaching everything by the book, correct on every matter of doctrine—but there was a lack of love. And because they were not acting in love, they were about to lose their salvation. Teaching the proper plan of salvation, worshiping without instruments, teaching the truth on the nature of the kingdom, etc... will not get you to heaven if you aren't showing love for others (by evangelizing) and for Christ (by spreading His word).

This warning points to a truth that the religious world deeply despises—just because a church claims to follow Jesus doesn't mean they are saved. Right actions, but wrong attitude gets you removed from the body of Christ—salvation is taken away. As we will see in later studies, right attitudes with wrong actions also removes a church from salvation. Are you sure about your church?

WHAT DOES THIS MEAN FOR US TODAY?

This is a message for us too!

Jesus concludes this letter with the words, "He that has an ear to hear, let him hear what the Spirit says to the churches." Jesus was writing this letter to us just as much as He was to Ephesus! We need to examine ourselves and make sure we are doctrinally pure—that is what Jesus commended! We need to examine ourselves and make sure we are showing the love of Christ—if we aren't, we won't be considered part of Christ's church.

Victors live forever!

"To him that overcomes, I will give to eat of the tree of life, which is in the midst of the paradise of God." Those who overcome, those who are victorious, those who faithfully follow what Jesus has said will have access to the tree of life. Eating of the tree of life would allow one to live forever—eternal life.

Faithful Christians have access to eternal life. Faithful Christians do the right things and do them in love. Are you a faithful Christian, doing the work of the Lord and doing it in love?

STUDY TEN:
JESUS' LETTER TO SMYRNA
(REVELATION 2:8-11)

Other than the fact that it's mentioned in the book of Revelation, do you know anything about the city of Smyrna? How old it is? What made it famous? What its most distinguishing features were? How these things fit into what Jesus wrote to the church in this city? For 99.99999% of the people on earth, the answer is "I have no idea." But never fear, all of those answers and more are contained in this very study!

There is no biblical information about the city of Smyrna, or the church there, so let's look at the historical evidence.

THE HISTORICAL BACKGROUND OF SMYRNA

Smyrna was in existence at least a thousand years before Christ. It existed as a city/state, completely self-governing. Homer, the famous poet (he wrote the Odyssey, the inspiration for the movie O Brother, Where Art Thou?) was supposedly born there around 800 BC. Around 700 BC, the city was captured by the Ionian Greeks and made subject to them.

In 580 BC, the city was destroyed by the Lydians (whose capital was Sardis), and it disappeared from history—*the city was dead*. In 334 BC, Alexander the Great re-founded the city, and it began to grow under the Seleucid Empire (a division of the Greek Empire)—*the city came back to life*.

Smyrna made a pact with the king of Pergamos in opposition to the Seleucid king. However, when Rome destroyed the Seleucids in 195 BC, Smyrna quickly abandoned Pergamos and announced her allegiance to Rome. Today, the city is called Izmir (as in *Zmir-na*), and is part of Turkey.

Smyrna was well-favored in the Roman Empire. Ephesus billed

itself as the second city in the Empire, only behind Rome—but Smyrna disagreed with that assessment. Smyrna was called "the flower of Asia" or "the ornament of Asia." Her coins called it "the first city of Asia."

In the year 195 BC, Smyrna built a large temple to worship the goddess Dea Roma (the personification of Rome itself). This was the first instance outside of Rome where anyone offered worship to Rome—and Smyrna did it voluntarily.

About a century later, during the winter, the citizens of Smyrna heard Roman soldiers did not have warm clothing. As a result, the citizens willingly took the clothes off their own backs and sent them to the soldiers.

The city prospered under Roman rule. In AD 26, Smyrna argued for and won the right to build a temple to worship Tiberius Caesar. Other cities wanted this right, but it was granted to Smyrna because of their early and overwhelming dedication to Rome. Later, this temple had its own priests, and the cult of emperor worship had begun. Though initially it was voluntary, worship of the emperor became compulsory, or forced, upon the people. It is suggested by some historians that the trend towards *mandatory* worship of Caesar have started in either Rome or Smyrna.

About the city itself during the first century.
The city had a population of 180,000-200,000 people. It had two harbors, one smaller and on the coast, and the other larger, but inland.

It was a "planned" city, designed (according to historians) by Alexander the Great himself. It was a city with long, straight, paved streets parallel to each other, set up as a grid. It was noted for its double-tiered colonnades. Aelius Aristides, living in the second century, described it as "shining [with its] mass of gymnasiums, markets, theaters, baths, fountains, and public walks…and running water in every home." It was well-known for its universities and was a great center of medicine.

On Mt. Pagos, the acropolis or citadel of Smyrna stood visible from the sea, and was called the "crown of Smyrna" and "the golden-lined palace." This image appears on many coins from Smyrna. Sloping down from the mountain was an amphitheater which sat 20,000 people.

Religious activity in the city of Smyrna.

One street, called the gold street (some believe it actually had gold as part of the paving) led to the temple of Zeus. Also in Smyrna were temples to Aphrodite, Apollo, Nemesis, and other well-known Greek gods.

The chief god of Smyrna was Dionysus. This Greek god (also called Bacchus) was the god of wine. The legend of Dionysus is that he died and came back to life. Every year, they held a great festival in which gruesome plays would reenact his death and rebirth. The priests of Dionysus worship received crowns afterwards. Many pagan worship centers had worshipers wear various types of crowns, depending on what god was being worshiped.

There was a huge Jewish population in Smyrna.

Things you should remember about the city of Smyrna before we get into the text:

- The history of the city was that it had died, and had been brought back to life.
- They worshiped Dionysus, the pagan god that legend said died, was buried, and arose from the grave.
- The city of Smyrna was known for its "crown" of buildings atop the mountain in the city.
- Pagan priests received corruptible crowns as part of the worship of Dionysus.
- There was an enormous Jewish population in Smyrna.

JESUS' DESCRIBES HIMSELF (2:8)

To the messenger of the church in Smyrna write; "These things say the first and the last, who was dead, and is alive."

I am "the first and the last."

Jesus existed long before Smyrna, and will continue to exist long after it disappears. Jesus reassures the Christians in Smyrna *He* is the true God to be worshiped, not any of the mythical Greek gods.

I am the one "which was dead and is alive."

As opposed to the popular pagan myth of Dionysus, Jesus is the *true* one who *was* dead, but *is* alive. Dionysus was *never* alive or dead or resurrected, for Dionysus is a mythical character.

The people of Smyrna (if they knew their history) could identify with the idea of something being dead, and then being brought back to life—their city had been dead and then brought back again centuries earlier.

In the midst of persecution Christians were enduring (and it was going to get worse—2:10) they needed to *know* Jesus rose from the dead. His resurrection is a promise of our own resurrection! (1 Corinthians 15). This should give us comfort today just as much as it did to them then!

WHAT JESUS KNOWS (2:9)

"I know your works, and tribulation, and poverty (but you are rich), and I know the blasphemy of those who say they are Jews, and are not, but are the synagogue of Satan."

Jesus knows their works.

Some translations omit this phrase, as some early Greek copies are missing those words. Given that the phrase "I know your works" appears in all seven of Jesus' letters, it is obvious someone accidentally omitted it in an early copy and that mistake carried over into some other old Greek manuscripts.

Jesus knows what they have done, how they live their lives, how they act as a congregation, etc... And He knows OUR works as well!

Jesus knows their tribulation.

Tribulation, as has been mentioned before, is immense outside pressure. It is like the pressure from the millstones grinding the wheat. It is like pressure from the heavy slab that crushes the blood out of the grapes in a winepress. This tribulation is not something in the future, but something they were presently undergoing. Jesus knows what His people are going through, and He cares.

Jesus knows their poverty.

It is assumed by most that this is a reference to their physical poverty. The poorest were usually the first ones to convert to Christ, because it gave them—the hopeless—hope.

There was also heavy persecution against them, because they rejected Caesar worship. The leaders of the city pushed the people to worship Caesar as "lord and god," but didn't make it an exclusive thing. Basically, you came and burned incense to Caesar, but then you were free to go worship the god of your choice down the street. However, Christians absolutely refused to do this, and as such may have had their property taken away, their employment taken, or their ability to do business in the marketplace (buying food, for instance) eliminated (Hebrews 10:34, perhaps?).

There was also heavy Jewish persecution. The religious Jews hated Christians (as is evidenced throughout the book of Acts), and they especially hated *Jews* who converted to Christianity. Because of the large Jewish population in Smyrna, and the fact Jews frequently were businessmen (having shops in the marketplace), it was easy to refuse to serve Christians and institute an economic persecution against them. These religious Jews would frequently turn fellow-Jews who became Christians over to the authorities.

However, it is possible Jesus means they were *poor in spirit.* "Blessed are the poor in spirit, for theirs is the kingdom of God" (Matthew 5:3). The word "poverty," used by Jesus in Revelation 2:9, means more than just "poor." It is the same word used in Matthew 5:3 when Jesus said "blessed are the poor in spirit..." One Greek word for "poor" means they have *nothing extra.* The Greek word in Revelation 2:9 means they have *nothing at all.*

In the midst of their poverty, they were still holding on to Jesus. Are you holding on to Jesus or just keeping Him around for when you need Him?

Jesus knows that they are rich!

This isn't earthly riches. This is a poor church—a church with nothing. What are these riches the poverty-stricken congregation had?

- They were rich towards God (Luke 12:21).
- True riches are found in Christ's poverty (2 Corinthians 8:9)
- God is rich in mercy towards His people (Ephesians 2:4).
- They were rich in good works (1 Timothy 6:18)
- They were rich in faith (James 2:5)
- They have the riches of God's goodness, forbearance, and longsuffering (Romans 2:4)
- They had the riches of God's grace (Ephesians 1:7)
- The riches are the spiritual blessings which are only found in Christ (Ephesians 1:3).

These Christians truly understood material wealth was unimportant; spiritual wealth was their goal. If you knew being a Christian would cost you everything you owned, would you have second thoughts?

Jesus knew the blasphemy of physical Jews in Smyrna.

These people *claimed* to be Jews, but weren't really. Now what does that mean?!? It means they claimed to be God's people, but really weren't.

- Romans 9:6—not all [physical] Israel is really [part of spiritual] Israel.
- Galatians 6:15-16—In Jesus Christ, Jews and Gentiles together were the Israel of God.
- Romans 2:28—one who is a Jew outwardly is not a real Jew, circumcision does not make one a true (spiritual) Jew.

You might remember Jesus interacting with some Jews back in John 8. They proudly proclaimed their lineage as children of Abraham, and that God was their Father—but Jesus basically said, "Not so fast. I can tell by the way you're acting, you are of your father, the devil" (see John 8:39, 41, 44). The Jews who rejected God's word and God's Son were following Satan, regardless of what they claimed.

As a side note, anyone who claims Jews today are still somehow God's people while they still reject Jesus are in heretical opposition to the Scriptures. You can't be God's if your father is Satan.

The Synagogue of Satan

The Synagogue of Satan (the Jews who opposed Christians) blasphemed Christians, Christ, and (by their actions) God. These Jews wanted it known that Christianity was *not* a sect of Judaism (which was a legal religion in the Empire), so Christians would be exposed to the punishment of the Roman Law, practicing an unauthorized religion.

The Jews were the largest persecutor of the church until Jerusalem was destroyed in AD 70. After that point, the Jews lost almost all standing within the Empire to accomplish anything against Christians. That didn't stop them from trying, but they lost their power to carry out widespread persecutions. But they certainly tried. In AD 156, Polycarp (an elder from Smyrna) was burned alive for not worshiping Caesar as God. This was done on a Sabbath day, and the

Jews in the area all broke the Old Testament Sabbath law by carrying load after load of firewood to make sure Christian burned up well. Their hatred for Christians was greater than their love for the Law of Moses.

JESUS' WORDS OF WARNING AND COMFORT (2:10)

"Don't fear any of those things which you will suffer: behold, the devil shall cast some of you into prison, that you might be tested; and you shall have tribulation ten days: be faithful to death, and I will give you a crown of life."

Don't fear the things which you will suffer.

They are already undergoing heavy persecution (tribulation). But this verse describes things which they are *about to* suffer (Greek word *mello* here indicates something which is about to happen). Their persecution was bad, but it was about to get worse.

The persecution against Christians got much worse beginning in AD 64 when Rome burned and Christians got the blame. The persecution was initially just in Rome, but local leaders throughout the Empire followed Rome's example—especially when the Jews (who were then still in good standing with the Empire) brought Christians forward as rebels—who refused to acknowledge Caesar as lord.

Beginning in AD 67 with the Roman-Jewish war, all Jews were subject to death as enemies of the Empire—even if they were Christians. And since Christianity was still viewed as a sect of Judaism, even Gentile Christians could be targets. Financial persecution would seem like a cakewalk compared to what was coming.

They were about to endure being cast into prison by the accuser.

The word "devil" is literally "accuser." Some believe it refers here to the Jews as a whole accusing (blaspheming) the Christians, causing imprisonment. Regardless, Satan is behind it, and it is because of people following Satan that these things were going to happen.

Their imprisonment was so they could be tested.

"The trying [testing] of your faith produces patience" (James 1:2-3). God allows us to be tested in order to strengthen our faith, but often people give in and give Satan the victory in their lives. Jesus knew the Christians of Smyrna had it within them to endure the hardship and tests that were coming (1 Corinthians 10:13).

They would have tribulation ten days.

Some believe this is a literal ten-day period where the persecution would reach its most vicious point. Others believe this is ten separate persecutions from Roman emperors starting with Nero. Still others believe that this is speaking of a figurative (symbolic) period of time. This last interpretation makes the most sense. It is a complete, but relatively short duration of time. Especially when one considers the reference to 1260 days in Revelation 12:5, "ten days" seems a very short period of time. This tribulation would not be pleasant, but Jesus gives them consolation that it would be relatively short.

But through all of this, Jesus says, "don't be afraid."

Why shouldn't they be afraid?

- Because those who can kill the body, cannot kill the soul (Matthew 10:28).
- Because they could endure it (1 Corinthians 10:13).
- Because Christ is the One who was dead, but is now alive and holds the keys of Hades—when His people die, He has the keys to set them free and grant them eternal life in heaven! (Revelation 1:18).
- Because that for which they endured (life in heaven) was their reward at death.
- Because if they remained faithful, even when it meant their death, they would receive a crown of life.

These all apply to us as well!

The "crown of life."

This is a crown which is made up of life; it never dies like the crowns worn by the pagan priests. This is a crown given to the victors, the ones who overcome. This is a crown far more valuable than the crown of rocks sitting atop Mt. Pagus in Smyrna. This crown is eternal life. This crown only comes from Jesus Christ—HE is the one who gives it.

Some of the Christians in Smyrna would not survive those things which must shortly come to pass. But those Christians—if they remained faithful during this trial—were promised eternity in the presence of Jesus.

WHAT DOES THIS MEAN FOR US TODAY?

Are you being persecuted?

The Letter to Smyrna is a letter for us as well (he that has an ear...)! How are you enduring pressure because of your Christianity? Do people even know you're a Christian?

If you're not suffering persecution and pressure because of being a Christian, then you are not living your life in a godly way, for the Bible clearly states *all who live godly in Christ Jesus WILL suffer persecution* (2 Timothy 3:12).

Are you spiritually rich? Are you rich in good works? Are you laying up treasure in heaven? Are you depending completely upon God like those in Smyrna were?

How do you speak about Christ and about other Christians? Jesus said that those who spoke against Christians were followers of Satan. We must take care how we speak about our brothers and sisters in Christ.

Do you fear the things which can happen to you? Do you worry about what other people will think of you if you stand up for Jesus? Are you more worried about your own comforts than in spreading the gospel to others?

How would you respond if faced with the choice of death or proclaim Caesar as God? They weren't being asked to deny Christ, but just to not be so exclusive, and worship Caesar too.

This is one of only two letters from Jesus which did not have anything negative about the congregation. If Jesus wrote a letter to your church, would He have anything negative to say?

Faithfulness means eternal life—and no second death.

If we overcome, if we endure the trials and temptations while remaining faithful, we will not be hurt by the second death. The second death is being cast into the lake of fire (20:14, 21:8). However, the opposite is also true: those who give in to the trials and temptations will suffer the second death—eternity in hellfire.

Will you overcome?

STUDY ELEVEN:
JESUS' LETTER TO PERGAMOS
(REVELATION 2:12-17)

What is a Christian to do in a culture where Christ is not respected, pleasure is the goal of most people, patriotism has become a religion, and learning and education is worshiped? That is actually a good description of America right now. This is also the perfect description of a city in the Roman province of Asia, almost 2,000 years ago.

Like Smyrna, we know nothing about the city of Pergamos (called Pergamum in some translations) or the church there outside of what is said in Revelation. Like the letter to Smyrna, if we want a deeper understanding of what Jesus says to the church at Pergamos, we need to know more about the city itself.

THE HISTORICAL BACKGROUND OF PERGAMOS

The city of Pergamos existed at least 400 years before Christ. In the period after the death of Alexander the Great (323 BC), the Greek Empire was divided among his four generals. One of these generals, Lysimachus, chose Pergamos as the place to store his vast wealth. Unfortunately for the general, he left his second-in-command, Philetaerus, in charge. Philetaerus took the money and established himself as king of Pergamos.

The Seleucids (under one of Alexander's other generals) joined forces with Pergamos until Lysimachus' "Empire" was destroyed. And to show their thankfulness, they turned on Pergamos, threatening to wipe them off the map. Pergamos actually held the upper hand until Antiochus the Great, a Seleucid king, came to power and nearly destroyed them. This king forcefully moved thousands of Jewish families from the Babylonian area into Asia Minor, but was very kind to the Jews of Judea, basically leaving them alone.[1]

In 190 BC, Antiochus was defeated by Rome, and Pergamos quickly threw their support to the victors (just five years after Smyrna did the same thing). As a result, Rome gave the king of Pergamos all of the territory conquered by Antiochus. In order to keep a civil war from occurring upon his death (in 133 BC), the king of Pergamos bequeathed the city and all he controlled to Rome. This guaranteed favor within the then-rising Roman Empire, as there would be no doubt about the loyalty of Pergamos.

In 29 BC, Pergamos became the first city outside of Rome to build a temple to worship Augustus Caesar, who died ten years after its completion. Some claim Emperor worship was not practiced until the time of Domitian (near the end of the first century), but it was going on almost 30 years before Jesus was born! And remember in AD 26, Smyrna was awarded the right to build a temple to worship Tiberius Caesar (who was still living at that time as well).

Pergamos was prominent as the headquarters of the imperial cult (Emperor worship) from before the birth of Christ until long after Revelation was written. The city still exists today (much smaller than during New Testament times), with the name Bergama.

THE GEOGRAPHICAL BACKGROUND OF PERGAMOS

The city lies about 100 miles north of Ephesus, or about 50-60 miles from Smyrna. It is not a seaport or coastal town, and it did not sit on one of the main trade routes.

---

[1] His son, Antiochus IV, is prophesied about in Daniel, and did horrible things in Jerusalem – His defeat and the cleansing of the Jerusalem temple which he had desecrated is the basis for the Jewish feast of Hanukkah.

So how did a city come to be here?

The city (the majority of it, at least) sat high atop a steep, rocky hill. Sir William Ramsey, an 1800s atheist-turned-Bible-apologist-and-archaeologist, said when he approached Pergamos, the small mountain rising up from the valley just screamed "royal city"!

The city being situated on a mountain made it nearly impenetrable. Many of the citizens lived lower in the valley, but when trouble arose, they could join the rest of the citizens on the mountain and rest safely.

THE RELIGIOUS AND CULTURAL BACKGROUND OF THE CITY

Like Smyrna and Ephesus, Pergamos was filled with temples to worship people and pagan deities.

- Emperor Augustus, and later (post-Revelation) Emperors Trajan and Severus (Pergamos was the first city to be awarded the temple for a current Emperor three times).
- Dionysus (Bacchus) the god of wine and entertainment.
- Athena (Greek) or Minerva (Roman), the goddess of mathematics and warfare. This temple was built in honor of her supposed help in defeating the Seleucid kings.
- Isis, the Egyptian goddess of motherhood and protector of the dead. Isis' name literally means "throne." Interestingly, the temple to Isis was later converted into a church building.
- Zeus, the chief Greek God (Jupiter, Roman name).
- Demeter, Greek goddess of the harvest
- Hera, Greek goddess of women and marriage
- Asclepius, Greek god of medicine.

The most prominent features in Pergamos were:

The Altar of Zeus.

This large building rested on a ledge on the mountain some 800 feet up, and could be seen clearly from the valley as you approached the city. One ancient writer declared this to be one of the Seven Wonders of the World. This structure was re-discovered by a German engineer in the late 1800s. He was planning a road through the valley town when one of the people said that if he needed some extra rock for the road, there was a bunch on top of the mountain. The altar was disassembled and transported to Berlin, Germany, where it now sits in the Pergamum Museum.[2]

The amphitheater.

This amphitheater (which sat 10,000 people) was built into the side of the mountain, and has the distinction of being the steepest amphitheater in the entire Roman Empire.

The Asclepieion.

The most prominent pagan deity in Pergamos was Asclepius, the god of medicine. The second-largest hospital in the world was here, but it was also the temple of Asclepius. The doctors were considered priests of this god. This temple was built near a natural spring, which was said to have healing powers. In the oldest images and carvings, Asclepius is portrayed as a serpent. Later images portray him as an old man who carries a serpent on a staff. The symbol for modern medicine is still a snake on a staff.

I am fairly confident the origin of this "god" can be found in the Bible. Numbers 21:8-9, Moses was commanded to make a brass serpent and put it on a pole, and any who looked upon it would be healed. 2 Kings 18:4, Hezekiah found and destroyed the brass serpent that Moses had made, for the people had begun to worship it.

---

[2] Adolph Hitler gave speeches in front of this building, apparently believing it gave him power. A replica of it was built for a 2008 speech of a well-known American political figure.

A serpent on a pole that had healing powers…I don't think that is a coincidence.

In this ancient hospital, they used natural remedies, prescribed exercise, and they used snakes… One section was filled with "harmless" snakes; patients would lie down, and if a snake slithered over them, it was a promise from Asclepius they would be healed. They also used the power of suggestion. The patients slept in special rooms with an opening overhead, where the priests (doctors) of Asclepius would tell them (in their sleep, of course) they were healed or were getting better. Some illnesses, then and now, are more in the head than anywhere else.

The Library of Pergamos.

This world-famous library was second only to the library in Alexandria, Egypt. The kings of Pergamos were avid readers, and commissioned many to copy books for this library. In all, there were over 200,000 volumes—*all handwritten*—in this library.

The king of Pergamos offered a great deal of money to the head librarian at Alexandria to come to Pergamos. However, the king of Egypt arrested the librarian so he could not accept the job offer. The library was getting so famous that Egypt refused to supply them with papyrus, the paper-like material made in Egypt. Left without anything to write on, the king of Pergamos issued a challenge to the citizens of the city to come up with a replacement. In response, one of the citizens introduced parchment, which, though more expensive to make, lasted much longer. The word *parchment*, in the original language, basically means "made in Pergamos." Because parchment didn't roll as well as papyrus, they began sewing the pages together, and it was in Pergamos that the first books were made.

By the time of John, however, the library had ceased to be famous, for Marc Antony had given the entire contents (all 200,000+ volumes) to Cleopatra for the Alexandria library as a wedding gift.

Now, you may wonder, "This is interesting, but do we really need to spend all this time going over it?" If nothing else, please remember these things:

- Pergamos was as Roman as it gets, and had been heavily involved in worship of the emperors for almost 100 years when Revelation was written.
- Pergamos had the altar of Zeus as its most visible building.
- Pergamos had a temple to Isis, whose name means "throne."
- Pergamos had a temple to worship the serpent-god.
- Pergamos encouraged people not to be exclusive with the god they worshipped.
- In short, Pergamos was pagan to the core.

JESUS IDENTIFIES HIMSELF (2:12)

To the messenger of the church in Pergamos write; "These things says he who has the sharp sword with two edges"

I am "he who has the sharp sword with two edges."

This is the heavy battle sword with which Jesus could destroy. Each time this sword is mentioned in Revelation, it is about Jesus' power and right to execute judgement and punishment.

Deuteronomy 32:39-42a –See now that I, even I am he, and there is no god with me. I kill, and I make alive. I wound, and I heal. Neither is there any that can deliver out of my hand. For I lift up my hand to heaven, and say I live forever. And if I whet my glittering sword, and my hand takes hold on judgment, I will render vengeance to my enemies, and will reward them that hate me. I will make my arrows drunk with blood, and my sword shall devour flesh...

From the start, the congregation in Pergamos should be scared—the one who has the power to destroy with His mere words (for the sword came from His mouth—Revelation 1:16) was writing to them. They needed to read, hear, and do what was commanded.

WHAT JESUS KNOWS (2:13)

"I know your works, and where you dwell, even where Satan's throne is: and you hold firm to my name, and have not denied my faith, even in those days when Antipas my faithful witness, was slain among you, where Satan dwells."

Jesus knows their works.

Jesus knows what is happening in every congregation. Their specific works will be mentioned momentarily.

Jesus knows that they dwell where Satan's throne is.

The word "seat" (KJV) is *thronos*, from which we get the word "throne." This is the same word used to describe God's throne throughout Revelation.

What is Satan's throne?

Some believe it is the altar of Zeus, the chief of the pagan gods. The Satanic influence in pagan worship was exemplified in this altar of Zeus.

Some believe it is speaking of the temple of Asclepius. The symbol of a serpent was repulsive to Jews and Christians alike, because the serpent is a representation of Satan (Genesis 3, Revelation 12:9). So a temple built to worship the snake-god could be interpreted as the seat of Satan worship.

Many believe emperor worship is under consideration. The idea of elevating a mere human to the status of deity is surely among the top of Satan's achievements on earth. Emperor worship was a strong weapon in Satan's arsenal during this time, and where it was concentrated, it was as though he ruled there.

Another option is the worship of Isis, the Egyptian goddess, whose name means "throne."

The best option, it seems to me, is this: Pergamos was so thoroughly pagan in its worship and in its daily life that Satan could be said to be ruling there. He ruled in the hearts and actions of almost all the people. It is similar to Las Vegas, known as "sin city" because sinfulness is so pervasive there. Jesus is telling the church at Pergamos He knows they are living in a place where it seems Satan has the complete authority.

Jesus knows that even in the midst of this thoroughly sinful city, they are holding to His name and have not denied His faith.
They did not forsake Jesus, nor did they stop identifying themselves as Christians. The desire to be accepted by people is so strong that some will deny Christ so they can still "fit in."

They did not deny His faith. They refused to recant their belief in Jesus Christ. But more than that, they stayed with Christ's doctrine, the system of faith that produces salvation.

They stayed faithful in these areas, even when Antipas, the faithful witness (testifier) of Jesus was killed amongst them, where Satan dwells. We know nothing about Antipas except for the fact that he was a faithful Christian, that he was spreading the word of Christ to others, and that he was murdered for it. Catholic Church tradition says Antipas was an elder (they say *the* bishop) at the church in Pergamos, and that he was roasted alive inside the bronze statue of a bull. Some have supposed that Antipas was dragged to one of the temples and there they tried to force him to deny Christ or burn incense to one of the pagan gods, and when he refused, he was made a public example and killed. The important part for us to remember is that he would rather die than deny Jesus Christ.

And even in the face of this event, the church refused to stop being Christians. Would to God that we could all be so dedicated! Do not cave in to the pressure to deny Christ in our words or actions!

WHAT JESUS CONDEMNS (2:14-15)

"But I have a few things against you, because you have there those that hold the doctrine of Balaam, who taught Balak to cast a stumbling-block before the children of Israel, to eat things sacrificed unto idols, and to commit fornication. So you also have those that hold the doctrine of the Nicolaitans, which thing I hate."

They were incredibly dedicated to Christ, but Jesus had "a few things against" them. A few is a small number, but even that small amount could cost them their souls! Don't ever try to convince yourself that you're "mostly faithful" and that that is good enough—because even those few things can be your condemnation.

There were some that held to the doctrine of Balaam.

Not all the Christians in Pergamos held to this doctrine, but all were held accountable for it. Jesus didn't say, "I have a few things against *some* of you." His condemnation was on them all.

Balaam (Numbers 22-24) taught King Balak how to cause God to curse the Israelites: by enticing them to sin by committing adultery and eating things sacrificed to idols (Numbers 25:1-2, 31:16). These two issues were a problem in the early church among Gentile converts (see the letter written to Gentile Christians in Acts 15:22-29, especially v. 29).

Peter and Jude both wrote about people who were following the ways of Balaam in the early church.

- 2 Peter 2:15—the way of Balaam was loving the wages of unrighteousness—speaking what people wanted to hear in exchange for money.

- Jude 11—Balaam spoke for reward, not for a love of God.

Some in the church at Pergamos encouraged participation in pagan worship, perhaps in order to "fit in" with the people of the city.

In prophetic writings, "fornication" is usually a reference to spiritual adultery—worshiping idols. Some of the pagan worship practices involved actual fornication as well, which would give this verse both a literal and a spiritual application.

There were some that held to the doctrine of the Nicolaitanes.

Jesus hated this doctrine (2:6, 16). But no one today is exactly sure what this doctrine entailed. Some believe it is another way of describing the doctrine of Balaam. Others (based on writings from the second century about this group) believe it was a group that said, "We have liberty to do whatever we want because we've been forgiven." If this is the case, this group took the false doctrine of "once saved, always saved" to its logical conclusion. This doctrine is hated by Christ. Paul condemned people who wanted to use their liberty in Christ as an excuse to sin (Romans 6:1-2).

The doctrine Ephesus hated was tolerated by Pergamos. What does this tell us about the church in Pergamos? They did not take a stand against false doctrines, but instead were showing their "love" by tolerating it. The condemnation wasn't because the false doctrine was being taught and spread from the pulpit, but because the false doctrine was held by some, and the whole congregation knew about it—but did nothing about it.

They did not deny Christ, but they certainly compromised with the world. This describes so many churches today. They won't deny Christ. But they will quickly compromise and tolerate false doctrine. All in the name of "love." Such churches were condemned in the first century, and they are condemned today as well.

WHAT JESUS PRESCRIBED (2:16)

Repent; or else I will come to you quickly, and will fight against them with the sword of my mouth.

In the city where it was basically "worship these false gods or else," Jesus says, "Repent—or else." Or else Jesus would come to them quickly. This isn't Jesus' final coming, but a coming in judgment against that congregation. The time for them to repent is NOW—if they didn't, Jesus' would come very quickly.

When Jesus came, He would fight against them with the sword of His mouth. Like the church in Ephesus, if they didn't repent, they would no longer be considered part of Jesus' church—they would be lost eternally. They would be judged.

THE PROMISE OF CHRIST FOR THE OVERCOMERS (2:17)

He that has an ear, let him hear what the Spirit says to the churches; "To him that overcomes I will give the hidden manna to eat, and will give him a white stone, and on the stone a new name written, which no one knows except he that receives it."

The one who overcomes will be given the hidden manna to eat.

Manna was given to the Israelites to sustain them in the wilderness before they got to the Promised Land (Exodus 16:35). There was manna hidden in the Ark of the Covenant as a reminder of what God had done for them (Exodus 16:33). Jesus is the manna from heaven (John 6:31-35).

This means those who overcome will be sustained by Jesus Christ. Have you ever considered that if you overcome temptation, Jesus is there to take care of you and sustain you? Ultimately, this is a reference to eternal life for those who repent and overcome.

A white stone with a new name.

In ancient times, white stones with a name on it were often given to show acceptance, and as a signs of friendship and of working together. One might give a stone as an invitation to a party. One might give a stone as a sign of "we welcome your business."

Also in ancient times, it was often the case that judgment was shown by a white stone or a black stone. White meant you were innocent and were free. Black meant you were guilty and were to be punished.

The "new name" may very well be "Christian" (Acts 11:26, Isaiah 62:2), because no one knows if someone else is truly a Christian except for that one and Jesus.

WHAT DOES THIS MEANS FOR US TODAY?

Tolerance of evil is sin.

YOU can live a faithful life, even in the midst of sinners. Don't let those you work with cause you to sin—be strong! Don't compromise and act as though what others are doing is just fine, because it isn't—and it can cost you your soul! Tolerance of evil is NOT showing kindness to those who hold false doctrines—instead it is giving your approval of them. Do not allow them into your house (the church) neither bid them God speed, because if you do, you become guilty of their evil (2 John 9-11). Compromising the truth is just as bad as denying the faith.

Be strong, my friends; you can stay faithful no matter what comes your way—you are THAT strong! Compromisers will face Jesus' wrath, but the ones who overcome will have His gentle aid and providence.

Which would you rather have?

STUDY TWELVE:
JESUS' LETTER TO THYATIRA
(REVELATION 2:18-27)

Have you ever felt unimportant? Insignificant? Small? Like you were a target for bullies?

Then you know how Thyatira felt.

It was a relatively unimportant city, much smaller than the other six mentioned in Revelation. Though on a major thoroughfare through Asia, is wasn't viewed as anything other than a stopping point on the way to a *real* city. Yet, in this small, unimportant city was the church Jesus wrote the longest of the seven letters to.

Jesus directs twelve verses to this church; including quite possibly the harshest condemnations of all of them. Don't forget: Jesus sees His people everywhere, and He knows what they are doing.

BIBLICAL BACKGROUND OF
THE CHURCH AT THYATIRA

Like the churches at Smyrna and Pergamos, the church at Thyatira is unknown in the Bible outside of Revelation. We don't know anything about this congregation except for what Jesus says about it in these twelve verses.

But we might know something about one of the members there.

Lydia, the seller of purple, was the first recorded convert after Paul came to Macedonia, and she was from Thyatira (Acts 16:12-15). Some speculate that after hearing the gospel, Lydia went back to Thyatira and brought some friends to the truth.

It is also possible (perhaps even more likely) that while Paul was at Ephesus, people from Thyatira (and Pergamos and Smyrna) came and were converted, taking the gospel back to their hometown (see Acts 19:9-10).

HISTORICAL BACKGROUND OF THYATIRA

Compared to the three cities we've already looked at (Ephesus, Smyrna, and Pergamos), very little is known of Thyatira.

Thyatira is situated on a very slight elevation.

It is surrounded by *very* short hills—not exactly a place that screams out "safety" or "this would be a good place for a city." In fact, these hills might be described as "glorified speed bumps," as the whole area was mostly flat. But it remains to this day a very fertile area of land.

It was built by Seleucus I, a general of Alexander the Great.

He was one of the four, referenced in Daniel 8:8. He built the city 40 miles southeast of Pergamos. Pergamos, if you remember, was originally under the control of one of Alexander's other generals, Lysimachus. Seleucus controlled Syria, the eastern majority of Asia Minor, and occasionally Jerusalem. His westernmost city of importance was Sardis, around 30 miles southeast of Thyatira.

It was built to be a buffer.

Because of its location, Thyatira became an important city—it was there to slow down attacking armies headed to Sardis. It was built to be a buffer against the king of Pergamos, keeping the invading armies busy while the *important* city, Sardis, prepped for battle. Because of this, Thyatira changed hands many times. People there got used to changes in leadership. It was almost like they woke up each morning wondering who was ruling over them that day.

They had no real kingdom pride, because they were continually taken by the competing kings. But they did have city pride, military pride, and would not give up.

Thyatira was known for its Olympic-type games.

The games were originally held in honor of their local god. After Rome seized control of the area, Thyatiran coins featured both their god and the Roman emperor presiding over the games.

Thyatira was a melting pot of people.

Multitudes passed through it while traveling the main east/west route. Seleucus gave Jews in his domain special status, granting them citizenship in any of the cities he controlled—many of them moved to Thyatira. It became a popular location during the time of Roman peace.

It was still a small city when Revelation was written.

It did not grow in size, importance, and wealth until the second and third centuries.

Thyatira was a city known for its trade guilds.

If something was "made in Thyatira," you knew you were getting a high-quality item. There were guilds of "wool-workers, linen-workers, makers of outer garments, dyers, leather-workers, tanners, potters, bakers, slave-dealers and bronze-smiths."[1]

The dyers (like Lydia) used the madder-root which is plentiful in that area to produce the bright reddish (called "purple") dye.

These trade guilds (similar in some ways to trade unions today) were very powerful within the city. If you were a tentmaker, you couldn't sell your tents or buy your material without being in the tentmaker guild.

THE RELIGION OF THYATIRA

Each of these guilds had their own god.

The guilds would eat many of their meals together, frequently consisting of food offered to that guild's god. Thyatiran coins were discovered with Hephaestus, the god of the bronze-smiths, on it. The bronze trade in the city was large and influential, because it was seen

---

[1] Sir William Ramsey, *Letters to the Seven Churches of Asia.* e-Sword edition.

as an emblem for the city. Each guild meal was prefaced by a statement about the origin of the food, and thanks were offered to the guild-god for the meal and their employment.

Now, tell me this: could a Christian participate in this in good conscience?

Apollo was worshiped there.

Apollo was the sun god, the son of Zeus (supposed "supreme" god of the Greeks), father of Asclepius (the snake god). Many images of Apollo show him with sun-rays emanating from his head or a crown he wore. Many statues of Apollo featured bronze feet, and some were entirely of bronze.

The Thyatiran version of Apollo was unique, though. The city, known for its military, made their version of Apollo into a war-like god (carrying a massive battle-axe) who brings peace (holding an olive branch).

As other people moved into Thyatira, they brought their religious ideas with them, and added legends and ideas to the main god of the city. The Apollo worshiped in Thyatira was at the same time Greek, Asiatic, military, and a number of other things that weren't ever seen in connection anywhere else.

THINGS TO REMEMBER ABOUT THYATIRA:

- The people had a history of taking orders from whoever took the city. They would follow whoever was leading.
- They were dedicated people and would not quit.
- They had pride in their work, never settling for doing something halfway.
- They were well known for their bronze-work.
- They worshiped Apollo, as well as many other guild-gods.

JESUS IDENTIFIES HIMSELF (2:18)

To the messenger of the church in Thyatira write;
"These things says the Son of God, whose eyes are
like a flame of fire, and his feet are like fine brass."

"These things says the Son of God."

Literally, the Greek reads "the Son of the God." This is the only time in Revelation Jesus is called by this description. From the outset, Jesus lets them know "I am the Son of THE God."

Think about this for a moment: Thyatira worshiped Apollo, the Greek god who was supposed to be the son of Zeus, the chief of the Greek Gods. Jesus, in one simple statement, declared Apollo irrelevant and unworthy. Jesus, in one simple statement, declared the pantheon of Greek gods to be fakes. Jesus, in one simple statement, declared there was only ONE God.

Some have said He is declaring Himself the "Son" to contrast with Apollo who was the "sun" god. And while that sounds convincing in English, the Greek words have nothing in common.

"whose eyes are like a flame of fire"

This shows complete vision and piercing knowledge. Unlike Apollo, whose rays of light came from the crown he wore, Jesus' light was from within. With this perfect vision, Jesus declares himself the perfect judge, because nothing is hidden from His sight.

Whose *"feet are like fine brass"*

In 1:15, it says, "like fine brass, as if they burned in a furnace." Micah 4:13 says feet of brass were for pulverizing many people (NASB). Malachi 4:3 says, "…treading down the wicked, making them ashes under his feet."

Most translations say "bronze" instead of "brass."

Do you think having feet made of the strongest alloy Thyatira could produce would strike a chord with the people? Remember this city was known for its bronze-smiths. And it was "fine" bronze: the highest quality, the most luster, the most strength.

Thyatira couldn't produce anything that came close.

Everything Jesus says about Himself is something that the people in Thyatira could identify with. That's something for us to keep in mind as we teach others: make it relatable to them.

WHAT JESUS KNOWS (2:19)

"I know your works, and love, and service, and faith, and your patience, and your works; and the last is more than the first."

He knows their works.

Jesus discusses their works at the end of the verse as well as the beginning. This is noteworthy.

He knows their love.

This is the word *agape*, a love defined by action and sacrifice. This is the only church commended for their love. Ephesus, on the other hand, left their first love. The Christians in Thyatira were showing love for one another, for Christ, for God, and for others.

He knows their service.

The word "service" is from the Greek *diakanos*, which is where we get the word "deacon." They had been performing service to God, Christ, and each other.

He knows their faith.

Like Pergamos, they did not deny Christ, but held firm to their belief and trust.

He knows their patience.

Like Smyrna, They were persevering under the trials, tribulations, and persecutions that came their way for being Christians.

He knows their works.

He repeats this part to express this: their later works are even more than their first works. Unlike many congregations who start strong then whimper out as years go by, Thyatira grew in faith and in works.

It makes sense, this was a city that took pride in their work, and would not quit. This is commended by Christ.

WHAT JESUS HAS AGAINST THEM (2:20-23)

"Nevertheless, I have a few things against you, because you permit that woman Jezebel, who calls herself a prophetess, to teach and seduce my servants to commit fornication, and to eat things sacrificed to idols. I gave her opportunity to repent of her fornication; and she would not. Behold, I will cast her into a bed, and those who commit adultery with her into great tribulation, unless they repent of their actions. And I will kill her children with death; and all the churches shall know that I am the one who searches the minds and hearts: and I will give to every one of you according to your works."

Jezebel is likely not her real name (though I guess it is possible).

This woman is compared to the wicked Old Testament queen who led Ahab, king of Israel, into complete idolatry. She also led almost the entire nation of Israel into idolatry and killed many of God's prophets.

This Jezebel was leading people away from worshiping God.

It is quite possible she was telling Christians that joining in the worship of the false gods in the trade guilds was fine—after all, you have to feed your family, right?

In several Greek manuscripts, Jezebel is called "your wife" instead of "that woman."

This has led some to the conclusion that she was married to one of the elders or to the preacher. If this is true, it helps explain in part why the congregation was tolerating her actions.

This Jezebel claimed to be a prophetess.

She wasn't one, but she would claim, "I am speaking for God," or "God has given me a message." She encouraged others to participate in pagan worship, and claimed God was okay with it. Picture this: she says, "God hath said, thou shalt worship Apollo and your guild-gods!" Can you imagine such insolence?

> *If there arises among you a prophet, or a dreamer of dreams... saying, "Let's go after other gods, which you have not known, and let's serve them," you shall not obey the words of that prophet, or that dreamer of dreams... And that prophet...shall be put to death because he has spoken to turn you away from the LORD your God... So shall you put the evil away from the midst of you (Deuteronomy 13:1-5).*

She was being permitted to teach.

This is something women are forbidden to do in the church. The word "teach" is the Greek *didasko*, which is the same word used when Paul said, "I do not permit a woman to *teach* or to have authority over a man [in the church]" (1 Timothy 2:12).

It seems this congregation was showing how *tolerant* they were (much like Corinth—1 Corinthians 5).

She led Christians astray into pagan worship.

She encouraged them to commit fornication. This is spiritual fornication (remember, Revelation is told in symbols), which would mean worshiping other gods—like the guild gods. She encouraged them to eat meats sacrificed to idols. This meat would have been eaten when the guilds came together, would have been dedicated to the gods, and thanks would have been given to the gods for it. A Christian eating in that setting would be—at the very least—condoning what was going on.

Jesus gave this Jezebel time to repent.

Somehow (it is not said specifically how), she had been made aware of her sinfulness. She knew she wasn't really a prophetess. Some of the members (we hope) would have pointed this out to her, but she did not and would not repent. She had no desire to repent, apparently because she enjoyed the power. Or perhaps her pride wouldn't let her repent (she'd have to admit she was wrong).

Are there things in your life that cause you to refuse to repent?

BEHOLD! Jesus is going to cast her into a bed.

This is a bed of punishment, a sickbed—a deathbed. Christians are to take notice, because they will see Jesus' judgment come upon her. But not just on her…

Jesus will cast those who commit adultery with her into great tribulation.

The punishment is not just on the leader (Jezebel), but on those who follow after her as well. This should give us all pause to stop and think about our lives. These people had no excuse; they couldn't stand before God and place the blame on Jezebel. Each one of us is 100% responsible for making sure our beliefs and practices are correct.

This great tribulation will end up with their death. Their only hope of escaping was to repent! They still had a chance! (YOU still have a chance to repent!)

Jesus will kill her children with death.

Her children are those who completely went over to her doctrine. Timothy was Paul's child in the faith, but these children of Jezebel were her children in sin—she had completely converted them.

What does it mean when Jesus says He will kill these corrupt Christians with death? Jesus gives a very vivid, violent, and striking statement here. What He is going to do will cause "all the churches [to] know that" He is the one who searches the hearts and thoughts. The only way this is possible is if it is something physical, something obvious that will cause the other churches to take notice.

Jesus is literally going to have these pagan Christians put to death for their sins. If these pagan Christians lived to a ripe old age and died natural deaths, would that send a strong message to any of the churches? Of course not.

In the Old Testament, Jezebel's violent death was foretold by Elijah, and in the New Testament, the Jezebel of Thyatira's violent death was foretold by Jesus Christ.

Each member in Thyatira would be repaid according to their own works.

The basic message here is, "If you're following Jezebel, I know it, and you will be punished for it." They were given one last chance to repent.

JESUS' COMMAND (2:24-25)

> *"But to you I say, and to the rest in Thyatira, as many as don't hold this doctrine, and which haven't known the depths of Satan, as they say; I will put on you none other burden. But hold fast to what you already have till I come."*

The faithful members in an unfaithful congregation.

To those in Thyatira who had not given in to Jezebel's false doctrine, Jesus says, "I will lay on you no other burden but that which you already have. Hold fast until I come."

These Christians were fighting to keep the church pure, and had not given in to this doctrine. Note: this proves beyond any doubt that there can be faithful Christians (considered faithful by Christ) in a congregation that has serious problems. Jesus never told them, "break off and start a new congregation."

The burden Jesus mentions is related to Jezebel and her influence. A burden is something you have to carry, that is unpleasant. Quite possibly, the burden was a command to withdraw fellowship from her and remove her from the church. They could tolerate her no longer.

Jesus' command was to hold fast to what they had until He came.
This is a command to hold on, because Jesus is going to take care of that which ails them. It isn't speaking about the second coming, because those Christians have been dead over 1900 years. They are to stay faithful in the face of Jezebel's influence until Jesus comes to remove her and her followers from the scene. Then their burden will be removed.

PROMISES TO THE ONES WHO OBEY (THE OVERCOMERS) (2:26-29)

He who overcomes, and keeps my works to the end, to him I will give authority over the nations, even as I received of my Father. And he shall rule them with a rod of iron; like the vessels of a potter they shall be broken to shivers. And I will give him the morning star.

He that has an ear, let him hear what the Spirit says to the churches.

The promises are given to…

- Those who overcome (endure through trials and are victorious over temptations)
- Those who keep (maintain) Christ's works until the end.

Poor, poor, delusional Jesus. He was under the impression that works were necessary for eternal life. Oh wait, He's the one who decides if works are important—not man! If you *ever* hear a preacher say works have nothing to do with salvation, you know you're not in Jesus' church.

The ones who overcome will receive power over the nations.

"Nations" is the same word as "Gentiles" in Greek, and is often used in Revelation to refer to non-Christians. The Christians of Thyatira, a small city who was always under the control of one nation or another, now had the prospect of being the rulers! The military might of Pergamos, Sardis, and Rome could not topple those who rule with Christ!

They will rule with a rod of iron, as the vessels of a potter they (the nations) shall be broken to pieces.

This is a quotation from Psalm 2:9, a Messianic Psalm foretelling Christ almost 1,000 years before He was born. They will rule or shepherd (this is the same Greek word used to describe the work of an elder).

The rod of iron is not a sword, but it is the weapon of a shepherd (Psalm 23). This rod will crush the enemies (imagine a shepherd using a rod of iron on a wolf's head). This rod if iron would crush the potter's works. Remember there were pottery guilds in Thyatira, so this imagery would have been especially appropriate.

Jesus says, "as I received of my Father"

Jesus received (past tense) His rule and power by the time Revelation was written. This is yet another verse which proves premillennialism wrong—Jesus was already ruling in the first century! And if we remain faithful, we will rule with Him!

The one who overcomes will be given the morning star.

The morning star is a bright star (actually, it is usually Venus) that appears clearly in the hour before dawn. It is the promise of a new beginning, a new day. Jesus identifies Himself as the bright and morning star (22:16). We have Jesus presently, if we keep His commandments, and He is the promise of the new day, the eternal day in heaven! (Revelation 22:5)

The promise is of eternal life!

WHAT DOES THIS MEAN FOR US TODAY?

What can we today learn from this letter?

- Growing in faith, love, and works will make us pleasing to God.
- We must not tolerate damnable false doctrine, regardless of who in the church is teaching it.
- We are each responsible to make sure we look to God's word to know what to believe and do—God will not accept the excuse of "but the preacher said…"
- Make sure you know whom you're following.
- If you refuse to repent of your sins, you will suffer the judgment of Jesus Christ.

There is still time for you to repent, right now! Don't let pride stand in the way of being right with God! All of us have sinned, but many won't admit it.

Don't let that be you.

Study Thirteen:
Jesus' Letter to Sardis
(Revelation 3:1-6)

Years ago, a man took the boxing world by storm. He came in, unheralded, defeating the heavily-favored champion, knocking him out in the first round. He kept winning matches, and usually they weren't even close. Then came one day when he was scheduled to face a nobody, someone who wasn't even thought of in the boxing rankings. Because he knew he was going to win, the champ didn't train much—everything had been so easy for him, so why bother against this insignificant opponent?

He was confident…too confident.

Mike Tyson lost to James "Buster" Douglas, and he was never the same after that.

Similarly, years ago, a great, powerful, and rich city knew it couldn't ever be taken. That city was Sardis. That city, and the letter to the church there, will be our focus for this study.

HISTORICAL BACKGROUND OF SARDIS

The background of Sardis is interesting, and helps us understand Jesus' words to the church there.

It is old.

Historians dispute when it was founded. Some think it was as early as 1200 BC (called Hyde) and mentioned by Homer, while others believe it was in the 6th century BC, around the same time the Jews were carried into captivity by the Babylonians. Regardless, it was an old city.

It was impenetrable.

Located 50 miles east of Smyrna, and about 30 miles southeast of Thyatira, Sardis was situated on a plateau, jutting out from Mt. Tmolus.

There was only one way to approach the city: a very steep, very easily defended pathway 1500 feet to the city. The rest of the city, surrounded by walls, was safe because it was atop very smooth, unclimbable cliffs that went straight down. Oh, and at the bottom of the cliffs was a river that served as a natural moat.

No one could take the city.

The city was the wealthiest in the entire world at one point.

Croesus, king of Sardis and the territory of Lydia, discovered gold amidst the sand in the Pactolus River, which flowed out of the mountain. When Cyrus, king of Persia, took the city (we'll get to that in a minute), he took the equivalent of $600 million in gold from the city. Sardis was the first city to make a standardized coin.

The city got overconfident…twice.

Sometime in 550s-540s BC, Croesus wanted to crush the annoying Persians who'd crept into Asia Minor. He had a habit of consulting the gods, and so went to the temple of Apollo at Delphi (in Greece). There, he asked the "oracle" (the priest) if he should attack the Persians. The answer, quite vague, was "if you do, you will destroy an empire." Croesus attacked the Persian army, suffered defeat, and was driven back to the city where he planned to regroup in safety.

Since a direct assault on the city would end in the slaughter of his army, Cyrus offered a reward to anyone who could find another way in. While searching around the base of the cliffs, some Persian soldiers saw a helmet fall from above. Shortly thereafter, a Sardian soldier climbed down a narrow crevice in the rock that was unnoticed before. He got his helmet and climbed back up.

This crevice was only wide enough for one person to climb up at a time.

The soldiers reported back to Cyrus, who must have smiled at this news. In the evening, after all had gone to sleep, Cyrus led his men, one-by-one, under the cover of night, up the crevice and into the city. The Sardian soldiers hadn't been guarding that area, because there was no way anyone could scale those cliffs and get into the city…except that's exactly what the Persian army did.

Croesus went to sleep prepared to destroy Cyrus the next day, and woke up to find his entire kingdom was taken from him.

320 years later, Antiochus the Great and the Seleucid army accomplished the same feat in remarkably the same way. The soldiers in the city had grown overconfident, and only guarded the main entrance to the city. From that point forward, Sardis was never again a free city.

What was their problem? They were not watching, and the enemy soldiers came upon them as a thief (stealing all their gold) in the night (both times).

Other Important Events in Sardis:

When Xerxes (Ahashuerus—Esther's husband), king of Persia, began to stage his attack against Greece, he gathered his immense army in Sardis.

The city was largely destroyed by an earthquake in AD 17. It was so bad that the Roman Emperor Tiberius declared they were free from taxes for five years, and also donated close to a billion dollars (in today's money) to rebuild it. By this time, the majority of the city was situated at the foot of the mountain and in the surrounding valley.

By the time Revelation was written, the city enjoyed some measure of wealth, but it was no longer of any importance—it was a city whose pride was in the past. According to Sir William Ramsey, "Thus, when the Seven Letters were written, Sardis was a city of the past, which had no future before it." *It was truly a city which still looked alive, but it was dying.*

The city continued to exist until 1405 when it was completely destroyed. Today a very small village called Sart exists in the valley near where Sardis once stood.

RELIGIOUS BACKGROUND OF SARDIS

Like most Gentile cities of the first century, Sardis had temples to a multitude of gods.

- Zeus (coins were minted mentioning him).
- Cybele (the earth-goddess, mother-earth) was the main object of their worship.
- Artemis

As a reaction to the generosity of Tiberius in helping to rebuild the city, they built a temple to worship him and his mother, Livia. This temple was not "official" and fell into decay within a few years of Tiberius' death.

The temple to Artemis.

This temple, though not as grand as the one in Ephesus, had been erected in the 400s BC. When the earthquake of AD 17 struck, part of the temple was destroyed, and much more of it was covered by a landslide. Though there was plenty of money available for the city's rebuilding, the temple of Artemis was never finished.

This pillars of this temple were 60 feet tall, each one (so it is said) made from a single piece of marble. After the pillars were erected, the carvers etched intricate details around them. But they never got around to finishing what they started. Keep that in mind as we read Jesus' words.

There was a large Jewish population in the city.

The largest synagogue ever discovered from the Roman Empire was found in Sardis. It was connected with the Marble Hall, the main gathering place for the city. This had a gymnasium, a pool, and many changing rooms. The synagogue was ornate, with mosaics all over the floor and walls, showing the Jews of the city were quite wealthy.

According to letters from the first century, Sardis was commanded to have Kosher food available for the Jews in the marketplace—something that makes Sardis unique. It also makes it seem that Sardis was extremely tolerant of every religious group—something that comes out in the letter.

THINGS TO REMEMBER:

- The city itself existed, but it was a shell of her former glory (a name that she was alive, but was really dead).
- They were well-known for being overconfident, and being taken at night when they weren't paying attention (like a thief in the night).
- What was once their grandest building had to be rebuilt, but they never finished it (I have not found your works completed...)

JESUS' INTRODUCTION (3:1)

To the messenger of the church in Sardis write;
"These things says the one who has the seven Spirits
of God, and the seven stars..."

He is the one with the seven Spirits of God.

The "seven Spirits" is a reference to the perfect or complete Spirit—the Holy Spirit. Jesus had authority over the Holy Spirit (John 16:12-15). The Holy Spirit is the one who delivered the word of God to us in written form. God's word comes from Jesus—with its commands, promises and punishments. Jesus had the Spirit "without measure" (John 3:34).

He has the seven stars.

The seven stars are the seven messengers (1:20). This is the same way He described Himself to Ephesus (2:1). He is showing He is the authority, and they needed to listen up. The message they speak must be *His* message.

WHAT JESUS KNOWS (3:1)

"I know your works, that you have a name that you're alive, and are dead."

Jesus knows their works.

If they were doing works for Jesus, this would be a commendation. But since I've read what comes next, I don't think that's what Jesus is talking about. In fact, it seems more like Jesus is saying, "I know you're not really working at all."

Jesus knows that they have a reputation (name) for being alive, but really they are dead.

Sardis had a reputation for being a great city, but they were a shell of their former glory—they were a dying city. The church in Sardis has a reputation for being a living, active, working church—but Jesus knew better.

We can make some educated guesses as to exactly what this means by noticing some things that are absent from this letter.

- Jesus doesn't speak of false doctrines being taught there.
- Jesus doesn't speak of persecutions against them (All who live godly *will* suffer persecution, 2 Timothy 3:12).
- Jesus doesn't commend them for their faithfulness, service, patience, or love.

The church in Sardis appears to be a harmless group who did no evangelizing, made no attempt to correct those living in the pagan lifestyle of the city—basically, they were just viewed as that harmless group down the street. This congregation did nothing to set themselves apart from the pagans, but tried to make it out like they were all ok.

In other cities, like Ephesus and Smyrna, the church separated themselves from their idolatrous neighbors, and everyone knew it. This is why they were persecuted heavily. When a church is not persecuted, it is time for that church to reevaluate what it is doing.

CHRIST'S COMMAND (3:2-3A)

> *"Be watchful, and strengthen the things which remain, that are ready to die: for I have not found your works complete before God. Therefore, remember how you had received and heard, and hold fast, and repent."*

WAKE UP! (NASB, NET, NIV)

The KJV/NKJV says "be watchful." The Christians in Sardis need to wake up out of their spiritual stupor and start being vigilant.

> *Be sober, be vigilant, because your adversary the devil walks about like a roaring lion, seeking whom he may devour (1 Peter 5:8)*

Remember the city of Sardis was taken twice in the night while men slept. The city was overconfident.

The church there was overconfident, thinking they were safe because they had become Christians.

Strengthen the things which remain, that are ready to die.

The fire they once had for the Lord dwindled to mostly ashes with only a few faint flickers among the embers. They needed to fan the flame, keep it from completely dying out. They needed to take a fresh and honest look at their life as a congregation, realize where they lacked, realize some of the members had fallen, and lift them back up while there was still a chance.

Christ had not found their works complete before God.

Remember that perhaps the grandest building in Sardis remained unfinished as they read this letter. Likewise, these Christians had begun the work in Christ, but were not seeing it to completion.

> *The trying of your faith works patience...Let patience*
> *have her perfect (complete) work (James 1:3-4).*

The Sardian Christians' faith wasn't being tested—most likely because they lived their lives in a way that made them no different than the rest of the city. They were just like everyone else, and blended in. No evangelizing. Even if they weren't involved with the pagan worship in town, they acted like the other religious groups were just fine. Does this describe you?

Remember how you had received and heard.

They received the word enthusiastically at first, but were now like the seed growing in rocky soil, dying because it had no depth. Some have suggested the gospel's arrival in Sardis was an unusual, noteworthy event (perhaps accompanied with many miracles).

Memories can be very strong. Nostalgia is powerful—remember the good old days? Some things from the past can still affect us decades later as though they just happened. Jesus asks them to look to the past, remember what it was like when they first became Christians, and compare it to what they're doing now.

Hold fast.

After bringing these things to mind, hold on to them! Don't let them go again! Cling to your excitement about the gospel!

Repent.

Look at how you were, and make up your mind to get back to it! Change your mind and your actions back to living for King Jesus Christ!

CHRIST'S WARNING (3:3B)

"If you will not be watchful, I will come on you as a thief, and you will not know what hour I will come on you."

Remember that Sardis was taken as a thief in the night TWICE in their history. Jesus is telling the church there the same thing will happen to them if they don't wake up and start watching their souls.

CHRIST'S COMMENDATION OF THE FEW (3:4)

"You have a few names even in Sardis which have not defiled their garments; and they shall walk with me in white: for they are worthy."

A few.

A few is a very small amount, a very small number. Most of the congregation is dead, but there are a few who have not defiled their garments (Zechariah 3:1-5 shows defiled garments represent sin).

There were only a few in the congregation at Sardis truly living for Jesus who hadn't gone back into worldly living. It may have been a congregation of 200 people, but if so, only about 15 of them would have been considered faithful.

This type of congregation is FAR more prevalent than you might think. In many congregations the majority of members just show up, while only a small handful actually care and study their Bible.

These faithful few will be counted as pure and innocent—walking in white—for they are worthy.

They are not worthy in and of themselves, but only as they live in and for Jesus. They are doing what they can for our Master.

JESUS' PROMISE (3:5)

"He that overcomes, the same shall be clothed in white raiment; and I will not blot out his name from the book of life, but I will confess his name before my Father, and before his angels."

Overcomers will be clothed in white.

The ones who overcome (those who wake up and repent, and those who stay faithful) will be clothed in white. Their sins will be cleansed and forgiven. Their garments would be washed in the blood of the Lamb. They will be given new, undefiled, pure garments (Zechariah 3) that show acceptance by God and Christ.

Blotted out of the book of life

Many cities kept a register of the citizens, and as citizens died, their names would be marked out.

The book of God, throughout Scripture, refers to those who are saved. After the golden calf incident, Moses went to God and said, "...forgive their sin—and if not, blot me, I beg you, out of your book which you have written" (Exodus 32:32). Deuteronomy 29:20 says those who don't obey will have their name blotted out. Paul said his fellow-laborers had their name written in the book of life (Philippians 4:3).

Those who overcome, then, will be counted by God as spiritually alive. They will receive eternal life! Jesus will confess them before the Father (see Matthew 10:32-33).

The "once-saved, always-saved" commentators have a very difficult time with this verse. John Walvoord (Baptist) went through some amazing mental gymnastics to try to say that the book of life isn't a record of the saved, but a record of every person on earth. He said it can't be a listing of saved people, because that implies your name can be removed. So, in essence, he's saying Paul was bragging on his fellow-laborers *for having been born* (because Paul said their name was written in the book of life)!

This is a book of those who are saved—but it isn't "once saved, always saved." Your name can be removed if you cease obeying the Lord!

WHAT DOES THIS MEAN FOR US TODAY?

Each of these letters is also a letter to us, for us to read, consider, and apply!

Sometimes it happens; you slowly let spiritual things slip away—but you must fight it! Each of you who has been baptized has been born again—given a new life. But if Jesus came today, would He find you spiritually alive, spiritually dead, or perhaps on spiritual life support?

It is time to re-ignite your fire for the Lord! It is time for faithful Christians to start being more active in encouraging those who are getting spiritually lazy!

If you don't wake up, you will find out too late that you have been judged as an enemy of Christ!

STUDY FOURTEEN:
JESUS' LETTER TO PHILADELPHIA
(REVELATION 3:7-13)

One definition of "maturity" is the ability to postpone pleasure. It is the ability to look past the possibility of immediate gratification and look to what will bring long-term happiness and stability. For Christians, it is the ability to not fall for Satan's temptations because we are looking for long-term happiness—in heaven!

The congregation in Philadelphia knew and lived this. They were steadfast in the midst of persecutions. They had a massive problem with Jews in the city. Yet they, of all the congregations addressed in Revelation, are given the highest praise from Jesus.

HISTORICAL BACKGROUND OF PHILADELPHIA

The city was established in the 150s BC, making it the youngest of all the seven cities. It was built by Attalus II, king of Pergamos. This king so admired and honored his brother (the previous king) that he received the nickname "one who loves his brother," or, in Greek, Philadelphius. When he built the city, he named it "Philadelphia" which means "the city of brotherly love."

It was a "missionary city" for spreading Greek culture.

The purpose of this city was to spread Greek culture to the surrounding area. It was situated in a prime location at the border between Lydia, Mysia, and Phrygia along one of the major roadways leading eastward into Asia Minor. It was known as "the gateway to the east." It was so successful at its Greek-missionary purpose that within a few years, the Lydian language was no longer spoken—everyone spoke Greek.

Given to Rome

When Attalus III (king of Pegamos) died in 133 BC, he had bequeathed his entire possessions (including Philadelphia) to the Roman Empire.

New names

It was destroyed by the AD 17 earthquake which had also flattened much of Sardis. Like Sardis, Philadelphia received aid from Tiberius Caesar in order to rebuild. In recognition of the aid, they changed their name to Neocaesarea (New-Ceasar-town). After the death of Tiberius, the city returned to the name "Philadelphia." When Vespasian ruled, he changed the name of the city to Flavia, after his wife. The city was not known as Philadelphia during that time. This is more evidence Revelation was not written during his reign.

Religion in Philadelphia

The city, with its many temples to the Greek gods, was known as "Little Athens." Because grapes grew abundantly here, their chief god was Dionysus, the god of wine. Though it is possible, there is no evidence that any form of emperor worship existed in Philadelphia until over 100 years after Revelation was written (during the reign of Caracalla). Oh, and there were Jews there too. The city is now called Alasehir, and very few remains of Philadelphia are left.

THINGS TO REMEMBER:

- Because of the constant earthquakes, stability and permanence would have been extremely important.
- The city was filled with temples to false gods.
- The city was built in order to spread a new way of life—Greek Hellenism.

The most important thing to keep in mind about Philadelphia is the Jewish population. The entire letter to the church at Philadelphia is filled with references to the Jews and things about the Jews. We also need to remember that the Christians in this area were largely Jewish.

JESUS' UNIQUE DESCRIPTION OF HIMSELF (3:7)

To the messenger of the church in Philadelphia write; "These things says the one who is holy, the one who is true, the one who has the key of David, the one who opens, and no man shuts; who shuts, and no man opens."

In the other letters, Jesus describes Himself in a way that refers back to Revelation 1. But in this letter, Jesus describes Himself in three ways—*none* of which appeared in that letter—and each of them held a very important meaning to Jewish Christians.

These things says he that is holy.

Literally, the Greek says, "These things says the Holy One." In the Old Testament, the phrase "the holy one" ALWAYS referred to God.

- 2 Kings 19:22
- Job 6:10
- Psalm 71:22, 78:41, 89:18
- Isaiah 10:20 "…upon Jehovah, the Holy One of Israel…" (Isaiah uses this phrase 27 times)
- Jeremiah 50:29, 51:5
- Ezekiel 39:7 "…the heathen shall know that I am Jehovah (the LORD), the Holy One in Israel."
- Hosea 11:9—"I am God, and not man, the Holy One in the midst of you."
- Habakkuk 3:3

To Jewish Christians (and any of the "synagogue of Satan" who might read it), this is Jesus laying claim to being God. To the non-Christian Jews, this was blasphemy (John 10:33). But to Christians (including Christian Jews), this was a statement of authority—follow me, for I am God.

These things says he that is true.

Literally, this is "the True One." While it is indeed the case that everything Jesus said was true, this is not what Jesus means here. Instead, Jesus is the True One, there are no others. The myriad of false gods in Philadelphia were just that—false.

This also says to the Jews, "The Old Testament is over with. Now you follow what I say to do." Jesus is the way, the truth, and the life (John 14:6). Jesus was the "true light" (1:9), the "true bread" (6:32-35), the "true witness" (8:14), the "true judge" (8:16), and the "true vine" (15:1). Jesus is the real deal, Jesus is completely truth (no falsehood in Him at all).

These things says He that has the key of David, He that opens and no one closes, and closes and no one opens.

This is a reference back to Isaiah 22:20-25.

> *And it shall come to pass in that day that I will call my servant Eliakim, the son of Hilkiah, and I will clothe him with your robe, and strengthen him with your belt, and I will commit your government into his hand: and he shall be a father to the inhabitants of Jerusalem, and to the house of Judah. And the key of the house of David I will lay on his shoulder; so he shall open, and none shall shut; and he shall shut, and none shall open. And I will fasten him as a nail in a sure place, and he shall be for a glorious throne to his father's house. And they shall hang on him all the glory of his father's house, the offspring and the issue, all vessels of small quantity, from the vessels*

of cups, even to all the vessels of flagons. In that day, says the LORD of Hosts, shall the nail that is fastened in the sure place be removed, and be cut down, and fall; and the burden that was on it shall be cut off, for the LORD hath spoken it.

Eliakim was given the keys to the house of David (the royal palace). No one could get in to see the king without going through him. If he decided to let someone in, no one could keep that person out. If he said a person was not allowed in, no one could force that person in.

This shows authority. Jesus said, "No one can come to the Father, except by me" (John 14:6). Jesus describes this action in the present tense, which shows He is continually active in determining who gets to the Father and who doesn't.

Eliakim was a type of Jesus Christ. Verse 25 is said by some to foreshadow Christ's rejection and the subsequent rejection of the Jewish people in AD 70.

It is in this description of Himself that Jesus proclaims he was already ruling His kingdom! This is not something yet to happen, Jesus was already ruling! He still is!

To the Jewish Christians in Philadelphia, Jesus is reiterating: "I am the Messiah!"

JESUS KNOWS... (3:8)

"I know your works: behold, I have set before you an open door, and no man can shut it: for you have a little strength, and have kept my word, and have not denied my name."

Jesus knows their works.

And these works must have been pleasing to Christ, because of what He says about them later.

He has set an open door before them that no one can close.

Some think this is a reference to a door of opportunity. Since Philadelphia was a city built to spread the Greek culture (a new lifestyle) to the area, the church there could spread Christianity (a new lifestyle) to the area. This is why many later writers call Philadelphia a "missionary city." Paul referred to doors of opportunity (1 Corinthians 16:9, 2 Corinthians 2:12, Colossians 4:3).

But what Jesus says here seems to be directed at Philadelphia specifically. After all, don't we ALL have opportunities to spread Christianity in our area?

The "open door" is a reference to what Jesus just said. Jesus controlled who had access to the Father, and says to these saints, "I've got the door open for you, and no one can close it." This is a reassurance of their salvation. They had complied with the conditions to gain access to the Father, and as such, Jesus has opened the door to welcome them.

Jesus knows they have little strength.

They are not strong within the city. They are either small in number, in finances, in influence, in abilities, or a combination of these.

But even though they just had a "little strength" (power—NASB), they didn't use it as an excuse to sit and do nothing. Many congregations say, "We're too small to do that work." Really?

Jesus knows that (even though they have "little power") they have kept His word and not denied his name.

People who are in a weak position often give in to outside pressure, but not this congregation. They stayed strong, faithful, sound, loving, and patient.

The words "kept" and "denied" are in the aorist tense, which means a one-time action in the past. Some believe that this means they went through a tribulation in the past already (perhaps at the same time that Antipas was killed over in Pergamos), and had come through it with flying colors. There are two choices: confess Christ or deny Christ—there is no third option.

JESUS KNOWS THE PROBLEMS THEY FACE (3:9)

*"Behold, I will make those of the synagogue of Satan,
who say they are Jews, and are not, but lie; behold,
I will make them come and worship before your feet,
and know that I have loved you."*

The Jewish source of persecution

Though other persecutions likely existed, the main difficulties in Philadelphia came from non-Christian Jews. Jesus again calls them the "synagogue of Satan" (as to Smyrna in 2:9). These claim to be Jews (right with God), but lie. True Jews are those who are circumcised in their heart (Romans 2:28-29), which Paul says happens at baptism (Colossians 2:11-12).

This "synagogue of Satan" could also include Judaizing teachers who crept into the church and caused much trouble in the first century.

These Jews would be made to come and worship before their feet, and made to know that Jesus loves the church.

This does not mean Jesus was going to make the Jews worship Christians, because only God is worthy of worship (Paul, Peter, and angels refused worship). Some believe this is a reference to those Jews who persecuted them in Philadelphia being converted to Christ and worshiping with that faithful congregation. Others believe that this is a reference to Judaism being crushed.

The destruction of Jerusalem in AD 70 was a loud and clear signal to any honest Jew that God had rejected them as His people, and that He could only be accessed in the New Jerusalem, the church. Honest-hearted and open-minded Jews—after that horrible event—would have bowed before the cause of Christ and submitted themselves to the one who loves the church. God's care and love is for the church, not physical Israel.

PROMISE OF BLESSINGS (3:10-11)

"Because you have kept the word of my patience, I also will keep you from the hour of temptation, which is about to come on all the world, to try those who dwell upon the earth. Behold, I come quickly..."

Because of their faithfulness in keeping Christ's word and following His example of perseverance, He would keep them from the hour of trial/testing/temptation.

A specific time is under consideration, a specific event. Not only is it a specific event, but it is one that Christians then alive in Philadelphia would live to see, otherwise this promise is meaningless. The literal wording is "which is about to come..."

The hour of temptation/testing/trial would come on all the world.
This is speaking of the Roman Empire (Matthew 24:14, Acts 11:28, 19:27, Colossians 1:6). Christians across the Empire would be affected by it.

This is directed at those who dwell upon the earth (the land).
This is a reference to the Jews. Don't forget that the word "earth" is the same in Greek as "land," and in Revelation usually (if not always) refers to the Promised Land—the home of the Jews. Shortly after Revelation was written, the Roman-Jewish war broke out and over a million Jews were slaughtered *throughout* the Roman Empire.

Jesus promised to keep them from (out of) this hour of trial.
It is possible Christians in Philadelphia would be unaffected by this event. At the very least, they are promised that in the upcoming wars, none of their number would be killed.

If there was any doubt, Jesus says "behold I come quickly."
The word "quickly" is the same as "shortly" in 1:1. Jesus said to *them, back then,* "I am coming soon!" Obviously this is not the final

coming of Christ, but a coming in judgment against the Jewish nation.

THE OVERCOMER'S REWARD (3:11-12)

"Hold fast that which you have, so that no man takes your crown. The one who overcomes I will make a pillar in the temple of my God. He shall go out no more. And I will write on him the name of my God, and the name of the city of my God, which is new Jerusalem, which comes down out of heaven from my God. And I will write on him my new name."

Hold fast what you have.

They had that open door, faithfulness, confession of Christ, salvation. They were told to hold tight to those things, don't let them go.

Make sure no one takes away your crown!

They had that crown of righteousness, the crown of victory. But they could lose it! Jesus doesn't believe the doctrine of once-saved, always-saved!

If one falls prey to the wiles of the devil, or the temptations of the world around him, he removes his crown, and gives up the victory with Jesus.

The overcomer will be a pillar in the temple of God.

In a city devastated by earthquakes, a pillar showed strength and permanence. Philadelphia had pillars standing with names of heroes inscribed on them. Jesus says His faithful overcomers would be a permanent fixture in God's temple (the church in heaven), and ...

He will not go out anymore.

When you overcome, you will have eternal life—never to leave, never to lose it! This is a promise not of an earthly reality, but of a heavenly one!

Christ will write three names on the overcomer.

- The name of God (showing ownership)
- The name of the city of God, New Jerusalem (showing citizenship)
- The new name of Jesus Christ (showing relationship)

And you certainly remember (don't you?) that the city of Philadelphia was used to being given new names. Jesus certainly knew how to connect with His audience!

WHAT DOES THIS MEAN FOR US TODAY?

The entire letter can be summed up in one short sentence: Stay faithful to Christ and you win! This entire congregation worked together and stayed faithful together. For you and the congregation where you are, it means this: Stay faithful to Christ and you win!

Don't deny Christ, but instead confess Him! Even if you're not in a large congregation, you still have strength to spread God's word!

Stay watchful! Don't fall into laziness, thinking you don't have to do anything anymore! Stay faithful and you win!

If Jesus came back right now, would He call you one of the winners?

Study Fifteen:
Jesus' Letter to Laodicea
(Revelation 3:14-22)

I get frustrated when I ask, "What do you want to do?" and the answer is "I don't know." We get annoyed when people won't make up their mind. They say, "I don't care, whatever you want."

Weird Al Yankovic did a song once describing a scene where a couple argues about what to eat, because neither one of them can make up their mind. In essence, it goes: What do you want to eat? I don't know what about you? I'm not really hungry, but I could eat. What do you want? What's in the fridge? The tuna's gone bad, and you ate the chili. Do you want something delivered? Why would I want liver? I said delivered. Anyway, what do you want to eat? I don't know, what about you? Do you want to go to this restaurant? No, it's too fancy and I don't feel like getting dressed up. What about this one? Nah, I'm not in the mood for that. Never mind, just forget about it. No, let's go somewhere. Where? I don't know.[1]

Then they finally go to a drive-thru, where they proceed to argue about what to order. And so it continues.

This same kind of attitude was described by Jesus when He wrote to the church in Laodicea. They were the "whatever" kind of people who didn't care one way or the other about spiritual things.

HISTORICAL BACKGROUND OF LAODICEA

Laodicea was established by Antiochus II, and named for his wife, Laodice. It is located around 40 miles southeast of Philadelphia, and about 90-100 miles due east of Ephesus. It was originally established as a garrison city, but grew to prominence because of its

---

[1] This is a highly summarized version of the first part of his song, "Trapped in the Drive Thru"

location along the main roadway from Ephesus to the East. It was among the cities bequeathed to Rome by the king of Pergamos upon his death in 133 BC.

Medicine and Springs

Laodicea was crushed by the earthquake in AD 17 and accepted the government's aid to rebuild. After rebuilding, the city quickly grew in power and prestige. Much of this was because of their central location between the hot springs of Hierapolis and the great medicinal center 13 miles outside of the city.

People from all over the Roman Empire would come here when they had eye diseases, for Phrygian powder, used in a salve, was well-known for curing many eye maladies.

Black Sheep

They were also well-known for their black-wool garments. Black sheep were plentiful in that area, and these garments sold at a very high cost throughout the empire, making the shepherds, the salespeople, and the garment-makers very rich.

Money. Money, Money

The city also had many banks. It has been called "The Wall Street of Asia" as well as "a city of millionaires."

In AD 60-61, the city was destroyed once again by an earthquake. This time, however, the city rejected aid from Rome and rebuilt itself from its own finances. They didn't need any help, thank you very much. Colossae (6 miles away) was destroyed and never rebuilt. Hierapolis (13 miles away), was rebuilt within the next decade.

Piped-in water

They had a very inventive system of clay pipes to bring water into the city. They piped in mineral water from the hot springs, but by the time it got to Laodicea, some miles away, it was no longer hot. They also, it is said, piped in cold water from an underground lake miles outside the city, but again, by the time it got to the city, it wasn't cold at all. Mineral water, especially lukewarm, is nauseating.

Today, there is no city on the site of Laodicea.

The people in Laodicea were:

- Generally healthy
- Financially rich
- Well-clothed.
- Independent and self-sufficient.
- Thought they had need of nothing.

BIBLICAL BACKGROUND OF THE CHURCH IN LAODICEA

The Bible gives us a lot of information about the background of the church at Ephesus, but none on any of the other six churches—well, except for Laodicea.

The church in Laodicea may have been founded during Paul's time in Ephesus (Acts 19:10). It appears Paul had never seen the majority of the members there (Colossians 2:1). Some old manuscripts of 1 Timothy close with the words "written from Laodicea...," but those are uninspired additions.

Some believe the congregation was started by Epaphras (Colossians 4:12-13). It is also possible that it was started by Philemon, who was converted by Paul.

Paul wrote a letter to the congregation in Laodicea (Colossians 4:16), but Bible students are divided on what happened to it. Some believe it is lost to time, and would not have contained anything we don't already have. Some believe this "letter from Laodicea" is what we know as Ephesians, because some ancient manuscripts don't say "at Ephesus" in 1:1. Personally, I think it is the letter to Philemon.[2]

---

[2] This is explained in an Appendix in my book, *The Prodigal Slave: A Study of the Letter to Philemon* (Charleston, AR: Cobb Publishing, 2013).

Archippus was a member of the church at Laodicea (see Colossians 4:16-17). He was part of the church that met in Philemon's house (Philemon 2). This being the case, Philemon was a member of the church in Laodicea.

It is surmised by some that after the great earthquake in AD 60-61 the churches in Hierapolis and Colossae merged into the congregation at Laodicea. This earthquake completely destroyed Colossae, probably within two years or less of their receiving the letter from Paul. Tradition says Philip the apostle (or Philip the evangelist) was crucified in Hierapolis.

But by the time Jesus wrote to the Christians in Laodicea, the congregation had become lukewarm.

How could this happen so quickly? I've seen it before with congregations who build new big buildings or have an influx of members from another congregation. They believe, "We're doing well, so God must be happy with us," then they stop doing anything and grow complacent. It doesn't take long for this attitude to permeate the whole congregation.

THE IDENTIFICATION OF JESUS (3:14)

To the messenger of the congregation in Laodicea, write, "These things says the Amen, the faithful and true witness, the Originator of God's creation."

These things says the Amen.

"Amen" means "So be it." What Jesus says is what will happen (evidence of this is seen momentarily). In Isaiah 65:16, God is called the "God of truth," but the word translated "truth" is the Hebrew word amen. Yet another clue that Jesus is God. Jesus is the absolute truth.

These things says the faithful and true witness.

Jesus was faithful in relating to man what God wanted relayed; as such, he was faithfully bearing the witness/testimony of God. The word "witness" comes from the word "martyr" in Greek, and we can also just as validly say Jesus was faithful and true to death. But the meaning here is this: Jesus is bearing accurate testimony about the church in Laodicea.

A faithful and true witness in court is one who:

- Has seen first-hand the events in question.
- Has the mental capability to recall and present those events accurately.
- Has the willingness to do so.

Jesus has seen what the church in Laodicea is, what they are, what they've done, and is about to relay it back to them accurately.

These things says the beginning of the creation of God.

This verse is one of the favorites of the so-called "Jehovah's Witnesses." Jesus is not saying He was the first thing created. Jesus stresses His authority over created things (the word "beginning" is the Greek word *arche*, which means "chief"), and the fact He is the one who created them all.

This same word (*arche*) is translated "principality" or "principalities" 8 times in the New Testament (KJV). ALL things were created by Jesus Christ, and without Him, nothing which was created came into existence (John 1:1-3). This means the only way Jesus could be a created being is if somehow, before He existed, He created Himself—an impossibility.

JESUS KNOWS... (3:15-16)

> *"I know your works. You are neither cold nor hot. I wish you were cold or hot. So, because you are luke-warm, neither cold nor hot, I will vomit you out of my mouth."*

Jesus knows their works.

Sure, they were doing things, but they weren't doing anything for Jesus. Remember, Jesus is faithfully reporting what He witnesses of them.

Jesus knows they are lukewarm.

They were neither cold nor hot (remember the water coming into Laodicea was neither cold nor hot).

Jesus states, "I wish you were cold or hot." We can understand easily that Jesus would want them to be hot, to be on fire for the Lord, to be zealous! But why would He add in there, "I wish you were *cold* or hot"?

Some believe this is a reference to the cool, refreshing water from Colossae. In which case, Jesus would be saying I wish you were a drink that was satisfying (we like cold drinks and hot drinks, but lukewarm drinks are rarely preferred).

I think it more likely Jesus would rather them not even claim to be Christians than to be lukewarm. Those who are cold don't put on a show of being religious, they don't come to worship, they don't participate in Christian activities. At least if they were cold, they wouldn't be a part of the local body and influencing others. It has been said that it is easier to convert someone who is cold towards Christ than to convert someone who is satisfied with where they are.

Because of their lukewarmness, Jesus will spew them out of his mouth.

Some translations say "I will spit you out…" However, it is much more graphic than that. Jesus takes a drink, swallows it, and then turns sideways, bent over in pain, and continually vomits the nauseating liquid out. He is about to *vomit* them out, because they are nauseated by them.

Literally, Jesus warns them: I've not yet cast you out of my body, but "I am about to." When Jesus says this, the lukewarm church is still in the body of Christ. But since they've been warned, since they've been shown their real condition, they have two options: repent or get cast out.

We need to remember Jesus still considered them as part of His church in this condition—apparently because they didn't realize their condition yet, but He would reject them if they *stayed* in that condition.

JESUS' LOVING ADVICE (3:17-19)

You say, "I am rich, and I have become wealthy, and I need nothing," but you do not know that you are wretched and pitiable and poor and blind and naked. I advise you to buy gold from me, purified in fire, that you may be rich; and white garments, that you may be clothed, and that the shame of your nakedness may not be seen; and salve to rub on your eyes, that you may see."

They claim to be rich, having need of nothing.
They were materialistic—like *sooooooo* many Christians today. Remember this city rebuilt itself with its own riches, refusing the aid of Rome because they didn't need it. *We're self-sufficient, we don't need anyone's help.*

Those who desire to be rich fall into many snares (1 Timothy 6:9-10). I've heard people say, "I'm rich, I've got everything I could possibly want. What do I need with Jesus? I'm happy right where I'm at!" It's nothing new: the rich young ruler chose earthly possessions over heavenly treasures.

They were the wretched ones.
This word describes slaves condemned to work in mines to the point of exhaustion. They weren't wealthy to Jesus, but spiritually destitute. They thought they were high and mighty, but Jesus says they were slaves.

They were the miserable ones.

This word describes people to be pitied, like the lame who can't do anything for himself. You really want to raise the ire of someone with a high opinion of himself? Tell him that you pity him.

They were poor.

This means destitute, a beggar without even enough for a morsel of bread. These Laodicean Christians were spiritually bankrupt, exchanging their own souls for money and possessions. They had cash, but they didn't have treasures in heaven.

They were blind.

They couldn't see their true condition; for they had hardened their heart to seeing the truth.

They were naked.

Oh, they were clothed with fine black Laodicean wool, but spiritually they were naked. They had put on Christ in baptism, but then took him off and hung Him outside their hearts.

Remember the parable of the wedding feast: a man was found without proper garments, and was cast into outer darkness.

Jesus counsels (a friend's loving advice) them to buy refined gold from Him.

Sure, they had lots of physical gold, but Jesus wants them to build up treasure in heaven! Notice Jesus wasn't just going to *give* them this refined gold, they had to *buy* it from Him. This required some kind of *effort* or *work* on their part. *True* riches can only be found in Christ.

Jesus counsels them to buy white garments so their spiritual shame would be covered.

They had the famous black clothing, but they needed to be clothed in white. They needed to be washed in the blood of the Lamb (1 John 1:7, Revelation 7:13-14).

The white garments are the righteous acts of the saints (Revelation 19:8). The Laodicean Christians lacked this. They didn't have the works that showed their faith (James 2:24).

Jesus counsels them to buy eye salve from Him so they could see.
John 9:39—Jesus came into the world so the blind could see (v. 41 shows that this means they were blind to their own sins). Jesus gives the Laodicean Christians His diagnosis, and prescribes a cure: take an honest look at your condition! (See also 2 Corinthians 13:5).

THE LOVE OF JESUS DISPLAYED (3:19-21)

"I correct and chasten as many as I love. Be zealous and change your heart. I stand at the door and knock. If anyone hears my voice and opens the door, I will come in to him, and I will dine with him, and he with me! The one who overcomes will sit with me on my throne, as I overcame and sat with my Father on his throne."

As many as I love, I rebuke and chasten.

The word "love" here is not *agape* (the sacrificial love), but instead is *phileo*. The word *phileo* is an affectionate kind of love, wanting to be with someone. We might even translate it better as "like." The noun form of it is translated "friend" 29 times in the New Testament. Jesus is saying, *I like you guys, that's why I'm trying to help you.*

He corrects them, but it is because He wants to be with them. He can't have fellowship with them when they've kicked Him out of their hearts.

Have you ever stopped and contemplated that Jesus Christ truly, sincerely loves you and wants to be in your presence? As Dave Ramsey says, "He's crazy about you!" Here's the catch: you've can't be in His presence if you're living in sin. Jesus says, *Hey, I want to spend time with you, but you keep saying no!*

Because Jesus loves you, be zealous and repent!

These lukewarm Christians are told to start being zealous! The Jews had a zeal without knowledge (Romans 10:2), but *these Christians had a knowledge without zeal.* How often have faithful Christians looked around their congregation and fervently prayed other members would show some signs of enjoyment and excitement out of being a Christian.

These lukewarm Christians are told to repent! You can't be acceptable to Christ by being content as you are. One preacher said it this way, "Yes, Jesus will accept you 'Just As I Am,' but He won't let you stay that way."

Because Jesus loves you, He is standing outside the door of your heart, knocking, saying, "Please, let me back in."

These Christians had shut Jesus out of His own church! He was begging them, *Please let me back in and we will eat together, we will have fellowship with each other, we can enjoy each other's company again!*

Pay attention here! This verse is <u>not</u> (did I make that emphatic enough?), I repeat, <u>not</u> telling a non-Christian to "invite Jesus into [their] heart" to be saved. This is the main verse that proponents of the "Sinner's Prayer" will appeal to in defense of their doctrine. This verse is about people who were *already Christians* who had locked Jesus out of their hearts. No non-Christian is ever told to pray in order to be saved—ever.

Unfortunately, the church in Laodicea is not the only church who has kicked Jesus out of their lives.

Those who overcome will be made to reign with Him on His throne.

Why is there rejoicing in heaven when one sinner repents? Because he has overcome sin, realized his condition, and did something about it! In this context, the overcomers in Laodicea would be any Christians who recognized their need for Jesus, and swung the door of the heart back open to welcome Him in!

Overcomers with Christ are part of the royal family, and get to share in Jesus' reign! This idea is addressed more later in Revelation.

WHAT DOES THIS MEAN FOR US TODAY?

My friends, I beg you today to take a look, an honest look at your life. Are you on fire for the Lord? Or are you a lukewarm Christian? Have you shut Jesus out of your time, your thoughts, and your actions?

Jesus desperately wants to spend time in your life; He loves you, He's already proven it by dying for you. But you need to make the next move.

STUDY SIXTEEN
THE HEAVENLY THRONE ROOM
(REVELATION 4)

Three times in the Old Testament, God's prophets were shown the throne of God.

Ezekiel 1

Ezekiel 1 contains a mind-boggling description of a fire, shooting out lightning bolts, and being carried around by four-faced beings (Cherubim) with four wings, each being a wheel of God's chariot. *This scene came shortly before Jerusalem was destroyed by Babylon.*

Isaiah 6

Isaiah 6 describes God's throne room, complete with beings (Seraphim) with six wings—with two wings they covered their face, with two their feet, and with two they flew. *This scene was to prepare Isaiah to preach the destruction of His people* (6:11-12).

Daniel 7

Daniel 7:9-10 describes a fiery stream going out from the throne, which had wheels of fire. *This is part of a vision describing events that would take place during the days of the Roman Empire* (the fourth beast in Daniel's vision).

What do we see in common with all of these visions? Every time the throne of God is seen in a prophetic vision, judgment is the context.

What does this have to do with Revelation?

The imagery in Revelation comes from the Old Testament. One writer counted over 350 allusions to the Old Testament in the final book of the Bible. With all these references to the Jewish Scriptures, who do you think the main audience was?

Remember our third study. The Christians in Asia were mostly Jewish, and the book deals with the end of Judaism and the fulfillment of many Old Testament prophecies. So, when they see a vision of God's throne, they should immediately realize this is a book that describes judgment on the Jews.

In Revelation 4, we have a view of God's throne in the heavenly temple.

Note some of the similarities between the Old Temple and the Heavenly Temple:

The Old Testament temple had twenty-four classes of priests that served (1 Chronicles 24:4). The role of these priests was to sing praises with their harps (1 Chronicles 25). Meanwhile, the heavenly temple had twenty-four elders around the throne, each with a harp, and they sang praises to the Lamb (Rev 5:8-9).

The Old Testament temple had a large laver, called a "sea for the priests to wash in" (1 Chronicles 18:8, 2 Chronicles 4:2-6). The heavenly temple had a "sea" of glass.

The Old Testament temple had cherubim (2 Chronicles 3:10-13). The heavenly temple had what most believe are Cherubim.

The Old Testament temple had the "mercy seat." The heavenly temple had a rainbow around it, a symbol of mercy (see Genesis 9:13-17).

This imagery would have been very important and notable for a Jewish audience.

A RECAP OF THE BOOK THUS FAR:

Jesus Christ is revealing things which had to shortly come to pass, and were "at hand" *when He first revealed them* (1:1, 3).

Jesus appears in a vision, and is eerily similar in appearance to the messenger that came to Daniel to announce the destruction of the Jewish people. This isn't a coincidence, because the destruction of the Jewish people was about to happen.

Jesus is dressed as High Priest among the true temple of God— the church!

When John was told "write the things which you have seen," it meant write down this vision of Jesus (Rev. 1:19).

Because of the impending events which are going to "try those that dwell on the earth/land" (the Jews), Jesus dictates seven short letters to seven very real congregations in Asia Minor, whose situations mirror the condition of congregations everywhere.

The letters were written to prepare the church for what was about to happen.

- The loveless must repent!
- The faithful must hold fast and remain faithful, even though some would die.
- The lukewarm were about to be vomited out of the body of Christ.
- The compromisers must recognize Jesus is in control.

Through it all, Jesus speaks of coming in judgment against those who are not with Him.

When John was told to write "the things which are," it meant the current condition of the churches, which Jesus dictated to him (Rev. 1:19). And now begins the last part of what John was told to write: "the things which shall be hereafter." The rest of the book contains those things which, in the first century, "must shortly come to pass."

Some have titled chapters 4-5 as "Believe in God" (ch. 4), "Believe also in Me" (ch. 5). Chapter four focuses on God, chapter five focuses on Jesus Christ.

THE THRONE SCENE

Look at this vision from John's point of view, and notice the big picture before we focus on the details. I really like the description given by David L. Roper:

The glory and grandeur of the vision exceeded anything that John could have imagined. Half-blinded by the brilliance and bewildered by the spectacle, he strove to sort out the scene before him. At center stage was a massive throne, the dais of the Almighty. Pulsating from the throne were the dazzling colors of the rainbow. Encircling the throne was a ring of smaller thrones. On those thrones were aged men, white-robed and golden-crowned, their craggy faces bathed in celestial radiance.

Without warning, an ominous rumbling of thunder and jagged flashes of lightning came from the throne. Then seven lamps flared up at the foot of the throne, startling John. Between him and that raw power was a shining expanse—and John was glad of the distance. His heart was pounding so hard that it seemed as if it might burst from his chest.

As John's eyes adjusted, his gaze was able to penetrate the glare surrounding the throne, and he saw four fantastic creatures. Their form...both beautiful and grotesque. All had wings, and were covered with eyes—unblinking, all-seeing eyes. Through the Spirit, John knew that they were the bravest, strongest, wisest, and swiftest beings in the universe. Then the apostle became aware of their song. As they praised the One who sat on the throne, their song filled the apostle's soul: "Holy, holy, holy, is the Lord God, the Almighty, who was and who is and who is to come." John was overcome with awe.[1]

---

[1] Roper, *Revelation, Vol. 1.*, pp. 206-207.

It would serve us well to read Ezekiel 1, looking at the fantastic imagery there (some of which is repeated in Revelation 4), and especially focus on the final verse of that chapter, which says everything Ezekiel saw and relayed was "the glory of God."

Yes, the details matter, but if you miss the big picture, the details won't help you. Let us look at this wonderful chapter with the throne of God being our main focus—because everything in chapter four revolves around the throne, or more specifically the one who sits upon the throne.

THE LOCATION OF THE THRONE (4:1-2)

After this I looked, and, behold, a door was opened in heaven: and the first voice I heard was like a trumpet talking with me; which said, "Come up here, and I will show thee things which must be hereafter." And immediately I was in the spirit: and, behold, a throne was set in heaven, and one sat on the throne.

A door is open in heaven, and John is told to "come up here."

In the Spirit, John is transported to the spiritual realm and he sees a throne "set in heaven." There is nothing on earth, no throne, no rule, no authority that can come close to the sheer power and grandeur of the throne of God.

The purpose of the vision is to show John the things which must be hereafter.

These are the same things that "must shortly come to pass." "Hereafter" means "from here, and afterwards" or from here on out. John is going to be shown visions describing things which were about to happen—the great tribulation followed by the destruction of Jerusalem. Those things are not specifically seen in chapter 4, but that is where the vision starts.

THE ONE UPON THE THRONE (4:3)

And he that sat [on the throne] was, to look upon, like a jasper and a sardius stone: and there was a rainbow round about the throne, in sight like an emerald.

The One on the throne is not described here. Instead John describes the radiance and glory emanating from the One sitting on the throne. (Note: Ezekiel's description was that He was like a man of fire.)

Holiness and judgment

He has the look of the jasper (most likely not the stone that we call jasper today, but instead a diamond—see Rev 21:11). This shows the intrinsic value, strength, purity, and holiness of God.

He has the look of the sardius stone. This is a fiery red gem that seems to glow with an inner fire. This brings the idea of God's fiery judgment.

A Rainbow

Around Him is an emerald-colored rainbow. The rainbow was a symbol of God's mercy after the flood (Gen 9:13-16). If God's judgment was all that existed, with no mercy, how many of us would still be here? This is why there was a "mercy seat" in the temple.

So in this description of God, we see His purity, His holiness, His fiery judgment, but we also see God's judgment tempered with His mercy.

THE ONES SURROUNDING THE THRONE (4:4)

Around the throne were twenty-four thrones: and on the thrones I saw twenty-four elders sitting, clothed in white raiment; and they had on their heads crowns of gold.

Around the throne of God sat twenty-four other thrones.

Thrones symbolize some kind of rule or authority. The KJV calls these "seats," but the Greek word is *thronos*—the same word used for God's throne in this verse.

Upon the thrones sat twenty-four elders.

These elders were clothed in white (a symbol of their purity) and wore crowns of gold (a symbol of their victory).

These elders are not literal old men in heaven—they are symbols of something else. But symbols of what?

Remember there were twenty-four classes of priests whose role in the Old Testament temple was to offer praise to God. This could be the source of the symbolism. These 24 elders represent the faithful under the Old and New Testaments. The twelve tribes (the sons of Jacob, representative of the Old Testament), and the twelve apostles (representative of the New Testament) are here combined.

Some might ask, how do you know these elders represent people?

- They are arrayed in white (which is promised to the over-comers—Revelation 3:3).
- They are wearing victory crowns (promised to those who stay faithful—Revelation 2:10).
- They are sitting on thrones (promised to those who over-come—Revelation 3:21; see also Matthew 19:28).

Daniel 7 describes the kingdom being given to the saints of the Most High. We reign presently with Christ!

As an alternate take, some see chapter 4 as a description of worship under the Old Testament, and chapter 5 a description of worship under the New Testament. I don't think I have a problem with that interpretation either.

COMING FROM THE THRONE, AND IN FRONT OF THE THRONE (4:5-6A)

And out of the throne proceeded lightnings and thunderings and voices: and there were seven lamps of fire burning before the throne, which are the seven Spirits of God. And before the throne there was a sea of glass like crystal.

Coming from the throne was lightnings, thunders, and voices.

This shows God as the source of the destructive judgments that are about to be pronounced. These descriptions are almost always, at least in prophecies, pictures of impending judgment. A storm was coming, and God was behind it.

In front of the throne were seven torches.

These torches (Greek word *lampas,* which is why some translations say "lamps") are the seven Spirits of God (the Holy Spirit). The Holy Spirit illuminates and sits ready before the throne of God to do the Father's will.

In front of the throne was a sea of glass like crystal.

Hugo McCord's translation says "a sea like glassy crystal." The Modern Literal Version says "a glassy sea, similar to crystal." The sea is not made of glass, but is clear (and probably smooth and peaceful) like crystal. Because of the function of the "sea" before the temple in the Old Testament, we can assume this sea is symbolic of the cleansing of the priests so they could be in the presence of God. *You have to go through the water to get to God.*

For no apparent reason, I think I should mention 1 Peter 3:20-21, Mark 16:16, Acts 2:38, 22:16, Romans 6:3-7, and Galatians 3:26-27. If you look them up, you'll see why they are noteworthy to mention here.

THE FOUR LIVING BEINGS IN AND AROUND THE THRONE (4:6-8)

In the midst of the throne, and around the throne, were four creatures full of eyes in front and behind. The first was like a lion, the second like a calf, the third had a face as a man, and the fourth was like a flying eagle. Each of the four creatures had six wings about him; and they were full of eyes within: and they do not rest day or night, saying, "Holy, holy, holy, Lord God Almighty, which was, and is, and is to come."

Part of the throne?

These are not beasts (KJV), but beings or creatures. They are both in the midst of the throne, and around the throne. This has led some to speculate that these beings are part of the throne itself, perhaps that which Ezekiel described as the wheels. They are also similar in description to those seen in Isaiah 6.

One was like a lion, one like a calf (ox-calf), one had the face of a man, and the other was like a flying eagle. If these are part of the throne, they are representative of God's inherent attributes: power, strength, intelligence, and swiftness.

Showing God's authority

Others say these are the highest of all forms of life, and that God is in control of all.

- Of wild beasts, the lion.
- Of domesticated beasts, the ox.
- Man
- Of fowls of the air, the mighty eagle.

Still others believe these are the highest forms of angels.

But we must remember these are symbols. This, like Ezekiel 1, is portraying the incredible glory of God and His throne.

WORSHIP TOWARDS THE THRONE (4:8-11)

They do not rest day or night, saying, "Holy, holy, holy, Lord God Almighty, which was, and is, and is to come." And when those creatures give glory and honor and thanks to him that sat on the throne, who lives forever and ever, the twenty-four elders fall down before him who sat on the throne, and worship him that lives forever and ever, and cast their crowns before the throne, saying, "You are worthy, O Lord, to receive glory and honor and power: for you have created all things, and for your pleasure they are and were created."

The four creatures continually chant "holy, holy, holy, Lord God Almighty, who was, and who is, and who is to come."

If there was any doubt as to whom this One on the throne was, this answers it. Those in the presence of God cannot help but praise, honor, and thank God. They proclaim both His holiness and His eternal nature.

The twenty-four elders, while the creatures are chanting, also worship the Father.

They bow down (showing reverence). They cast their victory crowns (showing they acknowledge God as the true source of their victory—they did not win on their own). They leave their thrones, counting their authority as nothing, for God has all authority. They worship Him (praising Him)

But why did they praise God?

- Because God is worthy to receive praise, glory, honor, and power.

- Because God created everything.
- Because everything was created for His purposes, or His will.

This has a direct bearing on what is revealed throughout the book—the things that "must shortly come to pass" are going to happen because it is God's will.

WHAT DOES THIS MEAN FOR US TODAY?

Imagine you were John, and you were shown this scene; what would your reaction be? It would be one of wonder, of awe, and of an amazing sense of "I am not worthy to be here."

God is awesome!

God is all-powerful, God is in control. People get into the rut of thinking God is just a guy somewhere with a lot of power that we can call on for help sometimes. We need to wake up to the awesome power of God, and show Him the honor, awe, and respect that He deserves. God is the Almighty, and even the other beings (who would be quite powerful) in the heavenly temple bow down to Him.

The picture of God on the throne is a fearsome sight when you realize He is about to pronounce judgment against an entire race of people.

The scary thing is that if you haven't taken hold of God's grace, and taken advantage of His mercy in baptism, then you are on His "judgment list" too.

STUDY SEVENTEEN:
THE LAMB AND THE SCROLL
(REVELATION 5)

Did you know the Bible records tears actually *have* been shed in heaven (and they were not tears of joy)? If you've read ahead in Revelation, you know what I'm talking about.

Last study, we looked at the amazing description of the Father on the throne and those who worship Him. You may have noticed the Father was there, as was the Holy Spirit, but Jesus was missing from the picture. Not anymore.

Revelation 4 described the heavenly setting, and some of the players in the rest of the book were introduced:

- The Father on the throne.
- The four creatures
- The 24 elders (one version calls them "ancient ones")
- The Seven Spirits (the Holy Spirit).

Revelation 5 introduces two more characters that come into play later in the book:

- The strong angel
- The Lion of Judah who was a slaughtered Lamb.

This chapter also introduces the sealed scroll that comes into play over the next few chapters. Once you understand what the scroll contains, and what comes from the seals being opened, you can better understand Revelation 5.

So, I will sit here and wait while you read Revelation 5:1 through 8.1. . . . . Back already? Okay, here we go!

THE SEALED SCROLL (5:1-4)

And I saw in the right hand of him that sat on the

throne a scroll written on the inside and the backside, sealed with seven seals. And I saw a strong angel proclaiming with a loud voice, "Who is worthy to open the scroll, and to undo its seals?" And no one in heaven, nor in earth, neither under the earth, was able to open the book, or to look on it. And I wept much, because no one was found worthy to open and to read the book, or to look on it either.

Remember John is seeing into heaven in a vision (these things all being symbols). He has seen the glory of the Father, seen the sea of glass, the 24 elders, the four creatures, the lightning and thunder and voices coming from the throne, and the seven torches. Though there's a chapter break, the vision of chapter 4 didn't stop with the beings in heaven worshipping the Father. It continues right on into chapter 5.

John looks, and sees in the right hand of God a scroll.

This scroll has writing on both the front and the back. You might ask, "How could he tell?" Scrolls were made with papyrus, which was usually just written on one side. When papyrus was rolled together (in a scroll), the writing would be on the inside, and the backside of the papyrus would be visibly blank. If writing was showing when it was rolled up, then both sides were used.

That it had writing on both sides show the importance of what was written. None of the papyrus was going to be wasted.

The scroll had seven seals on it.

Scrolls would usually be rolled up, then tied with a string or sometimes a leather strip, and then sealed with wax, to keep the contents from the eyes of others. It's similar to licking an envelope and closing it, but more tamper-proof.

The fact that it had seven seals on it shows that it was completely sealed. And no one was worthy to open even one of the seals, let alone all seven. This is shown more in the next verses.

"Who is worthy to open the scroll and remove the seals?"

Alas, there was no one. No one in heaven (not the angels, not the four creatures, not the elders), no one on earth (humans), and no one under the earth (those who have died, but whose spirits still exist) was worthy to open it. The point is this: *no created being is worthy to open the scroll and read its contents.*

The mighty angel asked this question with a loud voice (in Greek, it is *mega phone*), and his only answer was complete silence.

John wept bitterly.

Tears in heaven. Of course, this is a vision, not literal heaven. But why did John weep? It wasn't because his curiosity wasn't going to be satisfied. He wept because this was a revelation from God, and there was no one to deliver it.

But then...

THE LAMB APPEARS (5:5-7)

One of the elders says to me, "Don't cry, Behold! the Lion of Judah, the Root of David, has prevailed [overcome] to open the book and undo its seven seals." And I looked, and, behold! in the midst of the throne and of the four beasts, and in the midst of the elders, stood a Lamb like it had been slaughtered, having seven horns and seven eyes, which are the seven Spirits of God sent forth into all the earth. And he came and took the book out of the right hand of him that sat upon the throne.

One of the elders came to comfort John (v.. 5)

The elder here says one of the reasons Jesus prevailed was *so that He could open this scroll*. If part of the reason Jesus overcame (that is, died and arose on the third day) was to open this scroll, then you'd better believe it is important! Jesus died on the cross so we could have our sins forgiven, to show there is life after death, and to fulfill the Old Testament—which included promises about the destruction of the Jews and their rejection as God's people. Christ died and arose so this could be revealed to us.

John had already seen Jesus in a vision, as the High Priest, but new Jesus has changed. John turns around, looking for a lion (the Lion of Judah), but when he looked, he saw ... a lamb.

The slaughtered Lamb (v.. 6)

This Lamb appeared as though it had been slaughtered. Take a moment to think about that. How would a slaughtered lamb look? I doubt it was a nice, clean, white lamb. A slaughtered animal has wounds, and it probably had blood all over it. However, this once-slaughtered Lamb was alive!

The Lamb had seven horns.

Horns are generally a reference to power. In Daniel, the Medo-Persian Empire was represented by a ram with two horns, one higher than the other (Two united powers, the Persian half was more powerful than the Median half). The Grecian Empire was represented by a he-goat with one horn (Alexander the Great's concentrated power). The Roman Empire had ten horns, showing it had more power than any of the previous kingdoms.

Jesus, as the Lamb that was slain, but now living (a reference back to Revelation 1:18), has seven horns—complete power. The Father was said to be worthy of all power (Revelation 4:11). So this also shows equality with God, the deity of Jesus Christ!

The Lamb had seven eyes, which are the seven Spirits of God.

First, this shows omniscience—all-seeing ability.

Secondly, this shows that the Lamb (Jesus) had the Holy Spirit. This occurred at Jesus baptism (John 1). Jesus also received the promise of the Holy Spirit upon His ascension (Acts 2:33). Jesus had direct authority over the Holy Spirit (John 16:12-15). He had the Spirit without measure (John 3:34).

The description of Jesus as the Lamb shows that:

- Jesus is deity.
- Jesus did die, but is alive.
- Jesus was our sacrifice.

Some of the main truths about Jesus are found in the description of the Lamb in Revelation 5.

The Lamb took the scroll out of the right hand of God.

The Lamb is worthy! The scroll was spoken of in the very first verse of Revelation: "The Revelation of Jesus Christ which God gave Him to show to His servants things which must shortly come to pass." This scroll is that Revelation!

But notice that the Lamb "took" the scroll. If the Lamb wasn't worthy, or was acting presumptuously, the Father wouldn't have let it be taken.

- It reveals things which must shortly come to pass!
- And only Jesus could make it known!

WORSHIP TOWARDS THE LAMB (5:8-14)

And when he had taken the book, the four creatures and twenty-four elders fell down before the Lamb, each one of them having harps, and golden bowls full of incense, which are the prayers of saints. And they sung a new song, saying, "You are worthy to take the scroll, and to open its seals: for you were slaughtered, and have redeemed us to God by your blood out of every tribe, and language, and people, and nation; and have made us kings and priests to our God: and we shall reign on the earth."

And I stared, and I heard the voice of many angels around the throne and the creatures and the elders: and the number of them was ten thousand times ten thousand, and thousands of thousands; saying with a loud voice, "Worthy is the Lamb that was slaughtered, to receive power, and riches, and wisdom, and strength, and honor, and glory, and blessing."

And every creature which is in heaven, and on the earth, and under the earth, and such as are in the sea, and all that are in them, I heard saying, "Blessing, and honor, and glory, and power, to him that sits on the throne, and to the Lamb forever and ever."

And the four creatures said, "Amen."

And the twenty-four elders fell down and worshipped him that lives forever and ever.

Before we examine the form of worship here, we need to make something abundantly clear: This is in heaven, in the presence of God the Father. And beings in heaven begin to worship someone *other than* the Father.

- Unless Jesus is deity (God), this worship is blasphemous.
- Unless Jesus is deity, God allows worship to a created thing (something condemned in Romans 1 and in Revelation 22).

The fact Jesus is worshiped—in the presence of the Father—proves Jesus is God just as much as the Father is God! The Father would never permit worship to be given equally to Him and to some created being.

Instruments in heaven!

This is a vision—and these things are not to be taken literally. The harps are to identify the twenty-four elders as priests of God (1 Chronicles 24-25). We will discuss this more a bit later.

The golden bowls of incense

Golden—it shows the value and importance.

Incense—it is a sweet-smelling fragrance to God, in other words, it is pleasing and acceptable to Him.

These are the prayers of the saints. Catholic dogma (something required of all Catholics to believe) says this proves we pray to dead Christians who are in heaven, and that they then offer their prayers to God for us. Nowhere does this passage even hint at such nonsense! The prayers being presented before God are the prayers of the saints—and the Bible tells us who "saints" are: *Living, faithful Christians on earth* (Acts 9:13, 32, 41; Romans 1:7; 8:27; 12:13; 15:25-26, 31; 16:15; 1 Corinthians 1:2; 16:1-2; etc.).

"Now doesn't it at least prove prayer can be offered to Jesus?"

No, and here's why. These weren't offered to Jesus. It says they are in the hands of the elders (and possibly the creatures as well). Revelation 8:3-4 shows unambiguously these are presented before God the Father. If that's not good enough, consider what Jesus said:

> *Therefore pray this way:* **Our Father** *who is in heaven, your name is holy (Matthew 6:8).*

> *Whatever you shall ask* **of the Father** *in my name, he may give it you (John 15:16).*

Or consider Paul's words:

> *In everything by prayer and supplication with thanksgiving let your requests be made known* **to God***. And the peace of God, which surpasses all understanding, shall keep your hearts and minds through Christ Jesus (Philippians 4:6-7).*

> *And whatever you do in word or action, do all in the name of the Lord Jesus,* **giving thanks to God the Father** *through him (Colossians 3:17).*

Several other passages point to the same truth: Prayer is to be directed to God the Father.[1]

---

[1] For further study on this topic, see *To the Father—Through Jesus* by Gary W. Summers.

They sung a new song (5:8-10).

In chapter four, they sang a song praising the Father on the throne. Now, they sing a new song, praising the Lamb of God. The song includes these thoughts:

(1) Jesus is worthy to take, to open, and to reveal the things contained in the scroll.

> *God, who at various times and in diverse manners spoke in time past to the fathers by the prophets, has in these last days spoken to us by His Son, whom He has appointed heir of all things (Hebrews 1:1-2).*

- He is worthy because "He also, Himself, took part of the same [flesh and blood]; that through death, He might destroy him that had the power of death, that is the devil" (Hebrews 2:14).
- He is worthy because "He knew no sin" (2 Corinthians 5:21).
- He is worthy because "All authority has been given [to Him], in heaven and on earth" (Matthew 28:18).

(2) Jesus is worthy because he had been slain, and had redeemed people by His blood.

> *"Baptism doth also now save us…by the resurrection of Jesus Christ" (1 Peter 3:21).*

> *"The church of God which He has purchased with His own blood" (Acts 20:28).*

These people were from every tribe (Jews) and tongue (languages) and people (ethnicity) and nation (Gentiles).

(3). The identity of the four creatures and twenty-four elders?

Look at what they sang. They sang Jesus had redeemed "US" to God, and made "US" kings and priests, and "WE" shall reign on the earth. The creatures and elders were those redeemed by Christ's blood and made a royal priesthood and a holy nation (1 Peter 2:9).

Some translations (NASB, NIV) say "you have made **them**..." I don't believe these are based on the best manuscripts (the translators of those Bibles obviously disagree), but if they're right, then it completely renders the above paragraph worthless. Thankfully, our understanding of who they're singing about isn't going to be on the test come Judgment Day.

The elders and creatures were joined by 100 million angels, and millions more (5:11).

Literally, the Greek says "Myriads myriads." A myriad is 10,000. Most translations agree this means 10,000 times 10,000. But the words are both plural, meaning *multiple* 10,000s times *multiple* 10,000s. So the number I gave above (100 million) is actually—at best—*half* of what it should be. In other words, there's an awful lot of angels there.

These angels said, "Worthy is the Lamb that was slain to receive power, and riches, and wisdom, and strength, and honor, and glory and blessing." (5:12). These are some of the same things said about the Father (4:9-11).

- Jesus is worthy to receive the power (this isn't the word for authority, but for strength and dynamic power).
- He is worthy to receive the riches of heaven, for He lived sinlessly.
- He is now worthy to receive the wisdom and understanding of what is written in the book—that which no man could know, not the angels of heaven, not even the Son, but the Father only—Matthew 24:36, Mark 13:32.
- He is worthy to receive the strength that comes from His role as King of kings.
- He is worthy of honor and glory because of the sacrifice on our behalf.

All of creation joined in the chorus! (5:13-14).

Every creature in heaven, on earth, under the earth, and in the sea said, "Blessing and honor and power to him that sits on the throne, and to the Lamb forever and ever!"

Praise was given *equally* to the Father and the Son. The Son returned to heaven and received praise and glory from all of creation!

The four creatures said "Amen!"

Praise was offered, and creatures closest to the Father (perhaps even being representative of His attributes) shouted AMEN! This is God's divine approval of the worship offered to Him and to Jesus the Lamb!

As we leave this scene of praise and honor to the Father and the Son, let's not forget one little detail: The Lamb has the sealed scroll. And in the next study, the seals start to be opened, one by one, and those "things which must shortly come to pass" will be revealed!

WHAT DOES THIS MEAN FOR US TODAY?

Praise the Father and the Son!

Revelation 4 began by showing John the awesome glory of God. Revelation 5 continues the vision and shows the Son is worthy of the same praise and honor because He has overcome the world!

Jesus didn't stay dead

Regardless of modern skeptics who say Jesus never arose, the Scripture evidence (and historical evidence too, but that's a whole 'nother topic) proves without a doubt to any who have faith that Jesus rose from the dead. He is the Lamb slaughtered, but who came back to life to open the scroll of vengeance on His murderers.

Are you *sure* you're on His side? Because that Lamb isn't anyone to mess around with.

STUDY EIGHTEEN:
THE SEALS ARE OPENED (PART 1)
(REVELATION 6:1-8)

A large crowd gathers for a big event. They're waiting, waiting, waiting till the clock strikes the proper time. Then a man steps onto the stage, "The moment you've been waiting for has now arrived!"

This phrase seems appropriate. We've been reading, waiting for things to start. The promise from the first verse was *something* "must shortly come to pass." And now it begins.

Through the rest of the book, we get to see the prophecies given by Jesus Christ in fantastic imagery. But oh the fun!

There are differences of interpretation of specific details in chapters 1-5, even among members of the church, but that's nothing compared to the range of interpretations beginning with chapter 6. We will point out *some* of the different interpretations as we go through, and also point out which is correct—or at the very least, which is the most likely.

It will help you immeasurably if you read Matthew 24:1-34 before delving into this chapter. In that passage, Jesus discusses events leading up to the destruction of Jerusalem. You may notice some very striking similarities between it and Revelation 6.

Historically, here's how the destruction of Jerusalem happened.

(A good, short book on the topic, matching the destruction with Matthew 24, is Holford's "The Destruction of Jerusalem.")[1]

The Roman Army began its march through Asia Minor (heavily populated with Jews), and worked its way towards Jerusalem. Death and destruction followed the army as they slaughtered thousands of

---

[1] This book (in an illustrated edition) is available in print from this publisher, or a digital edition is available for free at www.TheCobbSix.com/Jimmie-Beller-Memorial-eLibrary/

Jews (some of them Christians) because of the uprising, where Jewish zealots had begun to assassinate Roman officials.

The armies came upon Jerusalem, and started a blockade—nothing in, nothing out. Just as it appeared Jerusalem would fall, Vespasian (the Roman general) was called back to Rome because the emperor had died. Vespasian took his armies back to Rome, and he was crowned Emperor of the Roman Empire.

The *Jews* in Jerusalem took this as a sign from God that they were saved. The *Christians* in Jerusalem took this as a sign from God to get out of the city as quick as possible. And historically speaking, all the Christians left. Early Christian writers speak of a mass exodus from Jerusalem during this time. They say not one Christian died in the events which followed.

Vespasian sent Titus (his son, and the next emperor) to finish the job in Jerusalem.

Why mention this? Because the seals match up with these historic events.

Before we get into this chapter and the opening of the seals, let's put things in context.

It was mentioned in passing a couple studies ago that some view chapter four as a description of the worship of Old Testament Israel. It had the 24 elders with harps (the 24 classes of priests who offered worship and incense to God on behalf of the people). It had the sea (the sea at the Old Testament temple was for the cleansing of the priests). It had what some believe are cherubim (there were cherubim in the Holy of Holies). The Spirit was at the front of the throne, showing that He is ready to do the Father's will. There was no Jesus to be seen.

This being the case, chapter five is a description of New Testament worship. Jesus is shown as the freshly-killed sacrificial Lamb. The scroll previously controlled by the Father is now controlled by the Son (the Lamb). Some have said this is the shift in power, the giving of the Kingdom to the Son. This scroll, written on front and back, was complete—no room for any additions!

After taking the scroll, all of those in heaven worship the Lamb *and* the Father. The conclusion of the two chapters is that Jesus is every bit as much God as the Father is.

And now the Lamb begins to open the seals of the scroll…

SEAL 1: THE VICTORIOUS ARCHER ON THE WHITE HORSE (6:1-2)

And I saw the Lamb open one of the seals, and I heard, like the noise of thunder, one of the four creatures saying, "Come and see." And behold! I saw a white horse. And he that sat on it had a bow; and a crown was given unto him: and he went forth conquering, and to conquer.

When the first seal is opened by Jesus Christ, the contents of the scroll leap out in the vision. John doesn't hear words being read, but actually sees it play out. When Jesus took the scroll, it showed His authority to *open* the scroll, to *reveal* the scroll, *and to cause the things in the scroll to take place!*

Throughout all of this, remember Jesus is the force behind the things described in the rest of the book. This is the "coming of the Son of man" spoken of in Revelation 1:7, because Jesus is the one directing and orchestrating it all.

First, there is the sound of thunder, as the first creature (apparently the one like a lion) said, "come and see."
Some translations leave out the words "and see," which would have the creature calling the horseman out of the scroll. If the KJV/NKJV reading is correct, then he is calling John to come look. This debate, while interesting to some, doesn't add much one way

or the other to our understanding of the vision. As such, there isn't a need to dwell on it.

The voice like thunder is often used in the Bible to describe God's presence, and frequently His judgments.

John saw a white horse.

Horses are symbolic of war. Pharaoh's army had horse-drawn chariots (Exodus 14:9). "The horse is prepared for the day of battle" (Proverbs 21:31). Jeremiah 4:11-14 describes God's judgment against Jerusalem, and in it He says His "chariots shall be as a whirl-wind: his horses are swifter than eagles..."

In pronouncing judgment upon Jerusalem, God says (through Habakkuk):

> *I raise up the Chaldeans [Babylon]...Their horses are swifter than leopards, and are more fierce than the evening wolves: their horsemen will spread them-selves, and come from far; they shall fly like the eagle that hastens to eat. They shall come for violence...*
> *(Habakkuk 1:6-9)*

Israel was warned not to import horses, because they would trust in those animals for their army instead of trusting in God (Deuteronomy 17:16). Israel was told not to fear the horses of the enemy [if they were following God] (Deuteronomy 20:1). God has armies with flaming horses (2 Kings 2:11, 6:16-17).

Hopefully, these passages are enough to prove to you that horses represent war. Because that will become a recurring theme in this chapter.

White

The color white is associated with victory. The ones who gain the victory will be dressed in *white* (Revelation 3:5). A *white* stone was given to overcomers (Revelation 2:17).

Therefore, this horse represents a war in which the rider is victorious. This is made clear because of...

The rider of the horse

Gerald Cowan states, "The riders of the horses are more important than the horses [themselves]."[2]

The rider of the white horse has a bow (as in bow and arrows). This is a symbol of warfare. Usually, archers were the first to begin the assault, doing it from a distance. This is the beginning of a battle.

The rider of the white horse was given a crown. This crown is not a crown of ruling or authority (Greek *diadem*), but a crown of victory (Greek *stephanos*). He was given the victory crown (we're not told by whom) *before he did anything*, showing this rider was guaranteed victory—Jesus made sure of it.

The rider went about conquering and to conquer.

One writer said "He was bent on conquest." This word "conquer" is the same root (in Greek) as "overcome." He went out to overcome, to conquer, to emerge victorious over his enemies.

Now that we know what the specific symbols mean, what does that say about what the first seal actually represents?

Here's where things get really fun.

Some say this rider represents the victorious Jesus Christ. After all, Jesus is represented as riding a white horse in chapter 19. However... Jesus is shown with many *crowns of authority* (not *victory crowns*) in chapter 19. Also, Jesus (the Lamb) is the one who opened the seal—am I the only one who thinks it would be screwy to have two Jesus's in the vision at the same time? This interpretation doesn't fit the context, because this rider must be understood in connection to the others

Some say this rider represents the Anti-Christ (I told you people varied widely on their interpretations). They claim the white horse is a *fake* white (like somehow the rider painted it white?!?). There is

---

[2] Unpublished commentary on Revelation.

no evidence for such an assumption. Nor does the Bible teach there will be someone known as "the Antichrist."[3]

Some believe this is the "spirit of conquest" in all ages. They say this so they can (and I quote) "avoid the need to assign the symbols a chronological sequence or historical setting; and avoid the need to identify the symbols with specific historic events or persons." But John was clear: he wrote about "things which must shortly come to pass."

This rider actually represents the Roman armies, about to march in conquest against the Jews (the Roman-Jewish war). They were guaranteed the victory (given the crown, riding the white horse). They went forth with military strength (the bow).

Some argue against this because white is always used to represent something holy in the rest of Revelation. But remember, this was a war where Rome was being used by Jesus Christ. *This was a holy war*: Christ against the now-rejected Jews. Jesus called Rome's attack on Jerusalem "the coming of the Son of man" (Matthew 24:27). If Jesus brings it about, then it *is* holy.

THE SECOND SEAL IS OPENED:
THE WARRIOR ON THE RED HORSE (6:3-4)

And when he had opened the second seal, I heard the second creature say, "Come and see." And another horse went out which was red: and power was given to him that sat on it to take peace from the land, that they should kill one another. And he was given a great sword.

---

[3] John, in the first century, said there were already "many antichrists" working (1 John 2:18). The word means "ones against Christ," and no passage speaks of a single individual with the title "Antichrist."

The red horse.

Again, a horse is a symbol of war. The color red indicates bloodshed, which goes along with war.

The first seal was The Roman army mobilized by Jesus Christ; the second seal is the war having begun.

The Roman Armies marched through Asia Minor, killing tens of thousands of Jews in close combat. Fifteen strongly fortified cities in Galilee were stormed, and all the inhabitants slaughtered (men, women, and children). In Caesarea, thirty-five thousand Jews were dead in the streets.

Bloodshed indeed.

The rider was given power to take peace from the earth.

This means to "take peace" means "to make war."

The "earth" is the "land" (aka, the Promised Land, Judea). The rider had permission from Jesus Himself to make war on Judea.

The rider was given power so they would kill one another.

Something interesting happened during this time: a Civil War broke out in Judea. Three different Jewish factions, fighting against each other for control of the city. One got wiped out, but there were still the other two—and they stopped at nothing to try to gain control. They killed each other, making the Roman Empire's job that much easier.

The rider was given a great sword.

This sword is not the *rhomphaia* or heavy Thracian battle sword used to hack people to pieces. This sword is the *macharia* or short-sword used for up-close and personal killing.

It also happens to be the sword the Roman army *always* used. And it is a "great sword," showing just how powerful their weapons would be.

THE THIRD SEAL OPENED: THE MAN WITH THE SCALES ON THE BLACK HORSE (6:5-6)

And when he had opened the third seal, I heard the third creature say, "Come and see." And I looked, and behold! a black horse; and he that sat on it had a pair of scales in his hand. And I heard a voice in the midst of the four creatures say, "A measure of wheat for a denarius, and three measures of barley for a denarius; and see that you don't hurt the oil or the wine."

The black horse.

This again is a horse, a symbol of war (are you noticing a trend here?). The first four seals are all about war or something connected to it.

The color black indicates mourning, sorrows. What do we think of when we say someone is dressed in black (other than "Johnny Cash")? Someone in mourning.

The black horse describes the sorrows that come with this war brought on by Jesus Christ against the Jews.

The rider held a pair of balances or scales.

This was used to weigh food. When someone got to the point they had to weigh out their own food, you know times were getting tough—they were rationing.

A voice in the midst of the four creatures said, "a measure of wheat for a denarius, and three measures of barley for a denarius; and you do not hurt the oil and the wine."

The denarius is the equivalent of one day's wages. A measure of wheat is what the average adult would eat in a day—one day's worth of food. You may say, "That's good, he has enough money to buy his food each day," but that misses the rest of the problem.

You are a hard-working man who makes a day's wages; you only have enough money to buy food for yourself. No money for food for your family (unless you all skip meals or eat next to nothing at each meal). Also, after buying the food, you have no money to pay for clothing, housing, fuel, or anything else.

This price for food is about 10-18 times the normal cost! If the cost of groceries increased by 10 times today, would your family be able to make it? Imagine that: eighteen dollars for a loaf of bread, thirty-nine dollars for a box of cereal. At those prices, you wouldn't even consider buying anything that wasn't a complete necessity, would you?

Three measures of barley could be had for a day's wages. Barley was considered animal-food, unfit for human consumption.[4] If you wanted to feed your *family* in this time of war, you had to buy animal feed.

When war breaks out, food becomes scarce. The people didn't care about the oil or the wine because they were too concerned about getting the things they needed to survive! And even then, they weren't getting enough to sustain them!

This horse and rider show the sad condition within Jerusalem during the initial siege. In discussing the destruction of Jerusalem by Babylon (600+ years earlier), God said:

> *"For thus saith the Lord GOD: How much more when I send my four sore judgments upon Jerusalem, the sword, and the famine, and the noisome beast, and the pestilence, to cut off from it man and beast?"* (Ezekiel 14:21).

Keep that in mind as we look at...

---

[4] This tells us something about the boy with five barley loaves and two fishes (John 6:9). He must have been exceedingly poor, yet willingly gave what he had to Jesus.

THE FOURTH SEAL OPENED: DEATH UPON THE PALE HORSE WITH HADES BEHIND (6:7-8)

And when he had opened the fourth seal, I heard the voice of the fourth creature say, "Come and see." And I looked, and behold! a pale horse: and its rider's name was Death, and Hades followed with him. And power was given to them over a fourth of the land, to kill with sword, and with hunger, and with death, and with the beasts of the earth.

The Pale Horse:

The horse is a symbol of ...? You guessed it, *war*.

The pale color is actually the Greek word for green. This pale green color might be ok for new grass, but not for humans. It is the color of a corpse.

And this is appropriate because...

The rider is Death.

This is the only rider that is given a name. And what happens in war? Death.

This refers to the result of pestilence and disease that comes during a famine, during times when people are malnourished. Death follows in the wake.

Hades follows after him.

It has been said that Death went out to collect the bodies while Hades went out to collect their souls. Hades (and its Hebrew equivalent, *Sheol*) frequently refers to the grave, as well as the state of the dead. Hades literally means "not-seen place."

They were given power over a fourth of the earth.

This isn't a fourth of the world or a fourth of the globe, but a fourth of the people in the Promised Land.

Was it a literal fourth? Well, consider this: When fifteen strongly fortified cities in Galilee (part of the Promised Land) are without citizens because the entire population was slaughtered, and you add the 35,000 lying dead in Caesarea, and the many others that died in the other cities, a fourth may well be literal.

But many believe this is a way of saying they only had power to take a *portion* of the lives. This part of the devastation was only partial, and served as a warning (this becomes clear later in the book).

Only a fraction of the people would meet death at this point. It was a large fraction, a noticeable fraction, but still only a fraction.

They were given power to kill with:

- The Sword—see Ezekiel 14:21
- With Hunger—see Ezekiel 14:21
- Death (pestilence, disease)—see Ezekiel 14:21
- Beasts of the earth—see Ezekiel 14:21

Remember, this isn't Christ sending out some hooded figure named Death on a literal horse. This is symbolic of what was going to happen in Judea during these times. A lot of people were going to die.

Now would be a good time to read Matthew 24:1-8…

MATTHEW 24:1-8

And Jesus went out, and departed from the temple: and his disciples came to him to show him the buildings of the temple. And Jesus said to them, "Do you not see all these things? Truly I say to you, there shall not be left here one stone upon another, that shall not be thrown down."

And as he sat on the mount of Olives, the disciples came to him privately, saying, "Tell us, when shall these things be? What shall be the sign of your coming, and of the end of the age?"

And Jesus answered them, "Take heed that no man deceive you. For many shall come in my name, saying, 'I am Christ'; and shall deceive many. And you shall hear of wars and rumors of wars: see that you are not troubled: for all these things must come to pass, but the end is not yet. For nation shall rise against nation, and kingdom against kingdom: and there shall be famines, and pestilences, and earthquakes, in diverse places. All these are the beginning of sorrows."

He is speaking to His disciples, forewarning them about the destruction of Jerusalem.

- Verse 6—You will hear of wars and rumors of wars.
- Verse 7—Nation will rise against nation (Rome vs. Judea)
- Verse 7—There will be famines.
- Verse 7—There will be pestilences.
- Verse 7—There will be earthquakes in various places (like Colossae/Laodicea/Hierapolis)
- Verse 8—*All these things are the beginning of sorrows.*

These four seals are just the beginning.

It is no wonder John called this "the final hour" (1 John 2:18). It is no wonder Peter said, "the end of all things is at hand!" (1 Peter 4:7). And since this is just the beginning, it is no wonder Jesus said this was "great tribulation such as was not since the beginning of the world, no, nor ever shall be" (Matthew 24:21).

WHAT DOES THIS MEAN FOR US TODAY?

Jesus is in control

As you contemplate these things, keep this in mind: Jesus Christ is the one in control, and this death and destruction is being brought against the people who rejected Him. Jesus Christ orchestrated this; He led the armies of Rome against the ones who were once God's chosen people!

His judgments are just and righteous. He will punish all who are opposed to Him.

My friend, where do you stand with Jesus?

STUDY NINETEEN:
THE SEALS ARE OPENED (PART 2)
(REVELATION 6:9-17)

A vision of heavenly glory and majesty was shown in Revelation 4. The Father sat on the throne in heaven, radiating glory, lightning, and thunder. The Holy Spirit sat before the throne in the form of seven torches.

The glory of Jesus Christ was shown in Revelation 5. He came as a Lamb, freshly slain. He had the Holy Spirit upon Him (in the form of seven eyes). He was worthy to take the scroll and open the seals which were on it. Praise and glory were heaped on the Father and the Son. Both were equally worthy of praise.

But then the mood changes, because the seals begin to be opened.

- Seal 1: the rider on the white horse—The Roman army, sent forth by Christ, guaranteed victory against the Jewish nation.
- Seal 2: the rider on the red horse—bloody war throughout Asia Minor and Galilee, and civil war in Jerusalem.
- Seal 3: the rider on the black horse—famine as a result of the destruction and the Roman blockade of Jerusalem.
- Seal 4: Death riding the pale green horse—disease, pestilence, and death caused by the famine and by the Roman attacks.

With the background firmly set in our minds, let's go to Revelation 6 and look at the next seal that is opened.

THE FIFTH SEAL: THE SOULS UNDER THE ALTAR (6:9-11)

And when he had opened the fifth seal, I saw under

the altar the souls of those who were slain for the
word of God, and for the testimony which they held.
And they cried with a loud voice, "How long, O Lord,
holy and true, do you not judge and avenge our blood
on those who dwell on the land?" And white robes
were given to every one of them; and they were told
they should rest for a little while longer, until their
fellow-servants and their brethren, that should also
be killed as they were, should be fulfilled.

Jesus said these things contained in the first four seals were only "the beginning of sorrows" (Matthew 24:6-8). The end was not yet (24:6). We need to remember this was just the beginning of the time of tribulation which came before the destruction of Jerusalem. This helps us place the vision of the fifth seal in context.

Souls under the altar

Whoever these souls are (and we'll get to that in a minute), they were ones who died faithful to God.

Under the alter

They were "under the altar." In the Old Testament, the priests killed an animal and drained its blood at the base of the altar (Leviticus 4:7, 18, 30, Exodus 29:12). Josephus said the blood at the base of the altar was ankle-deep for the priests on the Day of Atonement. God said Abel's blood cried out from the ground for justice (Genesis 4:10). Thus, these souls who had been murdered for faithfulness were crying out for justice.

Slain

These saints had been "slain." This word indicates one having been slaughtered or sacrificed. It is the same word used in Revelation 5:6 of Jesus as the Lamb that was slain.

They had been murdered, sacrificed for their faith. Romans 8:36 says, "For Your sake we are killed all the day long. We are accounted as sheep for the slaughter."

For the word of God and their testimony

They had been slain "for the word of God and for the testimony which they held." This is the same reason John was on Patmos (Revelation 1:9). At least one writer pointed out it does *not* say, "the testimony *of Jesus Christ*" here, and so he believes these are Old Testament saints. I tend to agree with that assessment. But at the very least, we can say these saints of God had been murdered because of their faithfulness to God.

Their cry: how long?

These martyred saints cried out "how long?" They weren't crying out of frustration at having to wait. After all, they were in Paradise. The first four seals showed the beginning, but these saints asked about the end. This is what Daniel enquired about while he was on earth.

> *...when he accomplishes the scattering of the power*
> *of the holy people, all these things shall be finished.*
> *And I heard, but I did not understand: then I said, "O*
> *my Lord, what shall be the end of these things?"*
> *(Daniel 12:7-8)*

These souls were asking God to fulfill His judgment on those who murdered them.

They called God "Lord."

The word here isn't the normal word for "Lord" (*kurios*). This word is *despotes*, from which we get the word "despot," meaning a complete ruler. Some translations render this word "Master," "Sovereign," "Ruler," "Sovereign Lord." God is in complete control, and all of His people recognize it.

They called God "holy and true."

Habakkuk proclaims God is too holy to look upon sin, and cries to God to punish the wicked Jews (Habakkuk 1:13).

He is the true One. This is something said of Jesus as well, showing their equality.

Avenge our blood on those who dwell on the land.

They asked God to carry out His justice. This question shows us undoubtedly whose destruction Revelation is about. After all, who did Jesus say was guilty of the blood of ALL the righteous, ALL the prophets, and ALL the ones sent (Gr. apostles)? Matthew 23:34 says it was the Jews.

Who are "those who dwell on the earth"? As we've mentioned several times, "earth" is the same word as "land" (as in "The Promised Land") in the original Greek. Those who dwell there are the Jews.

Jesus (again, in Matthew 23) said the blood of these souls would be avenged when judgment came on Jerusalem!

And if we skip forward in Revelation a bit, we can see Jerusalem (called Babylon) was destroyed because they were guilty of the blood of *ALL the righteous, the prophets, and the apostles* (Revelation 18:20-19:2).

In answer to their question:

(1) They were given white robes.

They were victorious! They were overcomers! (Revelation 3:4).

(2) They were told to rest for a little season.

When Daniel asked about the end of the Jewish system, He was told, "Go your way, Daniel: for the words are closed up and sealed [like a sealed scroll, perhaps?] until the time of the end" (Daniel 12:9). Daniel was then told, "Go your way till the end comes: for you shall rest…" (12:13). Like Daniel, the saints under the altar were told, "Be patient, the time is not yet." See Matthew 24:6.

(3) They were told to wait until their brethren to be killed was fulfilled.

It wasn't time yet, there was still more to come. The death of one of God's people is a wonderful thing, because they then have achieved the victory! Psalm 116:15—"Precious in the sight of the LORD is the death of His saints." More saints would die before the end.

Exactly who are these souls?

Look at Matthew 23:35-36. The Old Testament saints who had been killed would be avenged when Jerusalem (and her inhabitants) were destroyed.

Look at Matthew 24. The first four seals matched up with Matthew 24:3-8. Now look at what is said in the next verse (24:9). Speaking to His apostles, Jesus said the Jews would deliver them (the apostles) up to be afflicted, and would kill them. It sure seems these are the "fellow-servants and brethren" who were still to be killed.

The fifth seal shows one of the reasons for the destruction of Jerusalem was to avenge the blood of God's servants, the prophets.

THE SIXTH SEAL (PART 1): EARTHQUAKE, DARKNESS, AND FEAR (6:12-17)

And I saw when he had opened the sixth seal, and, behold! there was a great earthquake; and the sun became black as sackcloth of hair, and the moon became as blood; and the stars of heaven fell to the earth, like a fig tree casting her untimely figs, when she is shaken by a mighty wind. And the heaven departed like a scroll when it is rolled together; and every mountain and island were moved out of their places.

And the kings of the earth, the great men, the rich men, the chief captains, the mighty men, every slave, and every free man, hid themselves in the caves and in the rocks of the mountains. They said to the mountains and rocks, "Fall on us, and hide us from the face of him that sits on the throne, and from the wrath of the Lamb. For the great day of his wrath is come;

and who shall be able to stand?"

The contents of the sixth seal actually continue through chapter seven, but we will leave that chapter for the next study.

When the sixth seal was opened, there was a great earthquake!
Given that the context is full of obviously symbolic language, we should not assume this is a literal earthquake (though a major earthquake happened in Asia Minor in AD 60-61). Instead, this is a violent shaking and tearing apart of the Jewish nation—a natural result of the war that is going on.

The "heavenly signs."
The symbols themselves:

- The sun became as black as sackcloth of hair.
- The moon became as blood. It did not become blood, but it became *like* blood.
- The stars of heaven fell to the earth. This is obviously not literal, because stars are much larger than the earth. If one star fell to earth, the earth would burn up and cease to exist.
- The heaven (sky) departed like a scroll when it is rolled together.
- The mountains and islands were moved out of their places.

What the symbols meant in the Old Testament:
In order to make sure we understand these symbols, let's look to the Old Testament. In foretelling the destruction of the real Babylon, Isaiah said:

> *For the stars of heaven and their constellations shall not give their light. The sun shall be darkened in its going forth, and the moon shall not cause her light to shine. And I will punish the world for their evil, and the wicked for their iniquity...Therefore I will shake the heavens, and the earth shall be moved out of its place, in the wrath of the LORD of hosts and in the*

day of His fierce anger (Isaiah 13:10-13).

This does not describe a literal removal of heavenly bodies, but a description of the end of *the Babylonians'* world.

In speaking of the destruction of Jerusalem, Isaiah said:

> *The earth is utterly broken down, the earth is clean [completely] dissolved, the earth is moved exceedingly. The earth shall reel to and fro like a drunk, and shall be moved like a cottage; and its transgression shall be heavy upon it. It shall fall and not rise again... Then the moon shall be confounded, and the sun ashamed, when the LORD of hosts shall reign in mount Zion, and in Jerusalem, and before his ancients gloriously (Isaiah 24:19-23).*

Here we have earthquakes, the moon confounded (not giving its light), and the sun ashamed (not giving its light). All describing judgment against Jerusalem. One other thing to point out: these things would show God is in charge over Jerusalem and Zion "before his ancients" (the same word as "elders" in Revelation 4-5).

In speaking of the destruction of Idumea (Edom), Isaiah says:

> *All the host of heaven shall be dissolved, and the heavens shall be rolled together as a scroll: and all their host shall fall down as the leaf falls from the vine, and as a falling fig from the fig tree. For my sword shall be bathed in heaven: behold, it shall come down upon Idumea and upon the people of my curse, to judgment (Isaiah 34:4-5).*

These figures are used to refer to judgment upon a nation by God.

In speaking of the overthrow of Egypt, Ezekiel said:

> *I will water the land with your blood... I will cover the heaven, and make its stars dark; I will cover the*

sun with a cloud, and the moon shall not give her light. All the bright lights of heaven I will make dark over you, and set darkness on your land, says the LORD... For thus says the Lord GOD, The sword of the king of Babylon shall come upon you (Ezekiel 32:6-11).

This is a description of a *physical, temporal* judgment upon a nation by God.

In speaking of the destruction of Jerusalem, Joel said:

The earth shall quake before them; the heavens shall tremble: the sun and moon shall be dark, and the stars shall withdraw their shining (Joel 2:10).

In speaking of the "last days" of the Jewish nation, Joel said:

I will show wonders in the heavens and in the earth: blood, and fire, and pillars of smoke. The sun shall be turned to darkness and the moon to blood before that great and terrible day of the LORD come. And it shall come to pass that whoever shall call on the name of the LORD shall be delivered: for in mount Zion and in Jerusalem shall be deliverance... (Joel 2:30-32)

Notice God is the one reigning in Zion and Jerusalem when this prophecy is fulfilled. This lets us know it is talking about the same thing as Isaiah 24 (which we read a moment ago). We also know WHEN this was fulfilled, because Peter said "this is that which was spoken of by the prophet Joel" (Acts 2:16).

What the symbols mean in Revelation
Each time they appear in the Old Testament, these symbols speak of the overthrow of a nation.

The sun to darkness

This is a symbol of sorrow, of intense anguish and mourning (hence the sackcloth). The sun had set on the Jewish nation as God's people—Their day was over. According to Joel and Peter, this would happen *before* the great and terrible day of the Lord.

The moon to blood.

God has set the moon for seasons (Psalm 104:19). When their moon turned to blood, it meant their season was finished.

The stars of heaven fell to the earth.

The stars are the leaders of the nation, for they are the ones who guide. Daniel 8:10 uses it this way. The Jewish leaders were overthrown, some were murdered by the warring factions within Jerusalem, according to Josephus (Wars, 6.5.3-4).

They fell like a fig tree casts her untimely figs in a mighty wind.

These were figs that grew in the winter, but never came to maturity. A strong wind would dislodge them easily. A mighty wind was coming upon the Jewish nation, and they would be defeated easily—because they were against God and Christ!

The heaven departed as a scroll rolled together.

Their story was finished, as far as being God's people was concerned. The book is closed on them.

Every mountain and island were moved out of their place.

Josephus mentions that some mountains, while easy for footmen to climb, were difficult for the Roman army and their horsemen to traverse. Because of this, they (in four days) leveled some of the small mountains and took the rocks and dirt to use in building mounds to take the walled cities. Mountains are seen as a symbol of strength, yet this strength was moved.

The islands were the furthest reaches of an empire, yet they would be affected as well. The strongholds of the Jewish nation (the cities in Judea) would be taken. The furthest reaches of the Jewish nation (the Jews throughout the Roman Empire) would be taken as well. No Jew was left unaffected by these events.

The fear and reaction of the inhabitants of the land
All the people:

- Kings of the earth (the rulers of the Jews)
- The great men and rich men (influential Jews)
- The chief captains and the mighty men (the Jewish army)
- Every bondman and every free man (slaves and non-slaves)

These all hid themselves in the dens and in the rocks of the mountains. They said to the rocks and mountains, "Fall on us, and hide us…" Josephus records that many of the people hid underground in caverns underneath Jerusalem (which was built on seven mountains) when the Roman armies came (Wars 3.7.36).

When discussing judgment on Jerusalem and Judah, Isaiah said they would "Enter into the rock, and hide [themselves] in the dust, for fear of the Lord" (Isaiah 2:10).

In describing the destruction of the northern tribes of Israel, they said "to the mountain, 'Cover us,' and to the hills, 'Fall on us'" (Hosea 10:8).

On His way to the cross, Jesus spoke to women who were wailing and weeping because of how He was being treated:

> *Daughters of Jerusalem, weep not for me, but weep for yourselves, and for your children. For behold the days are coming in which they shall say, 'Blessed are the barren, and the wombs that never bore, and the breasts which never nursed.' Then shall they begin to say to the mountains, 'Fall on us,' and to the hills, 'Cover us' (Luke 23:28-30).*

Jesus quotes the prophecy of Hosea and applies it ultimately to the destruction of Jerusalem. See also Matthew 24:19.

They were trying to hide from the face of the Father and the wrath of the Lamb. The Jews understood when they were punished, it was brought on by God. John the Baptizer told them about the "wrath to come" (Matthew 3:7, Luke 3:7). Jesus told them unless they repented, they would suffer physical destruction as well (Luke 13:1-5). The first gospel sermon included talk of the destruction of Jerusalem (Acts 2:20-21) and the need to call on the name of the Lord in order to be saved "from this wicked generation" (Acts 2:40).

The great day of His wrath is coming upon them, and no one would be able to stand before Him.

The idea is no one would be left standing who was opposed to Christ. The Roman army was guaranteed victory against the wicked Jewish nation!

WHAT DOES THIS MEANS FOR US TODAY?

Nations can be taken down, even when they claim to follow God.

When God decrees that a nation will fall, it will fall. No one can withstand God's judgment. You need to be on the Lord's side so you will not have to face the judgment unprepared to meet your God!

Some people (falsely) call the United States a "Christian nation." It never has been. Claiming to be a nation of Christians isn't going to keep God from overthrowing the U.S. if He determines to do it. And the more wicked this nation becomes… I'll let you finish that thought.

Dying in the Lord means being in His presence!

The events revealed by the opening of the Fifth Seal can teach us today as well. Those who die faithful to the Lord will be in His presence! God will see that justice is always served, though it might not be on our timeline. We must have patience, and we must be ready to die for the LORD.

These seals had not yet come to pass, but were about to. Jerusalem, Judea, the entire wicked Jewish nation was about to be wiped out. But what about the *Christians* who lived in Jerusalem? That's in chapter seven!

STUDY TWENTY:
SEALING THE 144,000
(REVELATION 7)

When you're going through difficult times, do you ever wonder, "Does God care?" If so, you're not alone.

Now imagine you're a Christian living in the first century, and you're told the Roman army is about to march through Asia Minor and Galilee to slaughter thousands upon thousands of Jews on their way to Jerusalem. Do you think, as a Christian perhaps living in one of those areas—or even worse, in Jerusalem—you might ask, "God, don't you care about us?"

Consider something similar in the Old Testament. God said He was going to destroy Sodom and Gomorrah. Abraham bargained with God, trying to avert the destruction, hoping at least ten faithful people were there. Turns out, there wasn't. But God is not heartless. He carried out the destruction, but He permitted the faithful to escape before the destruction.

The first four seals described the advance of the Roman army at Christ's command to wage bloody war against the Jews. The fifth seal showed us the *reason* for the destruction to come—the innocent blood of the prophets, apostles, and righteous ones was crying out for justice upon the ones who murdered them. The first part of the sixth seal showed the reaction of the people as the Roman armies came upon them—fear and trembling because they knew it was a judgment from God.

But what about the Christians? Do they deserve this punishment as well?

Remember some of them would undergo tribulation for a short time, and some would even die for their faith (Revelation 2:10). Also remember that for a Christian, death is not a punishment!

For me to live is Christ, and to die is gain (Philippians 1:21).

God knows those who are His (2 Timothy 2:19), and this becomes abundantly clear in Revelation 7.

THE FOUR ANGELS (7:1-3)

After these things I saw four angels standing on the four corners of the earth, holding the four winds of the earth, so the wind would not blow on the earth, nor on the sea, nor on any tree. And I saw another angel ascending from the east, having the seal of the living God. And he cried with a loud voice to the four angels who were permitted to hurt the earth and the sea, saying, "Do not hurt the earth, neither the sea, nor the trees, till we have sealed the servants of our God in their foreheads."

After seeing the people of Jerusalem hiding in the mountains for fear of the Lord, John saw four angels. These angels were standing on the four corners of the earth. Most likely, this is a reference to north, south, east, and west. And since (as we've pointed out several times) the word translated "earth" means "land," as in the Promised Land, these angels are on the four edges of Israel.

Holding back the four winds
These are the winds of destruction being held in place ("hindered," says Foy E. Wallace).

At that time it shall be said to this people and to Jerusalem, "A dry wind of the high places in the wilderness toward the daughter of my people, not to fan nor to cleanse. Even a full wind from those places shall come to me." now also will I declare the sentence against them (Jeremiah 4:11-12).

Behold a whirlwind of the LORD has gone forth in a fury, even a grievous whirlwind: it shall fall grievously upon the head of the wicked (Jeremiah 23:19).

And upon Elam I will bring the four winds from the four quarters of heaven, and will scatter them toward all those winds; and there shall be no nation where the outcasts won't come. For I will cause Elam to be dismayed before their enemies, and before them that seek their life: I will bring evil upon them, even my fierce anger, says the LORD; and I will send the sword after them, till I have consumed them (Jeremiah 49:36-37).

Thus says the LORD, Behold, I will raise up against Babylon, and against those that dwell among them that rise up against me, a destroying wind (Jeremiah 51:1).

The four angels keep the destruction at bay until they are given orders to release the winds of destruction upon Judea. These angels are given permission to bring destruction (verse 2), but told not to do it just yet (verse 3).

Another angel came from the east with the seal of the living God.
Something coming from the east oftentimes was a symbol it was from God.

- Eden was to the east (Genesis 2:8)
- The tabernacle and later the temple both faced east.
- The rising of the sun is from the east.

This new angel, having God's official seal, had the authority to command the other angels to wait. This seal imprints a mark on something (like a letter or a scroll), and was about to be used.

the servants of God sealed in their foreheads

The word "servants" is the same word used in Revelation 1:1. These are the then-living Christians.

They were to be sealed (by this angel, apparently) in their foreheads. This means their minds were given over to Christ; they knowingly accepted and followed His teachings (and would remember Jesus' command to get out of town when the armies surround the city—Luke 21, Matthew 24, Mark 13). "They have this seal—the Lord knows them that are His" (2 Timothy 2:19).

This part of the vision also finds it origin in the Old Testament. In describing destruction upon Jerusalem in 586 BC, God said,

> *"Go through the midst of the city, through the midst of Jerusalem, and set a mark on the foreheads of the men that sigh and cry for all the abominations that are done in its midst." And to the others, he said in my hearing, "You go after him through the city and smite. Don't let your eye spare anyone, nor have pity. Slay old and young utterly, both maids and little children, and women. But don't come near any man upon whom is the mark; and begin at my sanctuary [temple]." Then they began at the ancient men which were before the house [temple]. And he said to them, "Defile the house, and fill the courts with the slain: go forth." And they went forth and slew in the city (Ezekiel 9:4-7).*

Now, here's a question for you to ponder (you may have already thought of it): In the midst of this turmoil from the first six seals, did God suddenly decide, "Oh, I'd better make sure I get some kind of mark on them so I know which ones are mine and which ones aren't"?

I'll go ahead and answer that for you. *No*, this is symbolic, and shows that even in the midst of destruction, God knows which ones are His—they are *not* the objects of His wrath. This shows up later in the book as well. In chapter nine, the locusts are given permission to hurt those who *do not* have the seal of God on their foreheads (9:4).

Though some may be killed throughout the initial siege, God knew which were his, and—as we will see momentarily—He takes care of them as well.

THE 144,000 SEALED SERVANTS (7:4-8)

And I heard the number of them which were sealed: 144,000 of all the tribes of the children of Israel. Of the tribe of Judah, 12,000 were sealed. Of the tribe of Reuben 12,000 were sealed. Of the tribe of Gad, 12,000 were sealed. Of the tribe of Asher, 12,000 were sealed. Of the tribe of Naphtali, 12,000 were sealed. Of the tribe of Manasseh, 12,000 were sealed. Of the tribe of Simeon, 12,000 were sealed. Of the tribe of Levi, 12,000 were sealed. Of the tribe of Issachar, 12,000 were sealed. Of the tribe of Zebulon, 12,000 were sealed. Of the tribe of Joseph, 12,000 were sealed. Of the tribe of Benjamin, 12,000 were sealed.

John did not *see* the people being sealed, but instead, he wrote what he *heard*. 144,000 were sealed. 12,000 from each of twelve tribes. *But pay attention to the tribes,* because something is definitely different.

- Judah is mentioned first (the only time this happens in Scripture), probably because this is the tribe of Christ.
- Dan is not mentioned at all. The most common explanation is Dan went into idolatry very early on, and cut themselves off from being part of God's people.

- Levi, which had no land, is mentioned.
- Ephraim is not mentioned, but Joseph (Ephraim's father, who didn't have his own tribe) is. The adulterous northern ten tribes of Israel were frequently called Ephraim in the Old Testament. Perhaps that is the reason Joseph's name is inserted here instead.

Who are these 144,000?

First, we need to realize this is not a literal number (regardless of what some of my "Jehovah's Witness" family members claim). Here are some reasons we can know this:

- Most of the tribes had shrunk so much that they were mostly non-existent by the time of Christ. So getting 12,000 from each of them would be quite difficult.
- Some of the tribes (such as Judah) were much larger than the rest, and it would be VERY unlikely that each tribe (regardless of size) would have the exact same amount of people converted to Christ.
- The 144,000 show up again in chapter 14—and it is there we discover each one of them is (a) a male, and (b) a virgin. If, as Jehovah's Witnesses teach, this means only 144,000 people will be in heaven, then (a) no woman will make it, and (b) the apostles (except perhaps Paul) will not make it either—for they were all married (1 Corinthians 9:5).

So what does it mean and who are they?

The most common view is that these are the faithful of all ages.

- The faithful under the Old Testament (12 tribes)
- The faithful under the New Testament (12 apostles)
- Too many to count (1000)
- 12 x 12 x 1000 = 144,000.

I do have some reservations about this view. First, the faithful under the Old Testament were long dead by the time of this prophecy. Second, since destruction on the Promised Land is being held back until these faithful were sealed (we have to keep this all in context), I can't see how it included many—if any—Gentiles. Third, it lists tribes of Israel, and is quite clear those who were sealed were a *portion* of those tribes—a *remnant*.

- Joel 2:32 (part of the prophecy quoted by Peter on Pentecost) speaks of the remnant of the Jews that would be saved.
- Micah 7:18 (part of a prophecy about Christ and the church) speaks of forgiving the sins of the remnant of the Jews.
- Paul said, "Isaiah also cries concerning Israel, 'Though the number of the children of Israel be as the sand of the sea, a remnant shall be saved'" (Romans 9:27).
- Later, Paul said the remnant was already in existence (Romans 11:5).
- Only a small portion of the Jews would be saved.

Because of the context of the vision (the destruction of the Jewish nation, and Jerusalem in particular), and the not-so-subtle clues given (that they are from the tribes of Israel), we can be assured these are Jews who made the decision to follow Jesus Christ.

So, how does this make 144,000? Similar to the more common interpretation, but slightly different.

- 12—Those of the twelve tribes
- 12—who followed the teachings of Christ through His twelve apostles.
- 1,000—Too many to count.
- 12 x 12 x 1,000 = 144,000

Why these? Because they (physical Jews living in the Promised Land) are in the direct line of attack! But they have been sealed.

They stand with the Lamb (Christ), and have been marked as belonging to the Father (Revelation 14:1).

Now, look at Matthew 24:29-31.

> *Immediately after the tribulation of those days the sun shall be darkened, and the moon shall not give her light, and the stars shall fall from heaven, and the powers of the heavens shall be shaken. And then the sign of the Son of man in heaven shall appear: and then shall all the tribes of the earth mourn, and they shall see the Son of man coming in the clouds of heaven with power and great glory. And he shall send his angels with a great sound of a trumpet, and they shall gather together his elect from the four winds, from one end of heaven to the other.*

I hope you can see in Jesus' words the connections to what we're looking at in Revelation 7.

THE GREAT MULTITUDE BEFORE THE THRONE (7:9-17)

> *After this I looked, and, behold! a great multitude, which no one could count, from all nations, and tribes, and people, and languages, stood before the throne, and before the Lamb, clothed with white robes, and palms in their hands; and cried with a loud voice, saying, "Salvation to our God which sits on the throne, and unto the Lamb."*

> *And all the angels stood around the throne, and around the elders and the four creatures, and fell before the throne on their faces, and worshipped God, saying, "Amen: Blessing, and glory, and wisdom,*

and thanksgiving, and honor, and power, and might, to our God forever and ever. Amen."

And one of the elders answered, saying to me, "Who are these which are arrayed in white robes? And where did they come from?"

And I said to him, "Sir, you know."

And he said to me, "These are those who came out of great tribulation, and have washed their robes, and made them white in the blood of the Lamb. Therefore they are before the throne of God, and serve him day and night in his temple: and he that sits on the throne shall dwell among them."

A great multitude, which no one could count.

Remember *John didn't see or count the 144,000*, but *heard* the number. This great multitude could have easily been 144,000, but no human had the capability of counting them all.

Who is this great multitude?

Various views exist, depending on which book you read.

(1) The 144,000 were Jewish Christians, and the great multitude is Gentile Christians.

The Greek word translated "nations" is also translated "Gentiles" throughout the New Testament; context must determine which one is appropriate.

This was the view I was leaning towards at one point as I was writing this. However, if—as many assert—this is a scene of heaven, then where are the Jewish Christians (the 144,000)? Don't they get to go to heaven too? This great multitude was comprised of people who came out of the Great Tribulation, which Jesus said would come upon Jerusalem and Judea—hardly a place filled with an innumerable amount of Gentile Christians.

(2) This is a picture of all the saved of all ages.

This cannot be the case, because this group came out of the Great Tribulation. Not one Old Testament saint went through this Great Tribulation. Very few—if any—Gentile Christians went through this Great Tribulation. Not one of the New Testament saints from AD 70 onward went through that Great Tribulation.

Additionally, these are ones who washed their robes in the blood of the Lamb—something that *only* applies to New Testament saints. Thus, it completely eliminates anyone from the Old Testament.

So what does it *actually* mean?

(3) This group is the same group as portrayed by the 144,000.

It is right after the 144,000 are sealed that John sees this great multitude before the throne. It is not a coincidence, since they're the same group. No human counted this multitude—God gave the number via His angels.

So how is this the same group? Here's how: The 144,000 are explicitly said to be from the tribes of Israel. The "great multitude" were people who went through the "great tribulation," which is the events leading up to the destruction of Jerusalem—thus they were Jews. The "great multitude" also washed themselves in the blood of the Lamb—thus they were also Christians.

OBJECTION!!!

The main objection to this interpretation is this: *This great multitude was from all nations, all kindreds, and peoples, and tongues.* Therefore, they say, this is universal of all Christians. Let's deal with that.

- Acts 2 tells us **Jews** from every nation under heaven were gathered in Jerusalem. Well, that explains the "all nations" part.
- The word "kindreds" (KJV) means "tribes" (as in Matthew 24:30—the tribes of earth shall mourn). What biblical people were known for their tribes? You guessed it—the Jews.

- The word translated "peoples" ("people," KJV) is interesting. Most of the times it appears in the New Testament, it refers to people of God—or at least, those who were *supposed* to be people of God (usually Israel in the Gospels, and Christians in the Letters). The main Bible dictionary definition is a people group, nation, or tribe who come from the same stock. This can easily apply to the Jews, who all came from Abraham, but who also traced their lineage to specific great-grandsons of Abraham.
- The word "tongues" means languages (not garbly-gook, but actual, spoken and understood human languages). Acts 2 says the Jews were from every nation, and each nation had its own specific language (Acts 2:11).

This great multitude and the 144,000 are the same: Then-living, national Jews who had become Christians. Since they had been sealed, they would make it through the Great Tribulation which preceded the destruction of Jerusalem. They didn't die in the destruction.

They stood before the throne and before the Lamb
We can come boldly before the throne only when we are Christians (Hebrews 4:16). God's ears are open to the cries of Christians (1 Peter 3:12).

The last verse of Revelation 6 says, "the great day of His wrath is come; and who shall be able to stand?" Revelation7:9 answers the question: *faithful Christians will stand, for they are on HIS side!*

They were clothed in white robes.
This is a symbol of victory, of overcoming (Revelation 3:5). This is spelled out in Revelation 7:14.

They had palms in their hands and cried out "Salvation to our God who sits on the throne, and to the Lamb."
This reminds me of Jesus' triumphal entry into Jerusalem, when the people took palms and cried "Hosanna! Blessed is the King of

Israel that comes in the name of the Lord!" (John 12:13). Hosanna means "save us," or "salvation." In Revelation, they are praising because they *have been saved.*

In John's gospel, Jesus entered the city as the King of Promise. In Revelation, Jesus is the King in Power.

The angels join in the worship.

They fell on their faces and worshipped God. They said, "Amen!" to the praise given by the multitude. They declared, "Blessing and glory and wisdom and thanksgiving and honor and power and might be to our God forever and ever! AMEN!" This is the same praise given to the Lamb in chapter five, with the exception of the word "thanksgiving." Why would they leave out the word "thanksgiving"? Probably because the Scriptures teach that in everything, we are to give thanks *to the Father* (Ephesians 5:20).

This praise is directed at God. In Revelation, "God" is the name given to the Father, while "the Lamb" is the name given to the Son. This is seen in verses 14-15.

Who are these people?

John certainly wondered who this multitude was, when one of the elders came and asked him that very question. John's reply was, "Sir, you know."

The elder (thankfully) explains it to John, and John wrote it so we can know as well.

- They came out of the Great Tribulation (the time preceding the destruction of Jerusalem).
- They washed their robes and made them white in the blood of the Lamb. [Notice they had to *do* something to wash their robes in the blood of the Lamb. It took action on their part, for *they* did the washing. Faith-only salvation is refuted by this passage (among many others in the Bible, both Old and New Testaments).]

Because they washed their robes in the blood of the Lamb, they are before the throne of God, and serve him day and night in His temple.

This describes Christians. The context is speaking specifically of Jewish Christians, even though this description is true of all Christians.

- Christians can come boldly before the throne of God because Christ's blood has made it possible (Hebrews 4:16).
- Christians offer service to God continually (Romans 12:1, Hebrews 13:15).
- Christians are the temple of God—the church! (1 Corinthians 3:16-17).

The one who sits on the Throne (the Father) shall dwell among them.

I know some might think I've lost my mind by saying this describes then-living Jewish Christians. "See!" they might say, "this shows it is speaking of heaven, because God is dwelling with them!"

To that, I reply: Not so fast. Look at 2 Corinthians 6:16.

> *And what agreement has the temple of God with idols? For you are the temple of the living God; as God has said, I will dwell in them and walk in them, I will be their God and they shall be my people.*

Christians, *living* Christians, were called the temple of God, and Paul said God dwelt in them. While they were alive on earth. So, no. I haven't lost my mind.

This great multitude consisted of faithful, living, Jewish Christians who had endured the Great Tribulation.

WHAT BLESSINGS DO THEY RECEIVE? (7:16-17)

> *"They shall hunger no more, neither thirst anymore; nor shall the sun light on them, nor any heat. For the*

> *Lamb which is in the midst of the throne shall feed them, and shall lead them to living fountains of waters: and God shall wipe away all tears from their eyes."*

They shall hunger no more, neither thirst anymore.

This is spiritual hunger and thirsting. Jesus told the woman at the well He could provide water for people to never thirst again (John 4:10-14). But He was talking about *living* water, the gospel, salvation! And who can forget that great Beatitude: Blessed are those who hunger and thirst after righteousness, *for they shall be filled* (Matthew 5:6).

The sun will not light on them, nor any heat.

This doesn't mean they will live in darkness. The idea is of the sun and heat burning, overwhelming, and striking them. This is a reference from the Old Testament.

> *They shall not hunger nor thirst; neither shall the heat nor sun smite them: for He that has mercy on them shall lead them, even by the springs of water shall he guide them (Isaiah 49:10).*

Revelation says the Lamb will feed them and lead them to living fountains of waters.

God shall wipe away all tears from their eyes.

> *He will swallow up death in victory; and the Lord GOD will wipe away tears from off all faces... And it shall be said in that day, "Behold, this is our God; we have waited for Him, and He will save us: this is the LORD; we have waited for Him, we will be glad and rejoice in His salvation" (Isaiah 25:8-9).*

This sounds just like what they were doing here in Revelation: praising God for His salvation.

These Jewish Christians have lost their homes, many of their friends and family, their hometown, but they remained faithful to God—and God will comfort them through it all.

WHAT DOES THIS MEAN FOR US TODAY?

God still cares for and comforts His faithful children
If you're a Christian, there is no need to be sad, because God is with you. Christ leads you through His word.

God brings comfort to all those who are truly His. All of our spiritual needs are fulfilled in Jesus Christ (Ephesians 1:3).

This chapter shows us the important truth that God knows those people who are truly living for Him, and He hears them, and comforts them.

Oh the wonderful joys of being a Christian!

STUDY TWENTY-ONE:
THE TRUMPETS SOUND (PART 1)
(REVELATION 8)

When we last left the apostle John, his mind must have been reeling. He'd seen the glory of God, heard the praises of fantastic beasts and elders, been driven to tears, seen a dead Lamb alive, saw colored horses thundering by him, saw many dead souls screaming for God to exact vengeance, saw death and destruction, and saw and heard an innumerable amount of people praising God.

With all of this happening, our mind can get lost in the images, and we can get confused just reading about it.

But imagine you were there, seeing all of this. Noise, power, fantastic scenes, and a tense anxiety as you look to see the final seal of the scroll opened. What could possibly come next?

Then you stand there, dumbfounded and even more confused. Because when the seventh seal was opened, there was complete silence.

Before we get into the text, remember the scroll given to Jesus by the Father was sealed with seven seals—it was completely sealed. When the seven seals are opened, the contents of the scroll are completely revealed.

Beginning in this chapter, we are introduced to seven angels with seven trumpets. Trumpets are used to warn (we'll get to that in a little bit), and so the seven trumpets represent a complete warning. Later in the book, come seven bowls of wrath—God's complete judgment.

The imagery in this chapter comes primarily from the book of Exodus, though there is also imagery from the prophets as well. We will also reference historical accounts of Josephus which go along with the descriptions of the first four trumpets.

THE SEVENTH SEAL: SILENCE IN HEAVEN AND THE GIVING OF THE SEVEN TRUMPETS (8:1-2)

And when he had opened the seventh seal, there was silence in heaven for about half an hour. Then I saw the seven angels which stood before God; and they were given seven trumpets.

A half-hour of silence

One of the joys(?) of preparing lessons like these is reading through commentaries and seeing the many different interpretations to certain symbols—even among those who agree on the overall picture.

One person said we should make a day equal a year, therefore an hour would represent a 24th of a year (he said, "approximately two weeks"), and since this is a half-hour, it is approximately a week of silence. His conclusion: this is the time between Jesus' ascension and the Day of Pentecost.

Another person said it was the time between Pentecost and the beginning of the Roman-Jewish war (approximately 37 years).

More than a few people said it is nothing more than a literary device used to build suspense.

Do you think the Bible might have the answer?

Look at Joshua 6.

- In verse 4, seven priests would have seven trumpets.
- In verse 10, the people were told to keep silent.
- In verse 20, they marched around the city seven times, then they all shouted and the priests blew the trumpets.
- In verse 20, the city fell.

Is the half-hour of silence in Revelation meant to grab attention? Of course it is. But is that *all* it is? Nope.

Is the half-hour of silence in Revelation reminiscent of the silence before the Jews took Jericho? Of course it is. That silence was a calm before the storm, an eerie silence before God allowed Jericho to be destroyed. This half-hour of silence is a brief pause in the action before Jerusalem is fully attacked.

This half-hour of silence is when faithful Jewish Christians in Jerusalem were to escape (as they were told to do in Matthew 24:15-21; Luke 21:20-22).

Historically, there's some interesting information about this.

> [Cestius Gallus, Roman ruler of Syria] encamped, at length, at the distance of about one mile from Jerusalem, On the fourth day he entered its gate and burnt three divisions of the city, and might now, by its capture, have put a period to the war; but through the treacherous persuasions of his officers, instead of pursuing his advantages, he most unaccountably raised the siege, and fled from the city with the utmost precipitation. The Jews, however, pursued him as far as Antipatris, and, with little loss to themselves, slew of his army nearly six thousand men. After this disaster had befallen Cestius, the more opulent of the Jews (says Josephus) forsook Jerusalem as men do a sinking ship. And it is with reason supposed, that on this occasion many of the Christians, or converted Jews, who dwelt there, recollecting the warnings or their divine Master, retired to Pella, a place beyond Jordan, situated in a mountainous country, whither (according to Eusebius, who resided near the spot) they came from Jerusalem, and settled, before the war (under Vespasian) began.[1]

---

[1] Holford, George Peter, *The Destruction of Jerusalem: Illustrated Edition* (Charleston, AR: Cobb Publishing, 2021) p. 40.

This event (at least to me) makes the most sense in context. But there is also another possibility…

When Rome committed fully to the war against the Jews, Vespasian and his son Titus marched their armies to Jerusalem. But during this time, Nero committed suicide (to avoid the death penalty), and the father-and-son generals pulled back and retired to Caesarea, awaiting word from the new Emperor on how to proceed. Eventually, Vespasian himself returned to Rome and took the throne (AD 69 saw four Roman emperors), and ordered his son back to finish the job in Judea. During that lull between Vespasian's pulling back and Titus' return, the Jews claimed victory. They thought the Roman army had given up the war and retreated.

The half-hour silence could be a reference to this, the final calm before the storm. I personally think the previous option fits the context better.

THE PRAYERS OF THE SAINTS ANSWERED (8:3-6)

And another angel came and stood at the altar, having a golden censer. And he was given much incense, that he should offer it with the prayers of all saints upon the golden altar which was before the throne. And the smoke of the incense, which came with the prayers of the saints, ascended up before God out of the angel's hand. And the angel took the censer, and filled it with fire from the altar, and cast it to the land: and there were voices, and thunderings, and lightnings, and an earthquake.

And the seven angels which had the seven trumpets prepared themselves to sound.

To put this into perspective, look at the prayers of the saints from chapter six.

- 6:10—they cried with a loud voice, saying, "How long, O Lord, holy and true, do you not judge and avenge our blood on them that dwell on the land?"
- 6:11—They were told "rest a little while" or wait just a bit longer.

Their prayer was for God to execute His justice on those that killed them. Their blood was crying out for justice. This was the prayer of the saints.

An angel stood at the altar.

Which altar? This altar is called the "golden altar," the altar of incense in the tabernacle next to the veil of the Most Holy Place or Holy of Holies (Exodus 30:1-10). The blood of the annual Day of Atonement sacrifice would be put on this altar (verse 10). It wasn't kept continually burning, but instead a coal would be taken from the brazen altar (*the altar of sacrifice*) and brought there.

The *altar of sacrifice* is where the "souls under the altar" were. The cries of those dead saints were being brought and offered as a sweet-smell in the presence of God. In the vision, the golden altar was before the throne of God, and from it, the prayers of the saints ascended to God.

The result of the prayers.

I know I said it just a few paragraphs ago, but you have to keep this in mind—the prayers of the saints were for vengeance to be rained down from God on those who killed them, that is, on the Jewish people (Matthew 23:34-37). What you're about to study describes the answer to that prayer.

The angel took the censor (bowl or vessel), filled it with fire from the altar, and cast it to "earth." The "earth" is the Promised Land.

And there were voices (great noises), thundering, and lightnings, and an earthquake.

Now would be a really good time to look at Exodus 19:16-18. Why? Because this is the same description of what happened when God gave the Law on Mt. Sinai.

- Thunders and lightnings (verse 16)
- Voice as a trumpet (verse 16)
- The whole mountain quaked greatly (verse 18).

In Revelation 4, lightnings, thunder, and voices (great noises) came from God's throne (4:5). These are symbols of God's presence, and of His direct action. The prayers of the saints are about to be answered!

Josephus records this:

> [A] prodigious storm in the night, with the utmost violence, and very strong winds, with the largest showers of rain and continual lightnings, terrible thundering, and amazing concussions and bellowing of the earth, that was in an earthquake. These things were a manifest indication that some destruction was coming upon men, when the system of the world was put into this disorder; and any one would guess that these wonders foreshowed some grand calamities that were coming. (Wars 4.4.5)

The seven angels prepared to blow their trumpets.

Trumpets are given as a warning, oftentimes warning of possible destruction. A watchman was to blow the alarm if enemies approached. But also remember the trumpets blowing prior to Jericho's destruction—it was used to announce "It's time to attack!"

If you want to better understand these seven trumpets, just remember the following sentence: *These seven trumpets are given as warnings to the Jewish nation to get them to repent* (see Revelation 9:20-21).

TRUMPET #1—HAIL AND FIRE MINGLED WITH BLOOD (8:7)

The first angel sounded, and there followed hail and fire mingled with blood, and they were cast upon the land: and a third part of trees was burnt up, and all green grass was burnt up.

The first trumpet is a reminder of the plagues that came against Egypt.

Exodus 9:23-25 describes the seventh plague in this way:

And Moses stretched forth his rod toward heaven: and the LORD sent thunder and hail, and the fire ran along upon the ground; and the LORD rained hail upon the land of Egypt. So there was hail, and fire mingled with the hail, very grievous, such as there was none like it in all the land of Egypt since it became a nation. And throughout all the land of Egypt the hail struck all that was in the field, both man and beast; and the hail struck every herb of the field, and broke every tree of the field.

Now, before we go on, we must ask a question: Were the plagues supposed to be *only* for punishment? Or were they designed to get Pharaoh to repent?

These trumpets in Revelation describe punishments, but not *complete* punishments. God was still trying to get the people to repent.

Now, what does hail and fire mingled with blood mean?

Hailstones are a symbol judgment carried out by God (see Ezekiel 13:11-16). Hail and fire are destructive, and the fact that it was mingled with blood shows that people would die as a result.

The result: a third of the trees were burnt up and all the green grass too. It wasn't a complete destruction; you might consider this a "warning shot" from God.

Josephus, the leader of the Jewish armies in Galilee before turning traitor and becoming a Roman historian of the Jews, said, "Galilee was all over filled with fire and blood" (*Wars* 3.4.1).

Speaking of the same attacks, he also said:

> [Vespasian] gave his soldiers leave to set the suburbs on fire, and ordered that they should bring timber together, and raise banks against the city (*Wars* 5.6.2).

And again:

> All the trees that were about the city had been already cut down for the making of the banks (*Wars* 5.12.4).

And again:

> They cut down all the trees that were in the country that adjoined to the city, and that for ninety furlongs round about (*Wars* 6.1.1).

The first part of the attacks on the Promised Land focused on Galilee (roughly a third of the Promised Land), and it was left in flames and blood—and was now tree-less.

TRUMPET #2—A BURNING MOUNTAIN CAST INTO THE SEA (8:8-9)

And the second angel sounded, and something like a great mountain burning with fire was cast into the sea: and a third of the sea became blood. And a third of the creatures which had life in the sea, died; and a third of the ships were destroyed.

***In Exodus, when the Law of Moses was given, Mt. Sinai appeared
to be on fire (Exodus 19:18).***

The Jews saw Mt. Sinai as a symbol for the Law of Moses. A
mountain on fire would have brought Mt. Sinai immediately into
their mind. That which was the basis of the Jewish way of life was
being destroyed. The Law of Moses was "decaying and waxing old,
[and] is ready to vanish away" (Hebrews 8:13).

Also, throughout the Old Testament, kingdoms are frequently
described as "mountains." So "something like a great mountain"
(NASB) is a kingdom that seemed great (but looks can be deceiving)
being cast into the sea.

Another passage to consider is Jeremiah 51:24-25.

> *And I will render to Babylon and to all the inhabit-
> ants of Chaldea all their evil that they have done in
> Zion in your sight, says the LORD. Behold, I am
> against you, O destroying mountain, says the LORD,
> which destroys all the earth: and I will stretch out my
> hand upon you, and roll you down from the rocks,
> and will make thee a burnt mountain.*

Every one of these ways of looking at the burning mountain cast
into the sea comes back to the same idea: *God is judging the Jews
and violently removing their place as a nation.*

The "Sea"

The "sea," according to some commentators, is a reference to
Gentiles. If so, then this passage means the kingdom of the Jews
(Mt. Sinai) was going to be destroyed, and what was left would be
scattered among the Gentiles.

The fact that the mountain would be "cast" into the sea means
someone had to do the "casting." That someone is God, through the
Roman armies the Lamb let loose on the Jews.

The sea to blood

The result of God's rejection of the people who looked to Mt. Sinai was that a third of the sea became as blood, and a third of the ships and a third of the creatures [people—see Mark 16:15] in the sea would be destroyed.

In Exodus, the first of the ten plagues was turning the water to blood (Exodus 7:20-21). That was a warning from God. In Revelation, it is a warning to the Jewish nation.

Let's again look to the Jewish historian, Josephus, and see what he says about the Jews on the sea:

> [The Jews] built themselves a great many ships, and turned pirates upon the seas near to Syria and Phoenicia and Egypt, and made those seas unnavigable to all men (*Wars* 3.9.2).

But then this happened:

> Now as those people of Joppa were floating about in this sea [the Mediterranean], in the morning there fell a violent wind upon them; it is called by those that sail there "the black north wind," and dashed their ships against the rocks and carried many of them by force, while they strove against the opposite waves, into the main sea; for the shore was so rocky, and had so many of the enemy [Romans] upon it, that they were afraid to come to land; nay, the waves rose so very high that they drowned them; nor was there any place whether they could fly, nor any way to save themselves; while they were thrust out of the sea by the violence of the wind if they stayed where they were, and out of the city by the violence of the Romans. And much lamentation there was when the ships were dashed against one another, and a terrible noise when they were broken to pieces; and some of

the multitude that were in them were covered with waves, and so perished, and a great many were embarrassed with shipwrecks. But some of them thought to die by their own swords was lighter than by the sea, and so they killed themselves before they were drowned; although the greatest part of them were carried by the waves, and dashed to pieces against the abrupt parts of the rocks, insomuch that the sea was bloody a long way, and the maritime parts were full of dead bodies; for the Romans came upon those that were carried to shore and destroyed them." (*Wars* 3.9.2-3).

Meanwhile, at the Sea of Galilee:

One might see the lake all bloody, and full of dead bodies (*Wars* 3.10.9)

Meanwhile, at the Dead Sea:

Not only the whole of the country through which they had fled was filled with slaughter, and Jordan could not be passed over, by reason of the dead bodies that were in it, but because the lake Asphaltitis [the Dead Sea] was also full of dead bodies that were carried down into it by the river (*Wars* 4.7.6).

TRUMPET #3—THE STAR CALLED "WORMWOOD" UPON THE RIVERS (8:10-11)

And the third angel sounded, and a great star fell from heaven, burning like a lamp, and it fell on a third of the rivers, and on the fountains of waters. And the name of the star is called Wormwood: and a third of the waters became wormwood; and many men died from the waters, because they were made bitter.

After Moses led the Israelites across the Red Sea, they came upon a body of water that was bitter, and they were unable to drink from it (poisonous?) (Exodus 15:23-25). God told Moses to cast a certain tree into the water, and it became sweet.

What we see in Revelation is a reversal of that blessing: the sweet water is now made poisonous—God is withdrawing His blessing, providence, and protection from the Israelites. He had given them nearly 40 years to repent and turn to His Son, and they instead persecuted His children (Christians).

Deuteronomy 29:18 shows God equated those who broke His covenant with poisonous wormwood.

This act of judgment was because they had broken His covenant.
Jeremiah 28:15 says (NASB):

> *Therefore, thus says the LORD of hosts concerning the prophets, "Behold, I am going to feed them wormwood and make them drink poisonous water, for from the prophets of Jerusalem pollution has gone forth into all the land."*

Because the leaders turned the people away from God and Christ, they were to be punished.

A star falling from heaven, burning like a torch, and fell upon a third of the rivers and on the fountains of waters.
Stars symbolically describe those who gave direction in a nation (usually the leaders of that nation, or leaders of the armies, etc…). The king of Babylon, a leader of the nation and her armies who was being cast down, was called "star of the morning" (Isaiah 14:12-22, NASB).

One writer described this falling star this way: "When this star fell, it would affect the very fountain heads of the nation of Israel which, in reality, meant that it would reach Jerusalem."[2].

Is there such an instance where a specific leader of the Jews fell and caused death and bitterness? I can think of two during this time period. And the first one may really come as a surprise.

(1) Josephus

Josephus was the general of 60,000 troops in Galilee whose job was to stop the Roman armies from advancing south towards Jerusalem. Josephus quit and defected to the Romans, and most of his 60,000 men were slaughtered.

Initially, it was reported he was slain in battle, and there was a great mourning of thirty days for him in Jerusalem. But when it was discovered he had turned traitor, the people were bitter and became even more determined to fight the Romans—and to kill Josephus too. As a result, many more Jews went to fight, and many more Jews were killed. The waters and rivers around the Promised Land were turned poisonous from all the blood (like we saw a couple pages back).

The people are left without anyone to lead/guide them (remember stars are used for guidance). The military leader is gone.

(2) Matthias ben Theophilus

I said I knew of two. Here's the second one, which while you may have never heard of him, *could* fit the context as well (I think Josephus is more likely, though).

Matthias ben Theophilus[3] was High Priest at the beginning of the war.

> During the troubles in Jerusalem which preceded the siege by Titus he was deposed, since he, like the

---

[2] Ogden, *Avenging of the Apostles and Prophets*, p. 226

[3] While unlikely, some have suggested this may be the "Theophilus" who first received the books of *Luke* and *Acts*.

other aristocrats, belonged to the peace party, one of his sons having even sought refuge with the Romans. Matthias was put to death as a dangerous character by the very Simon ben Gioras whom he had invited to Jerusalem to subdue the revolutionists. According to Grätz, it is he who is referred to in a Talmudic story which relates that once, on a Day of Atonement, a high priest remained in the Holy of Holies a longer time than usual praying for the Sanctuary, which was in danger of destruction by the Zealots.[4]

He wanted the Jews to stop fighting so there could be peace. His murder may have silenced the last voice of sanity in the city, leaving the Jews with pretty much no spiritual leader.

TRUMPET #4—A THIRD OF THE SUN, MOON, AND STARS ARE SMITTEN (8:12)

And the fourth angel sounded, and a third of the sun was smitten, and a third of the moon, and a third of the stars; so as a third of them was darkened, and the day did not shine for a third of it, and the night likewise.

As we've seen before, when there is a prophecy of the sun not shining, or the moon not giving its light (or turning to blood), and stars falling, or something similar, it's a reference to God's judgment upon a nation, usually resulting in its complete overthrow (Joel 2:10-11, Isaiah 13:9-11, and others for example).

However, in this prophecy (the fourth trumpet), only a *third* of the sun, moon, and stars were affected. This means it is a *partial* judgment, but still a significant chunk.

---

[4] Jewish Encyclopedia, 1906 edition, "Matthias ben Theophilus."

In the vision, it wasn't as though the sun was just 1/3 less bright. Instead, John says there were 1/3 fewer hours of daylight, and the evening was pitch black for 1/3 of the evening (no light whatsoever).

A full third of Israel had their light put out.

In Exodus, one of the plagues was three days of darkness. This was a warning of worse judgments to come if Pharaoh didn't repent. In Revelation, this partial darkening shows the lights are going out on the Jewish nation, and it warns of worse judgments if Israel doesn't repent. It's no coincidence the Egyptian plagues are used as the inspiration for this section, since Jerusalem is called "Egypt" in Revelation 11:8.

By the end of Vespasian's Galilee campaign, a third of the nation of Israel was conquered, and most of the inhabitants had been slaughtered.

THE ANGEL ANNOUNCING THE LAST THREE WOES (8:13)

And I beheld, and heard an angel flying through the midst of heaven, saying with a loud voice, "Woe, woe, woe, to the inhabitants of the land because of the other sounds of the trumpet of the three angels, which are yet to sound!"

Angel or Eagle?

In many newer translations, this word is translated "eagle," because some Greek manuscripts have *angellos* (angel) and some *aetos* (eagle).

If it is an *angel*, it would make sense because angel means "messenger" and each part of the vision has been given by an angel or angels.

If it is an *eagle*, then it goes along with what Jesus said in Matthew 24—"Where the carcass is, there the eagles will gather." So perhaps this eagle is announcing Israel is about to be made a carcass (dead body of people). It is interesting that the emblem of the Roman Empire was an eagle.

WOE, WOE, WOE ...because of what is still coming!

This "woe" is magnified because it is said three times. Each of the final three trumpets is a "woe," an event which causes great mourning and destruction upon the inhabitants of the earth (land, Promised Land).

The first four trumpets affected 1/3 of the inhabitants of the Promised Land, and should have been enough to get the rest of the people to repent—but they didn't. Now the rest of them will be affected.

The break in the action between the first four trumpets and the final three could point to the time Vespasian paused the attack to wait for instructions from the new Emperor.

In the book of Joel, we have something similar to what takes place in this verse.

Joel wrote after a locust horde decimated the land of Israel, stripping it of all its vegetation. Joel's message was basically, "If you don't repent, it's going to be far worse," and then described an invading army as locusts which could not be stopped (Joel 2:1-11).

You might find it interesting that the next trumpet (starting with Revelation 9) describes the enemies as locusts.

WHAT DOES THIS MEAN FOR US TODAY?

What can we, today, 1900+ years removed from the events, learn from this chapter?

We have everything we need—and will be held accountable for it.

God has completely revealed His will (seven seals all removed = completed revelation) for us, including the promises of blessings for obedience and punishment for rejecting His will.

God has given us every warning necessary (seven trumpets = complete warning). Sometimes God allows bad things to happen to us in order to get us to repent! If things aren't going the way you think they should, and you're doubting the truth of "all things work together for good to them that love God," perhaps you should re-examine your life, attitudes, and actions and see if perhaps God is trying to get you to repent of something you've been doing.

God is longsuffering...but...

He gave the Jews warning after warning, and gave incremental judgments against them, hoping that they would repent. But God's patience has an end, and His justice will be fully enforced—and WOE upon the person who doesn't obey God!

STUDY TWENTY-TWO:
THE TRUMPETS SOUND (PART 2)
(REVELATION 9:1-12)

Last time, we heard the fateful announcement: Woe, woe, woe upon the inhabitants of the Promised Land because of what will happen when the last three angels blow their trumpets (8:13).

They had already begun suffering death and destruction, yet the message was clear: In the book of Joel, things had gotten bad, but it was about to get much worse—and the "much worse" was described as an invincible army of locusts who would overthrow the nation of Israel (Joel 2:1-11).

So it should come as no shock when, in Revelation 9, the "much worse" is described as an invincible army of locusts out of the bowels of hell.

Before you look at our text in Revelation, read Joel 2:1-11 and see how the armies which would overthrow Israel are described.

- Their coming is described as a "day of darkness" (v.. 2)
- "a great people and strong" (v.. 2)
- "The appearance of horses" (v.. 4)
- "as horsemen, so shall they run" (v.. 4)
- "All faces shall gather blackness" (sorrow, mourning, in woe) (v.. 6)
- They work as a unit (v.. 7)
- They bring destruction (vv. 10-11)

Keep those things in mind, because the imagery of the locusts in Revelation 9 primarily comes from Joel 2, and has similar meaning.

THE FALLEN STAR FROM HEAVEN GIVEN THE KEY OF THE BOTTOMLESS PIT (9:1)

And the fifth angel sounded, and I saw a star fallen from heaven to the earth: and to him was given the key of the bottomless pit.

The most common interpretation is this symbol is a description of Satan being a fallen angel.

Nope, not Satan. Why, you ask? Consider these reasons:

- This "star" actively participates in doing God's will, bringing about God's judgments. Is Satan *ever* an active participant in working *for* God?
- Revelation 20:1 shows the "angel of the bottomless pit" is an *angel of God*, doing God's will.
- Revelation 1:18 says *Jesus* has the keys of Hell (Hades) and death. Yet, the key of the bottomless pit (which is part of Hades) was given to this star. Would Jesus give up some of His power and authority to Satan???

No, there is no way this star from heaven is Satan.

This star was not in the process of falling, but had already come down to earth (the land, Promised Land).

The word translated "fallen" is past tense, something that had already happened when John looked. It can also mean "alighted" or "landed." It doesn't necessarily mean it was cast down, but could mean it was something done willingly.

Contextually, there are only two viable options:

- Either this is the same as the "angel of the bottomless pit," the angel of God who was in charge of the beings in that pit. Or,
- This is a description of a leader of Israel whose overthrow instituted the events contained in this trumpet blast.

Remember the "star from heaven" imagery was used just four verses earlier to refer to a human leader. If this is the case, then perhaps the most likely candidate is the high priest who was murdered by the seditious Jews. His death would have ended one of the last things keeping the people somewhat focused on God, allowing for what is described next.

The "Bottomless pit" is "the abyss," and it appears multiple times in Scripture.

If we want to know what this pit is, then we need to look and see how it is used elsewhere.

The demons who were later cast into swine begged Jesus not to send them into "the deep" (Greek, *abyss*) (Luke 8:31). It is a place demons knew about, and desperately did not want to go to.

It is where the dead are, for Paul asked "who shall descend into the deep [abyss], that is, to bring up Christ again from the dead?" (Romans 10:7).

Thus, the "bottomless pit" is the place of the dead, and in Revelation is specifically the place of the *wicked* dead. This knowledge will help greatly with understanding the rest of this section.

THE BOTTOMLESS PIT OPENED (9:2)

> *And he opened the bottomless pit; and there arose a smoke out of the pit, like the smoke of a great furnace; and the sun and the air were darkened because of the smoke of the pit.*

The result of opening the bottomless pit was thick, black smoke rising from it (like out of a furnace), darkening the sun and the air.

The sun being darkened is a symbol of judgment from God, though this one was a temporary judgment—a warning (as we will see in verse 5).

In Joel, the locust attack was called a day of darkness (Joel 2:2).

THE LOCUSTS ARE GIVEN POWER (9:3-6)

And out of the smoke came locusts on the earth: and power was given to them, like the scorpions of the land have power. And they were forbidden to hurt the grass of the earth, or any green thing, or any tree; but they could only touch those who do not have the seal of God in their foreheads. And they were not permitted to kill them, but they could be tormented five months: and their torment was as the torment of a scorpion, when it strikes a man. And in those days men shall seek death, and not find it; and shall desire to die, and death will flee from them.

Just like the first four trumpets, this imagery harkens back to the book of Exodus. The eighth plague in Exodus was locusts (three final plagues, three final woes).

The locusts came out of the smoke, and upon the Promised Land.

Locust attacks were well-known in Canaan. When they came from the desert, locust hordes looked like a solid wall of smoke. One such invasion was described as pure blackness from the ground to the highest clouds, over a mile wide, and four miles deep.

When locusts came, it didn't matter what things looked like before—it could have been the Garden of Eden (Joel 2). When the locusts went through, it looked like a fire had destroyed everything. They would eat all the bark off the trees, every leaf, every crop, every plant, every blade of grass.

They would eat fabric—even though they wouldn't eat parts of a human, they would very quickly leave him without any clothing if he did not find a way to completely seal himself in a room. But Joel said the locusts could climb walls and enter into windows. There was really no hiding from them.

The locusts described in Revelation are figurative, not literal.

These locusts were commanded not to eat any plants at all, but to afflict specific humans (verse 4). This alone shows that we are dealing with something other than literal locusts.

Who are they? We'll get to that momentarily.

They were given power like scorpions of the land have power.

The scorpions in the Middle East are greatly feared, though their sting is not deadly except to the very young and the very old. But the pain is intense and long-lasting: and at that time, nothing could be done for it. So, whoever these locusts are, they had the ability to cause pain, and they were greatly feared.

These locusts would not affect plant life, but only certain humans

This shows they had some intelligence to be able to distinguish between a "sealed" human and a human without the seal of God. These sealed servants of God are the 144,000 in chapter 7 (the Jewish Christians living in the Promised Land)—they would be unaffected.

They did not have the power to kill, but could inflict great torment

The non-Christian Jews in Canaan would be tormented by the locusts for "five months." The life of a locust is, generally speaking, five months. So, whatever these locusts are, they were given permission to torment the non-Christian Jews for a limited time, until God decided they had fulfilled their usefulness.

Something that may be of interest is this: the final Roman siege of Jerusalem (before they entered the city) was five months.

The torment would be so bad the people would seek death, but could not find it.

This, perhaps, is one of the biggest clues we have as to what is happening and who the locusts are. Stay with me. This gets interesting.

The non-Christian Jews would wish for death, but would be unable to accomplish it.

Plenty of people committed suicide in the Bible (Judas being just one of many examples), but these people would be *unable* to do that. These people would seek death, desire death, look for death, but could not find it. They wanted to die, but were incapable of fulfilling that wish.

WHO ARE THESE LOCUSTS?

Remember how they are described:

- Number one: they come from the realm of the dead.
- Number two: they are greatly feared by the people in the Promised Land.
- Number three: they only affect humans who were not following God.
- Number four: they torment the humans they come in contact with.
- Number five: they keep people in torment, and make them unable to kill themselves to end their affliction.
- Number six: they had intelligence and personality—they were individuals (Revelation 9:7).

Now, consider this:

- Demons come from the realm of the dead—and they begged not to go back (Luke 8:31).
- Demons (and those possessed by them) were greatly feared by the people.
- Demons only affected people who were not following God (Matthew 12:43-45).

  When the unclean spirit is gone out of a man, he walks through dry places, seeking rest, and finds none. Then he says, I will return to my house from whence I came out; and when he is come in, he finds *it empty, swept, and garnished. Then he goes, and takes with himself seven other spirits more wicked than himself, and they enter in and dwell there: and the last state of that man is worse than the first. <u>Even so shall it be also to this wicked generation</u>.*

- Demons kept people in torment, and made them unable to kill themselves. One man had a demon-possessed son who continually threw himself into the fire and water, but was unable to kill himself (Mark 9:17-27). The demon-possessed man in the area of the Gadarenes frequently cut himself with stones, trying to end the torment, but was unable to kill himself (Mark 5:1-5).
- Demons had intelligence (they believe, yet tremble—James 2:19) and personality—they were individuals. They had names and they had fears.

In Zechariah 13, God foretold the end of miracles (prophecy shall cease), and the context is the time between the death of Jesus and the destruction of Jerusalem. But in the same passage, the same verse (Zechariah 13:5), God says He will cause the evil spirits to pass from the land.

If you remember back to the second study, miracles (including prophecy) would cease when Jerusalem was destroyed, but they would continue until then.

By the same token, that means *demon-possession would cease when Jerusalem was destroyed, but it would continue until then.*

Would God really allow evil spirits to possess people?
He did already many times in the gospel accounts and in Acts. Some even interpret various Old Testament passages to refer to God sending evil spirits to work in the lives of people back then (like King Saul—1 Samuel 16:14).

These people were tormented by the demons within themselves, but also by others who were demon-possessed.

WHEN DID THIS TAKE PLACE?

After Galilee was taken, the civil wars in Judea and Jerusalem really broke out. Various seditious groups struggled for supremacy and rule. Josephus states:

> For the present sedition, one should not be mistaken if he called it a sedition begotten by another sedition, and to be like a wild beast grown mad... (*Wars* 5.1.1)

> And now, as the city was engaged in a war on all sides, from these treacherous crowds of wicked men, the people of the city between them were torn in pieces. The aged men and the women were in such distress by their internal calamities, that they wished for the Romans, and earnestly hoped for an external war, in order to deliver them from their domestic miseries. The citizens themselves were under a terrible consternation and fear... The noise also of those that were fighting was incessant, both by day and by night; but the lamentation of those that mourned exceeded the [noise of battle]; nor was there ever any occasion for them to leave off their lamentations, because their calamities came perpetually one upon another, although the deep consternation they were in prevented their outward wailing; but, being constrained by their fear to conceal their inward passions, they were inwardly tormented [same as in Revelation 9:5], without daring to open their lips in groans... Everyone despaired of himself... [The seditious] omitted no method of tormenting or barbarity. (*Wars* 5.1.5)

> But these men, and these only [the seditious], were incapable of repenting of the wickedness they had

been guilty of; and separating their souls from their bodies, they used them both as if they belonged to other folks and not to themselves. For no gentle affection could touch their souls, nor could any pain affect their bodies... (*Wars* 5.12.4).

The madness of the seditious did also increase together with their famine, and both those miseries were every day inflamed more and more; for there was no corn which anywhere appeared publicly, but the robbers came running into, and searched men's private houses; and then, if they found any, they tormented them, because they had denied that they had any. And if they found none, they tormented [same word as in Revelation 9:5] them worse, because they supposed they had more carefully concealed it. (*Wars* 5.10.2)

They also invented terrible methods of torment to discover where any food was...and this was done when these tormentors were not themselves hungry; for the thing had been less barbarous had necessity forced them into it. But this was done to keep their madness in exercise (*Wars* 5.10.3).

Those that were thus distressed by the famine were very desirous to die; and those already dead were esteemed happy, because they had not lived long enough either to hear or to see such miseries. (*Wars* 6.3.4).

THE LOCUSTS DESCRIBED (9:7-10)

And the shapes of the locusts were like horses prepared for battle; and on their heads were as it were crowns like gold, and their faces were as the faces of men, but they had hair like women, and their teeth were like lion's teeth. And they had breastplates like iron; and the sound of their wings was like the sound of chariots, of many horses running to battle. And they had tails like scorpions, and there were stings in their tails: and their power was to hurt men five months.

They are like horses prepared for battle

Just like in Joel. This isn't a mere invasion for them: they mean to inflict severe damage.

They had crowns of gold.

This is a victory crown. They would not be defeated by the Jews.

Their faces were like the faces of men.

This shows intelligence, but also personality. These locusts were individuals.

They had hair like a woman.

"During this time…John [a leader of a sect of seditious Jews]…permitted them [his group of seditious Jews] to do all things that any of them desired to do. While their inclination to plunder was insatiable, as was their zeal in searching the houses of the rich; and for the murdering of the men, and abusing the women, it was sport to them. They…indulged themselves in feminine wantonness, without any disturbance, till they were satiated wherewith, while they decked their hair, and put on women's garments, and were besmeared over with ointments; and that they might appear very comely, they had paints under their eyes, and imitated not only the ornaments, but also the lusts of women, and were guilty of such intolerable uncleanness, that they invented unlawful pleasures of that sort... While their faces looked like the faces of women, they killed with their right hand." (*Wars* 4.9.10)

Their teeth were like lions.
They were fearsome.

They had breastplates like iron.
This keeps them from being defeated in their battle.

Their wings were like the sounds of chariots going into battle.
You would be unable to hear anything but the sound of these locusts.

They had tails like scorpions which allowed them to torment men for five months.
It was a temporary torment for the Jews.

THE KING OVER THE LOCUSTS (9:11)

And they had a king over them, which is the angel of the bottomless pit, whose name in the Hebrew language is Abaddon, but in the Greek language his name is Apollyon.

The king over the locusts is called "the angel of the bottomless pit."
This is one place where folks don't bother taking the rest of the book into consideration, because it seems most point to this and say, "This is Satan."

In Revelation 20:1, the "angel with the key of the bottomless pit" *chains* Satan and casts him into the pit. There is only one "angel of the bottomless pit," and it ain't Satan. The angel here in 9:11 is an agent of God, working to fulfill God's judgment and warning on the Jews.

The name of _____[?] is Abaddon and Apollyon.

The Hebrew word, *Abaddon*, is found in the Old Testament, and refers to the lowest depths of Hades. It is the place of torment. It is the place of destruction. It is hell.

The Greek word *Apollyon* appears only here, but it means a destroyer or destruction. There are some who believe this name refers to the name of the bottomless pit instead of the name of their king. In Greek, the words translated "whose name" could also be translated "its name." This would make a lot of sense, since the bottomless pit is the realm of torment and destruction. I think this is probably the correct interpretation.

Others believe this to be the name of the king of the bottomless pit. In the Old Testament, the angel of the LORD was sent to destroy in Jerusalem, and he was destroying until God said to stop. He was an angel of destruction (1 Chronicles 21:12-15). Many Bible scholars are confident the Angel of the LORD is Jesus Christ in a pre-incarnate form. If this is the case, and *Abaddon* is a reference to the destroying Angel of the LORD, then the king over the realm of the dead and one who rules the demons is Jesus Christ.

- The demons acknowledged Him as all-powerful (Mark 5).
- The demons believe in Him and tremble (James 2).
- The demons obey His commands (Mark 5).

Explanation of the fifth trumpet

The fifth trumpet, the first of the three great woes against the Jews, was this: God would torment the non-Christian populace with mass demon-possession for a short period of time (but remember, when you are being tormented, five months seems like forever) in an effort to get them to repent.

In Joel, after describing the invincible locust army, God tells the people to "rend your hearts, and not your garments," and to repent (Joel 2:12-13).

The goal of this (and the other trumpet judgments) was to cause the Jews to cease their rebellion and come back to God.

WHAT DOES THIS MEAN FOR US TODAY?

Hell is real, and worse than you can imagine.

Imagine that you are trapped in a city, and tormented by seditious soldiers who seem to be controlled by something from hell…and there is no escape. Imagine that you are trapped in a body under the massive influence of demons, unable to fight them off, wanting so bad to end the pain, feeling so helpless and hopeless that you want to kill yourself, but death continually escapes your longing grasp.

Now, as bad as those scenarios are, things can still get worse—much worse.

Imagine a life in an eternal hell where the torment is far worse than anything these people experienced. There is no hope, no escape, and no end to the torment. At least for these Jews, there was an end to the torment.

Now, imagine that there is a way to avoid the endless torment—THERE IS! Just as with then, the people of Jesus Christ are protected from the torment of an eternal hell!

And just like then, Jesus Christ knows which are His people. Make sure you are one!

STUDY TWENTY-THREE:
THE TRUMPETS SOUND (PART 3)
(REVELATION 9:13-21)

The now-opened seven seals showed what was going to happen and why.

- The Roman army was sent by Christ, guaranteed a victory in a bloody and deadly battle against the Jews.
- The Jews had murdered God's saints—whose souls were now crying for vengeance.
- It was indeed the day of the Lord.
- But God knew which ones were His, and He would take care of those faithful ones during this war.

The seven trumpets give insight into what started once the soldiers reached the Promised Land.

The Roman army, led by then-general Vespasian, destroyed the cities of Galilee, killing most of the inhabitants as they went (1/3 of the Promised Land). Those Jews who had fled to the sea were destroyed. The celebrated leader of the Galilean army (Josephus) defected and left his army to die. A third of the nation had fallen.

In Jerusalem, civil war broke out as various seditious groups began fighting with each other for control of the city. These had become so wicked that they were perfect hosts for evil spirits (demons). This happened mostly during the time when Vespasian took his army of 60,000 soldiers back to Rome to claim the throne.

But now, the focus shifts to the returning armies of Rome, led by Vespasian's son, Titus. He has been sent with orders to destroy Jerusalem, if need be, to squash the Jewish revolt. Vespasian, after destroying Galilee, had offered the Jews an opportunity to repent and thus end any further attacks from Rome. After surrounding Jerusalem, the offer of peace (delivered by none other than Josephus) was repeated—they refused.

A VOICE FROM THE GOLDEN ALTAR (9:13-15)

And the sixth angel sounded, and I heard a voice from the four horns of the golden altar which is before God, saying to the sixth angel which had the trumpet, "Release the four angels which are bound in the great river Euphrates." And the four angels were released, which were prepared for an hour, and a day, and a month, and a year, to slay a third of men.

After the sixth trumpet blast, a voice was heard.

This voice came from the golden altar, the altar of incense. This is the altar where the prayers of the saints were offered up to God. As such, this reminds us:

- The saints under the altar cried for vengeance.
- The prayers of the saints had been offered and heard by God.
- The prayer is being answered.

This voice said, "Release the four angels which are bound in the great River Euphrates.

The Euphrates River was important in Jewish history.

- It was one of the four rivers that flowed in the garden of Eden (Genesis 2:10-14).
- It was the northeastern border of the land promised to them by God (Genesis 15:18, Deuteronomy 1:7, 11:24, Joshua 1:4).
- It was the northeastern border of the land controlled by King David (2 Samuel 8:3. 1 Chronicles 18:3).
- On the other side of the Euphrates River were the Assyrians and later the Babylonians, both of whom took part of the Israelites into captivity.
- To the Jews, the Euphrates should have been the border of their land—this could be another symbol of God's protection

being removed: the revoking of the land promise.

The Euphrates was also an important part of the Roman Empire. It was *their* easternmost border. On the other side was the Parthian army, Rome's most powerful challenger (who later successfully helped overthrow Rome). The Romans had four legions of soldiers stationed at the Euphrates to keep the Parthians from invading.

When Vespasian sent Titus back to take Jerusalem, he gave him orders to take the four legions (24,000) of soldiers protecting the Euphrates River with him. These four legions are mentioned by Josephus when Jerusalem was surrounded. Instead of an army of 60,000 well-trained Roman soldiers, Titus came back with an army of around 84,000.

These four angels (messengers—perhaps messengers of God's wrath?) are the four legions of soldiers. You might think that sounds crazy, but just keep reading the text and see if you think it fits.

The angels were released, and had been prepared.

God had prepared the four legions of soldiers for *this* hour, day, month, and year. The KJV has "*an* hour, *a* day, *a* month, and *a* year," but the Greek says "*the* hour and *the* day and month and year" (see ESV, NET, MLV, etc.). God had prepared them for a specific time and for a specific purpose. They had been prepared by God to kill a third of men in the Promised Land.

Some interesting numerical facts for your consideration: When Jerusalem was destroyed, 1,100,000 Jews were killed out of the 3,000,000 that were said to have been in the city—that's about a third, wouldn't you say?

But then something interesting happens…

The angels are released, given a job for which they were prepared, and then you never see these angels again. What you see next is a massive army coming *to fulfill the charge given to the angels*.

I told you just keep reading and you'd see it.

THE DESCRIPTION OF THE ARMY (9:16-19)

And the army of the horsemen were numbered 200,000,000: and I heard the number of them. And this is what I saw in the vision: the horses and those who sat on them, having breastplates of fire, and of jacinth, and brimstone: and the heads of the horses were like lions' heads; and out of their mouths came fire and smoke and brimstone. By these three things a third of men were killed: by the fire, the smoke, and the brimstone, which came out of their mouths. For their power is in their mouth, and in their tails. For their tails were like serpents, and had heads, and with them they caused injury.

The number was 200,000,000 (two hundred million).

Various interpretations are given to this number, which is obviously figurative, because Rome's army was nowhere near that number (though to the ones they defeated, it might have felt that way).

The estimated population of the earth at this time was 200,000,000 people, and if this is intended, it was as though the whole world was against the Jewish nation (which was somewhat true as most non-Jews didn't care for the Jews).

This describes the massive amount of the forces available at God's command. He had the Roman army, but that wasn't all. He also has a massive army of horses and chariots of fire (2 Kings 6:16-17). The chariots of God are twenty thousand,[1] and thousands upon thousands of angels (Psalm 68:17). You may wonder why I bring up the heavenly armies here. I wouldn't have done it, except for some non-Christian historians who brought it up close to 2,000 years ago.

---

[1] Other translations render it "many thousands," "number in the thousands." The Hebrew word only appears one time in Scripture.

Multiple historians record the following incident in Jerusalem during the siege. The Roman historian, Tacitus, says:

> In the sky appeared a vision of armies in conflict, of glittering armor (Histories 5.13).

Josephus:

> A certain prodigious and incredible phenomenon appeared; I suppose the account of it would seem to be a fable, were it not related by those who saw it, and were not the events that followed it of so considerable a nature as to deserve such signals; for, before sun setting, chariots and troops of soldiers in their armor were seen running about among the clouds, and surrounding of cities (Wars 6.5.3).

Josephus agreed that this seems far-fetched, but he recorded it because it was reported by many reliable witnesses, and it was viewed as a sign of the utter destruction of Jerusalem.

They had breastplates of fire, jacinth, and brimstone.

Many of the newer translations (and much of the commentaries) believe this is speaking of the colors of their breastplates: fiery red, deep blue, and sulphur yellow. It just so happens the Roman soldier's breastplates matched these colors.

The heads of the horses were like lions.

Lions were the most feared animals in that area of the world. The lion would tear apart with his teeth, so it shows the destructive ability of this army. God described Babylon as a lion when He sent them to conquer Israel (Jer. 4:6-7).

Out of the horses' mouths (the lions' mouths) came fire and smoke and brimstone.

Fire and brimstone were used as a symbol of the judgment of God. Sodom and Gomorrah were judged/destroyed with fire and brimstone (Genesis 19:24). Consider also what David wrote:

Upon the wicked, he shall rain snares, fire and brimstone, and a horrible tempest. This shall be the portion of their cup (Psalm 11:6)

This collection of descriptions aptly describes the Roman army coming on Jerusalem:

The army appeared to be unbeatable (and they were in this war, because God was with them). They also invoked psychological warfare against the Jews by "displaying their military order, weaponry, and horses before the walls of Jerusalem in order to terrify the Jews"[2]

Josephus describes the four Roman legions around Jerusalem in this way:

> So the soldiers, according to custom, opened the cases wherein their arms before lay covered, and marched with their breastplates on; as did the horsemen lead their horses in fine trappings. Then did the places that were before the city shine very splendidly for a great way; nor was there anything so grateful to Titus' own men, or so terrible to the enemy as that sight; for the whole old wall and the north side of the temple were full of spectators, and one might see the houses full of such as looked at them; nor was there any part of the city which was not covered over with the multitudes; nay, a very great consternation seized upon the hardiest of the Jews themselves, when they saw all the army in the same place, together with the fineness of their arms, and the good order of their men" (*Wars* 5.9.1).

The army was made up of many armored horsemen. They used catapults to launch fiery boulders and arrows into the city and into

---

[2] Gentry, Kenneth, *A Preterist View of Revelation*, pg 64

the walls before the soldiers approached the city. Like fire and brimstone coming from the enemy.

Josephus:

> At the same time, such catapults as were intended for that purpose, threw at once lances upon them with great noise, and stones of the weight of a talent were thrown by the engines that were prepared for that purpose, together with fire, and a vast multitude of arrows, which made the wall so dangerous that the Jews dared not to come upon it (*Wars* 3.7.9-10).

It was by this power that they killed the third part of men.

They had power in their heads (the front) and in their tails (the rear). The front part of the army would attack, but the back part of the army was also just as prepared for hurting the enemies.

This might refer to the second third of the Promised Land to be taken (the first third was Galilee, this third would be the people destroyed on the way to Jerusalem, covering the middle third of the land of Israel).

THE END RESULT (9:20-21)

> *And the rest of the men which were not killed by these plagues still did not repent of the works of their hands—they would not stop worshipping demons, and idols of gold, and silver, and brass, and stone, and of wood: which can neither see, nor hear, nor walk. Nor did they repent of their murders, nor of their sorceries, nor of their fornication, nor of their thefts.*

Even with this destruction foretold, and shown in signs in the sky for the people to see, they did not repent. They continued in their sinful activities, because they refused to repent.

They continued to worship their idols of gold, silver, brass, stone, and wood.

Some might say, "Did the Jews really still have idols? I thought they stopped having idols after they returned from Babylonian captivity about 600 years earlier."

The groups running the city sold food at heavily inflated prices (a day's wages would only feed one person for a day—your family was left to starve), showing they worshiped money (gold and silver). Brass, stone, and wood were materials used for building weapons and armor—they still worshiped their own military strength—it had become their idol as well.

They continued in sorceries, fornications, and thefts.

These things describe the seditious Jewish groups (Josephus alludes to these sins). Nothing was getting through to these hard-headed Jews.

WHAT DOES THIS MEAN FOR US TODAY?

Don't be a stubborn knucklehead...

You'd think that when God sends warning after warning, and sign after sign, that these stubborn knuckleheads would get a clue and realize they are fighting a losing battle—because God isn't going to lose.

But if we can see the absolute stupidity of their stubbornness, why is it we can't see it in ourselves?

The stubborn knucklehead is the person who sits in the pews, week after week, and refuses to obey God by becoming a Christian. I'm saying it right now: if you are at the age where you are accountable for your own actions and decisions, and you've not become a Christian, you are a stubborn knucklehead just like the Jews 2,000 years ago.

If they would have just stopped and realized, "Oh, I'm not on God's side here," they could have changed and not been destroyed.

If you are not a Christian, then you are not on God's side, and you will be destroyed, painfully, for all eternity.

The stubborn knucklehead is the Christian who knows he is sinning, but thinks that if he doesn't acknowledge it, God won't notice it.

Don't be a knucklehead.

STUDY TWENTY-FOUR:
THE BREAK BETWEEN THE TRUMPETS
(REVELATION 10)

Let's be honest. Revelation 10 is extremely frustrating if you're a naturally curious person, like me. I love researching, digging, figuring out things. So when John hears seven thunders talking, then grabs his quill and starts to write it down, and then is told by God, "Don't write it down," I get frustrated. I want to know what was said. But no matter how many times I flip through the pages of Revelation, searching for the answer, it simply isn't there.

I know I'm not the only person like this. I have some commentaries that spend *pages* guessing at what was said. Same thing goes for that time Jesus wrote in the dirt—there is no shortage of people who will gladly tell you what Jesus wrote, even though we are never told. (Don't get me wrong, I have some ideas of what He *might* have written, but I fully admit it is just supposition). Ultimately, we have to remember Deuteronomy 29:29: "The secret things belong to God."

But, just to whet your appetite, I will let you know that by the end of the study, you will know the message from the seven thunders, without any need for speculation.

In this lesson:

- We will see a mighty messenger, bearing an amazing resemblance to someone we know.
- We will see commands are to be followed exactly.
- We will see a connection between the gospel and the destruction of Jerusalem.
- We will see John happily eating a scroll and then feeling nauseous after the fact.
- We will see what the seven thunders really said.

THE MIGHTY MESSENGER (10:1-3)

And I saw another mighty angel come down from heaven, clothed with a cloud: and a rainbow was upon his head, and his face was like the sun, and his feet as pillars of fire. And he had in his hand a little scroll open: and he set his right foot on the sea, and his left foot on the land, and cried out with a loud voice, as when a lion roars. And when he had cried out, seven thunders uttered their voices.

The trumpets have been sounding, but then there's a pause. In fact, the seventh trumpet doesn't sound until the middle of chapter 11. But the context hasn't changed.

A Mighty Messenger appeared.

The word "angel" isn't a translation of the Greek, but simply a transliteration (meaning they just changed the Greek letters to English). *Angellos* means "messenger." I know we said this when we covered chapters 2 and 3, but it needs to be repeated. The word "angel" means "messenger."

This messenger is "mighty" showing power and strength.

But who is this Messenger?

(1) He came down from heaven.

So this Messenger came with a divine message.

(2) He was clothed with a cloud.

Jesus promised to come in the clouds to judge Israel. Clouds were symbolic of judgment (look back at Study Seven for Scriptural evidence on this point). So this Messenger had the power of judgment.

(3) He had a rainbow around his head.

The rainbow, a symbol of mercy, surrounds the throne of God (Revelation 4:2-3). The judgment brought by the mighty messenger would be tempered with God's mercy. God would spare those who were His. He would not destroy every Israelite (see Isaiah 1:9). So this Messenger with a divine message of judgment also had the power of divine mercy.

(4) His face was like the sun.

Malachi 4:2 speaks of Jesus Christ and calls Him the "Sun of Righteousness." In Revelation 1:16, Jesus has a face that shines as the sun shines in its strength. This shows the glory of the one bringing the message.

(5) His feet were as pillars of fire.

The Angel (Messenger) of Jehovah in the Old Testament led Israel as a pillar of fire by night (Exodus 13:21-22, 14:19-20)—That was Jesus Christ.[1] Jesus has feet like burnished brass as though they burned in a furnace (Revelation 1:15). This shows complete indestructability. He could trample the ones marked for the divine judgment.

(6) He held a little scroll open.

We will look at the scroll itself in a few minutes.

(7) His right foot was on the sea and his left was on the land (Promised Land).

The Messenger has power and influence over both Jews (those from the Promised Land) and Gentiles (the sea). Quick question: Who rules over both Jew and Gentile?

> *There is no difference between Jew and Greek; for the same Lord over all is rich to all who call upon Him (Romans 10:12).*

(8) He cried with a loud voice like a lion roaring.

God roars when He is about to judge a nation (Jeremiah 25:30). This puts the Mighty Messenger in the same category as God, so far as how they announce their message of judgment. *And one person*

---

[1] This connection of Jesus and the Angel of the LORD will be discussed more in-depth in Study Twenty-Nine.

has already been described as a lion in Revelation: Jesus Christ (Revelation 5:5).

(9) When He roared, seven thunders uttered their voices.

As we saw before, the sound of thunder is a symbol of approaching divine judgment. Sounds of thunder issued from God's throne (Revelation 4:5) and were associated with judgment from God upon Jerusalem (8:5). This judgment comes from the Mighty Messenger.

So who is this Mighty Messenger? This is Jesus Christ Himself, announcing judgment on the Jews (it is the coming of the Son of man).

THE SEVEN THUNDERS UTTERED THEIR VOICES (10:4)

> *And when the seven thunders had uttered their voices, I was about to write. But I heard a voice from heaven saying to me, "Seal up those things which the seven thunders uttered, and do not write them."*

What did the seven thunders say???

- First, remember this was uttered from the mouth of Christ Himself. So, this was a divine message.
- Second, remember this is (in context) dealing with the destruction of the Jewish nation and Judaism.
- Third, remember seven is used throughout the book of Revelation to represent completeness.
- Fourth, remember thunderings represent judgment.

The seven thunders, then, was the proclamation from Jesus Christ that Jerusalem's complete overthrow was now completely set in stone.

The fifth and sixth trumpets were designed to get them to repent, but they refused. Because of their refusal to repent, their judgment was no longer a probability, it was guaranteed.

We don't know the exact words spoken by Jesus. It could have been specifics about the destruction. But we do know the gist of the message: no more chances—the Jews are doomed.

Throughout the Old Testament, God's promises of destruction were always conditional. If the people repented, God would forgive and not follow through with the promised destruction. But there comes a time when God's patience ends.

The voice of the seven thunders was the announcement that God's patience had ended.

Why wasn't John allowed to write it down?

First, God said not to, which by itself is enough reason not to write it down.

Second, there wasn't a need to, because after the people refuse to repent at the earlier warnings, God's patience with them ended. These things were spoken in advance, prophesying what would happen and what the reactions would be from the Jewish people. God is saying, "I will send them warning after warning, and they will not heed them. And then my patience will end."

No more warnings.

This is seen a bit better when we look into the Mighty Messenger's oath.

The secret things belong to God.

While curiosity may desire to know the exact words, we must be content knowing God has given us everything we need to know (1 Peter 1:3). God doesn't need to explain everything or reveal everything to us (Deuteronomy 29:29). Even if God did explain everything to us, some of it would be so far beyond our comprehension, we wouldn't understand it anyway (Isaiah 55:8-9).

We must trust God to know what is best and what we need—and He decided we didn't need to know the exact words of the seven thunders.

THE MIGHTY MESSENGER'S OATH (10:5-7)

And the angel which I saw standing on the sea and upon the land lifted up his hand to heaven, and swore by him that lives forever and ever, the one who created heaven, and the things in them, the earth, and the things in it, and the sea, and the things in it. He swore "There will be no more time. But in the days of the sounding of the seventh angel, when he shall begin to sound [the trumpet], the mystery of God should be finished, as he has declared to his servants the prophets."

This messenger raised His hand to heaven.

This is symbolic of taking an oath, showing the truth of a statement.

He swore by the one who is eternal, who created heaven and all its inhabitants, the Land and all its inhabitants, and the sea and all its inhabitants.

The mighty messenger is swearing by God—the eternal Creator. There are two ways of interpreting the description, both of which are true"

- God is the Creator of the sky (heaven) and the birds, the dry ground (earth) and all the animals (including humans), and the bodies of water (sea) with the marine life.
- God is the Creator of heaven (His abode) and the angels, creator of the Jews (those in the Promised Land), and Creator of the Gentiles (represented by the sea).

The second one seems to better fit the context of the vision, since the Mighty Messenger is standing on the land and sea, and raising his hand towards heaven. But both are true statements, so I'm not going to argue if someone disagrees with me on this one.

But some might object, "Wait a minute, this proves the mighty angel can't be Jesus, because He is swearing by the one who created everything—and Jesus created everything" (John 1:1-3). Let's look at that for a moment, because I don't want you to just take my word for it. Is it possible that God could swear by Himself?

> *"By myself have I sworn," says the LORD, "because you have done this thing, and have not withheld your son, your only son" (Genesis 22:16).*

> *"Look to me, and be saved, all the ends of the earth: for I am God, and there is no one else. I have sworn by myself, the word is gone out of my mouth in right-eousness, and shall not return, so that to me every knee shall bow, every tongue shall swear" (Isaiah 45:22-23).*

> *"But if you will not hear these words, I swear by my-self," says the LORD, "that this house shall become a desolation" (Jeremiah 22:5).*

> *"For I have sworn by myself," says the LORD, "that Bozrah shall become a desolation, a reproach, a waste, and a curse; and all its cities shall be perpet-ual ruins" (Jeremiah 49:13).*

> *For when God made promise to Abraham, because he could swear by no greater, he swore by himself (Hebrews 6:13).*

Why should we assume Christ could not do the same thing, since He is God?

The oath itself: there shall be time no longer.

The time of delay in carrying out judgment was over. God had been longsuffering, not willing that any should perish, but that all should come to repentance (2 Peter 3:9). And now all that would repent from among the Jewish nation had done so. Their wickedness was a slap in the face to Jehovah, and He is ready to execute His promised vengeance.

Please realize, the mighty messenger isn't announcing the end of the world (when time shall be no more), but the end of the Jewish system. Their time is up.

When will this oath be fulfilled?

The message is clear: it would be fulfilled during the days of the sounding of the seventh trumpet. The seventh trumpet sounds in Revelation 11:15. When we get there, the trumpets (and Jerusalem) will be finished.

The mystery of God will be finished

When the seventh angel blows his trumpet, "the mystery of God will be finished, which was declared to His servants the prophets." What is this "mystery of God"? Well, here's a *massive* clue: God only ever referred to the Old Testament prophets as "My servants the prophets" (2 Kings 9:7, 17:13,23, 21:10, 24:2, Ezra 9:11, Jeremiah 7:25, 25:4, 26:5, 29:19, 35:15, 44:4, Ezekiel 38:17, Daniel 9:6, 10, Amos 3:7, Zechariah 1:6). *The final trumpet is the culmination of things the Old Testament prophets had foretold.*

Jesus fulfilled a lot of those prophecies while He was on the earth. In fact, he said everything written in the Old Testament <u>about Him</u> had been fulfilled (Luke 24:44).

But Jesus said <u>all things written</u> in the Old Testament would be fulfilled during the days of vengeance on Jerusalem (Luke 21, especially verses 20-22 and 32).

The mystery of God was once concealed, but now is fully revealed. The specific words of the seven thunders were not recorded, because there was to be no more delay after the events of the fifth and sixth trumpets.

THE LITTLE SCROLL (10:8-11)

And the voice I heard from heaven spoke to me again,

and said, "Go and take the little scroll which is open in the hand of the messenger who stands on the sea and on the earth."

And I went to the messenger, and said to him, "Give me the little scroll."

And he said to me, "Take it, and eat it up; and it shall make your stomach bitter, but it shall be sweet as honey in your mouth."

And I took the little scroll out of the messenger's hand, and ate it up; and it was in my mouth sweet as honey: and as soon as I had eaten it, my stomach was bitter.

And he said to me, "You must prophesy again before many peoples, and nations, and languages, and kings."

John is told to take the little scroll from the Mighty Messenger.

God the Father gave this command, and it was a specific one. He said to *take it* from the hand of the specific Messenger, the one standing on the sea and the Land.

John went and said, "*Give it* to me."

But the Mighty Messenger reiterated what God said, "*Take* the scroll…"

And then John *took* the scroll.

When God gives a specific command, He expects it to be carried out in the way He specifically commanded it. This applies in all areas that God has given instruction.

What was the little scroll?

In one form or another, it was a message from God. There are various interpretations:

- Some believe it was the entire New Testament teachings of Christ.

- Others believe it was the book of Revelation (or at least chapters 11-22).
- Still others say is the gospel of Jesus Christ. Jesus said when the gospel was spread to the whole world (the Roman Empire),[2] the end [of the Jewish system] would come (Matthew 24:14).

The symbolism is from Ezekiel 3, where that prophet eats a scroll, ingesting the message he had to deliver. What was Ezekiel's message? *The destruction of Jerusalem was imminent.* So it should be no surprise to find that when John is asked to do the same thing Ezekiel did, the message would be the same thing.

It was an open scroll, showing nothing in it was hidden.

This scroll didn't contain any "hidden" things. No seals had to be broken. No special interpretive lens had to be applied. It was open and obvious for anyone who was familiar with the Old Testament. God's rejection of the Jews was foretold plainly by Moses 1500 years earlier:

> *If you do not carefully observe all the words of this law that are written in this book, that you may fear this glorious and awesome name, the LORD your God, then the LORD will bring upon you and your descendants extraordinary plagues, great and prolonged plagues, and serious and prolonged sickness. Moreover, He will bring back on you all the diseases of Egypt, of which you were afraid, and they shall cling to you. Also, every sickness and every plague which is not written in this book of the law will the LORD bring on you until you are destroyed. Only a*

---

[2] Luke 2 says Caesar taxed "the whole world," which is universally understood to be the whole Roman Empire. Regardless, Colossians 1:23 says the gospel was preached to "the whole world" by the time Paul wrote.

few of you will be left, whereas before you were as
numerous as the stars of heaven, because you would
not obey the voice of the LORD your God. And it
shall be that just as the LORD rejoiced over you to
do good and multiply you, so the LORD will rejoice
over you to destroy you and bring you to nothing.
And you shall be plucked from off the land which you
go to possess. Then the LORD will scatter you among
all peoples, from one end of the earth to the other...
(Deuteronomy 28:58-64).

John had to eat the scroll.

This is what Ezekiel had to do (Ezekiel 3). That prophet had to internalize the unpleasant message (God is about to destroy Jerusalem) and make it part of him so he could spread it to the Jews in Babylonian captivity.

John took the scroll and ate it. In his mouth it was sweet, because it was the word of God.

How sweet are your words to my taste! Yes sweeter
than honey to my mouth! (Psalm 119:103).

But eating the scroll made him nauseous.

The message was one of hope to Christians, but one of horror to the Jews. John had friends and relatives who would die. John had countrymen who would be slaughtered. John's nation would be overthrown and destroyed. And John's mission was to tell them they were doomed.

Yes, it was a bittersweet message: God is just, and Israel was about to experience that justice.

John was told he had to spread the word to others.

Specifically, he was to proclaim it before many peoples, nations, tongues, and kings. John wouldn't remain on Patmos, he would continue to spread the message. Tradition says he went to Ephesus and survived being boiled in oil (perhaps because he angered the Jews with this message?).

WHAT DOES THIS MEAN FOR US TODAY?

We have a message to spread

We have a similar message to spread today. God will destroy all who do not repent and come to Him! Have you truly internalized this message? Do you really believe it? If you do, why do you keep it secret? Why don't you tell others so they can be saved?

Eventually our time will run out

God is longsuffering, not wanting anyone to perish, but that all should come to repentance. But there will be a time for you when the seven thunders will utter their voice and there will be no more time to repent—the end will come and you will be judged…if you don't repent!

When God gives a command, He demands strict obedience

John was told to *take* the scroll, but asked the messenger to *give* it to him. The messenger reiterated, *take* the scroll. God had given a clear, simple command, and anything less than specific obedience was not tolerated.

When God commands "repent and be baptized, every one of you for the remission of sins" (Acts 2:38), only a fool would say "baptism isn't necessary." When God commands "sing, and accompany the singing with the heart" (Ephesians 5:19), who is so presumptuous as to say we can also add an organ, or guitars, or drums?

Jesus is the author of eternal salvation to all those who *obey* Him (Hebrews 5:9). Are you *really* obeying Him?

STUDY TWENTY-FIVE:
MEASURING THE TEMPLE
(REVELATION 11:1-2)

You read the text, scratch your head and wonder, *What does this mean?* So you grab a commentary. Then another. Then another. And they all say the same thing: *This chapter is probably the most difficult to interpret.* And nearly all the commentaries disagree with each other on the interpretations.

The reasons for the disagreements, primarily, are (1) approaching the book with the wrong interpretive model (see Study One), and (2) assuming the wrong date of composition (see Study Two). After all, if you're talking about a "temple," and you think this is something *spiritual*, it can't be an actual temple. If you take a *futurist* position, you have to assume it is a temple that doesn't exist yet. If you believe it was about something the Christians cared about in the first century, but after AD 70, then you almost have to assume it is the church. But if you follow the biblical data like we've presented here in this book... well, just keep reading and you'll see.

If we keep in mind the context of the book, then the identification and application of this passage should become clear. We must start by looking again at our foundation: the word of God.

- John wrote these inspired visions sometime during the reign of Nero, a little over thirty years after Jesus' death.
- It was *at that time* John was told these visions related to things "which must shortly come to pass" and were "at hand" (Revelation 1:1, 3).
- When the seventh angel sounded his trumpet, the mystery of God—given by His servants the prophets—would be finished. Jesus said everything in the Old Testament would be fulfilled at the destruction of Jerusalem (Luke 21:20-22). The measuring of the temple is done *in this context.*

One final thing: Chapter 11 isn't some brand-new, unrelated thought. Chapters ten and eleven form one continuous vision. John had to eat a little opened scroll which had a mournful message he was deliver (prophesy) before many people. This has a direct bearing on the incidents in chapter eleven.

MEASURING THE TEMPLE (11:1-2)

And a reed like a rod was given to me: and the messenger stood, saying, "Rise, measure the temple of God, and the altar, and those who worship in it. But the court which is outside the temple, leave out, and do not measure it; for it is given to the Gentiles. They shall tread the holy city underfoot for 42 months.

Right after John was told he would have to prophesy again, he was given a reed like a rod.

A reed grows by/in rivers, and is uniform in the distance between the "knuckles" of it. As such, it makes a good measuring stick.

Since it was "like a rod," this measuring stick was authoritative (Jesus rules with a rod of iron—Psalm 2:9). The measuring stick, this uniform reed by which an authoritative measurement could be found, is the word of God. All people of all times are measured by the word of God.

He was told to measure the temple of God, the altar, and those who worship in it.

The temple complex was a sprawling collection of connected buildings. But the Greek word here refers to the temple itself—not the entire temple complex. It included the Holy Place and the Most Holy Place.

In chapters 40-42 of his prophecy (given after the temple in Jerusalem had been destroyed by Babylon), Ezekiel saw a vision of a man measuring a new temple. Ezekiel 43:13-27 describes the new altar being measured. Ezekiel 44-46 describes the worshipers (priests) in this new temple.

John was told (literally) to "cast out" the outer court, because it was given to the Gentiles.

Don't even bother measuring the outer court, John. It has been utterly rejected.

There was a section of the temple complex called "the court of the Gentiles," where non-Jews were permitted to walk. But they could not go past that point. God isn't interested in that part. But all the buildings constructed by Herod to beautify the temple mount were given by God for the Roman armies to destroy. Jesus foretold in Matthew 24:1-3—"not one stone [would be] left upon another."

The Gentiles would tread the holy city underfoot for 42 months.

The "holy city" was a title given to Jerusalem because it housed the temple of God.

Jesus Christ said "Jerusalem shall be trodden down by the Gentiles, until the times of the Gentiles is fulfilled" (Luke 21:24). Jesus included that detail as part of the destruction of Jerusalem (see verses 20-23). The Gentiles (Romans) would tread down Jerusalem until such time as their work was done. According to Revelation, this was 42 months.

According to Josephus, the Roman armies began their invasion of Judea in February/March, AD 67. Jerusalem was destroyed in late August of AD 70. Guess how many months the Roman armies (the Gentiles) were in Judea fighting this war… If you said, "forty-two!" you're right.

But they didn't spend all that time in Jerusalem, so how can that fit? The judgment on Jerusalem was a judgment on the entire nation, not just that city.

- Jerusalem represented the entire nation.
- Jerusalem represented their entire worship system.

- Jerusalem represented the Jewish way of life nationally, socially, economically, spiritually, religiously, and politically.

Calling for judgment upon Jerusalem involved the judgment upon the entire Jewish nation—beginning with Galilee.

So how do we know what temple this is, and what it means?

Notice this: it had to be a temple that existed when John was living. This is because he was told to measure the people that *are* (present tense) worshiping in it. When John wrote, there were two temples: the physical temple in Jerusalem and the spiritual temple of God—the church.

Keeping this in context, there are two views offered (there are many others, but none of them attempt to fit it into the true context of the book):

Option One: This is the church (the spiritual temple of God).

If this is the case, God is saying His faithful Christians from among the nation of Israel would be measured for protection when Jerusalem was destroyed. This would make it synonymous with the sealing of the 144,000. It would mean the church (as a whole), their worship, and the individual members would be saved from extinction in the destruction that was coming.

In this view, the outer court (still part of the temple complex) would represent the half-hearted worshipers who would be rejected ("judgment must begin at the house of God," 1 Peter 4:17). The Gentiles are non-Christians who would persecute the "holy city" (the church).

Those who take this position say that 42 months is an incomplete period of time (the same as 3½ years, and since 3½ is half of seven, or a "broken seven," it means incompleteness.

Here are some problems with this view that render it impossible.

- If the church is marked for preservation, how is it God immediately says they *will be* trodden underfoot by the non-

Christians (especially when that represented death and destruction)?

- It ignores that the church has been persecuted since its inception—prior to Revelation being written, and continuing even through today.

Some have tried to tweak this view, and say the temple describes the church, but that the outer court and holy city refer to literal, physical Jerusalem. That doesn't jive. You can't have part of the symbol be literal and the other part figurative when there is nothing to demand such an interpretation.

Option Two: The temple in Jerusalem

God has John measure the physical temple itself for destruction, as well as all who still attempted to worship under the Law of Moses.

As such, this is God's announcement of:

- The end of the temple (it has never been rebuilt).
- The end of worship under the Old Testament (the altar hasn't existed since AD 70), and
- The end of the priesthood under the Old Testament (no priest has existed since AD 70, and no one has any proof of being a Levite).

It is as though God is saying, "I am personally and permanently destroying the Jewish worship system to show them they have been rejected."

The outer court was something added later, and was really unimportant so far as Old Testament worship was concerned. As far as that goes, the entire city of Jerusalem was unimportant to God (so far as Old Testament worship was concerned) except that it was the home of the temple. The important part was the temple.

Everything connected with forgiveness of sins in the Old Testament (the temple, the altar, the priesthood) was permanently removed, making it physically impossible for *anyone* to worship according to the Law of Moses.

WHAT DOES THIS MEAN FOR US TODAY?

God only has ONE acceptable way to come to Him.

Anyone who wishes to approach God by means of the Old Testament rituals and commands will be rejected (this includes Seventh-Day Adventists, modern-day Jews, and others like them). Anyone who tries has "fallen from grace" (Galatians 5:4).

The only way to approach God today is through Jesus Christ and His blood (John 14:6). The Jews rejected Jesus, and Revelation should make it very clear: God takes it personally when people reject His Son.

Look at your life; have you been rejecting God's Son?

STUDY TWENTY-SIX:
THE TWO WITNESSES
(REVELATION 11:3-14)

Remember how I told you commentaries say this is the most difficult chapter to interpret in Revelation? Then remember all the different interpretations of just what the temple was? That's nothing compared to the debate of who the two witnesses are. Briefly, let me list some of the various candidates.

- Joshua and Zerubbabel
- Moses and Elijah
- Enoch and Elijah
- The church
- The Old and New Testaments
- Ananas and Jesus (two Jewish high priests)
- Peter and James (the brother of Christ)
- Two specific popes
- Martin Luther and John Huss
- Jesus and John the Baptist
- The apostles and prophets
- The Law and the Prophets
- Jewish Christians and Gentile Christians
- The Bible and the Book of Mormon

And this doesn't even scratch the surface.

With all these different interpretations and guesses, can we know who the two witnesses are, or at least narrow it down to a couple reasonable options?

Yes, we can.

Before we even look at the text, we can eliminate a few options from consideration just from what we know of the context.

- Martin Luther and John Huss (two reformers from the

1500's) have nothing whatsoever to do with the final rejection of the Jewish people.

- The same is the case with any two popes, regardless of the era in which they lived.
- The Book of Mormon is a fraud, and was never prophesied in the Bible.

It is safe to say any suggestions for the identity of the two witnesses that include men born after the destruction of Jerusalem are false. We will eliminate other candidates as we go through the text.

CHRIST'S TWO WITNESSES (11:3)

And I will give power to my two witnesses, and they shall prophesy a 1,260 days, clothed in sackcloth.

In the Old Testament, something was verified as true under the testimony of two or three witnesses (Deuteronomy 19:15).

The same principle is true in the New Testament (2 Corinthians 13:1). Jesus admitted if He was the only one testifying about Himself, His testimony shouldn't be accepted (John 5:31-32).

The fact there are two witnesses verifies the truthfulness of the message they are proclaiming.

So at this point, remember *two witnesses were enough to establish their message as being true*, according to the Law of Moses and the Law of Christ.

Literally, it says, "the two witnesses of me."

Because of this, many scholars believe Jesus is speaking of two specific people (or entities) well-known to first-century Christians, instantly identifiable by the phrase "my two witnesses."

These are witnesses (or those who give testimony) of Christ.

If these two witnesses are individuals, they have to be Christians. Though two Jewish high priests (Ananus and Jesus) did try to get the Jews to cease rebellion during the Roman-Jewish war, they were still religious Jews in opposition to Jesus Christ. There is no way these two men could be called witnesses (testifiers) of Jesus. Jesus would not classify any individual since His death as *His witness* unless that person was a Christian.

If this is speaking figuratively (of something other than individuals), it must be something that bore witness to Jesus Christ. One such example would be the Law and the Prophets (the two recognized divisions of the Old Testament during the time of Christ).

> *Search the Scriptures, for in them you think you have eternal life, and they are they that testify [bear witness] of me (John 5:39).*

> *For had you believed Moses, you would have believed me, for he wrote about me (John 5:46)*

> *Paul reasoned with the Jews, teaching them of Jesus Christ from the law and the prophets (Acts 28:23).*

Some believe it is some specific Old Testament characters who would be brought back from the dead and then later killed again.

It is very hard to imagine God would pull some people out of Paradise so they could come to this sin-filled earth again to be murdered. Luke 16:31 says if the Jews wouldn't be convinced by Moses and the prophets, they wouldn't be convinced even if someone arose from the dead.

This eliminates the literal return of some Old Testament characters from the dead prior to the final end of Judaism.

They would prophesy

They would spread God's word, foretelling the destruction to come. Individual Christians could have done this, but at the same time, the Old Testament (Law and the Prophets) as well as the New Testament foretold this destruction.

The time of their prophecy would be 1260 days.

This is the same as 42 months (which we discussed last lesson). This is the time from the Roman invasion of the Promised Land to the final destruction of the temple. The reason for describing it in different terms might be because testifying about Jesus is something done daily.

So whoever these two witnesses are, they were actively prophesying during the time preceding the destruction of Jerusalem. This eliminates the duo of Jesus and John the Baptizer from consideration, for John had been dead nearly 40 years.

Specific Christians, or the Law and Prophets, or Old Testament and New Testament could be said to prophesy during that time, though.

They were clothed in sackcloth.

This was a sign of mourning or repentance. Their message was one of sadness (the end of their nation), but also one that called for the people to repent. This is the same message the apostle John was called to preach (10:10-11).

Does this eliminate anyone? If it is referring to two specific, *literal* individuals, it eliminates everyone who did not live during the time of the Roman-Jewish war.

- Joshua and Zerubabbel are eliminated (though we will mention them more later).
- Enoch and Elijah are eliminated (though we will mention one of them later).
- Moses and Elijah are eliminated (though we will mention both later).
- Jesus and John the Baptist are eliminated.

Anyone who came afterwards is eliminated.

THEY ARE OLIVE TREES AND CANDLESTICKS (11:4)

These are the two olive trees, and the two candle-sticks standing before the God of the earth.

This imagery is from Zechariah 4.

Zechariah was shown ONE lampstand (candlestick—KJV) being continually fed fuel by two olive trees. This represented the word of the Lord (Zechariah 4:5-6) which said "not by might, nor by power, but by my Spirit." God said the two olive trees are two anointed ones that stand by the Lord (master) of the whole earth.

So, the Old Testament imagery describes the lampstand/candlestick as the word of God. The two olive trees are two anointed ones. A large number of scholars say this is a reference to being anointed by the Spirit of God—being able to perform miracles (as is shown in the next verses of Revelation).

His two witnesses had their power from the Holy Spirit.

If this is speaking of individuals, then must have been able to work miracles and were inspired by the Holy Spirit. As such, it eliminates anyone whose work began after the end of miracles (AD 70).

If it is speaking figuratively, then it eliminates anything that is not inspired by God's Spirit. The Jehovah's Witnesses say the two witnesses were their commentary on Revelation and their six-volume doctrinal set called "Searching the Scriptures." Obviously, neither one is inspired, and neither one is under consideration.

THEY HAVE POWER TO KILL THEIR ENEMIES (11:5)

And if any man hurts them, fire proceeds out of their mouth, and devours their enemies. And if any man hurts them, he must in this way be killed.

So much for Revelation being literal…

For those people who demand all of Revelation must be literal, these must be fire-breathing people of God who kill their enemies by breathing on them. Anyone want to argue that God gave two Christians (or any Christians) the right to kill their enemies?

What is the "fire"?

This description makes it very difficult to apply to the "two witnesses" to any literal individuals, unless the "fire" from their mouth is figurative, describing their message of destruction upon the Jews. Even if the Jews tried to kill the messenger, the message would still come true.

The Old Testament and the New both describe destruction upon the Jews because they had become enemies of God. Deuteronomy 32 foretells the complete rejection of the Jewish people. Jesus made this clear in Matthew 23-24, as well as in many of His parables.

- The parable of the wicked husbandmen described the Jews' destruction because they rejected and killed God's messengers and His Son (Luke 20:9-16).
- The parable of the wedding feast described those rejecting the messengers of the King having their city destroyed, burned with fire (Matthew 22:2-14, specifically verse 7).

So we are still left with a few possibilities as to who the two witnesses are: individual Christians with a message of destruction, the church, or some aspect of the Scriptures.

THEY ARE DESCRIBED AS MOSES AND ELIJAH (11:6)

> *These have power to shut heaven, that it doesn't rain during the days of their prophecy: and have power over waters to turn them to blood, and to smite the earth with all plagues, as often as they want.*

"Now wait," you might say, "that verse doesn't say either one of those names!" That's true, so let's look at what it *does* say.

They have power to shut heaven so that it doesn't rain during the days of their prophecy.

How long were they said to prophecy? 1260 days, which is the same as 42 months, which also happens to be the same as 3½ years. Now do yourself a favor and read James 5:17—how long did it not rain when Elijah prayed? Which person would immediately come to mind to the Jewish Christians who read this section?—Elijah.

They have power to turn water to blood and to smite the land with plagues.

What famous Old Testament character is credited with turning water to blood and bringing plagues?—Moses.

Moses and Elijah both ceased their earthly existence hundreds of years before Revelation was written. There was no prophecy in the Old Testament that Moses would literally return. However, there was a prophecy (fulfilled in Jesus Christ) that a prophet *like* Moses would appear. There was a prophecy that Elijah would come before the day of the LORD, which Jesus said was fulfilled in John the Baptist.

Moses and Elijah both appeared during the transfiguration, but both faded away, and God said, "This is my beloved Son, you listen to Him!" (Mark 9:2-8). Moses and Elijah fading away, leaving only Christ, was a symbol the Law and Prophets (the two divisions of the Old Testament) were at an end, and Christ is the one people should listen to now. This matches perfectly with Hebrews 1:1-2.

So this cannot be *literal* Moses and Elijah, for they are both gone on to their reward, and the prophecies concerning both have been fulfilled.

Could this be two people (or groups of people) who come in the spirit of Moses and Elijah? Some believe so.

Is it likely this is the Law and the Prophets (the prophecies of the Old Testament)? This is in keeping with the context, the usage of the symbols, and Jesus' own words about the Old Testament testifying about Him (see Luke 24:27, 44).

Is it possible that the Old and New Testaments are under consideration? It's somewhat difficult to see how the New Testament could be described as Moses or Elijah (but more on this possibility later).

TESTIMONY ENDED—THEN THEY'RE KILLED (11:7)

And when they have finished their testimony, the beast that ascends out of the bottomless pit shall make war against them, shall overcome them, and kill them.

This verse eliminates several popular suggestions for the two witnesses, because the two witnesses finish their testimony.

This means their time of testifying or bearing witness has reached its conclusion. They *no longer testify* after this. The most popular suggestion within the Lord's church is the two witnesses are the church personified. But let me ask you a few questions…

- Does the church have power/authority to kill their enemies?
- Does the church have power to work miracles today?
- Has the church ever finished testifying of Jesus?

And let's not ignore that the testimony must be finished *before* Jerusalem is destroyed in AD 70 (Jerusalem still exists when they finish their testimony—verse 8).

This *cannot* be the church.

Another popular suggestion is that these are the Old and New Testaments. But has the New Testament ceased testifying about Jesus?—Absolutely not! Then this suggestion cannot be right either.

They will be killed by the beast out of the bottomless pit.

The bottomless pit is where the demon hordes came from (Revelation 9:1-3). They affected only non-Christian Jews in the Promised Land (9:4).

Generally speaking, in prophetic writings, a beast represents a nation (see Daniel 7:1-8, 17; 8:3-8, 15-26).

This beast (nation) will make war with the two witnesses. It has been pointed out by many people that it is hard to conceive of a nation declaring war on two individuals. But this beast (nation) will overcome and kill the two witnesses.

Let's summarize this description:

The two witnesses (whoever or whatever they represent) will complete their testimony, then they will be killed by a nation—and this happens before Jerusalem is destroyed.

The only nation mentioned in connection with the bottomless pit is Israel, and they are indeed the enemies of God, Christ, and anyone or anything that bore testimony for Him.

THEIR DEAD BODIES IN JERUSALEM (11:8)

And their dead bodies shall lie in the street of the great city, which spiritually is called Sodom and Egypt, where also our Lord was crucified.

One body? Or two?

The ancient Coptic New Testament, as well as the earliest Greek manuscripts in existence say "body" (singular). The Latin Vulgate, and majority of Greek manuscripts say "bodies" (plural).

Some (including me) have made a point of these two witnesses having one body. If this reading is correct, it heavily implies the two witnesses are actually one singular entity. The Law and the Prophets (two recognized sections) are the Old Testament (one singular entity). The New Testament and Old Testament (two recognized sections) make up the inspired Scriptures (the Bible).

If the plural form is correct, it doesn't eliminate either of these from consideration, it just requires other evidence to prove it.

The body (or bodies) of the witnesses would lie in the street (literally, it is the main street of the city) and be treated with shame and contempt (they would not be buried).

The city in question is spiritually called Sodom.

Isaiah 1:1, 9-10 shows God called Jerusalem "Sodom" (and these aren't the only places where that was done).

The city in question is spiritually called Egypt.

Egypt is the nation that kept God's people in bondage (Exodus 1). Since this is *spiritually* speaking, what city tried to keep God's people in spiritual bondage?

Galatians 2 speaks of false brethren who tried to put Christians in bondage by forcing them to keep the Law of Moses. What group of people tried to keep Christians in bondage throughout the New Testament books?—The Jews. What was their city?—Jerusalem.

The city in question is where Jesus was crucified.

Jesus was *only ever* crucified in one city: Jerusalem. Some argue, "Oh, Jesus was put to death by Pilate, the Roman ruler in Palestine, therefore Rome is the city under consideration." That is an attempt to *change the text* to say "the city *by which* our Lord was crucified."

The New Testament is clear: the Jews were guilty of murdering Jesus Christ.

- Acts 2:36—(speaking to Jews at Pentecost) "that same Jesus, *whom ye have crucified…*"
- Acts 3:12-15—(speaking to Jews at the temple) "*you denied the holy one… and killed the Prince of life,* whom God has raised from the dead…"
- Acts 4:8-10—(speaking to elders of Israel) "…by the name of Jesus Christ of Nazareth, *whom ye crucified*, whom God raised from the dead…"
- Matthew 27:25—(The Jewish crowd taking responsibility) "His blood be upon us and our children!"

Jesus was literally killed in only one city: Jerusalem. Only one group of people was held accountable by God for the death of Jesus Christ: the Jews.

3½ DAYS OF REJOICING JEWS (11:9-10)

And they of the people and tribes and tongues and nations shall see their dead bodies three and a half days, and shall not permit their dead bodies to be put in graves. And those who dwell on the land shall rejoice over them, and make merry, and send gifts one to another; because these two prophets tormented those who dwelt on the land.

The "peoples, kindreds, tongues, and nations" is a reference to the entire Jewish population of the world.
This was discussed back in Study Twenty.

- "Peoples" means groups of people who come from the same stock (The Israelites all descended from Abraham, Isaac, and Jacob).
- "Kindreds" are tribes (as in the tribes of Israel).
- "Tongues" are legitimate languages (Acts 2:5-8).
- "Nations" (Jews were from every nation, Acts 2:5-8).

They are all gathered in Jerusalem (like in Acts 2) likely for one of the Jewish festivals.

They would not allow the bodies to be buried.
This shows utter disgust and irreverence toward the two witnesses. The Jews rejoiced over their death.

They rejoiced because these two witnesses tormented [troubled] those who lived in the Promised Land.
Elijah proclaimed God's word and called for the people to repent. As a result, he was called "he that troubles Israel" (1 Kings

18:17). God's word troubles or torments all those who refuse to obey it.

So, the two witnesses tormented the Jews with their message.

RAISED AND BROUGHT TO HEAVEN (11:11-12)

And after three and n half days, the Spirit of life from God entered into them, and they stood on their feet; and great fear fell on those who saw them. And they heard a great voice from heaven say to them, "Come up here." And they ascended up to heaven in a cloud; and their enemies watched them.

"We won!" cried the Jews.

The Jews were sure they finally defeated the two witnesses, that the message they had been proclaiming (destruction to the Jews) was eliminated. But just when they thought they won, God raised the witnesses and took them to heaven; and all the people began to fear greatly. Though God's messengers may be killed, His word endures forever.

A great voice from heaven said, "Come up here," and the witnesses arose.

There is no historical record (whether church historians or Jewish historians) mentioning a resurrection of anyone prior to the destruction of Jerusalem.

While it is true that absence of evidence does not necessarily prove anything, you would think if God had miraculously raised up some of His leading Christians, *someone* would have mentioned it *somewhere*. This points away from the two witnesses being actual physical individuals.

If this is the Law and the Prophets, then though the Jews thought they had overcome the promised destruction, their supposed victory was short-lived—God followed through with it. It is the resurrection of the message, the resurrection of the cause of God.

WHO ARE THE WITNESSES, AND HOW DOES IT ALL FIT TOGETHER?

The witnesses are not specific, literal individuals who prophesied during the time of the Roman invasion and destruction of the Promised Land.

There are some interesting people who fit *some* of the qualifications, but not all of them.

Jesus, son of the high priest

He went about for the full 3½ years proclaiming woe upon Jerusalem, woe from the four winds. His final words were "Woe, woe to the city again, and to the people, and to the holy house, and woe, woe to myself also" before being killed by a boulder hurled by a Roman catapult (*Wars* 6.5.3). He testified of calamity, but he performed no miracles, nor was he resurrected, nor did he have power to destroy his enemies.

Peter and James (the brother of Christ)

According to Eusebius, James was murdered in Jerusalem by the Jews during the Roman-Jewish war for continuing to bear witness to Jesus being the Christ. He was thrown from the temple and then beaten to death. But according to the same church historian, James was buried on the spot (making it hard for it to be said that his body remained unburied).

Nothing is truly known of how Peter died outside of Jesus' statement in John 21:18-19 that Peter would be murdered. The tradition of Peter being crucified upside-down in Rome is uninspired and false (and comes from the same document that said a walking, talking cross came out of the tomb of Jesus). It is far more likely that Peter remained in Jerusalem trying desperately to convert the Jews and was then killed by them.[1] Regardless of where Peter was killed, no historian mentions the possibility of either one being raised from the dead.

Peter and John

Uninspired tradition says John lived to be 100 and died a natural death, but Jesus said James and John would drink of the same cup He did (a cup of suffering), and would be baptized with the same baptism He endured (a baptism of suffering and death).

James was murdered, beheaded by Herod, ruler over the Jews. If we are to believe Jesus, John had to die a martyr's death as well. Papias (a second-century writer) is cited as saying John, the brother of James, was murdered by the Jews.[2]

But regardless, there is no record of either being raised from the dead.

THE TWO WITNESSES ARE THE LAW AND THE PROPHETS, THE TWO SECTIONS OF THE OLD TESTAMENT AS RECOGNIZED BY THE JEWS

They are two in number.

I can't think of anything else to say here. There are two.

They testified of Jesus Christ

They were His witnesses (John 5:39)

---

[1] We will discuss Peter being in Jerusalem near the end of his life in a later study.

[2] Some ancient sources say he was killed and buried in Ephesus. An ancient calendar to celebrate martyrs said "The first confessor at Jerusalem, Stephen the Apostle, the chief of the confessors. John and Jacob [i.e. James], the Apostles, at Jerusalem."

Their message during the Roman-Jewish war was one of mourning and calling for repentance

They were clothed in sackcloth because they prophesied the final rejection of the Jews (see Deuteronomy 28:58-64; Luke 21:20-22).

They were inspired by the Holy Spirit and gave light.

Speaking of the Old Testament, 2 Peter 1:21 says, "Holy men of God spoke as they were moved by the Holy Spirit." They gave light as the two candlesticks/lampstands. Remember that the imagery of the candlestick in Zechariah was explained as it being "the word of God."

They contained the punishments for those who broke them

Deuteronomy 32.

They were Moses (the Law) and Elijah (the prophets)

Moses was the lawgiver. Elijah was foremost among the prophets.

They completed their testimony

The Old Testament was fulfilled when Jerusalem was destroyed (Luke 21:20-22).

They were ridiculed by the Jews.

They obviously thought the prophecies of God didn't apply to them.

Obedience to the Law of Moses ceased when they stopped offering the daily sacrifice.

In effect, they put the practice of the Law to death. This occurred just a few days (3½ days, perhaps?) before the final invasion of the Roman army into Jerusalem. Within a week, the temple was on fire.

The Jews thought they had overcome the promises of their destruction as recorded in the Law and Prophets

They rejoiced at 'overcoming' the prophecies of their demise. Josephus records the Jews killed a large contingent of Roman soldiers, and thought they turned the tide in the battle, only to have the Romans regroup and regain the advantage (*Wars* 6.3.1-2, 6.4.1).

In one instance, the Jews set fire to the section of Jerusalem the soldiers were invading, killing most of the Romans there. In another, the Romans had built battering rams and ramps and ladders to scale the walls, but the Jews killed almost every solder and took possession of the battering rams, causing the Roman soldiers to retreat. They celebrated. Then the very next day the gates of the temple complex were set on fire.

The promises in the Law and the Prophets, though (to the Jews) defeated, were brought back to life.

And the Jewish nation looked on in fear as the Roman armies began the final march, fulfilling these promises of God.

THE RESULT OF THEIR RESURRECTION (11:13-14)

> *And the same hour there was a great earthquake, and a tenth of the city fell, and in the earthquake 7,000 were killed: and the remnant were frightened, and gave glory to the God of heaven. The second woe is past; and, behold, the third woe comes quickly.*

In the same hour, there was an earthquake, and a tenth part of the city fell.

The earthquake may be a reference to judgment (which wouldn't be uncommon in prophetic books), or it may refer to the rumbling of the city as the Roman armies invaded with their battering rams, catapults, and chariots.

The temple complex (the first part of the city attacked by Titus after this temporary setback) comprised approximately 1/10 of Jerusalem.

Seven thousand people were killed.

Josephus estimated that ten thousand people were killed in the beginning of this final invasion. His estimate was likely three thousand people too many (after all, it isn't like he went around and counted the bodies).

Afterwards, those who remained were afraid and gave glory to God.

But by now it was too late. They still rejected Christ, and the time of their punishment had come.

This was the second woe, and the final woe was to come quickly.

The final woe is the complete destruction of Jerusalem and the temple (which is the focus of 11:15-19).

WHAT DOES THIS MEAN FOR US TODAY?

You can't reject part of God's message and expect God to be pleased with you.

Though this section isn't speaking about the church, we can absolutely apply the principles contained in it to the church.

No group of Christians can reject part of the word of God and expect to be acceptable to God. The Jews held firm to part of the Old Testament, but outright fought against another part (prophecies of Jesus, prophecies of their destruction). But God's word held true.

No Christians can reject part of the gospel message (the importance of baptism, the way to salvation, the proper way of worship, the qualifications for elders, the importance of evangelism) and be judged as worthy by God.—It won't happen!

When it seems like a church is dead, it can still be brought back

There are congregations stagnating and dying a slow death that could be brought back to a vibrant life if the members refocus their lives on God and seek His help! There are areas where the church is persecuted, and members are ready to give up, but they can be brought back if they refocus and let God work through them to spread His word.

Why? Because God's word is still true, and His promises are there for the taking.

We can't ignore the not-so-pleasant parts...

We have the responsibility to spread God's word, *including* the promises of punishment and the need for repentance. It has become popular in some churches to only preach happy things and tell people Jesus will take them "just as they are" without any need for them to change or repent. That's not the message of our Savior!

Our Savior makes great promises of love, hope, and reward, but they only comes to those who obey Him! (Hebrews 5:9).

Study Twenty-Seven: The Seventh Trumpet Sounds (Revelation 11:15-19)

Well, here we are, at the precipice of the halfway mark in the book of Revelation. It's been a while since we saw the previous six trumpets, so it might help to do a quick recap of how we got where we are.

- This book was revealed by Jesus Christ about things which were "shortly come to pass" (1:1) and "at hand" (1:3).
- Jerusalem was still in existence when the book was written (11:8), placing the date of writing prior to its destruction in AD 70.
- Seven churches of Asia (real congregations, but also representative of all congregations) receive letters from Christ to tell them where they stood (and what to correct) before this great tribulation hit them (chapters 2-3).
- We saw a heavenly scene of worship to God, and worship to the sacrificed-yet-alive Lamb, as well as a mysterious scroll with seven seals (chapters 4-5):
- The Lamb opened the seals, and war (carried out by Jesus via the Roman army) sprung from the scroll. It foretold of destruction of Jesus' Jewish enemies and their capitol city, and the rescue of God's people from this judgment (chapters 6-7).

After the seven seals were opened, seven angels appear, each with a trumpet. With each blow of the trumpet comes judgment and warning. Well… except for the seventh trumpet.

The seventh trumpet is just judgment.

God gave clues already about the seventh trumpet.

Revelation 10:7—when the seventh trumpet sounds, the mystery of God is completed, as He declared to His servants the prophets (the Old Testament prophets). Remember, Jesus said everything written (that is, the Old Testament) would be fulfilled during the days of vengeance when Rome destroyed Jerusalem (Luke 21:20-22). So thanks to Jesus' own words, we know the seventh trumpet deals with the destruction of Jerusalem, the temple, and the Law of Moses.

Revelation 11:14—the second woe (the final march into Jerusalem just a few days after the Jews ceased the Old Testament sacrifices) was finished, and the third woe (the seventh trumpet) comes quickly. Less than a week transpired between the beginning of the final march and the temple being in flames.

THE GREAT VOICES IN HEAVEN (11:15)

And the seventh angel sounded; and there were loud voices in heaven, saying, "The kingdoms of this world have become the kingdoms of our Lord, and of his Christ; and he shall reign forever and ever."

Loud voices shouted.

Who these great voices are is not as important as *what* they said. Some believe the great voices come from the four living creatures. Others believe it is simply the combined multitude of voices in heaven.

Since the text doesn't say or imply who it was, God didn't think it was important—what *is* important is the message..

kingdoms of this world have become kingdoms of our Lord

Wait, aren't all kingdoms subject to God throughout history? How can any kingdoms suddenly *become* God's? The point here isn't that there was some kingdom God *didn't* rule until this time.

The point is God is has now exercised and proven His dominion over the kingdom[s] in question.

The same idea is found in Daniel 4, where Nebuchadnezzar learned "[God's] dominion is an everlasting dominion, and His kingdom is from generation to generation" (Daniel 4:34).

Most newer translations say, "the kingdom [singular] of this world..." Greek manuscripts don't agree on whether this is singular or plural. If it is plural (kingdoms), then it means at the destruction of Jerusalem (the specific event under consideration) the church (God's kingdom) shook off the shackles of Judaism and truly became a world-wide religion—and today is overwhelmingly comprised of Gentiles, people from nations all over the globe..

If it is singular (kingdom), then it means Jesus' words in Matthew 21:43 were fulfilled.

> *Therefore I say to you," The kingdom of God shall be taken from you and given to a nation bringing forth the fruit thereof."*

The Jews ceased being God's kingdom people starting at Pentecost. Though they still followed the Law of Moses, it was no longer effectual—especially considering they rejected, persecuted, and killed Christians. The destruction of Jerusalem was the visible proof God had taken the kingdom from them.

Who is the one who shall reign forever and ever?

Two are mentioned (the Lord God, and His Christ), but then it says "*He* shall reign forever and ever." Some believe this shows the unity of the Father and the Son ("I and my Father are one"—John 10:30).

Others believe this describes the reign of Jesus Christ. As such, this would be the "sign of the Son of man in heaven" mentioned in Matthew 24:30 (which is dealing with the destruction of Jerusalem). It was the visible proof (the sign) that Jesus (the Son of man) was reigning in heaven.

Others believe it is speaking of the Father, to whom Christ would deliver up the kingdom (1 Corinthians 15:24).

PRAISE FROM THE 24 ELDERS (11:16-18)

And the twenty-four elders, which sat before God on their seats, fell on their faces, and worshipped God, saying, "We give you thanks, O Lord God Almighty, who is, and was, and who is to come; because you have taken to yourself your great power, and have reigned. And the nations were angry, and your wrath has come, and the time of the dead, that they should be judged, and that you should give reward to your servants the prophets, and to the saints, and those who fear your name, small and great; and should destroy them which destroy the land."

As in chapter four, the twenty-four elders fell down to worship God. Remember, regardless of the authority or place of honor one might have here or in heaven, God still reigns supreme!

They gave thanks to God, the eternal One, for taking the power and reigning.

Some translations (because of a difference in Greek manuscripts) omit the words "who is to come," leaving the strange description of God as He "who is and who was." It has been suggested that "who is to come" is missing because in context, God just came in judgment.

He has taken His great power and reigned.

God has shown His power and dominion in destroying the Old Covenant both effectively (through Christ's death) and visibly (through the destruction of the temple and city of Jerusalem).

And the nations were angry…

This is similar to Psalm 2:1-3:

Why do the heathen [same word as "nations" in Revelation 11:18] *rage, and the people imagine a vain thing? The kings of the earth set themselves, and the rulers take counsel together, against the LORD, and against His anointed, saying, "Let us break their bands asunder, and cast away their cords from us."*

There are several possibilities for what "the nations were angry" means:

(1) The Jewish nation was angry and attempted to cast off God's rule (through Christ) over them. The apostles applied this word ("nations/heathen") to the Jews in their prayer of Acts 4:23-27 (quoting Psalm 2). Psalm 2:12 says, "Kiss the Son, lest He be angry, and you perish from the way when His wrath is kindled…"

(2) The "nations" refers to citizens of the Roman Empire. The people throughout the Roman Empire hated the Jews. The Jews were given special rights and privileges that other conquered nations didn't get, causing envy and anger towards them. Thus they turned their anger on them. Not convincing, in my opinion, but there you have it.

(3) The "nations" refers to the multi-national Roman Army (referred to as "the Gentiles" throughout Revelation). The Jews, if you remember, had just won some major battles. Even then, Titus tried to hold back the armies because he didn't want to destroy the temple. But when some of his own soldiers died because he didn't want to destroy a "foreign" temple, he removed his mercy and gave the army permission to do whatever they wanted. The Roman army attacked, *and they were mad.* This one makes the most sense to me, in context.

God's wrath had come.

Depending on which of the interpretations you take of the phrase "the nations were angry," this either means:

- The Jews were angry at God's rule over them, so He poured out His wrath on them.

- The Roman citizens were angry, so God poured out His wrath upon the Jews (this really makes no sense).
- The Roman army was angry, and God used them as the instrument of His wrath.

Regardless, the wrath came upon the Jews, and it came quickly.

THE JUDGING AND REWARDING OF THE DEAD?

This, perhaps, is the most difficult part of the passage to understand. It is the time for the dead to be judged, and the righteous to be rewarded—that sure sounds like the resurrection, doesn't it?

Those who take the "spiritual" or "idealistic" view (where the book represents principles, with no reference to specific events) say this is the end of time—the final judgment.

The problem is, the seventh trumpet was the fulfillment of the Old Testament prophecies (which Jesus said was when Jerusalem was destroyed). So it can't be a reference to the end of time and a final judgment.

At least one person has said, "How can it be the final judgment if there is still 11 chapters to go?!?" While I appreciate the heart behind this objection, I think it is not a good one. There is a history of biblical writers describing something, then later describing the same thing again with other details. For example:

- Genesis 1 describes the creation week, and at the end of that chapter, the creation week has ended. But Genesis 2 goes back and describes the creation week again, but with a different emphasis.
- The book of Daniel describes four world empires (Babylon, Persia, Greece, and Rome), but does it in at least three different ways (Daniel 2—the statue; Daniel 7—the four beasts; Daniel 8—the ram, he-goat, and little horn).

As we go through Revelation, we will cover some of the same material (from a time perspective), but the emphasis or focus is different.

First, who are the dead being judged?

It seems the "dead" here are the spiritually dead, the Jews who were being judged.

However, some believe the dead here are the souls under the altar, the Old Testament saints, being judged worthy.

Some believe when Jesus' reign became visible through the destruction of Jerusalem, those who were in the Hadean realm were judged—the wicked into everlasting destruction and the righteous to everlasting life in heaven. To back this up, they connect this with chapter 20 which speaks of death and Hades giving up their dead and being cast into the lake of fire. They also connect it with Revelation 14:13 which says, "blessed are they that die in the Lord *from now on...*"

How were the righteous rewarded?

Remember the souls under the altar were told to wait just a little while longer to be avenged—the little while has been completed! Their blood has been avenged. Their time of waiting has ended.

The righteous were rewarded when God "should destroy them that destroy the land." This is how the righteous were avenged. The word "destroy" here doesn't mean "completely obliterate." Instead, the Greek word carries the idea of something being corrupted (like "moth and rust corrupts"), or something being brought to ruin.

So God is bringing to ruin those who corrupted the Promised Land—the Jewish nation. This is important because God nowhere said He was going to kill off every Jew and make it where they had no descendants.

Something to notice:

The seventh trumpet blows, and we are given no details at all about the final destruction. Instead, we are given the view from heaven when this event takes place.

Many authors view the first section (chapters 1-11) as being the view (for the most part) from heaven's vantage point, and the rest of the book (for the most part) is the view from the Promised Land itself.

THE ARK IN HEAVEN (11:19)

> *And the temple of God was opened in heaven, and there was seen in his temple the ark of his testament: and there was lightning, and voices, and thundering, and an earthquake, and great hail.*

Then the temple of God was opened in heaven...

The temple of God in heaven has been a focus of Revelation since chapter one.

- Jesus was wearing the garb of the high priest, surrounded by seven golden candlesticks (1:12-13).
- The church at Philadelphia was told they would be a pillar in the temple of God (3:12).
- The throne room in heaven (chapters 4-5) contained the "sea," which was a basin for priestly cleaning in the earthly temple.
- The throne room in heaven contained the altar of incense, which was always placed at the entrance of the holy of holies.

The temple in heaven has been a spiritual reality from the beginning. With the earthly temple out of the way, the true temple (the one made without hands—Hebrews 9:11) can shine forth.

More importantly, look at what was in the temple in heaven: the ark of His covenant.

The ark was a symbol of the presence of God. The Israelites carried it when they crossed the Jordan River, and when they marched around Jericho (Joshua 1-6). When it sat in the holy of holies (the most holy place), the high priest was in the presence of God.

Therefore, the imagery shows God's presence is no longer (and never will be again) in a physical temple in Jerusalem.

Do you remember what was in the Ark of the Covenant?

- *Aaron's rod,* which budded to show he was chosen for the priesthood. That is taken away—no more Aaronic priesthood. There hasn't been an Old Testament priest since Jerusalem was destroyed.
- *A canister of manna*—showing God's care and providence for the Israelites. That is taken away—the Jews no longer enjoy any preferred status with God…and anyone who says otherwise is confused at best and heretical at worst.
- *The Ten Commandments* engraved on two tablets of stone (Deuteronomy 10:1-5). This was representative of the entire Law of Moses—and it is taken away as well.

Then there were lightnings, and voices (great sounds), thundering, an earthquake, and great hail.

From the view of heaven, *this* was the final judgment against the Jewish nation. Each of these things represent judgment of God upon a rebellious people.

WHAT DOES THIS MEAN FOR US TODAY?

The whole theme of this passage is God is in control!

- God reigns supreme!
- God has dominion over every nation and can act to overthrow that nation if it fits His purposes.

- God has, and will continue to, reward those who are faithful to Him and punish those who are wicked.
- There is no way to be in the presence of God except to be in His church—the true temple of God (1 Corinthians 3:16).

STUDY TWENTY-EIGHT:
A WOMAN, A DRAGON, AND A BABY
(REVELATION 12:1-6)

So far in Revelation, we've seen a description of the Roman-Jewish war, ending with the violent consummation of the Jewish age.

At the seventh seal, there was silence (leading some to suggest it shows the Jewish nation was no more).

At the seventh trumpet, there was rejoicing in heaven because the Jewish nation (enemies of Christ) had been overthrown and God showed His power and dominion.

Now, we go into another vision which describes the same events, but in a different way than you might expect. This vision goes from chapters 12 through 14, and has seven main signs or characters featured.

1. The woman clothed with the sun
2. The great red dragon (identified as Satan).
3. The man-child
4. The sea-beast
5. The land-beast
6. The Lamb on Mt. Zion
7. The Son of man in the cloud.

Chapter 12 views Satan's part in this war. Chapter 13 views Satan's tools or weapons in this war. Chapter 14 shows God's people being saved and the enemies being destroyed, and it ends again with the destruction of Jerusalem.

This part of Revelation shows the spiritual conflict going on behind the scenes.

THE WOMAN (12:1-2)

And a great wonder appeared in heaven; a woman clothed with the sun, and the moon under her feet, on her head a crown of twelve stars: And she, being pregnant, cried, travailing in birth, and pained to be delivered.

In order to identify this woman, look at the things said about her.

- Clothed with the sun.
- Standing on the moon.
- Wearing a victory crown of twelve stars.
- About to give birth.
- Gave birth to a man-child who was to rule all nations with a rod of iron and who ascended to his throne in heaven.
- Fled into the wilderness to be nourished for 1260 days.
- The rest of her children are those who keep the commandments of God and have the testimony of Jesus Christ (12:17).

The most common guesses are as follows:

(1) Mary, the mother of Jesus

This view is taken by the Roman Catholic Church (surprise, surprise). However, there is no evidence Mary was persecuted after the ascension of her Son, nor that she had to hide in the wilderness for 3½ years afterwards either. She was left in the care of John the apostle, and the book of Acts (and Galatians) clearly places John in Jerusalem for many years after the ascension of Christ. No hint anywhere of he and/or Mary having to run to the wilderness. Additionally, Mary was never called or considered the mother of the church (which would be necessary, based on verse 17).

(2) The nation of Israel.

This makes sense because Jesus was born of Israel. However, after His ascension, the Jews were the persecutors, not the ones being persecuted. Also, the 1260 days of nourishment is (most likely) the same period of time called "1260 days" earlier, and is in reference to the Roman-Jewish war. The Jews were not *protected* and *nourished* by God in the wilderness during that time—they were the *target* of God's wrath.

(3) The New Testament church.

This is the most popular explanation, but it also has problems associated with it. In no way, shape, or form can the church of the New Testament be the mother of Jesus. The church came from Christ, not the other way around.

(4) A covenant.

This imagery is used in Galatians 4:23-31. Hagar is the Jerusalem below (physical Jerusalem), and represents bondage. Sarah is the Jerusalem above (the promised kingdom of God), and represents freedom. Paul says we are children of the free woman. Jesus is the fulfillment of the promise made to Abraham and Sarah though Isaac. This is a possible interpretation, though personally it seems a bit of a stretch, because most of the imagery in this book comes from the Old Testament instead of the New.

(5) Constellations

One writer online (I know, you can find *anything* online) really went out on a limb and said the woman, sun, moon, and stars were all references to constellations in the sky. Using a star chart, he determined that Revelation 12 gave us the exact position of the stars when Jesus was born, and therefore the exact day when Jesus was born: September 11th, 3 BC. Of course, this gives no explanation of the woman fleeing into the wilderness, or any of the other things discussing Mary.

Before we get to who the woman REALLY represents, let's look at the Old Testament and see what kind of imagery is being used here.

The Old Testament Imagery.

Much of the imagery in this chapter originates with the Exodus account, but not all of it.

In Genesis 37:9-10, Joseph had a dream regarding his family. His family was represented by the sun and the moon (Jacob/Israel being the sun) and eleven stars, all of which bowed down to him. Because of this Old Testament imagery, we should assume the vision of the woman/sun/moon/stars in Revelation 12 in some way, shape, or form, involves Israel.

In Isaiah 66, God promises to create a new people faithful to Him, and says:

> *Before she travailed, she brought forth; before her pain came, she was delivered of a man child. Who has heard such a thing? Who has seen such things? Shall the earth be made to bring forth in one day? Or shall a nation be born at once? For as soon as Zion travailed, she brought forth her children (66:7-8).*

This man child (verse 7) was called a nation (verse 8), and that nation would consist of Jews and Gentiles (verse 12), and be nursed by the holy Jerusalem (verse 13).

Immediately after saying this, God says He will "come with fire, and with his chariots like a whirlwind, to render His anger with fury, and His rebuke with flames of fire…and the [ones] slain by the LORD shall be many" (verses 15-16). The "new heavens and new earth" would be created and ever before Him, and at that time all flesh would come to worship before Him (verses 22-23).

Hopefully you can see the theme of this chapter in Isaiah 66 matches perfectly with the events described in Revelation.

SO, WHO IS THE WOMAN?

The woman is the New Jerusalem.

Isaiah pictured the New, heavenly Jerusalem as the mother of the saints. The inhabitants of physical Jerusalem were called "children of Jerusalem" (Joel 3:6), so it should be no surprise that the inhabitants of the new Jerusalem (the church—Revelation 21:9-10) are called her children.

The woman is God's faithful Israel.

It would include such notable people as Zacharias and Elizabeth, Joseph and Mary, and others faithful to God under the Old Covenant. After the ascension of Christ, God's faithful Israel was the faithful church. Paul said it this way:

> *For he is not a Jew, which is one outwardly; neither whose circumcision is outward in the flesh: But he is a Jew, which is one inwardly; whose circumcision is that of the heart, in the spirit, and not in the letter; whose praise is not from men, but from God (Romans 2:28-29).*

The woman is the true Israel of God.

To put it plainly, the woman represents God's faithful people as a whole.

- It was from His faithful people that the Christ was brought forth.
- It was His faithful people whom He protected during the 1260 days of the Roman-Jewish war.
- God's faithful Israel was clothed in splendor.
- God's faithful Israel was victorious in God's sight (hence John uses the word *stephanos,* a *victory* crown).

At the beginning of the vision, the faithful Israel of God is in pain, about to deliver a child, but then...

THE GREAT RED DRAGON (12:3-4)

Another wonder appeared in heaven. Behold a great red dragon, having seven heads and ten horns, and seven crowns upon his heads. And his tail drew a third of the stars of heaven, and cast them to the earth: and the dragon stood before the woman who was ready to be delivered, to devour her child as soon as it was born.

The dragon is "that old serpent...the Devil, and Satan" (12:7).

Satan is the one who tempted Eve in the Garden of Eden. Soon after that event, God gave the first prophecy about Jesus Christ.

And the LORD God said to the serpent, "Because you have done this, you are cursed above all cattle, and above every beast of the field; on your belly you will go, and dust you will eat, all the days of your life: And I will put enmity between you and the woman, and between your seed and her seed; it shall bruise your head, and you shall bruise his heel (Genesis 3:14-15).

Now fast-forward several thousand years to the impending birth of Jesus. Satan isn't stupid. He remembers the prophecy. Now he sees the fulfillment is imminent, and he's poised to stop it.

This dragon had 7 heads, 10 horns, and 7 crowns on his heads (12:3).

Seven represents completeness. So Satan had complete authority (seven heads and seven crowns). The crowns are not victory crowns (*stephanos*), but crowns of a ruler (*diadem*). Paul called Satan "the god of this world" (2 Corinthians 4:4) and the "prince of the power of the air" (Ephesians 2:2). Jesus called him "the ruler of this world" (John 12:31).

Ten represents fullness. So he had full destructive power. Later on, you will see a beast with the same attributes, given to it by Satan.

His tail drew a third of the stars of heaven and cast them to the earth.

We *MUST, MUST, MUST* keep this in context.

Some use this verse as "evidence" to prove Satan is a fallen archangel that took a third of the angels of heaven with him when he rebelled against God. Sounds good, as long as you ignore the context and the rest of the Bible.

(1) Satan was never EVER an archangel.

The word "archangels" (plural) is never found in the Bible. It is *always* in the singular. That means there is only one archangel. His name is Michael (mentioned later in Revelation 12).

(2) The Bible never says Satan was ever an angel.

Paul said Satan tries to make it appear as though he is an angel of light (2 Corinthians 11:14-15), but never says Satan ever *was* an angel. Passages used to claim Satan was once an angel (from Ezekiel and Isaiah) are descriptions of the kings of Tyre and Babylon—*not* Satan. And if you doubt me, look for yourself. The prophets tell us exactly who they are talking about (Isaiah 14:4-22; Ezekiel 28:12-19).

(3) The context of Revelation is the first century—*not* something thousands of years earlier.

So, even assuming the "Satan is a fallen angel" theory to be true, *this verse has ZERO to say about it.* The events in Revelation 12 take place in the first century, and Satan was already evil *at least* 4,000 years before these events took place.

It is extremely important that we not latch on to verses that *sound* close to something we already believe, without checking to see if those verses *actually teach it.*

What then is the "third of the stars of heaven"?

Stars symbolize rulers or leaders, and many leaders in the world have met their downfall because of Satan's influence (look at Ahab and Jezebel, for example).

This may simply be an example of Satan flexing his muscles and showing his strength, influence, and power over the rulers of the world.

He stood ready to devour the woman's child as soon as it was born.

Satan used King Herod (a ruler) to try to kill Jesus soon after He was born (Matthew 2). Of course, when that failed, Satan didn't just give up. In an attempt to keep God's prophecy from coming true, Satan tried to destroy Jesus in the wilderness by tempting Him (Matthew 4). He tried over and over to frustrate Jesus' work throughout His ministry. Satan thought he gained the ultimate victory in destroying Jesus at the cross, but instead brought about his own defeat.

The plans of Satan to destroy Jesus were foiled by what took place in Revelation 12:5.

THE BIRTH OF THE MAN-CHILD (12:5)

She gave birth to a man child, who was to rule all nations with a rod of iron: and her child was caught up to God, and to his throne.

This child "was to rule [shepherd] all nations with a rod of iron" and "was caught up to God, and to His throne."

Some argue this represents Christians as a whole. After all, the church in Thyatira was promised "power over the nations, and he shall rule them with a rod of iron" (Revelation 3:26-27). The church in Laodicea was told if they overcame, they would "sit with Me in my throne" (3:21). The glaring problem with this interpretation is that later on, another group appears, called "the rest of her seed [offspring]." If the man child represents all Christians, who are these other people?

The obvious identification of this man child is Jesus Christ.

He is the firstborn among many brethren (Romans 8:29). He is the fulfillment of the prophecy of Psalm 2:9 which says He will rule the nations with a rod of iron. He has ascended to His throne (Acts 2:30, 36).

Is this speaking of His literal birth?

Most think so (and I tend to agree), but it could also be speaking of the resurrection. Psalm 2:7 (the same Psalm that speaks of Jesus ruling with a rod of iron) says "Thou art my son, this day have I begotten thee." Look at what Paul (by inspiration) said about that prophecy:

> *God has fulfilled the same to us their children, in that*
> ***he has raised up Jesus again****; as it is also written in*
> *the second psalm, "Thou art my Son, this day have I*
> *begotten thee" (Acts 13:33).*

Of course, the reason I don't agree with this being His resurrection is because there was no woman (whether figurative or literal) involved in the process at all. And that would mean you'd have to ignore the context… which is *always* a bad thing.

Then the child ascended to heaven and to His throne.

Well, fast-forward 30+ years! We go immediately from the *birth* of Jesus to His ascension to heaven, decades later, in one short verse. Satan lost his opportunity to defeat the Messiah, and in this failure he knew he had lost the war.

THE WOMAN FLEEING INTO THE WILDERNESS (12:6)

> *And the woman fled into the wilderness, where she*
> *had a place prepared by God, that they should feed*
> *her there 1260 days.*

This event is mentioned with no reference to a passage of time. However, the same event is mentioned in verse 14, so we must take that into consideration when interpreting this.

1260 days in the wilderness

The woman (God's faithful people now embodied in the New Jerusalem, the church) fled to a wilderness prepared by God, and was cared for by Him for 1260 days.

Unless this is speaking of some *other* 3½ year period where God protected the church from harm, it should be seen as speaking of the 3½ years of the Roman Jewish war.

Some have suggested this describes God keeping the church safe during the first 3½ years of its existence, until the death of Stephen in Acts 7. It's difficult at best and impossible at worst to prove that 3½ years transpired between Acts 2 and Acts 7. Thus, this interpretation is only supposition.

Instead, we should see this as a look ahead at what was going to happen, described more in verses 14 and following. We will deal with that in the next study, but in case you are curious…

The Roman armies from Syria invaded Judea very late in AD 66 to quell the signs of Jewish rebellion. They surrounded the city, but for some reason unknown to us, they retreated and suffered heavy casualties as the Jews ambushed them. When Cestus Gallus (the general from Syria) left, there was a mass exodus of Christians from Jerusalem. They believed Jesus' words, "When you see Jerusalem surrounded by armies…then let he that is in Judea flee to the mountains" (Matthew 24:16; Luke 21:20).

The Christians fled past the Jordan River to a deserted place (a wilderness) called Pella, and remained there the entirety of the Roman-Jewish War—42 months. The area of Pella has two mountains with many caves, and has a stream flowing between the mountains which is fed by a spring—a perfect place prepared to house refugees from Jerusalem during the war.

This is what is under consideration when God nourished the woman (His faithful people) in the wilderness for 1260 days.

WHAT DOES THIS MEAN FOR US TODAY?

God keeps His word.

God promised Satan would be defeated by Christ, who was born of a woman—and it happened! We can trust EVERYTHING that God has said in Scriptures.

Satan has lost—act accordingly.

Though Satan is very powerful, he still lost the war to God—MAKE SURE you are on the right side!!!

Never ignore the context!

So many verses are violently torn from their context, and twisted to mean what God never intended. John 3:16 shows faith-only salvation? Only if you ignore Jesus' words earlier in the chapter about being "born again" and "born of water and spirit." Revelation 3:20 teaches the sinner's prayer to be saved? Only if you ignore that Jesus was speaking to people who were *already Christians*.

Context matters.

God will take care of His people.

God cares for His people and will take care of their needs (Matthew 6:33)! His faithful people were ready to obey, and received the comfort He provided.

Are you one of God's people?

STUDY TWENTY-NINE:
THE WAR IN HEAVEN
(REVELATION 12:7-11)

When we last left Revelation, we saw a woman (representing God's faithful people—His true Israel) giving birth to a man-child (Jesus Christ) while a dragon (Satan) tried to destroy Him to keep God's prophecy of Genesis 3:15 from coming true.

The child (Jesus) ascended to heaven and to His throne, as seen in Acts 1 and confirmed in Acts 2.

The last thing we saw was the woman fleeing into the wilderness for 1260 days to be protected and nourished by God. It is important for us to remember this "fleeing" takes place during the 1260 days of the Roman-Jewish war (AD 67-70). Also remember the same incident is re-stated, slightly differently, in verse 14 of this same chapter.

Why bring this up? Because the events in verses 7-17 *must fit somewhere between the Ascension of Christ and the destruction of Jerusalem.* (Did you catch that? Because a lot of people ignore it.)

This chapter was to help Christians understand *what* was happening/about to happen, and *why* it was about to happen.

Who are the fighters? (12:7).

In order to get a better grasp on this passage, we must know who is involved. So now introducing, combatant #1.

MICHAEL

> *And there was war in heaven: Michael and his angels fought against the dragon and his angels.*

Who is Michael? Well, let's let the Bible answer that for us.

Michael first appears by name in the book of Daniel.

He is called the "great prince who stands for your [Daniel's] people" (Daniel 12:1). Daniel was a Jew—so Daniel's people are... the Jews (I realize that's obvious, but I had to point it out).

A "prince" is a ruler, a leader, a chief.[1] So Michael (in some way) is a ruler, leader, or chief of the Jews.

Michael is next mentioned by name in Jude 9.

Here, we are told that Michael is *the* archangel. Nowhere does the Bible say there are "archangels," as though there is more than one. The word is only used in the singular—archangel.

So what does the word "archangel" mean?

- "Arch" is from a Greek word (*arche*) that means "chief" or "highest" or "primary."
- "Angel" (Greek, *angellos*) means "messenger."

So Michael, according to Jude, is the highest messenger of God.

Michael vs. Satan over the "body of Moses"

Jude describes Michael, contending with Satan over the body of Moses, and saying to Satan "the Lord rebuke thee, Satan." Many think this is the literal flesh-and-blood body of Moses after God killed him on Mt. Pisgah (Deuteronomy 34). However, look at Zechariah 3.

> *He showed me Joshua the high priest standing before the angel of the LORD, and Satan standing at his right hand to resist him. And the LORD said to Satan, "The LORD rebuke thee, O Satan; even the LORD that has chosen Jerusalem rebuke thee: is not this a brand plucked out of the fire?"*
>
> *Now Joshua was clothed with filthy garments, and stood before the angel.*

---

[1] Brown-Driver-Briggs Hebrew Dictionary.

And he [God] answered and spoke to those that stood before him, saying, "Take away the filthy garments from him." And to him he said, "Behold, I have caused your iniquity to pass from you, and I will clothe you with a change of clothing" (Zechariah 13:1-4).

So let's boil this down to the simple facts of the incident: In a vision, Zechariah sees Joshua the high priest, clothed in filthy garments (representing the sin of the nation of Israel). Joshua was standing before the Angel of the LORD. Satan stood and opposed (or accused) Joshua (who represented God's people) to the Angel of the LORD. The Angel of the LORD said, "the LORD rebuke thee, O Satan, even the LORD that hath chosen Jerusalem rebuke thee" (3:2).

Stick with me for a few minutes. Consider 1 Corinthians 10:1-2.

*Moreover, brethren, I do not want you to be ignorant of how all our fathers were under the cloud, and all passed through the sea; and were all **baptized into Moses** in the cloud and in the sea*

The Israelites were "baptized INTO Moses." Now consider something here. If baptism into Christ (Galatians 3:26-27) makes one part of the body of Christ, wouldn't baptism into Moses (via crossing the Red Sea) make one part of the body of Moses? Seems reasonable to me.

That means, Jude identifies Michael as the Angel of the LORD who rebuked Satan as they contended about the Israelites—the body of Moses—in Zechariah 3.[2]

And in case the parallels weren't clear enough, catch this: Zechariah shows Satan accusing the Israelites (God's people). Later in

---

[2] This is presented in more detail in *Fight for the Faith: A Study of the Letter from Jude*, by this author.

Revelation 12, when Satan is cast down, praise is lifted up because the "accuser of our brethren" is cast down!

Just one other passage mentions the word "archangel"—1 Thessalonians 4:16.

> *The Lord will descend from heaven with a shout,* **with**
> **the voice of the archangel**...

According to this verse, when Jesus returns, whose voice is He going to use?

What does "Michael" mean?

Since Michael is a heavenly being, this name *must have* been given by God, and not by any human.

The name "Michael" means "Who is like God." Some Bible dictionaries insert a question mark ("Who is like God?"), but that is their assumption. *God* is the one who called Him "Who is like God."

Michael defeats Satan

As you read Revelation 12:7-9, it is clear that Michael wins the battle.

Putting all of this together...

(1) Michael is the heavenly ruler of the Jews.

Who said He was born to be king of the Jews, and even had that title over His head as He was crucified?

(2) Michael is the highest messenger of God, "who is like God."

Who is the messenger through whom God speaks today (Hebrews 1:1-2), is superior to all other messengers, and who is also like God?

(3) When Jesus descends, it is Michael's voice that He uses.

Would Jesus speak with the voice of one LOWER than Himself?

(4) Michael is the Angel of the LORD from the Old Testament.

Exodus 3 shows the Angel of the LORD is deity—He was the one in the burning bush, whose presence made it HOLY GROUND, and who said "I am the God of Abraham, Isaac, and Jacob" (Exodus 3:1-6).

(5) Michael is the one who defeats Satan

Who is one who was prophesied to defeat Satan back in Genesis 3:15? Who, through His death, destroyed the devil (Hebrews 2:14)?

Michael the archangel is Jesus Christ.

Some folks get really upset when I point this out, because they think this makes Jesus a created being.

It doesn't.

The word "angel" has a meaning—and it isn't "created guys who wear white robes, carry harps, have wings, and wear halos." Angel means messenger—no more, no less. Jesus is the highest messenger, the one who brought the message of God's salvation to the world. He is not created. He is eternal deity (John 1:1-3).

Michael (Jesus Christ) is one of the two main combatants in this war; the other is...

THE DRAGON

There is no dispute over who this is. John states it plainly: this is Satan, the devil.

Satan is now, and always will be the enemy of God and Christ, and of all people who seek to do God's will.

> ***Our*** *adversary the devil, like a roaring lion, walks about seeking whom he may devour (1 Peter 5:8).*

Satan is *our* adversary—not just God's or Jesus' enemy.

Satan is angry, bent on destroying Christ, but he sees the war is slipping away from him. When Christ ascended into heaven, Satan's opportunities to destroy Jesus on earth had failed.

But Michael (Jesus) and the dragon (Satan) are not the only ones fighting this war.

MICHAEL'S ANGELS

*The key to understanding this is in remembering that the word
"angel" means "messenger."*

Who, after the ascension of Christ, were Jesus' messengers? On
the day of Pentecost, twelve messengers of Jesus stood in the temple
and proclaimed Jesus had ascended to sit on His throne (like Revelation 12:5).

The "angels" or messengers of Jesus Christ (Michael) are the
faithful proclaimers of His word, starting with—and perhaps specifically speaking of—the twelve apostles. It could also include all the
proclaimers of Jesus Christ throughout the book of Acts (like Stephen, Phillip, Paul, etc…).

We'll get to the interpretation of the war later.

THE DRAGON'S ANGELS

Given the context of Revelation, and history from the book of
Acts, who are the messengers of Satan? Since the messengers of
Christ were *people*, we should expect the messengers of Satan are
also people. 2 Corinthians 11:13-15 mentions false apostles, and
calls them the "ministers of Satan."

The messengers of Satan were opposed to, and fought against,
the messengers of Jesus Christ.

I see no better candidate for these messengers of Satan than the
Jews themselves. This is best exemplified in the Jewish leaders who
sought to kill Jesus and who later sought to overthrow Christianity.

THE OUTCOME OF THE WAR (12:7-9)

*And there was war in heaven: Michael and his mes-
sengers fought against the dragon and his messengers, and they [Satan and his messengers] did not*

prevail; nor was their place found any more in heaven. And the great dragon was cast out, that old serpent, called the Devil and Satan, who deceives the whole world: he was cast out into the earth, and his messengers were cast out with him.

Satan could not prevail.

In the battle between Jesus and Satan, Satan doesn't stand a chance (Genesis 3:15).

Their place was no longer found in heaven.

This is not speaking God's dwelling place, but of the spiritual realm. Satan no longer has any authority in the spiritual realm.

- He can no longer directly tempt people (as he did occasionally in the Scriptures—Genesis 2, Matthew 4).
- He no longer can stand before God and accuse all of God's people (like a lawyer) for breaking the Law.

Instead of living under the condemnation of the Law, we live under the covenant of grace, wherein the penalty for our sins has already been paid. As such, Satan is like a lawyer trying to convince a judge to find someone guilty and punished when the punishment has already taken place. Satan has lost his standing in the spiritual realm to accuse God's people.

Satan was cast down to the earth along with his messengers.

This is *not* talking about some pre-creation fall of Satan from being an angel to being an opponent of God. There is no 4,000(plus)-year flashback going on in the middle of this chapter. Remember, *context matters!*

When the seventy disciples returned from their mission, they were amazed, and told Jesus, "Even the demons are subject to us through your name!" (Luke 10:17). Jesus' immediate response was "I beheld Satan falling like lightning from heaven." Satan's power was weakening!

In the week leading up to Jesus' death, He said, "Now is the judgment of this world; now shall the prince of this world be cast out" (John 12:31), and John said this was a reference to Jesus' death (12:33).

Satan's authority was lost completely at the death, resurrection, and ascension of Christ. His power, much of which came through the Law of Moses (without law, there is no sin—Romans 5:13), ended when the Law of Moses was done away with.

Satan's messengers, the Jewish leaders, Pharisees and Sadducees who made excessive demands on the people and looked for every possible reason to condemn others, lost their power as well.

Think about it, you've spent your whole life being told you are worthless, you can't do anything right, you are a horrible, hell-bound sinner. And then the entire basis upon which those accusations are made is taken away, and Jesus says, "Come follow me."

The accusers no longer have an effect. The Pharisees tried to keep the people in line by berating them for being such horrible Jews (remember how they treated that man who was born blind in John 9?). But now their power was gone. They were like a snarling dog without teeth or claws.

The fact that Satan was defeated by "Michael" should be enough evidence that Michael is Jesus.

Hebrews 2:9-14 says that Jesus, through His death, might *destroy* him that had the power of death. Jesus is the one who defeats/destroys Satan. Since Revelation attributes that to Michael, then Jesus and Michael must be the same person. But don't take my word for it. Look at what happens next in the text.

WHEN DID THIS HAPPEN? (12:10)

And I heard a loud voice saying in heaven, "Now has come salvation, and strength, and the kingdom of our God, and the power of his Christ: for the accuser of

> *our brethren is cast down, the one who accused them*
> *before our God day and night."*

Going with the context of the book, there are two main options for when this war took place.

The first is AD 70, at the destruction of Jerusalem, when God's kingdom was seen in its glory, and Christ showed His power over the Jews by destroying them. While that may seem plausible on the surface, it doesn't account for the fact that verses 12-14 say it pre-dates the Roman-Jewish war (3½ years).

All we have to do is look at the immediate results of the war to know when this "war in heaven" took place. When Satan's power was taken away and he was cast down from his place of power, a loud voice announced the following:

(1) "Now has come the salvation."

When was salvation proclaimed and put into effect? On the day of Pentecost (Acts 2:21, 40, 47).

(2) "Now has come ...strength."

The word here is *dunamis*, from which we get our word *dynamite*. This word usually has reference to mighty works, specifically miracles. When did the time of miracles (prophesied by Joel) begin? According to Peter, in Acts 2:16-22, it was on the Day of Pentecost.

(3) "Now has come...the kingdom of God."

The kingdom of God existed prior to the destruction of Jerusalem (Colossians 1:13, Revelation 1:9), so this can't be speaking of AD 70. The Old Testament prophesied the kingdom would be established during the days of the Roman Empire (Daniel 2:44), and would be established in Jerusalem (Isaiah 2:2-4). The church is the kingdom that fits those descriptions, and was established in AD 30 in Jerusalem... on the Day of Pentecost.

(4) "Now has come...the power of His Christ."

The word *power* here is not *dunamis*, but *exousia*, which means authority. Jesus said very clearly, "All power [*exousia*] has been given [past tense] to me, in heaven and on earth" (Matthew 28:18).

Personally, I don't see how Jesus could say this in the past tense if it didn't really happen until forty years later when Jerusalem was destroyed. Again, remember Hebrews 2:9-14—through Christ's death, He might destroy the devil.

(5) "The accuser of our brethren is cast down, which accused them before our God day and night."

Some people use this section (verses 7-17) to argue Satan rebelled and was rejected from heaven at (or prior to) the beginning of time. But note: when Satan is cast out, *he had already been continually making accusations against humans day and night.* While Satan may well have rebelled against God at the beginning of time, *this passage is about first-century events*, and as such says *nothing* about Satan's initial rebellion.

When the church came into existence at Pentecost, the Old Testament ceased to be in effect, and the law of Christ took over. Imagine Satan as a massive sea-monster in an ocean filled with people, and he is enjoying devouring each and every one. But then people are pulled up and out of his grasp—people are being saved!

When Christ died, His death covered our sins, but it also covered the sins of those who died under the first covenant (the Old Testament) (Hebrews 9:15). So any accusations Satan could have brought against God's Old Testament saints were null and void at that point as well. Satan's power was taken away at Christ's death, but its effect was retroactive, and nullified Satan's power to accuse God's faithful from before the death of Christ as well.

HOW DID THE BRETHREN OVERCOME? (12:11)

And they overcame him by the blood of the Lamb, and by the word of their testimony; and because they did not love their lives to the death.

They overcame by the blood of the Lamb.

This includes those who became Christians by coming into contact with the blood of Jesus Christ in baptism, as well as Old Testament saints. Their sins had been washed away, and Satan no longer had a claim on them! We overcome the same way; and unless we forsake God, Satan has no claim on us!

They overcame by the word of their testimony.

Christians shared their faith with others (see Acts 8:1-4) and lived their faith. We overcome in the same way, by remaining faithful to Jesus Christ and sharing our faith with others.

They overcame because they didn't love their lives to the death.

To them, obeying Christ and receiving the eternal reward was much more important than saving their physical lives.

WHAT DOES THIS MEAN FOR US TODAY?

Be faithful unto death

Intense persecution came from the Jews throughout the book of Acts. Shortly after Revelation was written, the Neronic persecution broke out, and the Jews used it as an excuse to ramp up their own persecution of the Christians. Thousands upon thousands of Christians were murdered throughout the Roman Empire during this bloody time. But the overcomers stayed true to God and Christ.

How important is your physical life to you?

The War is over—Jesus won!

Jesus won the war – His kingdom is established, He has all authority, and He has brought salvation to all who will come to Him. Have you come to Him yet—the way He laid out?[3]

---

[3] For more information, see the Appendix, "Are You Saved?" at the back of this book.

STUDY THIRTY:
THE DRAGON ON EARTH
(REVELATION 12:12-17)

Satan has lost the war! Satan has lost the war!

One of the great teachings in Revelation is that Satan *has already lost!* He had overwhelming power to condemn people through the Law of Moses. Because if one is guilty of one part of the law, he is guilty of the whole thing (James 2:10). He stood before God day and night, accusing God's people and demanding condemnation be brought down upon them.

But when Jesus died, all the punishment due was taken.

Satan's power, his leverage, has been taken away. His power in the spiritual realm, his standing before God to accuse God's people is forever gone! My friends, Christ's death won *us* the victory, so long as we stay on His side!

This victory of Christ came at His death, resurrection, and ascension to His throne, and was followed with the pronouncement of salvation, the kingdom, of the outpouring of the Holy Spirit, and of the authority of Jesus Christ *at Pentecost.*

Satan has been cast down from his place of power, but he is not out of the fight. He's lost, but you couldn't tell that from the way he is fighting

Things were about to get very, very bad.

REJOICE AND BE AFRAID (12:12)

Therefore rejoice, you heavens, and you who dwell in them. Woe to the inhabitants of the land and of the sea! For the devil has come down to you, having great wrath, because he knows that he has but a short time.

Rejoice, you heavens and you who dwell in them!

The heavens is a description of the spiritual realm. God's true people are those who are spiritual, thus they are the ones who dwell in the heavenlies (spiritual realm).

- Ephesians 1:3—all spiritual blessings *in heavenly places* are in Christ Jesus.
- Galatians 6:1—you who are *spiritual*, restore such a one…
- 1 Peter 2:5—You…are built up a *spiritual* house.
- Romans 8:1, 4—We walk *according to the Spirit*, and not according to the flesh.

Why should the spiritual (God's faithful people) rejoice?

Because Satan's rule in spiritual things has been destroyed. Because we no longer have to fear death (Hebrews 9:14). Because if we continue to follow Christ (even making mistakes along the way), we can know we have eternal life (1 John 5:13)! That's something worth rejoicing over (Acts 2:40; 8:39).

Be afraid, inhabitants of the land and the sea, for the devil is come to you, having great wrath!

I'm not the first to say it: Satan is now a wounded animal—though defeated, he is perhaps more dangerous than before. Wounded animals oftentimes will attack anyone and everyone who gets near them. Satan is now ready to lash out at anyone and everyone who gets in his way.

"Earth" is the same word as "land" and refers to the Promised Land—Judea. Therefore, the inhabitants of the earth/land are the ones who live in the Promised Land—the Jews. I know I've said this about a dozen times so far in this book, but it really is important to remember.

The word "sea" describes the realm of the Gentiles. Therefore, the inhabitants of the sea would be Gentiles. It *could* also include the Jews of the dispersion (the diaspora), the Jews who did not live in the Promised Land (see James 1:1, 1 Peter 1:1).

Satan, as a defeated foe, is now going to use anything he can to attack all those who get in his path. After Pentecost, the focus of Satan's energies were in the Promised Land, trying to wipe out Christianity. For the most part, he used the Jews (the inhabitants of the Land) as his weapons.

When Christianity spread and began to include Gentiles, Satan's wrath was spread across the entire Roman Empire. From this point, he began to use Gentiles as well as foreign-born Jews to persecute Christians (see Acts 17:5-8).

Satan knew he had but a short time.

What does this mean? How could John record Satan only had a short time when he is obviously still among us today? How could 2,000 years be considered a short time?!?!?

Consider this:

It doesn't say Satan would only *exist* "a short time." It doesn't say Satan would only be able to *work* for "a short time." It doesn't say Satan would only be able *tempt* for "a short time." So what does it say? It says Satan knew he had "but a short time..." So after the death, burial, resurrection, and ascension of Jesus, and the establishment of the church on the Day of Pentecost, Satan knew he was on a time crunch. If he wanted to upset God's plans and still have hope to win the victory, he had better hurry and get to work—because there was only a short time period for him to do it.

With the ascension of Christ to His throne, Satan knew it was only a matter of time before the rest of the Old Testament prophecies would come to pass. Jesus said, "This generation shall not pass till all these things be fulfilled" (Matthew 24:34).—Satan knew it was a short time—he had one generation. When Jerusalem was destroyed, "all things written" would be fulfilled (Luke 21:20-22).

But if Satan could somehow *keep* those things from being fulfilled, he would again have the upper hand. If Satan could somehow wipe out the church before that time, then God would have no people when the Old Jerusalem was destroyed—there would be no New Jerusalem to shine forth in glory.

Once Jerusalem was destroyed and God's church was revealed in all its glory to the world, it was over—Satan would never be able to win. This was Satan's last stand, his final desperate attempt to keep God's word from coming to pass—and he was bringing in some heavy human reinforcements.

PERSECUTING THE WOMAN (12:13)

And when the dragon saw that he was cast to the earth, he persecuted the woman which brought forth the man child.

When Satan was cast to the earth, his focus was immediately on persecuting the woman (the faithful people of God—now embodied in the church).

This is a short, succinct description of the entire book of Acts.

- The apostles are threatened for preaching Jesus (chap. 4).
- The apostles are beaten (5:40-41).
- Turmoil in the church itself (6:1).
- Satan realizes threats and beatings aren't enough, so he influences the Jews to murder Stephen (7:58-60).
- Then Saul (influenced by Satan) institutes large-scale persecution against the church (8:1-4).
- Saul is converted, and Satan turns his attention to trying to kill him (9:23-24).
- James is murdered by Herod, king over Judea (12:1-2).
- Peter is arrested and almost executed (12:3).
- Paul and his companions are frequently targeted for beatings and death (chap. 13-28).

Had Satan turned his attention to persecuting the church after his defeat at Christ's ascension? ABSOLUTELY!

THE WOMAN (NOW THE CHURCH) IS KEPT SAFE (12:14)

And the woman was given two wings of a great eagle, that she might fly to the wilderness, into her place, where she is nourished for a time, and times, and half a time, from the face of the serpent.

God would not let His church be destroyed.

Satan's plan was to leave God without a people when Jerusalem was destroyed. And God knew it. So God gave her "two wings of a great eagle, that she might fly into the wilderness, into her place, where she is nourished for a time, times, and half a time, from the face of the serpent."

This imagery comes from the exodus from Egyptian bondage.

*"You have seen what I did to the Egyptians, and **how I bore you on eagles' wings**, and brought you to myself" (Exodus 19:4).*

Where were the Israelites taken care of by God after they crossed the Red Sea? *The wilderness*! The wilderness was not the easiest place to live, but it was there God provided for His people.

Isaiah 51:9-10 describes the Pharaoh from whom God rescued the Israelites as "*the dragon.*" In Revelation, God rescues His people from "*the dragon.*" No, that isn't a coincidence.

Psalm 74:13-14 describes the exodus and refers to the Pharaoh and his armies as *the heads of the dragon* or the Leviathan.

Satan used two main forces to destroy the church: the sea beast (the Roman Empire) and the Land beast (the Jewish rulers).

The identification of the sea beast as Rome is a common one. We'll discuss this again when we hit chapter 13, but in AD 64, Rome burned, and Nero blamed Christians. This led to an empire-wide persecution. Tacitus (early Roman historian) records this:

> Therefore, to scotch the rumor, Nero substituted as culprits, and punished with the utmost refinements of cruelty, a class of men, loathed for their vices, whom the crowd styled Christians. Christus, the founder of the name, had undergone the death penalty in the reign of Tiberius, by sentence of the procurator Pontius Pilatus, and the pernicious superstition was checked for a moment, only to break out once more, not merely in Judaea, the home of the disease, but in the capital itself, where all things horrible or shameful in the world collect and find a vogue. First, then, the confessed members of the sect were arrested; next, on their disclosures, vast numbers were convicted, not so much on the count of arson as for hatred of the human race. And derision accompanied their end: they were covered with wild beasts' skins and torn to death by dogs; or they were fastened on crosses, and, when daylight failed, were burned to serve as lamps by night. Nero had offered his Gardens for the spectacle, and gave an exhibition in his Circus, mixing with the crowd in the habit of a charioteer, or mounted on his car. Hence, in spite of a guilt, which had earned the most exemplary punishment, there arose a sentiment of pity, due to the impression that they were being sacrificed not for the welfare of the state but to the ferocity of a single man (Tacitus, *Annals*, book 15 ch. 44).

The Jews took advantage of this, and intensified their persecution of Christians as well.

But as political turmoil kept growing, the Jews revolted against Rome, leading to the Roman-Jewish War.

But during this time (year), times (years), and half a time (1/2 year), aka 3½ years, God protected His faithful people in the wilderness of Pella.

THE ATTACK OF THE DRAGON (12:15-17)

And the serpent cast water out of his mouth like a flood after the woman, that he might cause her to be carried away by the flood. And the land helped the woman, and the land opened her mouth, and swallowed up the flood which the dragon cast out of his mouth. And the dragon was furious with the woman, and went to make war with the remnant of her seed, which keep the commandments of God, and have the testimony of Jesus Christ.

The serpent cast a flood of water out of his mouth, trying to destroy the woman.

A flood destroys everything in its path, so if it got to the woman (God's people), she would be forever destroyed. When you read the verses, it seems like an almost insignificant thing, but this is very serious.

This is the attack of the Roman armies during the Roman-Jewish War, used by Satan as a weapon to destroy the Christians. How do we know this? By verse 16.

The flood went towards the woman, but the earth (the Promised Land) helped the woman, and swallowed up the flood completely.

The Christians (the church in Judea) had crossed the Jordan River, and left the Promised Land. The overwhelming attack of the Roman army never crossed the Jordan into Pella. The Roman army's goal was to destroy Jerusalem and to kill the rebels there. The focus of their mission did not extend past the Jordan River.

As the flood of the Roman army came, Satan was certain they would wipe out the church as well—but the church fled to the wilderness, while the Roman army's onslaught was contained in the Promised Land.

The dragon was furious with the woman (God's church), and went to make war with the remnant of her seed, which keep the commandments of God and have the testimony of Jesus Christ.

Before we decide what this verse means, we need to figure out *where* it fits in.

Beginning in chapter thirteen, we basically step backwards in time again. Whereas the days of the Roman-Jewish war (3½ years) were the topic of verses 13-16, chapter thirteen goes backwards to a time before it began. It fills in some details about the events in chapter 12:13-16. It is like Genesis 1 and 2—the facts are stated, and then immediately the story is re-told, with more specific details given.

The question is this: does 12:17 go with the previous verses (that we looked at in this lesson), or does it go with the events recorded in chapter thirteen?

If verse 17 goes with the previous verses, then this shows Satan knows (after AD 70) the war is over and he has lost, but he is still going after the members of the church individually. He knows he has no hope of destroying the church as a whole, so he tries to pick off individual members one at a time. If this is the proper interpretation, then this verse covers the time from AD 70 onward, and remains true today.

If verse 17 goes with the next chapter, it serves as an introduction to the beasts Satan will use in his war with the saints. Satan is making war with the Christians (12:17), and the Sea Beast is given the power to "make war with the saints" (13:7). This connection is enough (to me) to justify the interpretation that verse 17 serves as an introduction to the next chapter. But regardless, Satan's aim is to destroy as many Christians as possible.

WHAT DOES THIS MEAN FOR US TODAY?

Satan hasn't stopped trying to undermine God's plans. Be aware.

Satan has always been trying to undermine God's plans and God's people. That includes you. YOU are a target for Satan to aim at. Put on the whole armor of God (Ephesians 6) and know that he is out there.

God has given us protection—if we will use it!

Satan cannot tempt us directly. Satan cannot tempt us outside of the lust of the eyes, the lust of the flesh, and the pride of life. God has shown us who the enemy is, how he operates, and describes his weapons. God has given us the armor and weapons to defeat Satan in *every battle*! God has given us a way of victory *every day, every moment*!

If we resist the devil, he will flee from us (James 4:7). This means he doesn't have power over us. You can never claim, "The devil made me do it."

God has given us the victory—all we have to do is fight the fight! Never quit the fight against Satan, and you will gain eternal life!

STUDY THIRTY-ONE: THE SEA BEAST (REVELATION 13:1-10)

Satan has lost his power, he's down, and he's mad.

He has been cast from his spiritual perch, and he's planning to make war with the saints. He's going to use human powers to accomplish his goal of destroying the church before the prophecies of Christ can be fulfilled.

Chapter 13 introduces us to the two entities that Satan uses in this all-out attack on Christianity. The first is the beast from the sea (our focus in this study). The second is the beast from the land (aka the Promised Land) who encouraged people to put their trust and support in the sea beast.

Our mission in this study will be to identify the Sea Beast and see what he is going to do. As we go through this study, we will look at some passages in Daniel, as well as other parts of Revelation which also seem to mention the same beast.

With these things in mind, let's dive into our study! We will be identifying the Sea beast through a series of questions.

QUESTION #1—HOW IS THIS BEAST DESCRIBED? (13:1-4)

I stood upon the sand of the sea, and saw a beast rise up out of the sea, having seven heads and ten horns, and on his horns ten crowns, and on his heads the blasphemous names. And the beast which I saw was like a leopard, his feet were like the feet of a bear, and his mouth like the mouth of a lion. And the dragon gave him his power, and his throne, and great authority. And I saw one of his heads like it were wounded to death; and his deadly wound was healed: and all the world marveled after the beast. And they worshipped the dragon who gave power to the beast: and they worshipped the beast, saying, "Who is like the beast? Who is able to make war with him?"

He is a beast.

The literal translation of this Greek word would be a "wild beast." Whatever this beast it, it is something untamable by the Christians.

He comes from the sea.

This is in contrast to the next beast who comes from the land (13:11). This beast is from a different sphere/area than the land beast.

He has seven heads and ten horns.

The dragon has these same characteristics. Whatever the beast is and is doing, Satan is involved.

The seven heads are seven mountains.

In chapter 17, the same beast is described. There, the heads are called seven mountains on which the whore (a city called "Babylon") sits (17:9). Some say this means seven kingdoms (because mountains often represent kingdoms in the Old Testament—see Isaiah 2:1-4). However, this would require the angel in chapter 17 to interpret the symbol...by giving another symbol. Nowhere in the Bible is that done, and it shouldn't be tried here either. These are literal mountains or hills (the Greek word is translated both ways in the New Testament).

There are two cities of interest that were built on seven mountains/hills. One is Rome, well known for being the city on seven hills. The other is Jerusalem, also situated on seven mountains/hills—Zion, Acra, Moriah, Bezetha, Millo, Ophel, and Antonia; all of which are mentioned by Josephus in connection with the war against Jerusalem (*Wars* 5.5.8).[1]

The seven heads are seven kings (17:10).

Thus, the figure had a double meaning. Of those seven kings, five were gone (had passed away), one was then in existence (reigning), and another would come afterwards, but would only reign a short time (17:10).

Some (wrongfully, according to the context) have interpreted these seven kings to mean seven kingdoms that persecuted God's people. (1) Egypt, (2) Assyria, (3) Babylon, (4) Persia [which didn't necessarily persecute the people of God], (5) Greece [the last of the five], (6) Rome [the present kingdom when John wrote], and (7) ??? There is no real explanation for the seventh persecuting empire that would only exist a short time. This interpretation of the beast would make it simply civil/political powers of all times that persecuted God's people.

However, this book has a specific first-century context. And since there is no nation after Rome who persecuted all of God's people, this interpretation really falls apart. However, it is held by several well-meaning brethren who (sadly) take the late date view of Revelation. We will get to the interpretation of these seven kings a bit later.

From the information in chapter 17, we can know the beast represents an entity with kings. More than that, the beast is an entity the Christians of the first century would have recognized and been able to identify based on the descriptions of the kings.

It had ten crowns on its horns (13:1).

The Greek word here is *diadem*, and refers to crowns of authority or rule. From this, we can say whatever this beast is, some kind of ruling authority resides in it.

---

[1] Other lists give variations on the names: Scopus, Olivet, Mount of Corruption, Ophel, Old Zion, New Zion, and Antonia.

In chapter seventeen the ten horns are explained. They are ten kings (17:12). These ten kings don't have their own kingdom, but receive power with the beast (17:12). These ten kings work together and give their authority and strength to the beast (17:13). These kings have no authority outside of what the beast permits them to have.

From this, we see the beast represents an entity that had power over other nations and permitted those other nations to have certain authority.

It is scarlet-colored (17:3).

This is blood-red, and symbolizes the vicious bloody nature of the beast.

On its heads are the names of blasphemy (13:1).

Since we are told in chapter seventeen the heads are kings, then these kings wore blasphemous titles. A blasphemous name or title is claiming deity for himself, claiming to be a god.

So, whoever this beast is, its kings claimed the status of deity, or at least accepted the praises as such (see 13:4 where people worshiped the beast).

It was like a leopard, with feet of a bear and a mouth like a lion.

This looks, in backwards order, at the beasts mentioned in Daniel 7:3-6. There were four beasts mentioned in total, but the first three were Babylon (the lion), Persia (the bear), and Greece (the leopard). The fourth beast, mentioned in Daniel 7:7 was different that the others, and had ten horns as well.

The beast in Revelation has the strength of Persia, the power of Babylon, and the swiftness of Greece all wrapped into one.

Satan put his resources behind this beast.

He gave the beast his power (dunamis, forceful ability and power). He gave the beast his throne. He gave the beast his authority. Satan didn't give his own throne to the beast, instead the "his" refers to the beast. The *beast's* throne, power, and authority came from Satan.

QUESTION #2—WHO IS THIS BEAST?

In Daniel, the beasts all represented world-dominating kingdoms.
    What world-dominating kingdom existed in the days of Revelation?

The beast comes from the sea (realm of the Gentiles) as opposed to the Land (Promised Land).
    What national Gentile power (about to begin a persecution against them) would have been of importance to Christians in the first century?

The beast was influenced by Satan and its kings wore blasphemous names (titles).
    What Gentile kingdom had kings that were worshipped as gods? (Think back to some of the temples in the seven churches of Asia.)

The beast was on its sixth king, the previous five having died (chapter 17).
    What Gentile kingdom happened to be on king #6 when Revelation was written?

The beast had ten kings (or kingdoms) who served it and had no authority except that which was given to them by the beast.
    What Gentile kingdom in the first century had control over other nations and was the one who determined what kind of authority those nations could have?

The beast had the characteristics of Babylon, Persia, and Greece.
    What Gentile kingdom in the first century had aspects of these world empires?
    It is interesting that the entire statue of Daniel 2 (which Daniel interpreted as representing four successive kingdoms) was still standing until the kingdom of God arrived on the scene. The fourth kingdom was viewed as almost an extension of the first three; they

were all somewhat connected. The same idea is true with the beast in Revelation having aspects of the first three beasts/kingdoms.

Of course, the only kingdom that fits these qualifications is Rome.

One of its heads looked like it was wounded to death (13:3).

Some make a big deal about the words "as it were" (KJV) or "looked like," and say it wasn't *really* a death blow. However, Jesus appeared as the Lamb, "like it had been slain" (5:6). Jesus was actually slain.

The passage here describes the *head* (one of the kings) wounded to death, not the beast itself. Then it says the *beast's* deadly wound was healed.

In 44 BC, Julius Caesar, the first Roman Emperor, was murdered on the floor of the senate shortly after taking the title "dictator for life." The senate took back control of the Empire, and the dictatorship was over...so they thought. Fourteen years later, Octavius (Augustus Caesar) ascended to the status of emperor, and the Roman Empire was never the same again.

Why bring this up? Because the Greek word translated "one" in this verse could also be translated "first." Though the first Roman king was killed, the Empire was resurrected in Augustus Caesar. And the whole world looked on in amazement at what happened.

The whole world worshipped the beast.

Throughout the Empire, temples and shrines were built to worship Rome as a goddess, and to worship the various Roman Emperors as gods. These temples appear throughout the Roman Empire, including Asia Minor.

Note what the text says first: they all worshipped the Dragon (Satan). With all the pagan temples throughout the Empire, it is easy to see Satan being worshipped. Then they began to worship the Roman Empire and the emperors as well. Worshipping the Empire was the same as worshipping Satan.

Any time you put something ahead of the one true God, you are worshipping it and therefore worshipping Satan.

They said, "Who is like the beast? Who is able to make war with him?" Michael's name means "Who is like God," but the people were shouting "Who is like the beast?" Jesus had already won the war, but the people cried, "Who is able to make war with this great beast?"

THE BEAST'S AUTHORITY (13:5-7)

And there was given to him a mouth speaking great things and blasphemies; and power was given to him to continue 42 months. And he opened his mouth in blasphemy against God, to blaspheme his name, and his tabernacle, and those who dwell in heaven. And it was given to him to make war with the saints, and to overcome them: and he was given power over all tribes, and tongues, and nations. And all that dwell on the land shall worship him, whose names are not written in the book of life of the Lamb slain from the foundation of the world.

The beast was given a mouth speaking great things and blasphemies.

The kings of Rome (with only one possible exception) up to this point all wore titles declaring themselves gods. They declared themselves infallible and unbeatable.

He was given authority to continue for 42 months.

During those 42 months, the beast opened his mouth in blasphemies to God, to blaspheme the name of God, and his tabernacle, and those who dwell in heaven (Christians).

In Daniel 2, the head of the statue was Babylon, but it was *specifically* Nebuchadnezzar. The beast is Rome, but it is *specifically* personified in Nero. Nero was known as a beast (according to Suetonius, Tacitus, and Josephus). It is Nero that instituted the empire-wide persecution of Christians (see Revelation 13:7).

Rome obviously lasted longer than 42 months. But this refers to a specific period of time when war with the saints was made. Those who "dwell in heaven" are Christians, the ones the Roman Empire under Nero set out to persecute.

During those 42 months, the beast made war with the saints.

Now when did this happen? In June or July of AD 64, Rome burned, and the people blamed Nero. Nero, however (perhaps at the urging of some influential Jews?) placed the blame on Christians. A few Christians were arrested and confessed to setting the fire (most likely after a period of torture). Their confessions led to others being arrested as well.

In the middle of November of AD 64, Nero authorized a full-scale persecution of Christians throughout the Empire. This persecution, encouraged and authorized by the Roman Empire lasted until Nero's death on June 8, AD 68.

If you do the math (and I did), this adds up to almost 43 months of persecution (42½-42 ¾). It is possible the heavy persecution didn't start for a week or two after the proclamation (because it would need time to spread through the Empire). It is also possible the civil wars in Rome caused persecution to slack off prior to the death of Nero. Making 42 months right on the money.

Not only did the beast make war with the saints, he overcame them.

It was during this persecution that most (if not all) of the remaining apostles would be murdered. Paul was beheaded, Peter was killed, and many other Christians were slaughtered.

What was Satan's mission? To wipe out Christians before the Old Testament prophecies were fulfilled—leaving God with no people of His own. We don't often think about it, but the persecution under Nero almost fulfilled Satan's grand plan. It looked like Satan might win!

During those 42 months, those who dwelt "on the earth" (in the Promised Land) would worship the beast.

These are the Jews who encouraged and participated in the persecution and slaughter of Christians. When Christians were killed, Jewish leaders praised Rome and heaped accolades upon Nero. These Jews are those "whose names are not written in the book of life of the Lamb slain from the foundation of the world." Ones who encouraged persecution of Christians are not found in the book of life. Ones who participate in it are not written in the book of life. In fact, the only ones whose names *are* written in the book of life are faithful Christians.

WHAT DOES THIS MEAN FOR US TODAY?

If any man have an ear, let him hear. He that leads into captivity shall go into captivity: he that kills with the sword must be killed with the sword. Here is the patience and the faith of the saints (13:9-10).

If any have an ear to hear, let him hear.

This is Jesus saying *pay attention!* He that leads Christians into captivity will go into captivity, the one who kills Christians with the sword shall be killed with the sword. The Jews who turn Christians over to Rome (or kill them themselves) will go into captivity.

This is first and foremost a warning to Jews, but also to Christians. Christians who recant their faith will go into captivity in hell—forever. Christians who turn in fellow Christians for punishment are traitors and will go into captivity as well.

We may not be in such dire physical circumstances today, but the same things apply: recant your faith and you will pay for it with your soul. Turning against God's people will mean you have made God your enemy—and "it is a fearful thing to fall into the hands of the living God" (Hebrews 10:31).

This is the patience and the faith of the saints.

Things are going to be bad...*very* bad, but don't give in. Be patient and have faith. Don't renounce your faith. Don't turn on your brethren to save your own hide, because things will get even worse for you.

When Christians are persecuted, Satan is behind it. In the fiercest, most deadly persecution Christians ever had to endure, Jesus told them to keep the faith (be faithful to death...) and not to give up.

And some Christians today complain that the Christian life is just too hard.

Jesus wasn't about to give a pass to His followers if they stopped being faithful, *even in the face of being slaughtered.* What makes any of us think He will give us a pass today if we stop being faithful in the face of basically no persecution whatsoever?

Don't ever give up. Don't ever put anyone or anything ahead of God and His Christ.

> *Be faithful to death, and I will give you a crown of life (Revelation 2:10).*

STUDY THIRTY-TWO:
THE LAND BEAST
(REVELATION 13:11-18)

The Roman Empire, led by the maniacal tyrant Nero, is about to bathe the entire Roman Empire in the blood of Christians. But the Roman Beast isn't the only weapon Satan uses in this all-out war on the saints.

After seeing the first beast rising out of the water, bent on destruction, John sees another sight. Rising out of the ground comes another beast (almost like it's a creature rising from the grave). This one is deceptive and leads the people astray into worshipping the first beast.

And then there's that mysterious "mark of the beast."

But before we get to that mysterious number, we need to look at the beast from the land. Here's a quick overview:

- It is a beast
- It is from the Land
- It has two horns like a lamb, but speaks like a dragon
- It deceives the ones who dwell in the land with "miracles."
- It gets its power from the sea beast
- It gets people to worship the sea beast
- It had permission to give life to the image of the sea beast.
- It has permission to kill those who didn't worship the image of the sea beast.
- It causes all to receive a mark on their right hand or their foreheads—the mark of the beast: 666.
- It is called the "False prophet" (16:13, 19:20)

Ready to jump in and identify the Land Beast, and see how Satan used it in an attempt to destroy the church?

THE DESCRIPTION OF THE BEAST (13:11-12)

And I saw another beast coming up out of the earth; and he had two horns like a lamb, but he spoke like a dragon. And he exercises all the power of the first beast before him, and causes the land and those who dwell in it to worship the first beast, whose deadly wound was healed.

It was a beast.

Literally, a wild beast (same word as described the Sea Beast). Beasts in Old Testament visions represent nations (see Daniel 7). Thus, this beast from the land is a nation.

He came up out of the earth.

The word "earth" in Greek is the same word as "Land" and is a reference to the Promised Land. The only nation in the Promised Land was Judea—the Jewish nation.

He had two horns like a lamb, but spoke like a dragon.

In the Old Testament, Isaac (by then an old blind man) was deceived by his son, Jacob. Jacob wore the skins of a goat to trick his father into thinking he was Esau. Isaac fell for the deception, even though he recognized Jacob's voice (Genesis 27:22).

In the same way, this nation (land beast) tried to give the appearance of being pure (like a lamb), but its voice was as a dragon (like Satan). People were deceived by this beast when they could have known its nature by listening to its voice.

This nation was leading them further and further away from God, all the while crying "peace, peace" (like Ezekiel 13:10, 16). The Jewish nation (embodied in her religious leaders) caused the people to be lost, all the while saying they were serving God.

The two horns.

These may be a reference to the two high priests at the time (the legal high priest according to the Law of Moses, and the acting high priest, installed by Rome). These were the two most powerful men among the Jews. Some believe these two horns represent the Roman Procurator over Judea, Gessius Florus, along with the Jewish high priest (the political ruler and the religious ruler).

The sea beast had ten horns, while the land beast had two, showing the sea beast had a much greater power and authority.

The land beast (Israel) exercised the power (authority) of the first beast (Rome) who was before him (or in front of him) (13:12).

Some translations read "he executes the authority…" or "he used the authority…" of the first beast.

When Nero issued the edict against Christians, Jews throughout the Empire actively and enthusiastically carried out the order. They used authority given by Nero to kill Christians. But *they did not have this authority on their own* (see the trial and crucifixion of Christ), it could only be given to them by the Roman authorities.

This land beast (Israel, embodied in her leaders) served the sea beast (Rome, as embodied in Nero), and led people to worship it.

This should come as no surprise, since the gospels describe the Jewish leaders afraid to anger Rome and pledging their allegiance to the emperor.

> *John 11:47-48—Then the chief priests and the Pharisees gathered a council and said, "What do we do? For this man does many miracles. Therefore, if we leave him alone, all men will believe on Him: and the Romans will come and take away both our place and our nation."*

- John 19:15 has the Jewish leaders crying to Pilate: "*We have no king but Caesar!*"
- One of the charges against Jesus was that he was "*forbidding to pay taxes to Caesar*" (Luke 23:2).
- They told Pilate that if he released Jesus, he was *no friend of Caesar* (John 19:12).

The Jewish leaders led those who dwelt in the Land to worship Nero.

It wasn't necessarily that they encouraged the people to bow down before statues, but they did encourage the people to praise Nero and to throw their support behind him.

However, some believe the Jewish leaders *did* encourage the Jews who lived outside of Judea (the *diaspora*) to worship at the temples dedicated to Rome and her emperors to show their support for Rome and gain more influence. Thus it is no surprise that throughout most of Nero's reign, Jews were viewed as friends with Caesar, even carrying a certain degree of influence with him.

THE LAND-BEAST DID GREAT WONDERS (13:13-14)

> *And he does great wonders, so that he makes fire come down from heaven on the earth in the sight of men, and deceives those who dwell on the land by the means of those miracles which he had power to do in the sight of the beast; saying to those who dwell on the land, that they should make an image to the beast, which had the wound by a sword, and did live.*

It was as though he made fire come down from heaven in front of men.

However, notice verse 14 says he *deceived* people by means of these miracles that he did in front of the first beast. This shows the "miracles" were false.

Miracles were to prove something/someone was from God—these so-called "wonders" or "miracles" (same Greek word) were designed to deceive people into worshiping the Sea Beast (The Roman Empire, specifically Nero).

> *Deuteronomy 18:20—But the prophet, who shall presume to speak a word in my name, which I have not commanded him to speak, or that shall **speak in***

the name of other gods, even that prophet shall die.

Deuteronomy 13:1-5—If there arises among you a prophet, or a dreamer of dreams, and gives you a sign or a wonder, and the sign or the wonder comes to pass about which he spoke to you, saying, "Let us go after other gods, which you have not known, and let us serve them;" you shall not hearken to the words of that prophet, or that dreamer of dreams: for the LORD your God tests you, to know whether you love the LORD your God with all your heart and with all your soul.

You shall walk after the LORD your God, and fear him, and keep his commandments, and obey his voice, and you shall serve him, and cleave to him.

And that prophet, or that dreamer of dreams, shall be put to death; because he has spoken to turn you away from the LORD your God, which brought you out of the land of Egypt, and redeemed you out of the house of bondage, to thrust you out of the path which the LORD your God commanded you to walk in. So you shall put the evil away from your midst.

God warned long ago not to follow or worship *any* gods but Him, regardless of whether a false prophet could predict something that actually came to pass or not. And here in Revelation, there's a false prophet doing wonders, causing the people to worship the sea beast as a god.

Some people will say, "but it *says* that he worked miracles! How can you say they were *false* miracles?" I can say it, because *true miracles only come from God*. And because the Scriptures talk of others doing false miracles:

- 2 Thessalonians 2:9—"Power, signs, and **lying wonders**"

- Matthew 24:24—"false Christs, and false prophets, and shall show great signs and wonders...*they shall deceive*"

Interestingly, Matthew 24:24 discusses the same events as Revelation, and there Jesus calls them *false* prophets.

Notice one of the reasons why such praise was being heaped upon the sea beast.

Because it had received a deadly wound, but had been healed. This was billed as a resurrection, mocking the resurrection of our Lord and Savior, Jesus Christ. They would worship the resurrected Empire, but not the resurrected King, Jesus.

THE LAND BEAST GAVE LIFE AND TOOK LIFE (13:15)

[The land beast] had been given permission to give life to the image of the beast, so the image would speak and cause those who didn't worship the image of the beast to be killed (13:15).

The KJV and some other translations say the beast had "power," but literally, it says "it was given to him to make/give breath to the image of the beast." In other words, *permission* to act as though the image of the beast was alive (i.e., that it was a god to be worshiped).

What is this image of the beast?

Most believe this is speaking of a literal statue of, or temple to, the emperor of Rome. These temples with their statues were scattered throughout the Roman Empire. During the reign of Nero, anyone who did not declare their allegiance to him were marked as traitors and sentenced to death.

It is possible (I would argue *probable*) a literal statue isn't what this is talking about. Instead, it's talking about putting obedience to Rome and Nero ahead of obedience to God (thus making Rome their idol).

The Jewish leaders, through the synagogues, enforced submission and adoration for Nero. You can find images online of the Roman Eagle on benches from the synagogue of Sardis. The synagogues pushed economic boycotts for all who would not declare Caesar as Lord. They even went as far as putting to death those who wouldn't praise Caesar—whether by doing it themselves, or turning them over to Roman authorities as anti-Rome zealots..

- They did this to put down Jesus as the Christ, and to punish Christians.
- They did this to keep their favored status with Rome.
- They did this at Satan's bidding to thoroughly crush the church.

As the church is the image of the Son, so the Jewish synagogues were the image of the Beast (and thus called "the synagogue of Satan").

You can see how all of these ideas work together. The synagogues were bases of operation throughout the Empire to enforce Jewish submission to Nero. Those who didn't give complete heed to what the synagogues said were expelled, and most likely turned over to the Roman authorities for execution.

Oh, and one last *very important* detail. Jewish Christians frequently still met with the Jews on the Sabbath. The Christians in Jerusalem were "zealous of the law" (Acts 21:20). Paul met with Jews in the synagogues regularly (1 Corinthians 9:20; Acts 17:2; 18:4; 19:8). James used the word "synagogue" to describe the Christians' meeting-place (James 2:2). But perhaps the best evidence is found when Paul describes his Christian-killing days, and says, "Lord, they know that I imprisoned and beat in *every synagogue* those who believed in you" (Acts 22:19), and "I punished them frequently in *every synagogue*, and compelled them to blaspheme; and exceedingly raging against them, I persecuted them even to foreign cities" (Acts 26:11).

There were Jewish Christians meeting in "every synagogue" on the Sabbath. And they probably didn't hide that they were Christians. They were now targets, and had to decide whether to offend Rome or renounce Jesus.

THE LAND BEAST CAUSES ALL TO RECEIVE THE MARK (13:16-18)

And he causes all, both small and great, rich and poor, free and slave, to receive a mark in their right hand, or in their foreheads: so that no man might buy or sell, except he that had the mark, or the name of the beast, or the number of his name.

Here is wisdom. Let him that has understanding count the number of the beast: for it is the number of a man; and his number is Six hundred sixty six.

The mark is given by the land beast (Israel) upon all classes of people (small and great, rich and poor, free and slave).
The mark is equal to wearing the name of the sea beast or the number of his name (also called the number of the beast), thus it would indeed be the beast's mark.

What is the mark of the beast?
This mark is a mockery of the "seal" God places upon His people, marking them as His. Instead of being sealed by God, these people received the mark of the beast controlled by Satan. Thus, the mark of the beast is ultimately the mark of Satan. But what exactly *is* it? Consider the facts:

(1) The mark was given *by the land beast.*
This was a mark, then, given by Israel's leaders, and therefore would have *only* applied to Jews. Let me repeat: since it was given *by the Jewish leaders*, it could only apply to those who they had authority over: *Jews.*

(2) The mark is equal to wearing the name of the sea-beast or the number of the sea-beast (Rome, personified in Nero).

From this we know the mark had something to do with showing submission to Caesar, and belonging to him.

(3) The mark was on their right hand or their foreheads.

Both of these are always visible. The forehead is exposed for all to see. All business was conducted with the right hand (the left hand being viewed as "unclean" in most middle-eastern cultures), and it is also considered the hand of power (see Revelation 1:16).

When God sealed the 144,000, where were they sealed? In their foreheads! This was a sign their minds belonged to God. So if you are a first-century Jew with the mark of the beast on your forehead, who does your mind really belong to?

(4) The mark of the beast is not a literal marking.

It isn't literal any more than the sealing of God's servants on the foreheads was an actual wax seal on the forehead of every faithful Jewish Christian. My late father-in-law said this is probably speaking of the thoughts (forehead) and actions (right hand) of the people. I tend to agree. They would have to acknowledge Caesar as Lord and show it by their actions.

(5) Jews in the synagogue were "encouraged" (i.e. forced) to at least give lip-service (if not more) to Caesar as Lord.

The synagogue in Sardis had Roman emblems carved into some of its furnishings. Even during their times of study and worship, they also had praise for Rome all around them (sort of like a church today that has an American flag inside their worship area… Yes, I just said that.). Their morals were so corrupt by this time, they would blaspheme God if it would rid them of the Christians.

(6) Those kicked out of the synagogue for not calling Caesar "Lord" were kept from transacting business with other Jews.

When a Jew went to buy and sell, they would be asked, "Who is Lord," and the response expected was "Caesar is Lord." If they said it, they would be permitted to transact their business. If not, they were refused service.

The mark of the beast was a sign you honored Caesar, not Jesus. The "mark of the beast" was the Jewish recognition of Caesar as Lord—a full rejection of Jesus Christ, and therefore a full rejection of God.

WHAT IS THE MYSTICAL 666?

John pretty much tells us what 666 means.

It describes the beast
Rome, personified in Nero.

It is the number of his name.
Alphabets during the time of the Bible also doubled as their numbering system. Some people scoff at this idea, but surely you've heard of "Roman Numerals." I=1, V=5, X=10, L=50, C=100, M=1,000.

John told his readers the beast's name could be numbered, and that number was 666. This is not six-six-six, as in three separate sixes. This is six hundred sixty six.

It takes understanding/thought to figure it out.
It isn't something John was just going to come right out and proclaim. After all, he's in a Roman penal island, and anything he send out would be read by the guards first to see if there is anything that might encourage insurrection against Rome.

It is the number of a man.
In other words, the beast is a human. This alone would speak volumes to the Christian readers. *The beast worshipped as a god was still only a human*—and thus only as powerful as a human could be. He was not a god. This is a reminder for those who might be on the fence—this beast doesn't have the power that God does, because the beast is just a man.

It is related to the Roman Empire (the sea beast).

There are more than enough hints here for John's readers to know the answer.

So, let's put these things together:

What human, identified as the beast (thus of the Roman Empire), during the time Revelation was written, had a name whose letters (when added together) equaled 666?

The answer to that question is Nero!

John wrote primarily to Christians who were Jews (as shown in lesson six). He told them it would take "understanding" or "contemplation" to understand this mystery, so even though he wrote the book in Greek, he lets them know they need to look at it differently. In other words, they needed to use their historic language: Hebrew.[1]

Nero's name in Hebrew is spelled NRON KSR (Hebrew didn't have much use for vowels). The Hebrew letters that make up this name are

N = 50
R = 200
O = 6
N = 50
K = 100
S = 60
R = 200.

If you add those up, you come up with a total of 666.[2]

Possibly connected with this thought is that in the very height of his power, King Solomon received 666 talents of gold per year (1 Kings 10:14). Immediately afterwards, Solomon breaks God's laws about multiplying gold, multiplying horses, and taking foreign women as his wives (see Deuteronomy 17:16-17), which led to his

---

[1] This is noted by scholars from a wide range of denominational backgrounds.

[2] There are some ancient Greek manuscripts which read 616 instead of 666. Conveniently enough, the Latin version of Nero's name, in Hebrew letters is 616.

downfall. In Revelation, Nero is at the height of his power, and soon after this, he meets his downfall.

WHAT DOES THIS MEAN FOR US TODAY?

Keep things in focus

Just as Jesus gave a warning to stay faithful or suffer the consequences when discussing the sea beast (Rome), he closes this section with a reminder to *keep things in focus*. Yes, things are going to be very hard on Christians, but remember Nero is just a man; your eternity lies in God's hands, not Nero's. The same is true with any person today, regardless of how powerful they may be. *Your eternity lies in God's hands, not the hands of a politician.*

Keep your eyes on God.

It doesn't matter how smooth someone talks, or what wonderful things they claim to do, *if they lead away from God they are the enemy. Never worship anything or anyone but God.*

Persecution is real—and is part of being a Christian.

Don't give in to persecution, and know it is going to come. "Those who live godly in Christ Jesus <u>will</u> suffer persecution (2 Timothy 3:12).

You are marked. But you get to decide by whom.

You are either marked by God or marked by Satan—there is no middle ground. But each person chooses whose they are. Do you belong to Christ?

STUDY THIRTY-THREE: THE LAMB ON MT. ZION (REVELATION 14:1-5)

I am in a strait betwixt two; having a desire to depart and be with Christ, which is far better (Philippians 1:23).

But you have come to Mt. Zion, and to the city of the living God, the heavenly Jerusalem, and to an innumerable company of angels (Hebrews 12:22).

"...don't hurt the earth, neither the sea, nor the trees, till we have sealed the servants of God in their foreheads." And I heard the number of those who were sealed, and there were sealed 144,000 of all the tribes of the children of Israel (Revelation 7:3-4).

Nevertheless, the foundation of God stands secure, having this seal: the Lord knows those who are His, and, let everyone that names the name of Christ depart from iniquity (2 Timothy 2:19).

...That the name of our Lord Jesus Christ may be glorified in you (2 Thessalonians 1:12).

And I looked and behold, a Lamb stood on the Mt. Zion, and with Him 144,000, having His Father's name written in their foreheads (Revelation 14:1).

As you look back on the previous chapter, you've seen Satan bringing Nero and the Roman Empire (the Sea Beast) into the battle, as well as the leaders of the Jewish nation (the Land Beast). The Jews were "encouraged" (by threats of expulsion or death) to offer praise and worship to Rome. Those who praised Nero (whether they meant it or not) had the mark of the beast—the mark signifying they belonged to Nero. But as a marked contrast, in chapter 14, John sees another sight: the Lamb on Mt. Zion surrounded by the 144,000 who had the name of *God* on their forehead.

THE LAMB ON MT. ZION (14:1)

And I looked and behold, a Lamb stood on the Mt. Zion, and with Him 144,000, having His Father's name written in their foreheads (Revelation 14:1).

Who is the Lamb?

As you saw in chapter 5, the Lamb is Jesus Christ, the Lamb slain for the sins of the world (5:5-6). His death was ordained before the foundation of the world (13:8).

What or where is Mt. Zion?

There was a physical Mt. Zion in Jerusalem, where the temple was built by Solomon.[1] To Jews, Zion was the holiest place of all. In fact, the name Zion became virtually synonymous with Jerusalem. For example: Isaiah prophesied "out of Zion shall go forth the law, the word of the Lord from Jerusalem." (Isaiah 2:3). And in fulfillment of that prophecy, on the day of Pentecost, the apostles preached from the temple— on Mt. Zion!

However, there is also a spiritual Mt. Zion. Many this passage in Revelation describes heaven, but it doesn't. Take a look at what another inspired writer said about it.

Hebrews 12:22-24—But you have come to Mt. Zion, and to the city of the living God, the heavenly Jerusalem, and to an innumerable company of angels, to the general assembly and church of the firstborn ones, which are written in heaven, and to God the

---

[1] As way of confusing people, there are two mountains/hills in Jerusalem called Mt. Zion. One is the "old" Mt. Zion, and the other is "New Mt. Zion." Why they couldn't have picked a different name, I don't know.

Judge of all, and to the spirits of righteous men made perfect, and to Jesus, the mediator of the new covenant, and to the blood of sprinkling, that speaks better things than that of Abel.

The writer of Hebrews told living, breathing, not-yet-dead Christians *they had already come* [past tense] *to Mt. Zion.* They weren't in heaven, but they were already at this new Mt. Zion. According to the writer, Mt. Zion is the same as the "church of the firstborn ones."[2] All Christians are counted as firstborn ones, and so each receives a full inheritance.

This image of Christ on Mt. Zion may be two-fold.

It most definitely pictures Christ among His church, the saved, the redeemed (see v.. 4). But it may also picture Christ standing with His people, ready to judge Jerusalem by means of the gospel which was proclaimed (see v.. 6).

THE 144,000 (VERSES 1-5)

And I looked and behold, a Lamb stood on the Mt. Zion, and with Him 144,000, having His Father's name written in their foreheads. And I heard a voice from heaven, like the voice of many waters, like the voice of a great thunder, and I heard the voice of harpers harping with their harps. And they sung something like a new song before the throne, and before the four creatures, and the elders: and no man could learn that song but the 144,000 which were redeemed from the land. These are those who were not defiled with women; for they are virgins. These are those who follow the Lamb wherever he goes. These were redeemed from among men, being the first-

---

[2] The word "firstborn" is plural in Greek, so it is literally the *firstborn ones*.

fruits to God and to the Lamb. And in their mouth was found no guile: for they are without fault before the throne of God.

These 144,000 have the name of God on their foreheads.

These are the same ones who—in chapter 7—were sealed by God on their foreheads. They wore God's name proudly. Since the 144,000 is the same group mentioned in that chapter, let's remember what was said about them.

- They were from the house of Israel—they were physical Israelites.
- They were servants of God, sealed before destruction was let loose on the Promised Land.
- The 144,000 was representative of all Israelites (twelve tribes) who became Christians (as taught by the twelve apostles), too many to count (the figurative use of the number 1,000).

Now, back to chapter 14.

The 144,000 were redeemed (purchased) from the land.

Acts 20:28 says *the church* is purchased by God. God hasn't purchased anyone else. This confirms these 144,000 are Christians.

These were purchased from the earth—the land—the Promised Land, confirming the 144,000 are specifically Jewish Christians.

They stand on Mt. Zion for all the other Jews to see.

They are an example of holiness. They wear the name of God as opposed to the name of the beast. Everyone is marked by one or the other.

They were not defiled with women, for they were virgins.

It is important that we remember this part of the verse, for it helps us to understand *we are dealing with figurative language.* The "Jehovah's Witnesses" take chapter seven and say that literally only 144,000 people will be in heaven. However, the 144,000 are all men!

Which means (if their doctrine were true) no women will be in heaven. Also, the 144,000 are all virgins! Which means, with the possible exception of Paul, none of the apostles will be in heaven! Obviously, God does not intend us to take this *literally*.

These 144,000 were *spiritually* pure, spiritually virgins. They were betrothed to Jesus Christ.

> *I have betrothed you to one husband, that I may present you as a chaste virgin to Christ (2 Corinthians 11:2).*

They were redeemed from among men.

The word for "men" here is *anthropos* (as in "anthropology"), and it means mankind, humanity. They responded to Jesus' invitation.

These are the first-fruits to God and the Lamb.

What does first-fruits mean here? Romans 1:16 has the answer.

> *For I am not ashamed of the gospel of Christ, for it is the power of God unto salvation to every one that believeth to the Jew first and also to the Greek.*

Who were the first ones to hear and respond to the gospel? The Jews. Therefore, who were the first-fruits to God and Christ? The Jews who obeyed the gospel.

These are the Jews who—even under the persecution and pressure put on them by Rome and the Jewish leaders—would not bow down their knee to Baal (or Rome). These are the ones who stood with Christ (they are standing with the Lamb), regardless of what came from their fellow-countrymen.

In their mouth was no guile, and they are without fault before the throne of God.

This means they were Christ-like (1 Peter 2:22). Being without fault means they had been forgiven by the blood of the Lamb, and were now blameless before God. In other words, these were faithful and forgiven Christians.

The conclusion of these two symbols (the Lamb on Mt. Zion and the 144,000) is this: Jesus stands with His true disciples.

Picture this in context: John describes scary beasts, leading people away from God, killing and persecuting Christians. Any person standing there, seeing what he is seeing, would feel stress, worry, maybe even *hopelessness*. But then he looks another direction, and sees the hero—the Lamb—surrounded by 144,000 faithful followers, and it sounds like singing from heaven filling the air.

John must have felt relief, joy, courage. *The war is not over. We have not lost.*

This war is for the minds (foreheads) of men. It's a war between being marked for God and being marked for Satan. The ones on Mt. Zion made their choice to stand with the Lamb, and are completely forgiven in the sight of God.

What about you? Have you truly given your mind over to God in faithful obedience? Are you truly in the spiritual Mt. Zion, the heavenly Jerusalem, the church of Jesus Christ?

THE SOUNDS (VERSES 2-3)

> *And I heard a voice from heaven, like the voice of many waters, like the voice of a great thunder, and I heard the voice of harpers harping with their harps. And they sung something like a new song before the throne, and before the four creatures, and the elders: and no man could learn that song but the 144,000 which were redeemed from the land.*

There was a voice as of many waters that came from heaven.

It was loud, roaring, some might say majestic. Jesus' voice was described the same way (Revelation 1:15).

The sound was like the voice of great thunder.

Every time a voice of thunder or thunders is mentioned in the Bible, it originates with God or Christ (Job 40:9; Psalm 77:18, 104:7; see Revelation 6:1).

The sound was like harpers harping with their harps.

This sound was (1) like many waters, (2) like great thunder, and (3) like professional harpists playing harps. This isn't three different sounds, but three different ways of describing how it sounded to John (sorry to those who thought we all get harps when we get to heaven).

Though it was loud and thunderous, it was beautiful and melodious. It was coming *from heaven*, and was heard by the 144,000 on Mt. Zion. Thunder can be scary—and what God describes in Revelation can be scary, to those who reject His Son. But the judgment of God is sweet, sweet music to those who follow Jesus Christ.

They sang a new song—the Song of Moses.

The only ones who could learn it are those 144,000. This song is later called "the Song of Moses the servant of God and the song of the Lamb" (Revelation 15:2-3).

Before we go any further, remember this song is coming *from heaven*, and it sounds scary (voice of thunders) to the lost, but sounds sweet (beautiful harp music) to the righteous. With that in mind—especially the *scary* part—let's continue.

The "Song of Moses" is recorded in Deuteronomy 32:1-43, and ends with these words:

> *He will avenge the blood of His servants, and will render vengeance to His adversaries, and will be merciful to His land and to His people.*

In Revelation 15:4, the song includes the words "Your judgments are made manifest [openly displayed, shown to all]."

This is a song of judgment *against the Jewish nation,* promised by God in the Old Testament, and fulfilled by Christ when Jerusalem was destroyed and the Jews were completely rejected.

WHAT DOES THIS MEAN FOR US TODAY?

Don't give up—Jesus the hero has this under control.

Satan is on the warpath, Christianity is under attack, but **the** faithful stand with Jesus Christ.

Judgment doesn't have to be scary—if we are faithful.

The faithful hear a song of judgment against the enemies of the cross, and a song od salvation for God's true people.

Faithful Christians have been redeemed from the enemy's camp.

Jesus purchased us with His own blood. That blood completely forgives our sins. So long as we are following and standing with Christ, we can rest assured of our salvation (1 John 1:7, 9; 5:13).

Only the faithful win the victory with Jesus Christ!

Study Thirty-Four:
Three Angels and a Blessing
(Revelation 14:6-13)

In the first century, Christians evangelized with a sense of urgency. They taught, "Repent or perish" (like Christ in Luke 13:3). They taught the urgent need to "save yourselves from *this* wicked generation" (Acts 2:40). They warned people to flee from the "wrath to come." They taught about the results of rejecting Christ: "Judgment to come" (Acts 24:25).

Why did they preach with such urgency? Because they had a deadline—an hour of judgment was about to come, and once it did, millions of souls would no longer have a chance to hear the gospel.

THE FIRST ANGELIC MESSAGE:
PREACH THE GOSPEL! (14:6-7)

And I saw another angel fly in the midst of heaven, having the everlasting gospel to preach to those who dwell on the land, and to every nation, and tribe, and tongue, and people, saying with a loud voice, "Fear God, and give glory to him; for the hour of his judgment is come: and worship him that made heaven, and earth, and the sea, and the fountains of waters."

Another angel flies in the midst of heaven.
This is a reference back to Revelation 8:13, where an angel had flown in the midst of heaven proclaiming "woe, woe, woe." Some translations have "eagle" in 8:13, but this verse indicates that "angel" is the proper translation there.

This angel had the everlasting gospel.

Heavenly angels don't do the preaching (see Acts 8:26, 10:3-6). This is something reserved for human messengers of God (2 Corinthians 4:7).

This everlasting gospel was to be preached to...

Those who dwelt on the land (Jews who lived in the Promised Land). And every nation, tribe [see Matthew 24:30], tongue, and people (a.k.a. Jews who didn't live in the Promised Land—see Acts 2:5-6). The reason given by the angel proves the Jews are the objects of the preaching.

Preach because the hour of God's judgment has come.

God's judgment had arrived—but against whom? Not the entire world (which is still here nearly 2,000 years later), but on one specific group of people: the Jews. But God, in His grace and mercy, wants them to have another chance to repent before they are destroyed.

Some scoff at the idea that this is directed only to the Jews, because aren't the Gentiles supposed to hear the gospel too? Of course they are (Acts 10-11 proves it). But Gentiles aren't under consideration in this context—this is a specific mission to preach to a specific group of people. This isn't a new concept either. Jonah was told to go preach to Nineveh—not Israel, not Egypt, not Greece, not Persia, but just Nineveh. God was going to destroy Nineveh in 40 days, but gave them one last chance to repent. In the same way, the angel gives a commission for the gospel to be preached again to the Jews, as one last chance for them to repent before God brings down the judgment-hammer.

The message is, "Fear God, and give glory to HIM! Because the hour of His judgment has come!"

Remember, at this point the Jews were throwing their support behind the beast—Nero—and joining him in opposition to God and His Christ. They were giving glory to *Rome*, and as such were about to become the victims of God's vengeance.

If they didn't repent, they would perish (see Luke 13:1-5).

The first angel's message helps identify the topic of Revelation.

> *Matthew 24:14—This gospel of the kingdom shall be preached in all the world for a witness to all nations; and then the end shall come.*

Immediately after saying this, Jesus said the "abomination of desolation" (Luke 21:20 calls it "Jerusalem surrounded by armies") would happen, and the church was to flee to the mountains. The context of Matthew 24 describes Jerusalem's destruction after the gospel had been preached throughout the "whole world." The "whole world" there is a reference to the Roman Empire (Luke uses the same word to refer to the Roman Empire in Luke 2:1; Acts 11:28; 17:6; 19:27; 24:5).[1]

The angel's message is the gospel must be preached because the hour of God's judgment *against Jerusalem* had come.

So here is the question: Did the gospel of Christ, including the warnings of judgment and the call to repentance, get preached to the whole world (the Roman Empire)? It sure seems so, since Paul, around AD 60-61, said, "…the gospel, which you have heard, and which was *preached to every creature under heaven*" (Colossians 1:23). Paul said it was done *before Jerusalem fell.*

THE SECOND ANGELIC MESSAGE: BABYLON IS FALLEN, IS FALLEN! (14:8)

> *And there followed another angel, saying," Babylon is fallen, is fallen, that great city, because she made all nations drink of the wine of the wrath of her fornication."*

---

[1] The idea *may* also be under consideration in Revelation 12:9; 20:2.

It's important to realize the messages of these three angels are connected—one unified message.

The call to repent, the "hour of His judgment" arriving, both included the announcement that Babylon has fallen. This is known as the "prophetic perfect," where something that hasn't happened yet is spoken of as though it already occurred. This is used in the Bible to describe something so certain, there was no doubt—so certain, there was no changing it.

Who is Babylon?

This is a loaded question, and you'll find all kinds of answers both in books and online. But let's ignore all them, and just stick with the Biblical information.

(1) Babylon is "that great city."

The only "great city" mentioned in Revelation was in 11:8—the "great city...where our Lord was crucified." What city was Jesus crucified in?

(2) Babylon is connected with the preaching of the gospel message of God's judgment.

What city's destruction was connected with the first-century gospel message? (see Matthew 24:16ff, Acts 2:16-21)

Some say Babylon is Rome—but Rome wasn't taken until 400 years later; this can hardly be described as "the hour of God's judgment has come."[2]

Babylon is Jerusalem, the great city in which Jesus was crucified, the one whose destruction was foretold by Jesus and the apostles (Matthew 24; Luke 21; 1 John 2:18; 1 Peter 4:7).

Jerusalem was the city to which all Jews looked for their religious identity, their social identity, their national identity, their cultural identity—to them, Jerusalem was the only real city of importance. That is why its destruction would cause all the tribes (of Israel) to mourn (Matthew 24:30).

---

[2] We will deal with this idea with more detail when we cover chapter 18.

I know there are objections to this identification, but don't worry. We will address them when we get to chapter 18 and the destruction of the whore Babylon. We'll also show even more evidence that it *is* Jerusalem.

Babylon made all nations drink of the wine of the wrath of her fornication.

The "wine of wrath" is the wrath of God (see verse 10). Thus, this is better understood as: "Babylon made all nations [partakers of] the wine of the wrath [of God], by [joining in] her fornication."

Jerusalem (embodied in her leaders) held sway over all the Jews across the entire Roman Empire, throughout all the nations. It was the Jewish leaders who enforced Caesar-worship through the synagogues. In this way, they made Jews throughout the Empire engage in spiritual fornication. In the Old Testament (under which Israel was made the "wife" of God), the punishment for fornication and adultery was death (Leviticus 20:10-ff).

Jerusalem, throughout her existence, had engaged in spiritual fornication with many other nations. Egypt, Assyria, Canaan, Philistia, Syria, Babylon, Northern Israel, Rome, etc… This isn't anything new. But it is the final straw. They led people away from Jesus, and toward Rome, giving accolades to King Nero instead of King Jesus.

THE THIRD ANGELIC MESSAGE:
JUDGMENT ON THOSE WHO WORSHIP THE BEAST
(14:9-11)

And the third angel followed them, saying with a loud voice, "If any man worships the beast and his image, and receives his mark in his forehead, or in his hand, that one shall drink of the wine of the wrath of God,

*which is poured out undiluted into the cup of his in-
dignation; and he shall be tormented with fire and
brimstone in the presence of the holy angels, and in
the presence of the Lamb. And the smoke of their torment ascends up forever and ever: and they who worship the beast and his image, and who receive the
mark of his name have no rest day nor night.*

Though Jerusalem encouraged reverence to Caesar and Rome in
an attempt to eradicate Christianity, it was still up to each individual
what he was going to do.

*"If any **man** [individual] worships the beast or his
image...or receives his mark..."*

*"We ought to obey God rather than man" (Acts
5:29).*

Truly pious Jews refused to submit to Caesar worship, were
kicked out of the synagogues, and were turned over to the Roman
authorities. Not every Jew was branded with the mark of the beast.
However, because they rejected Christ, these religious Jews were
still guilty of the fornication of their nation. But also remember,
Christian Jews still met with other Jews in the synagogues on the
Sabbath (Acts 22:19, 26:11), so they were put under the same pressure.

The three angels warned Christians that the gospel message,
which they had obeyed, had been carried to the whole world. The
time for God's judgment upon Jerusalem (and therefore the Jews)
was here.

Christians needed to be aware of where they stood. There is no
straddling the fence! You're either with God or with Jerusalem. One
way you live, the other you die!

The ones with the mark of the beast would be forced to drink the undiluted wine of the wrath of God.

This term is used in the Old Testament when God's about to overthrow a nation (see Obadiah 16).

They would drink God's wrath unmixed (undiluted) in the cup of his indignation, and receive the full power of God's wrath. It wouldn't be mixed with mercy, but poured out in pure vengeance.

The ones with the mark of the beast would be tormented with fire and brimstone in the presence of the holy angels and in the presence of the Lamb.

Notice the smoke of their torment ascends up forever and ever, and they have no rest day or night (v.. 11). This describes an endless punishment for these wicked ones who rejected Christ.

Jehovah's Witnesses proclaim when wicked people die, their existence simply ends—no punishment, no pain, no suffering. The Scriptures here (and in Matthew 25) show, after destruction on earth, there is torment in hell.

Perhaps even more significant, this torment is in the presence of the holy messengers and in the presence of the Lamb. Ultimately, Jesus Christ is in charge of hell! Hell is not a place where Satan punishes people, but is a place prepared for the punishment of Satan and his messengers (Matthew 25:41). The Jews opposed to Christ were messengers of Satan, and hell was their destiny.

Worshiping the beast is ultimately worshiping Satan instead of God—and the guilty will have their place in the lake burning with fire and brimstone.

The wicked appear to go immediately to torment/hell upon dying. The rich man, in Jesus' story of the rich man and Lazarus, died and went to torment (Luke 16)—obviously he was judged. Here in Revelation, the enemies of Christ receive God's wrath (destruction here on earth) and go to be tormented forever—there is no indication of an intermediate place between death and punishment.

Great trials, tribulations, and sufferings are coming, but if the Christians give in, the torment gets worse, because it comes from Jesus Christ, and it never ends!

In the face of the Roman and Jewish threats, Christians might be tempted to save their own selves by assenting to worship Caesar. In doing so, they invite torment far worse than anyone on earth could possibly enact against them, for they have made themselves enemies to Jesus Christ.

SEVERE JUDGMENT UPON REJECTERS OF CHRIST (BOTH ON EARTH AND IN ETERNITY), AND A REMINDER TO CHRISTIANS (14:12-13)

Here is the perseverance of the saints, they keep the commandments of God, and the faith of Jesus. And I heard a voice from heaven saying to me, "Write, Blessed are the dead who die in the Lord from now on. Yes," says the Spirit, 'that they may rest from their labors; and their works follow them."

Here is the perseverance of the saints: they keep the commandments of God and the faith of Jesus.

Christians, have patience! Christians, don't give in, just keep God's commandments and hold tight to your faith in Jesus! "Be faithful to death, and I will give you a crown of life!" (Revelation 2:10)

Blessed are the dead who die in the Lord from now on…that they may rest from their labors; and their works follow them."

God lets Christians know, if you die in this Satanic persecution carried out by Rome and Israel, it is a wonderful thing! Because if you die as a Christian, you have rest from your labors, and your works follow you! In other words, your "treasures in heaven" await! You don't have to worry!

The stress and anxiety we have in this life, the struggles we go through, trying to live right while the culture shoves us toward sin—all of this pressure goes away. We have rest. And God, who sees all we have done in His service, who sees our fighting against sin in our own lives, welcomes us into His eternal rest.

So…now we have to figure out what "from now on" means. After all, it has to mean *something*, otherwise God wouldn't have put it in there. There is some blessing that comes to those who die in the Lord *from this point forward* that wasn't given to those who came before.

Some believe (especially with the idea of the wicked going immediately to torment) at AD 70, when the Old Covenant prophecies were fulfilled, Hades was emptied (Revelation 20:13), and all who were there were judged. If this is the case, all who die after that point are judged at their death and immediately go to heaven or hell (see Hebrews 9:27, Philippians 1:23). Thus, the blessing promised in this verse would be immediate transportation to heaven with the Father and Son, without a time of waiting in Hades.

While I'm not completely sold on this interpretation, it is the only one I have found that makes sense in context.

WHAT DOES THIS MEAN FOR US TODAY?

Understanding the post-death timeline is irrelevant.

Let's say we are mistaken on the logistics of what happens when we die—what *really* matters is how we live our lives here! If we are faithful to God here, we are promised Heaven!

If we have to spend some time in a paradise while waiting for it (ala Jesus' promise to the thief on the cross), I'm not going to complain one bit. If we go immediately to heaven, I'm not going to complain, "Hey God, I wanted to spend time in paradise first before I came to see you!"

However, if we aren't faithful to God here, we will suffer the same fate as those who rejected Jesus Christ: eternal torment!

And even if you don't go immediately to hell, you *still* experience fiery torment while waiting to go there (see the rich man and Lazarus in Luke 16)! It is pain beyond your comprehension, beyond man's ability to accurately and fully describe—and there is no end to it, no getting numb to it.

The good news of Jesus Christ is that you don't have to go there. *You have a choice* in the matter! You get to choose heaven, if you want! But you have to give yourself over to Jesus Christ.

Have you?

STUDY THIRTY-FIVE:
THE SON OF MAN ON THE CLOUD
(REVELATION 14:14-20)

In Matthew 24 (discussing the destruction of Jerusalem), Jesus said the tribes of the Land would mourn when they saw Him coming in the clouds. In Revelation 1:7 (in reference to things which were then "shortly come to pass"), John says the same thing.

Now, in Revelation 14, "the Son of man" appears on a cloud, and the end result of the actions is the entire Land covered in blood. In other words, this is the culmination of Jesus' prophecy about coming in judgment upon the rebellious Jewish nation.

THE SON OF MAN WITH A GOLDEN CROWN (14:14)

Then I looked, and behold, a white cloud, and seated on the cloud one like a son of man, with a golden crown on his head, and a sharp sickle in his hand.

Who is this "Son of man"?

This is Jesus. He is the "Son of man [who came] with the clouds of heaven and came to the Ancient of Days…and there was given him dominion, and glory, and a kingdom…which shall not be destroyed" (Daniel 7:13-14).

Jesus called Himself the "Son of man" 85 times in the four gospels, making it His favorite title. It's also noteworthy that the first time He appears in Revelation, that's how John describes Him (Revelation 1:13).

Why is He on a cloud?

As we saw over and over again in the Old Testament (see the section on Revelation 1:7), God coming in the clouds always indicated judgment.

Christ coming on the cloud indicates judgment—this time against the Jewish nation (the same ones referenced in Matthew 24:30 and Revelation 1:7).

Why is He wearing a golden crown?

The crown is golden, showing its lasting value—nothing was as precious or valuable as gold.

It is a *victory* crown (Greek *stephanos*), not a ruling crown. Later on (19:12), Jesus appears wearing many *ruling* crowns (Greek *diadem*). But in this passage, the emphasis is on His victory. He conquered death. He conquered Satan. And now He comes to fight against the rebellious Jews—and His victory is assured.

Why is He holding a sharp sickle?

This is explained in verses 15-16.

THE HARVEST OF THE EARTH (14:15-16)

And another angel came out of the temple, crying with a loud voice to Him who sat on the cloud, "Thrust in your sickle, and reap: for the time has come for you to reap; for the harvest of the land is ripe." And He who sat on the cloud thrust His sickle in the land; and the land was reaped.

Before we go any further, you need to realize there are *two* reapings in this chapter. Look at the differences to see for yourself.

Reaping 1 (Verses 15-16)	Reaping 2 (Verses 17-20)
Jesus does the reaping	Angel does the reaping
Angel comes from the temple	Angel comes from temple *in heaven*
Harvest of grain?	Harvest of clusters of grapes
Harvest is "ripe"	Harvest is "fully ripe"
(Greek means "dried")	(different Greek word)
No negative effects	Floods the land with blood

Now, on to the text!

An angel came out of the temple.

This angel came out of "the temple," but the next angel came out of "the temple *in heaven*." This first angelic messenger came from the temple John was most familiar with: the temple in Jerusalem.

The angel's announcement: "Thrust in your sickle and reap: for the time has come for you to reap...the harvest of the land is ripe."

And immediately, Christ (the One sitting on the cloud) thrust in his sickle, and the earth/land was reaped. But what is this reaping? What does it mean? When did it happen?

Some (wrongly) believe this is the same "reaping" or "harvesting" as the one in verses 17-20, making this a description of the destruction of the Jews and their temple. But as we noted on the previous page, the differences show these are two different events.

The word "ripe" in verse 15 could also be translated "dried." In fact, of the 16 times this word appears in the New Testament, this is the *only* time it is translated "ripe." There is a crop that is ripe and ready to be harvested when it is dry: *wheat*. Interestingly, Jesus gave a parable of "the wheat and the tares," in which the wheat represented His people: faithful Christians (Matthew 13:24-30, 36-40). They were supposed to be gathered first.

In Matthew 24:30-31, speaking of events preceding the destruction of Jerusalem, Jesus says:

> *"And they shall see the Son of man coming in the clouds of heaven with power and great glory. And he shall send His angels with a great sound of a trumpet, and they shall gather together His elect from the four winds, from one end of heaven to the other."*

This describes Jesus gathering His people together and taking them to safety. This happened when Christians around Jerusalem saw the signs Jesus foretold and ran to the mountains and the wilderness called Pella.

The first harvest in Revelation 14 is Jesus gathering His people together so that they can avoid the wrath of God about to be poured out. Notice the "ripe/dried" crops harvested are just gathered—nothing is done to them afterwards. And they are collected from the "earth" (land, Promised Land). In the second harvest, the harvested grapes are crushed with God's wrath.

The first harvest is Jesus removing Christians to safety out of the Promised Land, much like the woman taken to the wilderness to be nourished by God in chapter 12.

THE SECOND HARVEST AND THE CRUSHING OF THE GRAPES (14:17-20)

And another angel came out of the temple which is in heaven, also having a sharp sickle. And another angel came from the altar, which had power over fire; and cried loudly to him that had the sharp sickle, saying, "Thrust in your sharp sickle, and gather the clusters of the vine of the earth; for her grapes are fully ripe."

So the angel thrust his sickle into the earth, and gathered the vine of the earth, and cast it into the great winepress of the wrath of God. And the winepress was trodden outside the city, and blood came out of the winepress, even up to the horse bridles, for 1,600 furlongs.

The angel from the temple in heaven.

The text does not leave us to guess where this angel came from. This angel was sent with a mission from God. He had a sharp sickle, everything he needed to complete his job.

The angel from the altar.

This angel "had power over fire." I think we've seen this angel before. After the seventh seal was opened, an angel stood by the altar, holding a golden censor, filling it with fire from the heavenly altar, and casting it down to the earth (Revelation 8:3-5). Since it's the same angel, we are expected to connect the two events.

In chapter 8, he acted immediately before the seven trumpets were blown (8:5-7). In chapter 14, he acts immediately before the seven bowls of wrath are poured out (14:17-chapter 15).

In chapter 8, the fire from this angel was a sign of judgment coming from God. In chapter 14, the cry of this angel was a sign of judgment coming from God.

The command from the angel: "Thrust in your sharp sickle, and gather the clusters of the vine of the earth, for her grapes are fully ripe." The grapes were fully ripe: their time had come.

What is this harvest?

First, let's look at a couple Old Testament passages which will shine some light on the situation.

Genesis 15:16—"the iniquity of the Amorites is *not yet full.*" There was a time when, although they were opposed to God, they hadn't reached a level so bad God was through with them. But when their sin reached a certain point, God destroyed them. Leviticus 18:24 (speaking of the Amorites and others)—"the nations *which I cast out before you* are defiled." I Kings 21:26—the *Amorites, whom the LORD cast out* before the children of Israel. They were fully ripe for the uprooting.

But even more eye-opening is this:

> *...My well-beloved has a vineyard on a very fruitful hill. He fenced it, and removed the stones that were there, and planted it with the best grapevine, and built a tower in the middle of it, and also made a winepress in it. And he looked for it to produce grapes, but it produced wild grapes.*

And now, O inhabitants of Jerusalem, and men of Judah, judge, I ask you, between me and my vineyard. What could have been done more to my vineyard, that I have not done? Why, when I looked for it to produce grapes, did it produce wild grapes?

And now come, I will tell you what I will do to my vineyard: I will take away its protection, and it shall be eaten up; I will break down its wall, and it shall be trodden down. And I will lay it waste: it will not be pruned, nor tilled; but briars and thorns will come up. I will also command the clouds that they do not rain upon it.

For the vineyard of the LORD of hosts is the house of Israel*, and the men of Judah his pleasant plant. He looked for justice, but behold oppression; He looked for righteousness, but behold a cry.*

Woe to them that join house to house, that lay field to field, till there is no room, that they stand alone in the middle of the land!

I heard the LORD of hosts say, "Truly many houses will be desolate, even big and fancy houses, without inhabitant.

God's vineyard (His grapevine) is "the house of Israel, and the men of Judah" (v. 8). And because of their actions, God said "I will lay it waste" (v. 7). Any Jewish reader of Revelation would immediately recognize what God meant here. They, the Jews, had been God's vineyard, His grapes. And things were about to get very bad.

Now, let's look back at Revelation.

"Gather the clusters of the vine of the earth, for her grapes are fully ripe."

The "vine of the earth" is Israel, God's vineyard which He planted over a thousand years earlier. The grapes are fully ripe—the time had come to remove them.

The vine cast into the winepress

> *"And the angel thrust his sickle into the earth and gathered the vine of the earth and cast it into the great winepress of the wrath of God."*

It wasn't just the grapes—*the entire vine* was uprooted and thrown into the winepress of the wrath of God. The entire plant was now worthless to God. No grapes were spared. God uproots Israel, removing them completely as His people.

Then they are crushed in the winepress of God's wrath. This is parallel to their being forced to drink of the wine of God's wrath from the cup of His indignation (14:10).

The crushing of the grapes in the winepress

Who did the treading? God said:

> *I have trodden the winepress alone; none of the people were there with me: for I will tread them in my anger, and trample them in my fury; and their blood shall be splattered on my garments, and I will stain all my clothes (Isaiah 63:3).*

Revelation 19:13-16 describes Jesus in an interesting way:

> *...clothed with a garment covered in blood: and his name is called the Word of God...and he treads the winepress of the fierceness and wrath of God. And he has on his robe and on His thigh a name written, King of Kings and Lord of Lords.*

In Isaiah, God says He alone treads the winepress. In Revelation, it is Christ. This is yet another proof Jesus is God.

But it also shows who is behind the Jews' destruction. This is the "coming of the Son of man" described in Matthew 24:30—a coming in judgment upon the rebellious Jews who had murdered Jesus.

Outside the city

It is appropriate it was "outside the city," for that is where Jesus was crucified. Now the man on the cross, "the stone that the builders rejected," would crush them—"And whoever falls on this stone will be broken: but when it falls on someone, it will grind him to powder" (Matthew 21:42-44).

The measurement of blood

The blood was around five feet deep (give or take), and stretched for 1,600 furlongs. That is approximately 200 miles. And it just so happens to be the size of the Promised Land.[1] In other words, this is a figurative way of saying Jesus will cover the Promised Land with the blood of His enemies, the Jews who rejected and killed Him and His followers.

WHAT DOES THIS MEAN FOR US TODAY?

Salvation is NOT once-saved always saved.

Jesus Christ is the judge of all (2 Timothy 4:1), and He will give eternal rest or eternal destruction (Matthew 25:31-46). Revelation teaches us if God's people reject Him, they will be rejected *by* Him.

God is a God of love, and was long-suffering to the Jews, desiring that they repent. But God is also a God of justice, judgment, and vengeance towards those who will not repent (see 2 Thessalonians 1:8).

---

[1] This fact is noted by such scholars as Charles Wesley, Albert Barnes, B.W. Johnson, A.T. Robinson, John Gill, and Matthew Henry

God controls the downfall of nations

God has no qualms destroying an entire nation if they reject Him. Just because a nation claims to be a "Christian" nation doesn't make it so. America is not immune from being overthrown by God.

Get to be friends with the Judge.

Because Christ is the judge of all, we should want to be on His side. If you want the final Judge to be your friend, to proclaim you innocent and free, you must come to where He is. You must "obey the gospel." Jesus said, "You are my friends, *if you do what I have commanded you*" (John 15:13-14).

Have you?

STUDY THIRTY-SIX:
THE SPIRITUAL EXODUS
(REVELATION 15)

Glimpses of the Old Testament flash across the pages of Revelation. Characters who mirror Old Testament figures. Apocalyptic imagery (fire, rainbows, lightning, thunder, coming in a cloud, etc…) that originated in Old Testament books. And who can forget the reference to "Egypt" in chapter 11—the ones who had kept God's people in bondage?

As we move on to chapter 15, keep the Exodus from literal Egypt in your mind, because starting here, God presents "The Spiritual Exodus." The events are not a perfect chronological match with the original Exodus, but the figures, ideas, and principles are the same.

THE GREAT SIGN IN HEAVEN (15:1)

> *And I saw another sign in heaven, great and marvelous, seven angels having the seven last plagues; for in them is filled up the wrath of God.*

It was sign "great and marvelous".

The Spoken English New Testament (SENT) says "awesome and amazing."

A sign *always* points to something. John calls it a sign because we are to *interpret* it, to see what it symbolizes or points to.

Seven angels having the seven final plagues.

Seven represents completeness or fullness. So the seven final plagues contain the complete or full wrath of God.

The text doesn't say if John somehow *saw* the plagues being carried by the angels, or if the angels embodied these plagues, or if the angels just had the power to enact these last plagues.

Literally, the text says the seven angels have "the seven plagues— the final ones."

Plagues aren't a foreign idea in Revelation (two are mentioned in 9:20). Those plagues were meant to get the Jews to repent, but they wouldn't.

The plagues here are the final ones in which God pours out His wrath on them—and there is no escape. Let us all learn from the judgments of the past so we can avoid judgment to come!

THE GATHERED SAINTS BY THE SEA OF GLASS AND FIRE (15:2-4)

And I saw something like a sea of glass mingled with fire: and those who had gained the victory over the beast, and over his image, and over his mark, and over the number of his name, stand on the sea of glass, having the harps of God. And they sing the song of Moses the servant of God, and the song of the Lamb, saying, "Great and marvelous are Your works, Lord God Almighty; righteous and true are Your ways, You King of saints. Who will not fear You, O Lord, and glorify Your name? For You alone are holy: for all nations shall come and worship before You; for Your judgments are made clear.

In the vision, John saw the sea of glass.

This sea has appeared before (Revelation 4:6). The Old Testament temple also had a "sea" where the priests had to wash in order to be acceptable in service to God. Like then, like now, you got to go through the water to get to God!

In this image of the sea of glass is the idea of "the washing of regeneration" (Titus 3:5), baptism. How can I know this? Stick around and it will become clear.

This sea of glass was mingled with fire (we'll hit this point in a minute).

The saints stood by the sea of glass.

The KJV says "*on* the sea of glass," while others say "*by* the sea" (ASV, NET) or "*beside* the sea" (ESV, NRSV, NIV). One translation[1] had a footnote which said, "on the shores of the sea of glass." Given the Old Testament imagery from this chapter, *beside* is probably the most accurate understanding.

The ones standing there had won victory over the beast, and over his image, and over his number of his name. Literally, the Greek says "the victors *out of* the beast, and from his image, and from the number of his name." The beast had persecuted them, tried to devour them, but they escaped from his clutches!

This image of the saints in the presence of God by the sea of glass comes from the book of Exodus. The LORD saved the Israelites *out of* the hand of the Egyptians (Exodus 14:30). Immediately after crossing the Red Sea, they sang a song of praise to God (Exodus 15:1-19).

- It was a song led by Moses (v. 1).
- It was a song of triumph over their enemies (2).
- It was a song praising God's conquering powers (3-10).
- It was a song praising God as over all other things which are worshiped (12).
- It was a song of mercy on the redeemed (13)
- It was a song of establishment for God's people (17)

In this chapter of Revelation, immediately after they are delivered *out of* the hand of the enemy, the saints by the sea sang a song of praise to God (Revelation 15:3-4).

- It was "the song of Moses" (v. 3).

---

[1] Spoken English New Testament (SENT)

- It was a song of triumph over their enemies (v. 3). God delivered them from the Romans and the Jewish nation. 12:11 calls it "the song of the Lamb"—the one whose blood gave them the victory.
- It was a song praising God as the one over all things which are worshiped (4).
- It was a song of God's mercy on His people (3).

Back to the sea of glass mingled with fire.

In order to be where God was, they had to go through the sea (the water). It was a difficult time, being slaves in Egypt, but once they crossed the Red Sea, they had peace and were free. The apostle Paul described the crossing of the Red Sea as a baptism (1 Corinthians 10:1-2).

Here in Revelation, echoing Exodus, the sea symbolizes the spiritual Exodus and salvation from the bondage of the Jews (spiritually called Egypt, Revelation 11:8). Christians are saved by water (1 Peter 3:20-21), and are safe on the other side.

But now, it is mingled with fire—representative of God's judgment. It is possible this points to the baptism of fire (Matthew 3:10-12)—a prophecy of the violent end of the whole Jewish system, which would be carried out by Jesus Christ. The baptism of fire idea fits the context in the following ways:

- Water freed the Israelites during the Exodus, but also destroyed their enemies.
- Water saved Noah and his family (1 Peter 3:20-21), but also destroyed the enemies of God.
- Salvation and judgment at the same time.

The sea of glass represented salvation for God's people, but it represented destruction for God's enemies. Part of the song they sang while by the sea of glass was "Your judgments are made clear" (v. 4).

In the Old Testament Exodus, the song was sung after the plagues, after the enemy had been completely broken.

In the Revelation Exodus, the song was sung *before* the final plagues, *before* the enemy had been completely broken. But the song was sung with assurance—because they knew the outcome before it happened.

Wouldn't it be best to learn the lessons BEFORE the bad things happen?

The wonderfully gracious God of heaven revealed we can be in His loving presence forever, if we become one of His people. But He also revealed the full weight of His destructive powers on those who reject Him.

Basically, the choice is: "do you want a million dollars, or do you want to lose everything you own and be tortured with fire?" But people *still choose the fire*!!

THE TEMPLE IN HEAVEN, THE COMPLETE WRATH OF GOD, AND THE PRESENCE OF GOD (15:5-8)

And after that, I looked, and behold, the temple of the tabernacle of the testimony in heaven was opened. And the seven angels came out of the temple, clothed in pure white linen, having the seven plagues, and having golden sashes around their chest. And one of the four creatures gave to the seven angels seven golden bowls full of the wrath of God, who lives forever and ever. And the temple was filled with smoke from the glory of God, and from his power; and no one was able to enter into the temple, till the seven plagues of the seven angels were fulfilled.

After the song concluded, John saw the temple of the tabernacle of the testimony in heaven was opened.

The "tabernacle of the testimony" refers to the first tabernacle, built by Moses after the Exodus from Egypt (Numbers 9:15). It was a temporary, movable building, filled by the presence of God.

The "*temple* of the tabernacle of the testimony" was the permanent dwelling place of God.

This scene is a connection. At the end of Revelation 11, the seventh trumpet had sounded, judgment upon Jerusalem and her people was announced, and the temple of God in heaven opened up (11:15-19). Now, we are again shown the temple opening up—reminding us what is happening: judgment against Jerusalem has been announced, it is as good as done.

In a way, chapters 12-14 summarize what led to this point, and now we continue where we left off at the end of chapter 11. What follows is seven last plagues—the final actions against Jerusalem, her temple, and her people.

Seven angels came out of the temple.

These are the angels mentioned in verse 1. The pure white linen shows purity, holiness.

The golden sashes around their chest are like Jesus' attire in chapter 1. There, Jesus was shown as the true High Priest in the heavenly temple. The angels wear the clothing of their Master; doing the bidding of Christ. In a way, they were serving as priests of God in His holy heavenly temple.

The golden bowls are distributed.

One of the four creatures (which one is unknown) handed each of the angels a golden bowl. These bowls were filled with the wrath of God, who lives forever and ever—He will never be defeated. He is eternal, and cannot be destroyed.

I'm not quite sure what bowls of wrath look like, but I bet it isn't a pleasant sight.

In chapter 14, the Jews were made to drink the wine of the wrath of God from the cup of indignation, and were crushed in the wine-press of His wrath. We now see wrath from three directions:

- The wine would kill them from the inside—God's wrath exercised through the Jewish civil wars.
- The winepress would kill them from the outside—God's wrath exercised through the Roman armies.
- The golden bowls poured the wrath from above—God's direct action in the destruction of the city, temple, and people.

The glory of God filled the temple.

When the tabernacle (a temporary house) was built, the glory of God filled it like a cloud (Exodus 40:34). When the temple (a semi-permanent house) was built, the glory of God filled it like a cloud (1 Kings 8:10-11). And now, the glory of God fills the temple in heaven (the true permanent house of God). This was a symbol of the presence of God.

No man could enter into the temple until the seven plagues were fulfilled.

When the cloud filled the tabernacle, no man could enter—not even Moses (Exodus 40:34-35). When the cloud filled the temple, no man could enter—not even the priests (1 Kings 8:10-11). When the cloud fills the heavenly temple, no man could enter (Revelation 15:8).

But why couldn't anyone enter in until the plagues were completed?

The plagues culminated in the complete destruction of Jerusalem and the earthly temple, and the complete, permanent rejection of the Jewish people as God's chosen ones.

While Christ's earthly work was completed at the cross, the work of redemption was not completed until all Old Testament prophecy was completed. Jesus said this would take place when Jerusalem was destroyed (Luke 21:20-22).

When John the baptizer began preaching, he connected Christ's mission with redemption and of baptizing in fire (destruction of the Jewish nation and their capitol city). Jesus proclaimed salvation, but also His coming in judgment upon Jerusalem (Matthew 24). The beginning of the church started with a prophecy which mentioned (in apocalyptic language) the overthrow of a nation (Acts 2:16-21), so the two were connected.

It was when Jerusalem was finally destroyed that the prophesied work of Jesus was fulfilled completely.

Imagine if Jesus had died on the cross, been resurrected, but then had been unable to carry out His prophecies about destroying Jerusalem in the lifetime of that generation (Matthew 24:34). Jesus would've been a false prophet! And we have to ask this—if Jesus became a false prophet, what about our salvation?

The destruction of Jerusalem was the final redemptive act, the final and ultimate proof Jesus was the Christ. The doors to heaven, to the temple, to the most holy place Jesus had entered on our behalf were officially wide open to all His people; and they could not be shut! Until Jerusalem's destruction, things hadn't become "official," because it was still awaiting the promised fulfillment.

Is it any wonder Revelation is about "things which _must_ shortly come to pass"?

It _had_ to happen because it was a moral necessity. It _had_ to happen because if it didn't, Jesus would have been a false prophet, and our salvation would be voided!

WHAT DOES THIS MEAN FOR US TODAY?

Thank God the things Jesus prophesied _did_ come to pass! We can have faith in our salvation, knowing we have eternal life, if we are one of His people, separated from sin and brought into the presence of God through the washing of regeneration—baptism.

Have you been to Jesus for the cleansing flood?

Study Thirty-Seven:
The Bowls of Wrath (Part 1)
(Revelation 16:1-11)

A former preacher's son was brutally raped and murdered by a so-called Christian. The murderer then turned the gun on himself and fired. The preacher's anguish was indescribable, but there was also a deep yearning for vengeance—a vengeance he would never be able to carry out.

He said he wanted to raise that man from the dead and brutally kill him, and then do it over and over again.

You may say, "That's a horrible attitude to have!" but I ask you this: what would your feelings be if someone you had trusted, someone who you had invited into your home as an honored guest, had done this to your own child?

Why do I bring this up? God had treated Israel with love and kindness, invited her into His presence. Gave them everything they could've ever needed. They were his special people. And then they brutally beat, mocked, and murdered His Son.

I ask again, how would you have reacted?

Now let's place ourselves back in the first century.

God did not execute judgment immediately against the Jews. Instead He amazed the world by freely offering them His grace! For close to forty years, God's grace was preached to the people who brutally murdered His Son.

However, God is also a God of judgment, thus judgment had to come. They deserved God's vengeance—after all, they murdered His Son. But realize this: God's vengeance was only upon one group of people—Jews who *did not repent* of having murdered Jesus Christ. I mention this, because some of the Jews *did* repent, and became Christians. They escaped before Jerusalem fell. Just like us,

God's attitude toward someone who exhibits true remorse and repentance is massively different from His attitude toward those who refuse to repent.

In this lesson, we look at the bowls of God's wrath, the seven final plagues which culminate in the utter destruction of the Jewish system. You will see God's vengeance poured out, but also see glimpses of God's mercy and grace as well.

Remember, events in Revelation are not all in Chronological order, but are sometimes repeated with different aspects emphasized, and from different vantage points. The comparison of the seven trumpets with the seven bowls of wrath is quite interesting.

1. Trumpet 1—directed towards the land
    Bowl 1—directed towards the land
2. Trumpet 2—a third of the sea became blood
    Bowl 2—all of the sea became as blood.
3. Trumpet 3—star fell and affected the rivers
    Bowl 3—wrath fell and rivers turned to blood.
4. Trumpet 4 - 1/3 of the sun smitten
    Bowl 4—bowl poured on the sun
5. Trumpet 5 –inhabitants of the land tormented but not killed
    Bowl 5—tormented with pain, but not killed.
6. Trumpet 6—deals with the Euphrates
    Bowl 6—deals with the Euphrates.
7. Trumpet 7—final judgment upon Israel from God
    Bowl 7—final judgment upon Israel from God.

One writer said that while the trumpets showed the vision Israel's point of view, the bowls show it from the view of the Roman Empire. This may be the case, though it seems like the bowls of wrath are more intensified (1/3 of men in the sea died in trumpet 2, whereas *all* in the sea died in bowl 2). The trumpets were the warning, the bowls are the final steps to destruction.

THE FIRST BOWL OF WRATH POURED OUT (16:1-2)

And I heard a great voice out of the temple saying to the seven angels, "Go your ways, and pour out the bowls of God's wrath on the land. And the first angel went, and poured out his bowl on the land; and a wicked and evil sore came on the men who had the mark of the beast, and on those who worshipped his image.

First, a voice from the temple commands all the angels to go pour out the bowls of wrath.

This voice was God Himself. The previous verse (15:8) says "The temple was filled with the smoke from the glory of God…and no one could enter it until the seven plagues…were fulfilled." He is the One in the temple.

The angels were commanded to go, pour out their bowls "upon the earth."

This sets the stage for the entire chapter. "Earth" is the same word as "Land" and means "Promised Land." The plagues (all of them) were on the Promised Land and her inhabitants—The Jews.

This may seem confusing, since the angels pour them out on the sun, the sea, the rivers, the "throne of the beast," and the air. But the command from God was to pour out His wrath "upon the Land." Regardless of where it was poured, the result affected the Jews.

The first angel poured his bowl on the land, causing sores on all who wore the mark of the beast.

These seven bowls are also called the seven final plagues (15:8). Any Jew hearing the word "plagues" would've instantly thought back to the ten plagues God sent against Egypt. Because of this, we should expect to see similarities to the plagues of Egypt.

This plague involved "noisome and grievous sores" (KJV) on the ones who worshiped image of the beast and had the mark of the beast. One of the plagues on Egypt was sores on all the Egyptians

(Exodus 9:8-12). The word for "sores" is the same word used in Exodus for "boils."[1]

God sends a plague of horrible sores/boils on the ones who worship the Roman Empire (embodied in Nero). The Jews were almost completely on Nero's side. Any who wouldn't pledge allegiance to Nero as Lord were kicked out of the synagogues, and became outcasts. Just as *physical* Egypt was plagued with boils, *spiritual* Egypt (the Jews, see 11:8) was plagued with gruesome sores.

While these passages are figurative ways of describing the events, there's a reason God describes it this way. Boils are effects of God's wrath on them. And while boils are irritating, bothersome, and painful, they are not deadly. It is a warning that things are going to get worse if they don't repent (and they didn't—Rev. 16:11).

Isaiah 1:6 describes the Israelites' spiritual condition as "putrefying sores."[2] Those who had physical boils were unclean until the boil was healed (Leviticus 13).

This first bowl of wrath is God declaring the Jewish nation unclean in His sight.

THE SECOND BOWL (16:3)

And the second angel poured out his bowl on the sea;
and it became like the blood of a dead man: and
every living soul died in the sea.

Every person in the sea died.
When we discussed the trumpets, we mentioned a passage from Josephus about a great storm which destroyed a significant portion

---

[1] The Greek translation of the Old Testament, done approximately 250 years before Christ, is called the Septuagint, and is abbreviated LXX. It seems to be the preferred translation of the New Testament writers. The first-century Jewish readers would have caught that the same word was used for "boils" in Exodus was used for "sores" in Revelation.

[2] Isaiah 1 sounds eerily like Israel's condition at the time of Revelation.

of Jewish ships and sailors. But what is described here is more than a significant portion, this is a complete destruction.

A large contingent of Jews living near the sea of Galilee had built many ships, knowing the Romans would probably win the battle on land, but they planned to escape into the sea and wage war against the Romans in the water. Vespasian hurriedly built ships, and went after these Jews.

> "As for those that endeavored to come to an actual fight, the Romans ran many of them through with long poles. Sometimes the Romans leaped into their ships, with swords in their hands, and slew them; but when some of them met the vessels, the Romans caught them by the middle [of the ship], and destroyed at once their ships and themselves who were taken in them. And for such as were drowning in the sea, if they lifted their heads up above the water, they were either killed by darts [arrows], or caught by the vessels; but if, in the desperate case they were in, they attempted to swim to their enemies, the Romans cut off either their heads or their hands; and indeed they were destroyed after various manners everywhere, till the rest being put up to flight, were forced to get upon the land, while the vessels encompassed them about (on the sea): but as many of these were repulsed when they were getting ashore, they were killed by the darts upon the lake; and the Romans leaped out of their vessels, and destroyed a great many more upon the land. One might then see the lake all bloody, and full of dead bodies, for not one of them escaped." (Wars of the Jews, 3.10.9)

This bowl marks the beginning of the complete destruction as the Romans marched towards Jerusalem.

THE THIRD BOWL (16:4-7)

And the third angel poured out his bowl on the rivers and springs of waters; and they became blood. And I heard the angel of the waters say, "You are righteous, O Lord, who is, and was, and shall be, because you have judged in this way. For they have shed the blood of saints and prophets, and you have given them blood to drink; for they are worthy." And I heard another out of the altar say, "Even so, Lord God Almighty, true and righteous are your judgments."

The angel poured out wrath on the rivers and springs of water, and they became blood.

This "bowl of wrath," as well as the one before it, mirror the first plague upon Egypt: waters turned to blood. In Exodus, it was a miraculous changing of water to blood. In Revelation, the waters turned to blood because of all the people killed in them.

With the rivers and springs turned to blood, the whole water supply was ruined. No surprise, then, that the angel says God was giving the Jews "blood to drink."

While this is another way of saying that God forced them to drink the wine of His wrath from the cup of His indignation (14:10), there's more to it. Josephus records the horrible condition within the nation during Rome's invasion, when food became scarce.

> "...they drank the blood of the populace to one another, and divided the dead bodies of the poor creatures between them" (Wars, 6.10.5).

This punishment was deserved. The angel said, "They are worthy." Jesus, in Matthew 23:37, said Jerusalem was the city guilty of killing the apostles and prophets. They deserved this destruction. The time of God's grace on them was quickly coming to an end.

Another voice spoke from the altar

The voice from the altar may have been one of the martyred saints (6:10-11) or the angel of the altar who announced the destruction in 14:18. Either way, it was agreement that the Jews deserved what God was dishing out. When judgment comes on us from God (whether in this life or the next), it is deserved and righteous.

THE FOURTH BOWL (16:8-9)

And the fourth angel poured out his bowl on the sun; and power was given to him to scorch men with fire. And men were scorched with great heat, and blasphemed the name of God, who has power over these plagues: and they did not repent to give him glory.

The angel poured the wrath on the sun, which then was used as a weapon upon people in the Promised Land

This is different from the fourth trumpet which symbolically represented a third of the nation being destroyed (1/3 of the sun, moon, and stars were turned to darkness). Here, the sun is turned into a weapon against the Jews.

Isaiah 49:10 was a promise of blessings—"neither heat nor the sun shall smite them." Revelation 7:16-17 spoke of blessings upon the 144,000 (the Jews who became Christians), and included in it was "neither shall the sun light on them, nor any heat." But on the wicked Jews, God turns the sun (symbolically) into a weapon.

Some (like Ogden) believe this is a reference to the fire which the Romans used to destroy many of the cities and the people. Others believe there may also be a reference to a drought that went through the land, the heat being overwhelming.

Instead of repenting, they hardened their hearts and blasphemed.

In one way, we might say God hardened their hearts, because it was through His actions it happened. But ultimately, the choice belonged to the people—and they made the wrong one.

Examine your life and make the choice to repent of your sins and follow God!

THE FIFTH BOWL (16:10-11)

And the fifth angel poured out his bowl on the throne of the beast; and his kingdom was full of darkness; and they gnawed their tongues from pain, and blasphemed the God of heaven because of their pains and their sores, and did not repent of their deeds.

The fifth angel poured his bowl on the throne of the beast, and his kingdom was full of darkness.

The beast was the Roman Empire, embodied in Nero. His "seat" (KJV) or "throne" (NIV) was Rome itself. The war against the Jews began in early AD 67, but by the middle of AD 68, the Roman Empire was in great turmoil. Things were so bad that the senate decreed Nero must die. Most historians say instead of facing death at the hands of the senators, Nero murdered himself.

After this event, civil war erupted throughout the Roman Empire. The Celts revolted, the Gauls began to fight back. Three more emperors took the throne and were either killed or committed suicide before AD 69 was over. Vespasian halted the campaign against the Jews and returned to Rome where he took the reins of the government and brought back stability.

It was about this time of turmoil Josephus says,

"Those Jews…were also in a flourishing condition for strength and riches" [during this year of reprieve, they stockpiled gold and built weapons] "for the Jews hoped that all of their nation which were beyond the Euphrates would have raised an insurrection together with them. The Gauls also, in the neighborhood of the Romans, were in motion, and the Celts were not quiet; but all was in disorder after the death of Nero."

The Jews in Palestine were trying to start a massive uprising of all Jews throughout the Empire while Rome (and the whole Empire) was in chaos.

History shows very clearly that Rome (the seat of the beast) was in darkness, and remained that way till Vespasian took the throne and brought stability back to the Empire.

They gnawed their tongues…and blasphemed God because of their pains, and their sores, but did not repent of their deeds.

"They" refers to the object of the plagues/wrath: the Jewish nation. They had pains (from the heat) and sores (see bowl of wrath #1), but still refused to repent.

The turmoil in Rome did not allow the Jews to prevail. Instead they divided among themselves, different warring factions fighting for control.

Instead of asking "What have we done that is causing God to not be with us?" they blamed God for the problems since Nero declared war on them. But whose fault was it really?

WHAT DOES THIS MEAN FOR US TODAY?

When you have problems in your life, stop trying to blame others.

Instead, first look to yourself and ask *honestly*, "What did I do to contribute to the problems I am now experiencing?" Teenagers complain about their parents, but seem to ignore that they aren't a bargain to live with either. You need to consider that *you* might be part of the problem, instead of always looking for someone else to blame.

You may find yourself in a mess at work, or at home with your spouse. But you need to remember, odds are you could have done things differently that would have kept the mess from getting to where it is now.

What do I do now?

Secondly, ask yourself *honestly*, "What can I do right now that will bring resolution to the problems I'm experiencing?" The Jews? They could have repented and followed Jesus Christ.

If you're a husband experiencing problems at home, the solution is probably to treat your wife with love and patience, and admit you've not been a bargain to live with either and accept your part of the blame. If you're a wife experiencing problems at home, the solution may well be to show true love, honor, and respect to your husband and admit you could have handled things better.

Imagine what would happen if *both* husband and wife did these things…

Judgment is coming on all people, and we'd best be ready.

Like God showed with Israel, He is longsuffering, but like God showed with Israel, His vengeance is required to all those who know not God and who obey not the gospel of our Lord Jesus Christ.

STUDY THIRTY-EIGHT:
THE BOWLS OF WRATH (PART 2)
(REVELATION 16:12-21)

PAY ATTENTION!

How many times have you heard that? Many mistakes and accidents could've been avoided if someone simply paid attention. I didn't mean to break my toe, but I didn't pay attention to the door that turned my toe upside-down. My kids didn't mean to knock stuff over, but they weren't paying attention. People don't mean to end up in hell, they just aren't paying attention to what they're doing.

But what we're talking about in Revelation isn't something accidental. Christ reveals things which were about to happen. His people who paid attention would see the signs and act accordingly.

The first-century Jews, however, didn't pay attention, and Christ came upon them as a thief.

Frogs, Beasts, Armageddon, Demons, Thunders, Lightnings, Earthquake, Hail, and God's wrath! Quite the assortment of events —all found in Revelation 16:12-21.

THE SIXTH BOWL OF GOD'S WRATH (6:12-16)

The sixth angel poured out his bowl on the great river Euphrates; and its water dried up, so the way of the kings of the east might be prepared. And I saw three unclean spirits, like frogs, come out of the mouth of the dragon, and out of the mouth of the beast, and out of the mouth of the false prophet. For they are the spirits of demons, working miracles, which go forth to the kings of the earth and of the whole world, to gather them to the battle of that great day of God Almighty. Behold, I come like a thief. Blessed is he that watches, and keeps his garments, lest he walk naked, and they see his shame. And he gathered them to-gether into a place, called in the Hebrew tongue, Ar-mageddon.

Remember, these were all meant to have an effect on "the earth," that is "the land," AKA the Promised Land (16:1).

The angel poured out the bowl on the Euphrates River.

This river was the northeastern border of the land promised to Abraham's descendants (Genesis 15:18). So to the Jews, this was part of *their* land.

The river dried up, making an opening for the kings of the east.

When Vespasian sent his son, Titus, back to finish the job, Titus removed the border guards (some 24,000 soldiers) from the Euphrates River to join with him. The Judean Jews had hoped their fellow Jews living outside the Promised Land would come join them in an uprising. With the border guard gone, those Jews had an opening—but never came.

However, this bowl of wrath is talking about something else that might have initially given the Jews some hope. The Parthians (a continual thorn in Rom's side) controlled everything east of the Euphrates River. With the border guard out of the way, the Parthians could invade and attack the Roman army.

So, even though the border guard meant another 24,000 troops (around 80,000 total) marching towards Jerusalem, the Jews had hope it would prove to be Rome's downfall.

The three unclean spirits.

These three unclean spirits looked or acted like frogs. They went all over the place, jumping in every direction.

They came out of the mouths of the dragon (Satan), the beast (Rome), and the false prophet (the Jewish nation). Since they came out of the mouth, it represents a message (verse 14 confirms this).

Their purpose: to gather the kings of the earth and of the whole world to battle.

The "kings of the earth" were the leaders in the Promised Land (see Acts 4:26-27). The kings of the "whole world" were the lesser kings throughout the Roman Empire (rulers of the various provinces).

Satan encouraged this gathering for war, because he thought that by wiping out the Jews, the Christians would be destroyed as well. Remember back in chapter 12, Satan sent a flood to destroy the woman (God's faithful people), but the flood was swallowed up by the land—the Roman army didn't chase after the fleeing Christians, they focused on Jews in Palestine.

Rome called for the kings of the "whole world" (a phrase describing the whole Roman Empire—see Luke 2:1) to assist in crushing the Jewish rebellion.

The Judean Jews called for aid from the Jews throughout the Empire, from the Parthians, and from the rulers of all the provinces to come help as a united stand against Rome—though the Jews only cared about their own freedom.

They worked "miracles."

These are not real miracles, for real miracles only come by the power of God. We must remember Revelation is highly figurative. Perhaps this means each one (Satan, Rome, and Israel) made every effort to muster support on their side. Though it would not be surprising if they claimed miraculous means.

These may be the emissaries of Satan, Rome, and Jerusalem proclaiming that God (or "the gods") was on their side, "Come join the battle!"

Even though each party gathered troops for battle, *God* was ultimately in charge of the gathering (verse 16). Satan was unwittingly playing according to God's plan. Rome was fulfilling God's will. Jerusalem—the one slated for destruction—was inadvertently helping to bring it about.

They gathered the kings together for the "battle of that great day of God Almighty!"

This is the same as "the great and terrible day of the Lord" spoken of in Acts 2:20. We will get into it more in chapter 19, but this is the gathering of the armies to Armageddon (see verse 16).

Armageddon means "the mount of Megiddo." It is frequently called "Mount Carmel" in the Old Testament. It was the location of some of the most decisive battles in Israel's history.

- Gideon and his 300 men defeated the Midianites there.
- Barak and Deborah defeated the Canaanites there.
- Elijah met the prophets of Baal there.

But not all of the events there were happy.

- The Philistines killed King Saul and his son Jonathan there.
- Pharaoh Necho killed possibly the most godly king Judah ever had there—Josiah.

The Jews knew this place well—and not for the happy times (see Zechariah 12:11).

Before we go on, it is worthwhile to notice something important: the Bible *nowhere* speaks of "the battle of Armageddon." Instead, it speaks of the armies gathering there, in preparation for the battle of the great day of the Lord—which took place *in Jerusalem*.

What does this gathering to Armageddon mean?

Just this: When Titus came back with his army, he waited at Caesarea for the heads of the other military units to arrive. When they arrived, they gathered at—you guessed it—Mt. Carmel, preparing for the final assault on the capital city of Jerusalem. Ain't history great?

Jesus speaks.

Around forty years earlier, Jesus told His Jewish audience, "Watch, because you don't know what hour your Lord is coming. If the master of the house had known which hour the thief would come, he would have watched, and would not have let his house be broken into" (Matthew 24:42-43).

Here in Revelation He interrupts the vision of impending doom to remind His followers to watch so they aren't caught unaware. In Matthew 24, Jesus gave His followers *signs to look for* so they would know when to flee Jerusalem. In Luke 21, He specifically says, "When you see Jerusalem surrounded by armies...flee to the mountains."

And here in Revelation, armies are gathering, and Jesus reminds His people to pay attention so they won't be taken by surprise.

He says, "I come like a thief."

Thieves come unannounced, and *never have good intentions*. It is important to remember *both* those facts. Most preachers I have heard speak on this phrase leave out the second fact, and only focus on the unannounced part.

Jesus told His people to watch so they can see when He is coming against Jerusalem. For Christians, that coming in judgment *wasn't* "as a thief," because it had been announced 40 years earlier. Jesus would only come "as a thief" for the ones not paying attention.

Look at 1 Thessalonians 5:2-4—Paul says the day of the Lord will come as a thief, and that sudden destruction will come upon *them*, but "*you* are not in darkness that the day of the Lord should overcome you like a thief." Jesus wouldn't be surprising His followers, nor would they suffer from His destructive intentions.

Blessings on those who watch, so they don't lose their garments.

They put on Christ as a garment (Galatians 3:27). They wore figurative robes of white by means of their salvation. But if they chose to not believe Jesus Christ, those garments are lost, leaving them spiritually naked, ripe for death in the impending battle.

So, in the midst of armies gathering for the great day of destruction, Jesus basically says, "Remember what I told you, and watch so you know when to get out of the city!"

THE SEVENTH BOWL OF WRATH (16:17-21)

And the seventh angel poured his bowl into the air; and a great voice came out of the temple of heaven, from the throne, saying, "It is done." And there were voices, and thunders, and lightnings; and there was a great earthquake—since men have been on the land, there was never so great and mighty an earthquake. And the great city was divided into three parts, and the cities of the nations fell: and great Babylon came in remembrance before God. He gave her the cup of the wine of the fierceness of his wrath. And every island fled away, and the mountains were not found. And great hail fell out of heaven upon men, every stone about the weight of a talent: and men blasphemed God because of the plague of the hail; because its plague was exceedingly massive.

The final angel poured out the wrath on the air.

Generally speaking, this is the lower part of the atmosphere; the place where people walk, talk, and breathe.

When this bowl was poured out, the voice from the temple (God) said, "It is done."

The word "done" is past tense—it is completed. It is a form of the same word used in 1:1—must "shortly come to pass" or some versions say, "must soon be done."

This section describes the completion of those things which had to "shortly come to pass." Thus, the seventh bowl of wrath describes the destruction of Jerusalem, the temple, and the nation of Israel in AD 70. This is confirmed by other things mentioned in this section.

Voices (noises), thunders, lightning, and a great earthquake.

These are symbolic ways of describing God's judgment (see 8:5, 11:3, 19).

The earthquake (Land-quake, a shaking of the Promised Land) was the fiercest and mightiest that had ever come since men had been on the earth (land). Think about that for a moment…how many times had God acted against people who dwelt in that land?

He cast out the Canaanite nations by means of the Jewish armies—instructing them to kill every single inhabitant. He sent the Babylonian army in to displace all the Jews, killing off thousands upon thousands of them, and destroying Solomon's temple.

But what He did in AD 70 was far greater in scope and power than anything that had ever happened before—or since.

The great city (Jerusalem—11:8) was divided into three parts.

During the final year of the Roman-Jewish war, three warring factions tried to gain power in Jerusalem. The city was in a three-way civil war. The leaders were Eleazar (who led the first sedition), John of Galilee, and Simeon (the leader of the Idumeneans/Edomites) (Josephus, *Wars* 5.1.4).

The city itself was also literally divided into three parts. It was walled into three sections: the upper city, the lower city, and Ophel (according to Josephus, *Wars* 5.1.1-5).

Ezekiel 5:2 prophesies of the destruction of Jerusalem by Babylon: "You shall burn with fire (pestilence) a third part in the midst of the city, when the days of the siege are completed. And you shall take a third part and strike it with a knife (sword). And a third part you shall scatter in the wind (exile); and I will draw out a sword after them." This may well have had a final fulfillment in AD 70.

And the cities of the nations fell.

Almost immediately after taking the throne, Vespasian had his troops go through the Empire and squash any rebellion (Jewish or otherwise). Jerusalem was the last one to deal with.

Babylon came into God's remembrance.

Babylon shows up in Revelation first in chapter 14 with the announcement: "Babylon is fallen, is fallen!" As we've seen before, and will see again in chapters 17-19, Babylon is Jerusalem. Peter—whom the Bible locates in Jerusalem—sent greetings from the church in "Babylon" (1 Peter 5:13). Note: there is no scriptural evidence that Peter ever set foot in Rome—*none.*[1]

This destruction of "Babylon" is the same as drinking of the cup of the wine of the fierceness of His wrath (see 14:10).

The islands fled away, and the mountains were not found.

One writer said the islands represented common individuals, and the mountains represented the mighty individuals. In the sixth seal, the islands were moved out of their place, but now they are not found—they are gone. His interpretation is that the Jews throughout the Empire had come to Jerusalem for the Passover, and so when Jerusalem was destroyed, none of the people (great or small) could be found.

The Roman armies parted to allow pilgrim Jews inside. At the same time, Christians made their escape. After this point Rome tightened the grip around the city and would not let anyone out.

Some view the "islands" as the furthest Jewish communities from Jerusalem, and the "mountains" as the major cities within the Promised Land. After this event, there were no Jewish-run cities in the Promised Land, and the Jewish population throughout the Empire was decimated and without influence.

And great hail fell out of heaven on men, every stone about the weight of a talent.

These weigh 75-100 pounds, depending on whose book you're reading. Josephus records the Roman army, in their assault on Jerusalem, using catapults to launch stones. Look at how he describes them:

---

[1] When Paul wrote to the Roman church, he greeted a *lot* of people—Peter wasn't mentioned. Paul said he wanted to get to Rome so he could give the Christians there some "spiritual gift." If Peter was there, they wouldn't need Paul to show up for this purpose.

"[They weighed a] talent, and were carried two furlongs and further. The blow they gave was in no way
to be sustained, not only by those that stood first in
the way, but by those that were beyond them a great
space. As for the Jews, they at first watched the coming of the stone, for it was white in color" (*Wars*,
5.6.3).

What color is hail? It's white. Just like the stones catapulted by
Rome into Jerusalem.

***And they blasphemed God because of the plague of the hail, for
the plague was exceedingly massive.***
Even to the end, while God was destroying them, they blamed
Him for abandoning them, when the truth is they had abandoned
Him!

WHAT DOES THIS MEAN FOR US TODAY?

Check your allegiances.
Some turn away from God when things go bad instead of stick-
ing with Him through it all. Are you a fair-weather friend to God, or
are you truly dedicated to Him?

Just like then, we need to remember the things Jesus taught.
- He taught us how to live.
- He taught us what to do to become a Christian.
- He showed us how to treat others.
- He showed us how to have compassion.
- He taught us to be watchful so when our end comes, we are
  prepared for it.

Don't ignore the things Christ has taught you through His word!

Study Thirty-Nine:
The Whore, Babylon
(Revelation 17)

Some say if you understand Revelation 17, you have the key to understanding the entire book. But in the same vein, if you misunderstand chapter 17, your interpretation of the entire book will likely be off. So, with such a serious proposition before us, let us consider this chapter.

There are two main characters in this vision: the *beast* and the *whore*. There is a relationship between the two, but *they are not the same*—remember this, because some claim the harlot is Rome, and so is the beast. Read the chapter and see how such an interpretation makes no sense. The beast and its ten horns hate the harlot, shall make her desolate, eat her flesh, and burn her with fire. So Rome hates and destroys…Rome??? Really???

The text makes it very clear that we are dealing with two separate entities.

In this lesson, we will identify the whore called Babylon. I know we've already covered who "Babylon" is; but now we dig into the details that prove it beyond any reasonable doubt.

HER JUDGMENT FORETOLD (17:1)

And one of the seven angels which had the seven bowls came and talked with me, saying, "Come here; I will show you the judgment of the great whore that sits on many waters:

The whore sits on many waters (this is explained in verse 15).
While many translations use the word "harlot" (NKJV, ASV) or "prostitute" (NIV, ESV), those words do not convey the disgust God

has for the sins of this city like the word "whore" (KJV, Message, NRSV) does.

Not only is this city called a *whore*, she is called "the *great* whore." The Greek word for *great* is *mega*. She is a *mega* whore. This city has repeatedly, and continually, gone after everything except God. If you want God's very graphic way of describing their national disgrace, read Ezekiel 16:24-52.

The "many waters" are explained in verse 15 as multitudes, peoples, nations, and tongues. Remember that Acts 2 describes the Jews gathered in Jerusalem as multitudes of people from every nation under heaven, each hearing in their own language.

Revelation focuses mainly on judgment against one entity, and this chapter describes it.

This chapter gives insight into the reasons *why* the judgment is deserved and coming. It also informs us what city is under consideration. If you have any doubt, just keep reading.

HER JUDGMENT EXPLAINED (VERSES 2-5)

"[...the great whore] with whom the kings of the land have fornicated, and the inhabitants of the land have been made drunk with the wine of her fornication."

So he carried me away in the Spirit into the wilderness: and I saw a woman sitting on a scarlet-colored beast full of blasphemous names, having seven heads and ten horns. And the woman was dressed in purple and scarlet, and decked with gold and precious stones and pearls, having a golden cup in her hand full of abominations and filthiness of her fornication.

And on her forehead was written a name, a mystery: BABYLON THE GREAT, THE MOTHER OF WHORES AND ABOMINATIONS OF THE EARTH.

Why she is being judged.

(1) First, she is THE great harlot (verse 1).

The biggest spiritual fornicator in history.

(2) Second, she committed fornication with the "kings of the earth" (verse 2), that is, the rulers of the Promised Land.

This could be a reference to their active involvement in the Roman persecution of Christians, enforcing the "mark of the beast." But you can't forget the Israelites' history of idolatry, dating back to before they even received the Ten Commandments (remember the golden calf incident in Exodus 32?). Their kings and leaders (rulers of the Promised Land) were mostly wicked, leading the people into worshiping Baal, Molech, Asteroth, and other pagan deities.

(3) Third, she made the inhabitants of the Promised Land drunk with the wine of her fornications.

The inhabitants didn't make themselves drunk—it wasn't something they decided to do on their own. Instead, they were influenced, coerced, and in some cases *forced* to partake in the whore's actions. Power-hungry leaders demand unquestioned obedience from their followers—or they will inflict consequences on them (see the punishments inflicted on those who refused to accept the mark of the beast). And frequently, corrupt leaders influence the people to be corrupt as well.

The city = whore motif isn't a new concept.

God called three cities "harlots" in the Old Testament: Tyre, Nineveh, and Jerusalem. What do these three have in common? Each one of them were—at one time—in a covenant relationship with God.

Tyre was in a covenant with God (seen in 1 Kings 5:1-12, 9:13, Amos 1:9), but later forgot God and was called a "harlot" (Isaiah 23:15-18).

Nineveh was converted to worshiping Jehovah by Jonah (Jonah 3:1-5), and was later called a "harlot" (Nahum 3:1-5).

Jerusalem was in a covenant with God, and was called a "harlot" repeatedly.

- Twice in Isaiah 1 (verses 1, 21).
- Twice in Jeremiah 2 (verses 2, 20).
- Three times in Jeremiah 3 (verses 1, 6, 8).
- Seven times in Ezekiel 16 (verses 2, 15, 16, 28, 31, 35, 41).
- Three times in Ezekiel 23 (verses 4, 19, 44).

And this is nowhere near a complete list.

When John wrote this, only one city existed which had been in a covenant relationship with God—*Jerusalem.*

The visual description helps identify her.
(1) She sits upon a scarlet colored beast—the Roman Empire

This whore used the beast to accomplish her desires. For example, the Jews were guilty of murdering Jesus Christ (Acts 2:23, 36), but they did it through manipulating the Roman ruler, Pilate (John 19:12-15), and demanding Jesus face a Roman-run execution (Matthew 27:22-26). They also worked with the Romans to persecute Christians throughout the Empire.

(2) She wears purple and scarlet, and is decked with gold and precious stones and pearls.

In the Greek version of the Old Testament, the *exact same words* describe the purple and scarlet clothing of the high priest of Israel (Exodus 39:1). The high priest was also decked with gold and precious stones (Exodus 28:4, 6).

(3) She has a name on her forehead.

She has a name, a mystery, written on her forehead: BABLYON THE GREAT, THE MOTHER OF WHORES AND ABOMINATIONS OF THE EARTH. The high priest of Israel was supposed to have, written on his forehead, "HOLY TO THE LORD" (Exodus 39:30). The city that was once "holy to the Lord" has now become "the mother of whores and abominations of the earth."

After Jerusalem was destroyed, Josephus made this observation:

"If the Romans had delayed any longer in attacking these villains, the city would certainly have been swallowed up by the earth or flooded or destroyed by lightning, as Sodom was, for it had brought forth a generation more atheistic than those who had previously suffered such punishments" (*Wars* 5.13.6).

The word "mystery" shows this name is not meant to be taken literally, but instead is something the readers were supposed to decipher.

She was drunk with the blood of the saints and the witnesses (martyrs) of Jesus.

Which city bore the guilt of the blood of the apostles and prophets and saints? Matthew 23:34-37 is unambiguous—Jerusalem.

HER JUDGMENT CAUSES SHOCK (VERSES 6-7)

And I saw the woman drunk with the blood of the saints, and with the blood of the martyrs of Jesus: and when I saw her, I stared in great amazement. And the angel said to me, "Why were you amazed? I will tell you the mystery of the woman, and of the beast that carries her, which has the seven heads and ten horns."

John was in shock at the sight—because he knew who it was.

In chapter 12, a woman that represented Israel gave birth to a Son (Jesus), who then ascended into heaven. That woman was then carried to the wilderness where God protected her for 3½ years.

So imagine John's utter shock when this angel carries him to the wilderness (where he last saw the Israel-woman) and he sees a drunk, murderous whore in her place. The once-faithful woman had completely corrupted herself.

The angel told him he shouldn't be amazed. It shouldn't have come as a shock.

The woman in chapter 12 was *faithful* Israel. When the Jewish nation ultimately rejected Jesus' offer of salvation, they ceased being *faithful*, and became a whore. But that doesn't mean there wasn't still a *faithful* (spiritual) Israel. There was—she is called "the Lamb's bride" and "New Jerusalem" in chapter 21.

After verse 7, the angel describes the Roman Empire (the beast), which we will examine in the next study. But now, we will skip to verse 15.

HER JUDGMENT IS DESCRIBED (VERSES 15-17)

> *And he said to me, "The waters which you saw, where the whore sits, are peoples, and multitudes, and nations, and languages. And the ten horns which you saw on the beast, these shall hate the whore, and make her desolate and naked, and shall eat her flesh, and burn her with fire. For God has put in their hearts to fulfil His will, and to agree, and give their kingdom to the beast, until the words of God shall be fulfilled."*

The "many waters" are "peoples, multitudes, nations, and languages"

Again, see Acts 2 and see how the description of the Jews matches this. The whore/city is over the Jewish people.

The beast (Rome) and its ten horns (vassal kings of Rome) will attack the great whore, make her desolate and naked, and shall eat her flesh, and burn her with fire.

Jesus said Jerusalem would be left <u>desolate</u> within the days of "this generation" (Matthew 23:36-38).

Ezekiel 16:39 and 23:29 describe God's judgment on Jerusalem, saying He will strip them <u>naked</u> and bare—meaning they will be left with no walls, no protection, no anything.

When Jerusalem was destroyed by Rome, the surviving Jews were paraded naked through the streets of Rome in Titus' victory parade.

Jesus, speaking of the destruction of Jerusalem, said wherever the carcass was, the eagles would gather—to <u>eat the flesh</u> (Matthew 24:28).

The baptism of fire spoken of by John the Baptist was a reference to the destruction of Jerusalem (Matthew 3:10-12). The Romans <u>burned the temple and the entire city with fire</u>.

This describes complete death of the Jewish way of life. And God is behind it. He called the kings together to join with Rome and utterly destroy the Jewish people.

THE WHORE IS IDENTIFIED (VERSE 18)

"And the woman you saw is that great city, which reigns over the kings of the earth."

The whore is the great city.

There is only one "great city" described in Revelation, and that is the one in which Jesus was crucified (11:8)—Jerusalem.

The kings of the earth are the rulers of the Promised Land.

The city that held sway in the Promised Land was…Jerusalem!

WHAT DOES THIS MEAN FOR US TODAY?

The one thing that we need to get out of this chapter, more than anything else, is this: Just because you used to be faithful doesn't mean you're saved now! It is possible for a once-faithful follower of God to leave the faith, and become an object of God's wrath and judgment. "Once saved, always saved" is a lie from the pits of hell.

STUDY FORTY:
THE BEAST WITH SEVEN HEADS
(REVELATION 17)

When dating the book of Revelation, some immediately point to chapter seventeen. They point to the beast "with seven heads, which are seven kings," and then proceed to "prove" their preferred date by this "evidence."

The problem is, it's often done arbitrarily, ignoring the evidence from the rest of the book.

Last study, we looked at "the Whore, Babylon," and saw how all the descriptions pointed to first-century Jerusalem.

- She was drunk on the blood of the saints.
- She was once in a relationship with God, but had turned into a whore.
- She caused the abominations in the land, and influenced the inhabitants of the Promised Land to engage in spiritual adultery (becoming the "synagogue of Satan").

In this lesson, we will examine what chapter seventeen says about the scarlet-colored beast.

Almost every teacher of Revelation agrees that this—in some way—represents the Roman Empire. They may differ greatly on which aspect of the Empire, and especially *when* this takes place, but in general, they all agree it somehow represents Rome. The disagreement (and it is a significant one) comes when they try to identify the seven heads.

We will focus on four things:

- The identity of the beast in chapter 17 with the beast of chapter 13.
- The beast's actions with the woman.

- The explanations of the "seven heads which are seven mountains" and the "seven kings."
- The explanation of the ten horns.

IDENTIFYING THE BEAST (17:3, 12, 14)

So he carried me away in the spirit into the wilderness: and I saw a woman sitting on a scarlet-colored beast, full of blasphemous names, having seven heads and ten horns…

"And the ten horns which you saw are ten kings, which have received no kingdom as yet; but receive power as kings one hour with the beast…"

"These shall make war with the Lamb, and the Lamb shall overcome them: for he is Lord of lords, and King of kings: and they that are with him are called, and chosen, and faithful."

John was shown a woman sitting on a beast.

The beast was full of blasphemous names and had seven heads and ten horns. It would also make war with the saints. These describe the beast from the sea in chapter 13—which was the Roman Empire of the first century. Note the connections:

- 13:1—a beast rises up out of the sea, having **seven heads**, and **ten horns**, and upon his horns **ten crowns**, and upon his heads the **name of blasphemy**.
- 17:3—a scarlet colored **beast**, full of **names of blasphemy**, having **seven heads** and **ten horns.**
- 13:7—And it was given to him to **make war with the saints.**
- 17:12, 14—the **ten horns** that you saw are **ten kings**… they shall **make war with the Lamb**.

In other words, we are dealing with the same beast. The Roman Empire.

THE BEAST'S ACTIONS WITH THE WOMAN (17:3, 12, 16)

> *So he carried me away in the spirit into the wilderness: and I saw a woman sitting on a scarlet-colored beast, full of blasphemous names, having seven heads and ten horns.*
>
> *"And the ten horns which you saw are ten kings, which have received no kingdom as yet; but receive power as kings one hour with the beast..."*
>
> *"And the ten horns which you saw on the beast, these shall hate the whore, and shall make her desolate and naked, and shall eat her flesh, and burn her with fire."*

It carried the woman (17:3).

The woman (Jerusalem) was able to do her drunken deeds—being drunk with the blood of the saints—because she used the beast (the Roman Empire). Jerusalem used the Roman Empire to her advantage:

- In murdering Jesus.
- In murdering James, the brother of John (Acts 12).
- In persecuting Christians throughout the Empire (how many times in Acts are government officials involved as Jews go after Paul and other Christians?).
- In carrying out a massive, bloody persecution on the Christians via Nero's edict.

The beast turns on the woman and utterly destroys her (17:12, 16).

It is important to remember the horns of the beast were still *part of the beast*. The horns did not act on their own accord. The ten horns (ten kings) gave their authority to the beast, and they all joined together to destroy Jerusalem. The armies of Rome were comprised of soldiers from every Roman province.

Rome realized it was being used, and—at God's urging—turned their attention to destroying the Jews.

THE BEAST DESCRIBED, AND THE DESCRIPTION EXPLAINED (17:3, 7-14)

So he carried me away in the spirit into the wilderness: and I saw a woman sitting on a scarlet-colored beast, full of blasphemous names, having seven heads and ten horns…

And the angel said to me, "Why were you amazed? I will tell you the mystery of the woman, and of the beast that carries her, which has the seven heads and ten horns. The beast that you saw was, and is not; and it shall ascend out of the bottomless pit, and go into perdition: and those who dwell on the land, whose names were not written in the book of life from the foundation of the world, shall be amazed when they behold the beast that was, and is not, and yet is.

"And here is the mind which has wisdom: The seven heads are seven mountains, on which the woman sits. And there are seven kings: five are fallen, and one is, and the other is not yet come; and when he comes, he must remain [or wait] a short time. And the beast that was, and is not, he is the eighth [king], and is of the seven[th], and goes into destruction.

"And the ten horns which you saw are ten kings, which have received no kingdom as yet; but receive

*power as kings one hour with the beast. These have
one mind, and shall give their power and strength to
the beast. These shall make war with the Lamb, and
the Lamb shall overcome them: for he is Lord of
lords, and King of kings: and they that are with him
are called, and chosen, and faithful."*

It was scarlet-colored (17:3).

This is the color of blood. Rome was a bloody empire (very few
of the emperors died natural deaths).

It was full of names of blasphemies (17:3).

Octavius changed his name to Augustus, which means "The Supreme One." Every emperor after him added "Augustus" to their
name when they took the throne—declaring themselves supreme.

With only one possible exception, all the Caesars from Augustus
onward demanded worship. Historical evidence shows various first-
century Caesars were called "Lord and God."

The beast "was, and is not, yet is."

The Roman Empire was enduring a massive civil war, and it
looked as though it was going to fall apart—the empire was, but "is
not," because it was in darkness during this time of great upheaval.
Yet the Roman Empire still existed ("and yet is").

Some Greek manuscripts say, "was, and is not, yet shall be." If
these are correct, it means even though the Roman Empire was in
darkness, it would come out of it (which it did when Vespasian took
the throne).

It ascended out of the bottomless pit.

The beast (the Roman Empire) appeared to be dead, but it came
roaring back to life. During the turmoil, the Jews in Jerusalem believed they would defeat Rome—they probably thought this was
God overthrowing Rome for them. But when Vespasian took the
throne (17 months after Nero's death), he focused his attention on
Jerusalem. And the inhabitants of the Promised Land, whose names

were not written in the book of life, were scared—and for good reason.

It would go into perdition (destruction).

This means the beast (specifically the eighth king—more on that momentarily) would go forth and destroy the woman (Jerusalem) with the help of the ten horns.

Grammatically, it could also mean the beast (the eighth king) would lead himself to his own destruction. The problem is that the result of the beast's "going into destruction" is the Jews being shocked and fearful. If it was talking about the downfall of Rome, the Jews would have been rejoicing. Some will point out the eighth Emperor, Otho, committed suicide after reigning three months (destroying himself). However, as you will see in a few moments, this isn't who is under consideration.

It had seven heads (17:3).

These seven heads are defined for us in verses 9-10, and the angel says they have a double-meaning.

They represent seven mountains on which the woman sits. Rome and Jerusalem both sat on seven literal mountains. But also remember that mountains, throughout Old Testament prophecy and frequently in Revelation, refer to kingdoms—and that seven is a number used to represent completeness. So which nation ruled over all the kingdoms in that area?—Rome.

They represent seven kings. There are many different interpretations to this:

(1) Some say these are kingdoms

Specifically: (1) Egypt, (2) Assyria, (3) Babylon, (4) Persia, and (5) Greece are the five that have fallen, (6) Rome is the one that "is" at the time John writes. They believe the seventh kingdom is the Christian dispensation, and the "short time" is the rest of the world's existence.[1] They believe the eighth king, which is one of the seven,

---

[1] Coffman, Hendrickson, Plummer, and other "Idealist" interpreters.

is apostate Christianity (frequently cited as the Roman Catholic Church) which will rule until Christ comes again. This interpretation cannot be right for the following reasons:

- Christianity already existed when Revelation was written—but Revelation says the seventh "king[dom]" had "not yet come."
- Christianity has existed for 2,000 years—hardly a "short time."
- Christianity (if it is part of the beast) would have to try to kill itself (the beast made war with the Lamb).

(2) Some say these are the seven Roman rulers over Judea

Under Caligula and Nero, after Judea was again made a Roman province, there were (it is said) seven rulers. While it would fit the timeframe, and shows the relationship between Rome and Jerusalem, it seems rather contrived, and doesn't give any suggestion for the interpretation of the eighth king who is one of the seven.

(3) The majority believe these are Roman emperors

But—surprise, surprise—even then they disagree over which ones should be counted. Some interesting mental gymnastics are used to explain who counts and who doesn't—all because the evidence doesn't fit some preconceived ideas about when the book was written. Let's look at the evidence:

Five are fallen, one is (reigning at that time), and another one hasn't yet come to the throne, but when he does, he will continue or wait "a short space." Here John gives us inspired evidence as to the timeframe of this book.

- Five kings of the Roman Empire had already died.
- One was currently reigning.
- The seventh one would only reign a short time—or another possible translation is that the seventh would have to wait a short time (before taking the throne).
- The beast himself is the eighth, though he is also of the

seven, and also goes into destruction.

First, we have to know where to start counting.

Ancient writers, including the Roman historian Suetonius (*Lives of the Twelve Caesars*) and the Jewish historian Josephus, start their numbering of the kings of Rome with Julius Caesar, and count Domitian as the twelfth. Some claim, "Julius wasn't ever an emperor!" but the ancient writers (who would be in a better position to speak on the matter) said he was. Julius turned the Roman republic into the Empire, and was declared supreme dictator for life. He wasn't given the title "emperor," but other than not having the official name, he was emperor in every way—which is why every emperor of Rome was named after him: Caesar.

So, in order, the five kings who had died must be:

1. Julius Caesar
2. Octavius (Augustus)
3. Tiberius
4. Caligula
5. Claudius

That means the king when John wrote ("one is") was Nero.

What about the seventh king, and the beast who is the eighth, but of the seven?

There are two possible answers to this question, and which one it is depends on how you translate the Greek word *meno*. It can mean "to remain, to continue" but it also can mean "to wait for, await."[2]

(1) "continue"

If we are to translate it as "he must *continue* a short space," then the verse means the seventh king would only reign for a short amount of time. The seventh king was Galba, the man who took the

---

[2] Thayer's Unabridged. Strong's definition says "to stay (in…expectancy)" and "to tarry" (or wait). The *Complete Word Study Dictionary* says, "to remain for someone, wait for, await."

throne after Nero's suicide—and was killed six months later. The eighth king was Otho, who had been a close companion with Nero. Otho was the eighth, but was strangely like one of the seven ("of the seven").

When Otho took the throne (after murdering Galba), he raised up the statues of Nero, and the ancient historians agree he was very much like Nero in appearance and demeanor. He brought back all of Nero's freedman, officers, and servants. The populace called him "Nero" because of the similarity of their appearance and their love for the late emperor. (Otho also brought back Nero's castrated lover as his own…)

Could Otho, the eighth king, be said to be "of the seven"? In his looks, mannerisms, and actions it can. Can it be said of him that he goes into perdition [destruction]? Yes, he committed suicide three months into his reign.

The problem with this interpretation is John says the eighth king is the beast, who—along with the ten horns—destroys the woman (Jerusalem). Otho was never involved in any way with Jerusalem, and if he is the one described as the beast, the passage makes no sense.

(2) "wait"

However, if we are to translate it as "he [the seventh king] must *wait* a short space," then the verse means that after Nero dies, another king would arise, but would have to wait before taking the throne. Vespasian, the Roman general leading the troops against Israel, was declared emperor by his troops, but he did not go back to Rome and take the throne until 17 months after Nero's death. This would make Vespasian that seventh king.

The eighth king [the beast] would be Titus, the son of Vespasian. Titus, as the beast, was the one who gathered the troops from across the Empire to destroy Jerusalem in AD 70. He embodied the return of the beast (going into destroying mode). Also, the text could be translated the eighth king is "of the seven<u>th</u>," and Titus (the eighth) was the son of the seventh king.

This is what this section is talking about:

When Nero committed suicide, the war on Judea came to a screeching halt, as Vespasian pulled back, awaiting orders. The "seat of the beast" (Rome) was thrown into darkness (16:10-11). This lasted 17 months, during which time Galba, Otho, and Viltellius each took the throne. It was at this point that the beast (the Roman Empire) "was, but is not." It still existed, but just barely.

Vespasian was the seventh king, the one who had to wait a short season, but took the throne at the end of AD 69—after having been declared emperor much earlier by his troops. When he took the throne, he made it his business to squash all rebellion, and sent his son Titus to take Jerusalem.

Titus was the general of the multinational army [the armies of the ten Roman provinces] which completely obliterated Jerusalem. Titus was the beast, the head of the fierce, destructive power of Rome. He was the eighth (he would ascend to the throne after his father died), who was "of the seventh"—the SON of the seventh.

He used the ten horns [the ten rulers who gave their authority to the Empire] to destroy the woman, Babylon. These ten rulers were over the same provinces in which they carried out the war on Christ and the Christians.

Revelation clearly states they made war with the Lamb, but the Lamb overcame them. Revelation clearly states the Roman Empire made war with the Jews, but the Jews did not overcome. This was a clear statement of God's rejection of the Jews and the acceptance forever of Christians as His people.

WHAT DOES THIS MEAN FOR US TODAY?

The Bible can be trusted

One thing missed a lot in the discussion of Revelation is this: When John wrote the words in this book, the Roman Empire was strong and flourishing; Nero was a solid, strong, popular leader, surrounded by many wise advisors. Everything was looking up.

So, when John wrote of Rome shortly being engulfed in a civil war, of another king waiting in the wings, and of the temporary disappearance of the Empire, it would have been viewed as complete foolishness. Outside of the Christians, no one would have taken it seriously.

And yet what happened just a few years later? All of it came true. This is yet another proof the Bible is from God—no man could have predicted the amazing upheaval.

Since the Bible is from God, we would all do well to examine its pages to find out what He wants us to do.

- He wants us to hear His word (Romans 10:17).
- He wants us to believe it (Hebrews 11:6).
- He wants us to repent of our sins (Acts 3:19).
- He wants us to make the good confession that Jesus Christ is the Son of God (Romans 10:9).
- He wants us to be immersed in water for the forgiveness of our sins (Acts 2:38).
- He wants us to stay faithful to Him (Revelation 2:10).

Have you put your trust in God, His Son, and His inspired message?

Study Forty-One:
"Come Out of Her, My People!"
(Revelation 18:1-8)

What happens if you have one rotten apple in a bushel? "One bad apple ruins the whole bunch," right? Perhaps a better question is: What happens when you have a bushel of rotten apples and you place a few good ones in the middle of it? The answer is if you don't pull those apples out soon, they will be corrupted and ruined.

Why bring this up? Because God cried out to the Christians in Babylon, "Come out of her, my people, so that you aren't partakers of her sins, and that you don't receive her plagues!" He didn't want them ruined by the rotten apples filling Babylon.

THE ANNOUNCEMENT (18:1-3)

And after these things, I saw another angel, having great authority, come down from heaven; and the land was illuminated by his glory. And he cried forcefully with a mighty voice, saying, "Fallen, fallen is Babylon the great, and has become the habitation of demons, and the cage of every unclean spirit, and a cage of every unclean and hateful bird. For all nations have drunk of the wine of the wrath of her fornication, and the kings of the earth have committed fornication with her, and the merchants of the land have become rich through the abundance of her delicacies."

"After these things, I saw…"

Some might get confused, because John said, "after these things," right after Babylon's destruction was described (17:16-17).

Yet now there comes an announcement that the people of God could escape Babylon without being destroyed.

Remember, John hadn't *seen* Babylon's destruction, instead he heard an angel explain what *was going to happen* (it was still future tense, 17:16-17). After this *explanation* was given, John saw the angel descend, crying out: "Fallen, fallen is Babylon."

Another messenger descends from heaven.

This angel is called "another angel," meaning he was not one of the angels with the seven last plagues (mentioned in chapter 16, and including the angel that spoke to John in chapter 17).

This angel had great power (KJV), or authority (NKJV). Some suggest this is a symbolically describing New Testament prophets who announced Jerusalem's destruction. I don't see any reason to make that assumption. Whoever this heavenly messenger is, his authority derives from Jesus Christ (Matthew 28:18).

This messenger brightened the land with his glory.

Because of the great authority and immense glory, some have speculated this is another description of Jesus Christ. I find this hard to believe, since this messenger is called "another messenger" or "another angel," which seems to equate him with the seven angels of chapter 17, except he apparently has more authority. Jesus is not equal to the angels—He is superior to them in every way.

Probably we aren't supposed to read anything into the identity of this angel, because the focus is on the message—not the messenger.

The angel cried out his message with a strong voice: "Fallen, fallen is Babylon"

The same message was given in Revelation 14:8. This is also the same message spoken against literal Babylon hundreds of years earlier in Isaiah 21:9.

But what is meant by "Fallen, fallen is Babylon"? It means one of two things: (1) Mystical Babylon (Jerusalem)'s destruction was so certain that it was spoken of as an already-happened event (this is called "the prophetic perfect" tense). This is the same way Isaiah spoke of *literal* Babylon, over a hundred years before the Babylonian Empire was overthrown by Persia. (2) Mystic Babylon (Jerusalem)'s spiritual condition was so bad (based on the rest of verse 2 and 3) the angel declared them ripe for judgment.

I lean toward the first interpretation, but both work in tandem—Jerusalem is so spiritually fallen and opposed to God that they are ripe for judgment—and their destruction is certain.

Babylon has become the habitation of demons, and the cage of every unclean spirit.

Given that spiritual gifts ended by AD 70 (as per biblical prophecy), and that Zechariah 13 said evil spirits and prophecy would end at the same time (13:3-5), then this MUST be a description of the state of Jerusalem BEFORE AD 70.[1]

The interpretation we gave of the army of locusts that infested the land (the fifth trumpet, Revelation 9:1-2) was that of a mass demon-possession. Josephus described the inhabitants of Jerusalem before its destruction as the most atheistic group of people in history. Even if demon-possession is not under consideration, the people themselves could have been called evil spirits, wicked as they were.

Babylon has become a cage for every unclean and hateful bird.

This is also a reference to the sinful character of the inhabitants of Jerusalem. But also note the word "cage"—they were now unable to escape, gathered together in Jerusalem and surrounded by the Roman army.

They are caged because of the fornication of Jerusalem.

All nations were influenced by her actions (there were Jews in all the nations under heaven—Acts 2:5). The rulers of the land were

---

[1] For more on this topic, see Study Two: When was Revelation Written?

involved in the spiritual fornication—rejection of Christ. The merchants of the land had made themselves rich through their relationship with the adulteress, Babylon. Jews far away, along with the Jewish leaders and merchants, were united in this rejection of Christ and persecution of the saints.

This "Babylon" sounds like a really bad place.

But the world today is not much different, is it? The world is spiritually fallen! It is full of evil people who are unclean and hateful! It's full of people antagonistic toward Jesus Christ and His people. And the same fate awaits them: destruction!

THE CALL FROM HEAVEN (18:4-5)

And I heard another voice from heaven, saying, "Come out of her, my people, so that you don't become partakers of her sins, and that you don't receive her plagues. Because her sins have reached up to heaven, and God has remembered her iniquities."

"Come out of her, My people!"

God has repeatedly called for His people to separate themselves from the wicked.

- Lot (from Sodom).
- Israelites (from Egypt).
- Christians (from the world).

And now, God calls His people to come out of Jerusalem (see Matthew 24:15-22). The destruction of Jerusalem was an absolute certainty—and to be spared, God's people had to leave.

Cestus Gallus, the Roman General in late 66/early 67 AD was about to take Jerusalem, but for some unspecified reason he just retreated (Matthew 24:22—unless the days are shortened, no flesh would escape, but for the sake of the elect, the days will be shortened). Most likely, it was during this point the Christians left.

But why would they need to flee? Surely God wouldn't destroy the city if there were still ten righteous souls in it (see Genesis 18), right? They were told to flee the city for two reasons:

So they would not become partakers of Jerusalem's sins.

Even good apples, when thrown in a bushel of bad ones, will quickly rot. Evil companions corrupt good morals (1 Corinthians 15:33). If they had stayed, they would have been packed in with bloodthirsty murderers and those who were described as "atheistic" by Josephus. It is best to get out of a sin-filled situation as quick as possible so it does not influence you for evil.

So they would not receive the plagues which were going to come upon Jerusalem.

This is why Jesus told them to flee for the mountains: because a great tribulation was coming upon Jerusalem, worse than anything that had ever happened or ever would happen. If you believed Jesus, you'd get out and quick!

The sins of Jerusalem had reached up to heaven, and God remembered their iniquities.

Imagine the sins stacking up higher and higher until they finally reached God's feet in heaven. This is the imagery to keep in mind when you think about the sins of Jerusalem.

And if Christians stayed in the city, they would receive the same punishment—because *nothing* was going to save Jerusalem from destruction.

THE CURSE (18:6-8)

"Give her back what she gave, and double it to her double according to her works: in the cup she has filled, fill to her double. However much she glorified herself, and lived deliciously, give her torment and sorrow: for she says in her heart, 'I sit as a queen,

and am not a widow. I shall see no sorrow.' There-
fore her plagues shall come in one day: death, and
mourning, and famine; and she shall be utterly
burned with fire: for the Lord God who judges her is
strong."

God will punish them according to what they have DONE.

"Double it to her double according to her works! In the cup she has filled, fill it to her double!" Some try to justify sinful behavior by saying, "God wouldn't punish someone throughout eternity for a short time of sinfulness." But those who reject Christ are worthy of *double* the hate they have shown to God.

If you argue God shouldn't punish someone eternally for a relatively short period of sinfulness, then logically you must argue God shouldn't reward someone eternally for a relatively short period of faithfulness. You can't have it both ways. The last verse of Matthew 25 shows that hell will last every bit as long as heaven will. God knows what He is doing.

She had glorified herself—not God.

People not living for Christ glorify themselves instead of God, and are worthy of the same destruction.

She had lived "deliciously" (KJV) or "luxuriously" (NKJV). That is, according to her own desires. And God's message: however much she lived for herself and built up her own pleasures, that is how much torment and sorrow she deserves—then double it.

Jerusalem had said, "I sit as a queen, and not a widow." When Nebuchadnezzar (king of the Babylonian Empire) threatened to destroy Jerusalem, the Jews were overconfident, proclaiming God would never let the temple be destroyed. They basically thought they were "Once chosen, always chosen," and that God could never reject them. They were proud and boastful like an egotistical queen, instead of mourning over their horrible sin and separation from God.

Because of her attitude and actions, plagues would come upon her all at once: death, mourning, famine, burned with fire.

Each one of these things features prominently in Josephus' account of Jerusalem's destruction.

What happens if our time comes to an end, and we have not been faithful to the Lord? The plagues of eternal death, constant mourning, lacking the bread of life (a spiritual famine), and burned forever in the fires of hell!

The judgment is guaranteed because no one is stronger than God.

God knew Jerusalem wouldn't repent, and judged her worthy of total destruction. This matters because God is the one true Supreme Court—No power can over-rule His judgment, and no force can keep it from happening.

WHAT DOES THIS MEAN FOR US TODAY?

If we are friendly with the world, we will be corrupted and doomed to destruction.

Destruction comes to everyone who does not obey the gospel (2 Thessalonians 1:8). And the destruction is guaranteed, because God, the one who judges all, is powerful.

Salvation from destruction is available—if you answer the call.

God cries out to a lost and dying world, doomed for eternal destruction, "Come out of her, My people!" He doesn't want you to meet destruction. But you have to answer the call—"Repent, and be baptized, every one of you, for the remission of sins" (Acts 2:38).

In AD 70, when Jerusalem was obliterated and over a million Jews were killed in less than a week—there was not one faithful Christian among them, for they had all escaped the destruction by leaving the sin-filled city behind.

When judgment comes and billions face the judgment of God Almighty, will you be saved by having left the sin-filled world behind?

STUDY FORTY-TWO: REACTIONS TO DESTRUCTION (REVELATION 18:9-19:6)

Do you remember the sadness that engulfed the country when the World Trade Centers were attacked on September 11th? People sat frozen in shock, glued to their television sets, overwhelming sadness and fear washing over them. The stock market dropped quickly before they halted trading; and when the stock market re-opened a few days later, it plummeted. For the first time in forty years, the NFL cancelled its scheduled games for the week.

If you are old enough to remember it, you will never forget.

But what happened then was nothing compared to what happened in Jerusalem in AD 70. The mourning resulting from that event is described in Revelation 18:9-19. But the mourning was much different, as we will see.

THE REACTION OF THE WORLD (18:9-19)

And the kings of the land, who committed fornication and lived luxuriously with her, shall wail [for] her, and lament for her, when they see the smoke from her burning. Standing afar off because they fear her torment, [they are] saying, "Alas, alas, that great city Babylon, that mighty city! for in one hour your judgment has come!"

And the merchants of the land shall wail and mourn over her; for no one buys their merchandise any more: the merchandise of gold, and silver, and precious stones, and pearls, and fine linen, and purple, and silk, and scarlet, and all citron wood, and all kinds of vessels of ivory, and all kinds of vessels of most precious wood, and of brass, and iron, and marble, and cinnamon, and incense, and ointments, and frankincense, and wine, and oil, and fine flour, and wheat, and beasts, and sheep, and horses, and chariots, and slaves, and souls of men.

(Tthe fruits that your soul desired have departed from you, and all things which were sumptuous and radiant have departed from you, and you will not find them anymore—ever.)

The merchants who sell these things, who were made rich by her, shall stand afar off because they fear her torment, weeping and wailing, and saying, "Alas, alas, that great city that was clothed in fine linen, and purple, and scarlet, and decked with gold, and precious stones, and pearls! Because such great wealth has been destroyed in a single hour!"

And every shipmaster, and all those who travel by ship, and sailors, and all those who trade by sea, stood afar off, crying, when they saw the smoke from her burning, saying, "What city is like this great city!" And they threw dust on their heads, and cried, weeping and wailing, saying, "Alas, alas, that great city in which all who had ships in the sea became rich because of her wealth! Because in one hour is she made desolate!"

Let's look at the mourners, and why they were mourning.

The kings of the earth/land

These are the leaders throughout the Promised Land—probably the Roman rulers in Judea (because they see the destruction from *outside* the city). They stand back (so they aren't caught in the destruction) and wail when they see the smoke of Jerusalem burning because:

- *They committed fornication with her.* They were closely connected with Jerusalem, and pointed people to honor Caesar instead of Christ
- *They had lived luxuriously ("deliciously," KJV) with her.* They had used their political power to get rich, exploiting Jerusalem and the worshipers who came there. Now that Jerusalem is no more, they are in anguish—not because people are dead, but because their source of financial gain is gone.

Why, as they mourn, did they call it a "great city"? Over a decade before Jesus was born, Herod the Great had begun a massive reconstruction of Jerusalem, starting with the temple complex. The project wasn't finished until AD 63—and the entire city was a glory to behold. This city was very wealthy, and for a time had a favored status in the Roman Empire. By all earthly measures, it was indeed a "great city."

Why did the rulers of the Promised Land mourn the destruction of Babylon (aka Jerusalem)? It had nothing to do with being sad over the loss of life, or the destruction of architectural marvels, or art, or history, or the most important religious center for worship of the true God of heaven—nope, Jerusalem's only value in the eyes of the "kings of the earth" was as a source of money and power.

The merchants of the Promised Land

This is probably traveling merchants who made a living selling their wares in Jerusalem. They wept and mourned because there was no one left to buy their merchandise. The list of merchandise bought and sold in Jerusalem is quite illuminating:

- Gold, silver, precious stones, pearls.
- Fine linen and purple material, silk and scarlet material.

- Citron [scented] wood and all kinds of vessels of ivory, precious wood, brass, iron, and marble.
- Cinnamon, incense/spices, ointments, frankincense.
- Wine and oil, fine flour, and wheat.
- Beasts and sheep.
- Horses and chariots.
- Slaves and the souls of men.

Each of these things had been brought to Jerusalem over the previous 75+ years for the building and expanding of the temple complex and beautifying of the city. Merchants were literally making a fortune while Jerusalem built these fabulous buildings (see Matthew 24:1-2). Slaves were brought in for manual labor, the beasts and sheep for sacrifices, the horses and chariots for the rich citizens to travel around the city in style. The temple was completed in AD 63—and seven (the number for completeness) years later, it was permanently destroyed.

The merchants stood afar off to avoid the destruction, and said, "Alas, alas, that great city that was clothed in fine linen (the priestly wardrobe), and purple and scarlet (the colors of royalty), and decked with gold (temple was covered in gold), and precious stones and pearls (decorated the interior of the temple complex)."

The merchants were more upset at the destruction of the *merchandise* than the *people*. And they were only upset about the people dying because of the financial hit to their business.

The Seamen

They mourned because they were losing a massive source of revenue. If you're like me, you picture Jerusalem and the Promised Land being like it is now: a hot, dry desert. But remember the Promised Land was once called "the land flowing with milk and honey" (and is called such repeatedly in the Old Testament—Exodus 3:8, 17; 13:5; 33:3; Leviticus 20:24; Numbers 13:27; 14:8; 16:13-14;

Deuteronomy 6:3; 11:9; 26:9, 15; 27:3; 21:30; Joshua 5:6; Jeremiah 11:5; 32:22; Ezekiel 20:6, 15).

When you consider the value of the buildings and the wealth of the citizens, it was actually one of the wealthiest cities in the entire Roman Empire!

The seamen cried because they had gotten rich by bringing merchandise to Jerusalem, and now their source of income was gone.

Why did each of these groups mourn?

None of them mourned the loss of people—they mourned because they were financially affected by it. Does that tell you how the world viewed the rebellious, atheistic Jews at this time?

It reminds me of a song from the 1970 movie, "Scrooge." The crowds are all singing a song to Ebenezer Scrooge, "Thank you very much! Thank you very much! That's the nicest thing that anyone's ever done for me. It sounds a bit bizarre, but things the way they are, I feel as if another life's begun for me." The problem is, they are all people who owed Scrooge money, and their joyous song is thanking him… because he was dead.

THE REACTION OF THE RIGHTEOUS (18:20-24)

> *"Rejoice over her, heaven, and you saints, and apostles, and prophets; for God has avenged you [by destroying] her."*

> *And a mighty angel took up a stone like a huge millstone, and cast it into the sea, saying, "In this way, with violence, that great city Babylon will be thrown down, and shall not be found anymore—at all. And the sound of harpists, and musicians, and pipers, and trumpeters, shall not be heard anymore in you—at all. And no craftsman, of whatever craft he is, shall be found any more in you; and the sound of a millstone shall not be heard anymore in you—at all. And*

the light of a candle shall not shine anymore in you—
at all. And the voice of a bridegroom and bride shall
not be heard anymore in you—at all. Because your
merchants were the great men of the land; and be-
cause you deceived all nations with your witchcraft."

"And in her was found the blood of prophets, and of
saints, and of all that were murdered on the land."

Rejoice!

The voice from heaven (God) is still speaking (18:2 and 4), and says, "Rejoice over her, heaven, and holy apostles and prophets; for God has avenged you on her."

When Osama Bin Laden (the mastermind behind the attack on the Twin Towers) was killed, spontaneous celebrations erupted across the country. But some questioned: is it right for Christians to celebrate when a wicked person is killed? The answer is in this verse: *Yes*, a Christian can be happy—in fact is *commanded* to re-joice—that justice has been served according to God's design (see also Romans 13:1-5).

Literally, the voice says, "You rejoice over her, heaven, and the saints [holy ones], and the apostles, and the prophets." These three groups of people encompass God's faithful under the Old Testament and New Testament up to that point. The reason they were supposed to rejoice was because God had avenged their blood by destroying the city that was guilty of shedding it. We've covered this before, but which city was guilty of the blood of the apostles, prophets, and saints?

Matthew 23:34-37—I send [Greek apostello] to you
prophets…some of them you will kill and crucify, and
some of them you will scourge…and [you will] per-
secute them from city to city, so that all the righteous
blood shed on the land will come upon you…O Jeru-
salem, Jerusalem, that kills the prophets, and stones

those which are sent [Greek apostello] to you…

When Jerusalem was destroyed, the blood of the martyrs had been avenged—as per Jesus' explicit words. This is what the souls under the altar cried for (Revelation 6:9-11).

God will take vengeance on those who persecute His people—"Vengeance is mine," says the Lord, "I will repay" (Romans 12:19). It is not our responsibility, nor our right to get revenge.

The destruction was violent

The destruction of Jerusalem would be violent (18:21-23). Verse 21 proves Babylon is not Rome—because Rome has never suffered a violent destruction. It was sacked and looted in 410, and a few buildings burned, but nothing that could be described as a violent destruction.

> "The sack was nonetheless, by the standards of the age (and all ages), restrained. There was no general slaughter of the inhabitants and the two main basilicas of Peter and Paul were nominated places of sanctuary. Most of the buildings and monuments in the city survived intact, though stripped of their valuables."[1]

And when Rome finally fell in 476, there was no destruction. They allowed the invaders to come in without opposition.

> "On the last day of the empire, [Odovacar,] a barbarian member of the Germanic tribe Siri and former commander in the Roman army entered the city unopposed."[2]

---

[1] https://en.wikipedia.org/wiki/Sack_of_Rome_(410) (accessed 10/27/2021)

[2] Wasson, Donald, "Fall of the Western Roman Empire" in *The World History Encyclopedia.* https://www.worldhistory.org/article/835/fall-of-the-western-roman-empire/ (accessed 10/27/2021)

The destruction would be complete.

The city shall not be found anymore <u>at all</u>. The voice of joy (harpers, musicians, pipers, trumpeters) would not be heard anymore <u>at all</u>. No craftsman, regardless of the craft, would be found any more in the city. No workers (people who used the millstones) would be heard anymore in the city <u>at all</u>. The light of a candle will not shine in the city <u>at all</u>. No marriages in the city <u>at all</u>. The entire city would be laid waste, without inhabitant AT ALL.

Jerusalem will never to be rebuilt again as God's city, or even as the city that once was—with the temple and the priesthood.

The destruction was just (18:23-24).

The merchants of Jerusalem were the great men of the land, and by their deceptions (witchcraft) all nations were deceived. It was because of the Jews that persecution against Christians spread to all nations in the Roman Empire. Jerusalem had also deceived the majority of the Jews throughout the Empire to join in their rebellion.

In her was found the blood of the prophets, and the saints [holy ones], and all that were slain on the land. Again this goes with Jesus' statement that Jerusalem was guilty of **all the righteous blood shed on the earth [land]** (Matthew 23).

Rejoice, don't weep.

When evil is destroyed, God expects His people to rejoice—and at the very least not show sympathy for the evil ones.

- God told Aaron not to show sorrow when his sons Nadab and Abihu were killed by fire from heaven (Leviticus 10:6).
- The Israelites complained about God squashing Korah's insurrection against Moses, so God sent a plague among them, killing many of them (Numbers 16-17).
- God instituted governments to punish the evil—it is His design, and His plan for it to happen (Romans 13:1-ff).

God expects His people to rejoice when evil is stopped and when the wicked are punished.

HEAVENS' REACTION (19:1-6)

And after these things I heard a great sound of many crowds in heaven, saying, "Hallelujah; Salvation, and glory, and honor, and power, to the Lord our God: because his judgments are true and righteous: because he has judged the great whore, who corrupted the land with her fornication, and he avenged the blood of his servants at her hand." And again they said, "Hallelujah."

And her smoke rose up forever and ever.

And the twenty-four elders and the four creatures fell down and worshipped God who sat on the throne, saying, "Amen; Hallelujah."

And a voice came out from the throne, saying, "Praise our God, all you his servants, and you who fear him, both small and great."

And I heard something like the sound of a great multitude, and like the sound of many waters, and like the sound of mighty thunderings, saying, "Hallelujah: because the omnipotent Lord God reigns."

Praise to God

After the angel's announcement of Jerusalem's overthrow, John hears praise heaped upon God. A united voice of many people [literally, many crowds] in heaven cry out "Hallelujah! Salvation and glory and honor and power to the Lord our God!"

This is in response to the command to rejoice over the destruction of Jerusalem (18:20). The praise was because "He has judged the great whore [Jerusalem]… and avenged the blood of His servants at her hand." Don't miss the importance and impact of this:

God's wife, Israel, had just suffered capital punishment because she was unfaithful to God.

We should praise God because all His judgments are correct, holy, and righteous. They praised again, "Hallelujah," which literally means, "Y'all praise Jehovah."

The smoke of Jerusalem rose up forever and ever.

There will never be a third temple built. Jerusalem will never again be the city of God.

The current city of Jerusalem shares a *name* with the ancient city, and is built on part of the same land—but it is not the same city. Consider this:

- Jerusalem was scraped clean by the Romans, and a new city built in its place sixty years later, called "Aelia Capitolina." Jews were forbidden to enter under penalty of death.
- In 614, a revitalized Persia destroyed much of the city with help from Jews. But 15 years later, it was back in Roman hands.
- In 634, the Muslims captured and destroyed part of the Roman city, and renamed it Iliya.
- For the next 400 years, various Arab groups fought over the city, causing destruction at various intervals, and building new buildings.
- The Crusaders came in and massacred all the inhabitants, and filled the city with non-Jews from all over the place who also began to remake the city in their own image.
- The Muslims, under Saladin, retook the city, but by the 1200s, the city was nothing more than a village.
- For the next 400 years, the city changed hands many times, with much destruction coming with each attack (Muslims, crusaders, Mongolians, etc…).
- The area was also devastated by many earthquakes during this time.

The modern city of Jerusalem is a Muslim-built city built on top of a partially destroyed Muslim city, built on top of a partially destroyed Roman city, built on top of a partially destroyed Muslim city, built on top of a partially destroyed Roman city, built on top of the completely destroyed Roman-built Hebrew city.

Modern Jerusalem is NOT the same city as ancient Jerusalem—which was God's once-holy city. If my house burned down, and I built another one in its place, it isn't the same house, even though it is in the same location and has the same address. Jerusalem of today is *not* the Jerusalem of first century.

The twenty-four elders fell down and praised God, saying "Amen! Hallelujah!"

They shouted their agreement of God's execution of the harlot Jerusalem.

A voice from the throne, commands praise to God

Since it comes from the throne, one might think it is God's voice. But since it says "praise *our* God," it may be the four creatures. Regardless, the command originates with God. And the command/encouragement is for *all* people—praise Him for His judgments and power!

Then another voice praises God.

This voice or sound (same word in Greek) is like others that have appeared before in Revelation. This voice is like the sound of a great multitude, like the sound of many waters (1:15), like the sound of mighty thunderings (thundering proceeded from the throne frequently).

Though tempting to say this is Jesus (because of the similarities to other parts of Revelation), verse 10 shows that interpretation cannot be accurate, for this messenger says, "I am…one of your brothers, having the testimony of Jesus" (verse 10). This heavenly messenger says, "Y'all praise Jehovah (Hallelujah), for the omnipotent (all-powerful) Lord God is reigning!"

WHAT DOES THIS MEAN FOR US TODAY?

What is your reaction to God?

Some people only look at what they lose, while others look at what is right. The city of Jerusalem rejected God, and killed His Son—and God executed them for it. But His persecuted people rejoiced in Him, and praised Him for His justice. Do you complain about life, or do you rejoice in the God who will make everything right?

God rules

God's destruction of Jerusalem was an irrefutable proof that He rules in the affairs of men, and uses whoever He wants to carry out His plans (see Daniel 4). God didn't send fire from heaven on Jerusalem, but instead used the Roman armies as His chosen instrument. Do you recognize God's rule in your life and in the world? Or do you try to make yourself the all-powerful center of your universe?

God deserves praise

We need to praise God for His mighty power, for His judgments, for His kindness, and for caring about us—His people! Yes, God does care about you—you are made in His image! He loves you, and He wants to be a part of your life, but you've got to let Him in by coming to Christ and submitting to His rule and the laws of His kingdom.

Jesus spoke a lot of parables while on earth. One dealt with a marriage supper and the destruction of a city. Take a look at it:

> *And Jesus spoke to them again in parables, and said, "The kingdom of heaven is like a certain king, who made a marriage feast for his son, and sent out his servants to call those who were invited to the wedding, but they would not come.*

> *"Again, he sent out other servants, saying, 'Tell those who are invited, "Look, I have prepared my dinner: my oxen and my fatlings are killed, and all things are ready: come to the marriage feast."'*

> *"But they made light of it, and went their way, one to his farm, another to his business. And the rest of them took his servants, and treated them spitefully, and murdered them.*

> *"But when the king heard this, he was livid, and he sent out his armies, destroyed those murderers, and burned up their city.*

> *"Then he said to his servants, 'The wedding feast is ready, but those who were invited were not worthy. Therefore, go into the highways, and invite to the marriage everyone you find.' So those servants went out into the highways, and gathered together all they found, both bad and good: and the wedding feast was furnished with guests.*

> *"And when the king came in to see the guests, he saw*

a man there who was not wearing a wedding garment. And he said to him, 'Friend, how did you come in here without having a wedding garment?' And he was speechless. Then the king said to the servants, 'Bind him hand and foot, and take him away, and cast him into outer darkness; there shall be weeping and gnashing of teeth. Because many are called, but few are chosen.'" (Matthew 22:1-14)

The Jews received the primary invitation to follow Christ and be part of the church. Instead of accepting the invitation, they continually rejected it and even killed some of the messengers (the apostles) who were inviting them. As a result, God destroyed them and their city was burnt with fire (verse 7). According to that parable, after the destruction of the city, the wedding feast took place and the invitation was open to everyone.

This parable appears to form the background for what takes place in the rest of Revelation 19.

Before we get into the text, we need to remember that in the Old Testament, Israel was pictured as the wife of God (Isaiah 54:5—"Your maker is your husband"; Jeremiah 3:14—"I am married to you"). But Israel committed adultery and was given a bill of divorce from God (Isaiah 50:1-ff). The book of Hosea shows God had put away Israel, but would later attempt to woo her back. But the Jews rejected God's attempts to bring them back into a relationship with Him through Christ—and as a result, they were destroyed along with their city, Jerusalem.

Isaiah 62 prophesies of things in the church. The Gentiles would see the righteousness of the New Jerusalem, and the followers of God would be called by a new name (62:2). That was fulfilled in Acts 11:19-26—after the Gentiles heard the gospel, the disciples began to be called "Christians." In Isaiah 62:5, God compares this restoration to the joy of a groom rejoicing over his bride.

And let's not forget the New Testament refers to the church as the bride of Christ (Ephesians 5:23-32).

With these things in mind, let's dive in!

THE BRIDE OF CHRIST DESCRIBED (19:7-8)

Let us be glad and rejoice, and give honor to Him: for the marriage of the Lamb has come, and His wife has made herself ready. And it was granted to her that she should be dressed in fine linen, clean and white: for the fine linen is the righteousness of saints.

The marriage of the church to Christ is a fact worth celebrating.

Jesus Christ—the most powerful, kind, loving, righteous, and perfect man—has chosen His bride: the church. Weddings were a cause of great joy and celebration, especially when royalty was involved.

The time of the marriage had come.

(More on this in just a bit).

The wife has made herself ready.

Faithful Christians (aka the church, the bride) have dedicated themselves to a lifetime of loving and serving Jesus Christ. The bride/church has been cleansed with the washing of water by the word (Ephesians 5:25-27). It is through baptism *and* faithful living that the church/bride is made ready (1 John 1:7).

She is clothed in fine linen, clean and white.

Fine linen first appears in the Bible as a garment of honor and prestige—Pharaoh made Joseph the 2nd highest ruler in the whole kingdom, and clothed him in fine linen (Genesis 41:42).

God chose fine linen for holy use. The tabernacle covering, outer fence, veil, and curtains all included fine linen (Exodus 26:1, 31, 36;

27:9, 16, 18). All the priests' garments were made of fine linen (Exodus 39:27-29). The church is called the *temple*[1] of God (1 Corinthians 3:16), and all Christians are *priests* (1 Peter 2:5, 9)

This color (pure and white) shows purity. Unlike the harlot, Old Jerusalem, the church is a virgin bride for Christ (2 Corinthians 11:2).

The white garments are the righteousness of the saints (Revelation 19:8). Saints are made righteous by being clothed in Christ in baptism, being washed by His blood (Galatians 3:27, Revelation 1:5).

The church today is still the bride of Christ.

Anyone who cheats on their spouse should be ashamed and stands condemned before God (Galatians 5:19-21). How much more serious is it to cheat on Jesus Christ?

So many congregations have committed spiritual adultery and tried to join themselves with the world, and with denominations—and then claim their husband—Christ—is okay with it! Would you be okay with it if your spouse cheated on you?

The church must remain pure, saved exclusively for Christ Jesus her husband!

THE TIMING OF THE WEDDING

There are two main views about the wedding of Christ and the church.

(1) The marriage of Christ to the church began at Pentecost. (2) The marriage of Christ to the church has not yet taken place, but will take place when Christ returns.

Joseph was called the "husband" of Mary when they were betrothed (in an official, legally binding engagement period). She was

---

[1] The tabernacle was designed to be portable because the Israelites did not at that time have their own land. It was retired and replaced by the temple built by Solomon.

technically his wife (going by Jewish custom), but they had not yet had their formal ceremony, nor had they yet consummated the marriage.

In a similar way, the church became Christ's chosen bride at Pentecost, but did that make the marriage complete? Paul told the Christians in Corinth that they were "betrothed" to Christ (2 Corinthians 11:2). Some believe Ephesians 5:25-27 speaks of a time before the church is "presented" to Christ as His bride.

So, if the church during Paul's time was "betrothed" to Christ, when did/when will the marriage be completed?

The most common view in the church is that it becomes complete at the final coming of Christ. This would make us presently engaged/betrothed to Christ.

A second view is based on the parable of the marriage feast and on the context of Revelation. The Jewish wedding feast, according to some Jewish sources, came after the marriage was consummated. In the parable of the marriage feast, the feast came after the destruction of the wicked city. In Revelation, the marriage feast comes after the destruction of the wicked city, when the king returns triumphant after smashing His enemies (which we will get into momentarily). This would make a 40-year betrothal period.

While the first view is popular, the second is the one that fits the context of Jesus' parable and the context of Revelation the best.

While interesting to think about and discuss, the truth is whether "betrothed" or actually "married" to Christ, we still have the responsibility to live for Him, keep ourselves pure for Him, and be faithful to Him.

THE BLESSING (19:9-10)

And he said to me, "Write, 'Blessed are those who are called to the marriage supper of the Lamb.'" And he said to me, "These are the true sayings of God."

And I fell at his feet to worship him. And he said to me, "Look, don't do that! I am your fellow-servant, and of your brethren that have the testimony of Jesus: worship God: for the testimony of Jesus is the spirit of prophecy."

"Blessed are those who are called to the marriage supper of the Lamb."

Remember the parable of the wedding feast (Matthew 22:1-14). The Jews had been called, but they rejected the call. Afterwards, all people were called, both good and bad.

Receiving a wedding invitation has long been a sign of honor and respect. It shows the bride and/or groom thinks you're special or important. That is how Christ views everyone—as special, or important enough to be invited to participate. This is how the church *should* view everyone.

Being invited to the wedding feast isn't the same as accepting the invitation.

The Jews, for the most part, rejected the call. People are called today, but most still reject the invitation. Some sneak in, but are not wearing the wedding garments (they either pretend to be a Christian, but never put on Christ in baptism, or they are not wearing the white robes of righteousness).

These are the true sayings of God.

People are blessed when they accept the call—God gives His word. Do we want people to be blessed? Go call them to Christ! Tell them "All things are ready, come to the feast!"

John was so overwhelmed he fell down to worship the messenger.

Angels are not to be worshiped (though some still do it today!). John did the same thing later, and was again rebuked for it (Revelation 22:8-9). Angels are fellow-servants who have the testimony of Christ, which is the spirit of prophecy. This means that angels were involved in prophecy—both in revealing it and in bringing it about as aids of Christ (see Matthew 24 and throughout Revelation). God is the only one to be worshiped.

THE KING DESCRIBED (19:11-16)

And I saw heaven opened, and behold, a white horse; and the one who sat on it was called Faithful and True, and in righteousness he judges and makes war. His eyes were like a flame of fire, and on his head were many crowns; and he had a name written, that no man knew, but him alone. And he wore a cloak baptized in blood: and his name is called The Word of God.

And the armies which were in heaven followed him on white horses, and were clothed in fine linen, white and clean.

And out of his mouth goes a sharp sword, so that he would smite the nations with it: and he will rule them with a rod of iron: and he treads the winepress of the fierceness and wrath of Almighty God. And he has on his cloak and on his thigh a name written, KING OF KINGS, AND LORD OF LORDS.

The bride is prepared and waiting, and now the king returns.

He sat upon a white horse.
White is a symbol both of purity and of victory.

The horse is a symbol of war. The king—Jesus Christ—judges and makes war with righteous judgments. Jesus Christ is guaranteed victory in every war He wages.

He is called "faithful and true."
Since He is pictured as the groom coming for His bride, it is appropriate that His character as a Husband is described. He is completely faithful and trustworthy, He is true to His wife. This is the

way every man should be toward his wife. Christ is trustworthy in everything He has said.

His eyes were a flame of fire.

This description also appears in Revelation 1. It means He sees everything (omniscient), and needs no light to see into the heart of men, because His eyes have their own light.

He wore many crowns.

There are two words translated "crown" in the Bible: stephanos (a victory crown), and diadem (a kingly, or ruler's crown). The word here is *diadem*. Christ here is seen wearing many *ruling* crowns, showing He is superior to all rulers on earth—He is King of kings.

He had a name written that no man knew except for Him.

This name is revealed in verse 16: "King of kings and Lord of lords." Jesus was born to be king of the Jews, and died with the name "king of the Jews" over His head (Matthew 2:2; 27:11, 37; John 18:33-37).

Until Jerusalem was destroyed, Jesus had not yet been fully revealed as the overpowering ruler over all earthly rulers. His universal dominion was fully set forth when Jerusalem was destroyed. And we'll see it set forth in another event later in the chapter.

He was clothed in a garment/cloak/robe dipped in blood (19:13).

The word "dipped" is *bapto*, and means "to immerse" or "to dye." It is the root of the word "baptize."

Christ returns as the conquering king whose clothing is immersed, soaked, stained, dyed red with the blood of His enemies. When you think of Christ, do you picture the triumphant king who personally leads His armies in battle, destroying the enemies so fiercely that His clothes are covered in blood?

My friends, this is Jesus Christ!

His name is called "the Word of God."

As we saw in Revelation 1:2, John had already given His testimony about the life of Christ (a reference to the book of John). It is in that gospel account Jesus Christ is called "the Word" who "was God" (John 1:1, 14).

Though there was no mistaking who this conquering king in heaven was, John gives many different descriptions which can only describe one person: Jesus the Christ.

The armies in heaven followed Him.

Some believe these to be the angelic armies of heaven who aided Christ in the overthrow of the beast and the false prophet. This is because they are riding on white horses (victorious war), and because this is still a scene which involves the King coming to the wedding feast (see verse 17). If this is the case, then it shows the majesty of Christ who leads the armies of heaven (see Joshua 5:13-15).

More likely, these are Christians (the bride of Christ) being brought to the feast by their new husband. Think about it: the armies are clothed with fine linen, white and clean—the same clothing as the bride of Christ. (And it seems noteworthy that the only one with blood-splattered garments is Christ—He did all the work.) And Jewish marriage customs involved the husband bringing his wife *to* the wedding feast (which took place after the wedding itself).

The picture here is really of a powerful king whose bride was being held captive by an enemy. He charges in, slaughters the enemy, rescues her, and then escorts her to the wedding feast.

Out of His mouth came a sharp sword.

This is the same way He is described in Revelation 1. This shows His words have the power to destroy and judge (see John 12:48). He uses this sword (the power of His word) to smite the nations and rule them with a rod of iron.

Some believe the *Jews* are being referred to here as "the *nations*" (the same Greek word as *Gentiles*) because of how wicked they had become. It is more likely this represents Christ's universal power and authority to destroy any and all that try to hurt His bride—the church. If you had absolute power, and someone tried to harm your wife, they'd be dead, right?

He treads the winepress of the fierceness and wrath of Almighty God.

In Isaiah 63:3, God says, "I have trodden the winepress alone…I will tread them in my anger, and trample them in my fury, and their blood shall be splattered on my garments, and I will stain all my clothing." Jesus treads the winepress, and His clothes are stained with their blood. So…why is it again that some people say Jesus isn't God?

KING OF KINGS AND LORD OF LORDS.

We hear this phrase often, especially in some of our hymns, but what does it mean? Some have said that this means He is the "kingliest king" and the "lordliest lord,"—basically that of all the kings, He is the most regal, most king-like. While this may capture part of the idea, I think it is showing His universal dominion over all kingdoms.

> The mountain of the Lord's house shall be established on the top of the mountains—Isaiah 2:2.

In other words, His kingdom is above every other kingdom. Christ is the King who rules over all other kings. All kings and masters on earth are still subservient to Him.

THE FEAST AND THE WAR (19:17-21)

And I saw an angel standing in the sun; and he cried with a loud voice, saying to all the birds that fly in the midst of heaven, "Come and gather yourselves together to the supper of the great God; so that you may eat the flesh of kings, and the flesh of captains, and the flesh of mighty men, and the flesh of horses, and of their riders, and the flesh of all men, both free and bond, both small and great."

And I saw the beast, and the kings of the land, and their armies, gathered together to make war against him who sat on the horse, and against his army. And the beast was taken, and with him the false prophet that worked miracles before him, with which he deceived those who had received the mark of the beast, and those who worshiped his image. These both were cast alive into a lake of fire burning with brimstone.

And the rest were killed with the sword of him who sat on the horse, which came out of his mouth: and all the birds were filled with their flesh.

Come here, birds. Time to eat!

They were gathered so they could eat the flesh of kings, captains, mighty men, horses and horsemen, and all: free and slave, small and great (19:18). This describes the entire Jewish population in Jerusalem.

Back in Genesis, Joseph interpreted a dream, while in prison, for Pharaoh's baker, and said in three days Pharaoh would have him put to death, and the birds would eat his flesh (Genesis 40:19). Goliath threatened David: "Come to me and I will give your flesh to the fowls of the air" (1 Samuel 17:44).

The angel's message meant a great destruction was coming, and the birds would have a feast on the dead bodies. The great supper appears to take place at the destruction of Jerusalem, though it was announced ahead of time.

The beast and the kings of the land and their armies gathered together to make war against Christ and His army.

Here, the *reason* for the bird's feast is given. It refers back to the massive persecution instituted by Nero beginning in AD 64 in which the Romans—but especially the Jews—throughout the Empire made war on the saints—the bride of Christ. Remember what I asked before: If someone attacked your wife, what would your response be?

The beast (Nero) and the false prophet (the beast from the Promised Land—the Jewish nation) were cast alive into the lake of fire burning with brimstone.

Remember that Nero was the embodiment of the beast—and he was destroyed when Christ had the angel pour out the vial of wrath upon Rome (Revelation 16:10). There is a growing number of Christians (myself among them) who believe Nero is also the "man of sin" described in 2 Thessalonians 2 that would be destroyed at Christ's coming. When Christ came in judgment against the Jews (beginning with the start of the Roman-Jewish War), he also came in judgment against Nero.

The false prophet was the Jewish leadership that deceived the Jews into throwing their support behind Nero and against Christ—thus wearing the mark of the beast.

They were cast alive into a lake of fire burning with brimstone. That they were cast *alive* into hell shows that hell is not annihilation, but it is a constant punishment.

The remnant (the rest of the wicked Jews) were killed with the sword of Christ which comes from His mouth.

It was under the command of Christ that Rome went forth conquering and to conquer (Revelation 6:1-2). The destruction of Jerusalem is called "the coming of the Son of man" to judge them (Matthew 24:30-34). They were judged and killed because Christ said so.

The birds were filled with their flesh.

The buzzards and vultures of the area would have eaten all they could, and there would still be plenty more (see Matthew 24:28).

WHAT DOES THIS MEAN FOR US TODAY?

The faithful bride of Christ—the church—anxiously awaits the return of her King.
The King—Jesus Christ—remains faithful to her, and will destroy all the ones who seek to do her harm. Here is a vision of absolute love and faithfulness from both sides.

You really ought to consider being god friends with Jesus.
When you look at Jesus Christ, and you realize He is the Savior of mankind, shouldn't you want to be His friend? When you look at Jesus Christ, and you realize He is a warrior-king whose clothes are soaked with the blood of the enemies He has killed, don't you think it would be a good idea to be His friend instead of His enemy?

Jesus said it very plainly, You are my friend *if* you do whatever I have commanded you (John 15:14). We sing, "I'll be a friend to Jesus," but have you done what Jesus commanded?

- He commanded us to believe He is the Christ, the Son of God (John 8:24).
- He commanded us to repent of our sins (Luke 24:47).
- He commanded us to confess Him before others (Matthew 10:32-33).
- He commanded us to be baptized in order to be saved (Mark 16:16).
- He commanded us to be faithful to Him even to the point of death (Revelation 2:10).

Does that describe you?

Study Forty-Four:
The Thousand-Year Reign?
(Revelation 20:4)

The look of shock and utter confusion was apparent on the woman's face. Until this point, she felt like she was in control, calling the shots, making sure nothing and no one got in her way. One simple statement destroyed all of her confidence, and the momentum she thought she had.

She was a Jehovah's Witness, and—like almost every other denomination—bought into the idea of a thousand-year reign of Christ on earth. She was making one of her points, not even really dealing with the millennial reign, but just mentioning it in passing (they are taught to do that, to mention things in passing that are widely accepted to get people to let their guard down).

That's when I made the innocent statement, "There's no such thing as a thousand-year reign of Christ." You would have thought I had just told her that pizzas actually came from the nostrils of purple Martians.

The idea of a literal thousand-year reign of Christ on earth is so ingrained in some religious folks that they've never stopped to consider, "Does the Bible really teach that?" This woman was in such shock by that statement that after another two minutes of stammering, trying to prove that such was the truth, she left.

If you don't think this idea permeates the denominational world, consider that many identify themselves based on their interpretation of this one verse! Premillennialists, post-millennialists, transmillennialists, amillennialists, and non-millennialists.

Pretty much everyone who has come to an opinion on the second coming of Christ falls into one of these categories, whether they realize it or not. So, before we go on with the lesson, let's define these terms.

THE DIFFERENT "MILLENNIALIST" BELIEFS

Premillennialism.

Premillennialists take the view that Jesus will come, "rapture" the faithful and raise the dead saints, and then within the next seven years,[1] *He will begin to literally reign on a literal throne in literal Jerusalem.* This is called "pre-millennialism" because they believe Christ's return is *before* the thousand years.

As we will discuss in more detail later, Premillennialism has major problems, one of which is that Scriptures *never* teach Jesus will reign on a literal throne in literal Jerusalem. In fact, quite the opposite is true. Just follow the biblical evidence:

- Jeremiah 22:28-30 says that NO descendant of Jeconiah will prosper, sitting on the throne of David and ruling from Judea.
- Matthew 1 says that Jesus was a descendant of Jeconiah.
- Therefore, if Jesus sat on the throne of David *and* ruled in Jerusalem (which is in Judea), then His rule would be a miserable failure.

Post-millennialism.

Post-millennialists are the opposite of the pre-millennialists. They believe in a thousand-year reign of Christ, but that it is carried out *through His people here on earth.* They believe that after a thousand-years of intense evangelism wherein almost the entire world is

---

[1] There are many different flavors of Premillennialism, that generally fall under two categories: Classic and Dispensational. In the Dispensational category, there are different camps, who dispute the specific timing of the so-called "Rapture" (before, during, or after a seven-year "tribulation" period). Each of these varieties still violate the context of the book of Revelation, which described things which were "shortly come to pass" and "at hand" when John wrote (see Revelation 1:1, 3; 22:6, 10; as well as studies 1 and 2 of this book).

converted to Christ, He will return to judge the world. Hence, they have Christ's return as *after* the millennium.[2]

They claim that Old Testament prophecies about Israel (which they say is the church) and great blessings (which they view as coming in a 1,000-year "golden age") still must be fulfilled so Christ can come back.

Transmillennialism.

This is one that most of you probably have never heard of, and for good reason. Trans-millennialists believe Christ will never return, but instead that He reigns *eternally* on the earth *through Christians*. They believe the millennium figuratively means eternity (usually beginning with AD 70, which they claim was when all the "second coming" prophecies were fulfilled). They also believe there is no judgment for anyone after Jerusalem was destroyed—in essence, meaning universal salvation to everyone who has lived after AD 70, whether they believe in Jesus or not.

This belief is called "transmillennialism" because they believe the representative reign of Christ transcends the millennia, and that it represents the *trans*ition from Old Testament to New (at AD 70). This interpretation has many problems, perhaps most glaring of which is that Revelation 20:4 says headless, dead Christians are the ones who reign with Him—not living Christians here on earth. And it makes the entire Bible irrelevant after AD 70, since no one would be lost. That's heretical.

It is also a trademarked term. Transmillennialism®. So make of that whatever you wish.

Amillennialism.

This describes the belief that there is no *literal* period of a thousand years described—that it is a *figurative* number, representing the *entire Christian dispensation from Pentecost until Jesus returns*

---

[2] Some modern post-millennialists believe that the "thousand years" is figurative, and just means a long period of time.

again. This is the view held by most in the church of Christ today. Unlike Post-millennialists, amillennialists usually deny any sort of universal revival before the final coming of Christ—in fact, many amillennialists believe things will continue to get worse and worse until Christ finally comes in judgment upon all. In this way, they are in some cases polar opposites of the Post-millenialists.

Non-millennialists.

This group believes Revelation 20:4 and 6 says absolutely *nothing* about a thousand-year reign of Christ—neither literally or figuratively. Not in heaven or on earth.

They do believe Christ is and will continue to be reigning, but believe the term "thousand years" in these verses don't apply to *Christ's* reign at all. If that seems odd to you, just keep reading.

THE TEXT (REVELATION 20:4, 6)

> *And I saw thrones, and they sat on them, and judgment was given to them. And I saw the souls of those who were beheaded for the witness of Jesus, and for the word of God, and who had not worshiped the beast, nor his image, neither had received his mark on their foreheads or in their hands; and they lived and reigned with Christ a thousand years.*

> *Blessed and holy is he who has part in the first resurrection: on such the second death has no power, but they shall be priests of God and of Christ, and shall reign with him a thousand years.*

I realize we skipped verses 1-3. We'll deal with them in the next study.

Who is "them"?

In verse 4, John said he saw thrones, and *they* sat on them, judgment was given to *them*, even the souls of *them* who were beheaded... neither had [they] received the beast's mark on *their* foreheads, or in *their* hands.

The verse is clearly talking about Christians who had been killed for their allegiance to Christ. Some believe this also includes those who died natural deaths, but who had lived faithfully, which could be possible as well.

But notice _the subject of every clause is the group of faithful dead Christians_. Why is that important? Because they are also the subject of the last part of the verse too.

<u>THEY</u> lived and reigned with Christ a thousand years.

Who is it that "lived and reigned" a thousand years?—the dead saints! The phrase "with Christ" describes *how* they were reigning.

Before you think I've lost my mind, let me ask you a question. A man and woman get married. Obviously, after they got married, they lived together. If I said, "She lived with him thirty years," does that tell you how long *he* lived? If you follow the "logic" of most of the millennial camps, you would have to answer that it meant the man only lived 30 years. But you and I both know that saying "she lived with him thirty years" only tells you how long they lived *together*, and says nothing at all about how long he lived before or after those thirty years.

The same thing is true with this statement in Revelation 20:4— The only thing it tells us is the length of time that the dead saints lived and reigned *with* Christ. *They* lived and reigned a thousand years. It says nothing at all about the length of Christ's reign, or of the length of His life.

Verse 6 says the same thing. *They* reigned a thousand years.

We will deal more with the "thousand year" issue next study (spoiler alert: it isn't a literal number), but for now, we need to realize *the idea of a thousand-year reign <u>of Christ</u> (whether literal or* *figurative) isn't taught in the Bible.* A thousand-year reign of saints, however, *is*.

THE PREMILLENNIAL PROBLEMS

Premillennialists teach the book of Revelation is to be interpreted literally, and so the reign of Christ is literally a thousand years. However, this verse actually disproves that doctrine and their entire approach to the book itself. Let's look at just some of the problems they face with this verse.

Christ must die after the thousand-year reign.

What??? The text clearly states the dead saints "lived and reigned" with Him a thousand years. If this text limits Christ's *reign* to a literal thousand years, then it also limits His *life* to a literal thousand years. You can't separate the verbs "lived and reigned" and say that only *one* of them is a thousand years—both of them cover the same period of time.

You can't live with Christ if you have a head.

The only ones, according to the text, who would live and reign with Christ are the ones beheaded for being a Christian. And if we take this absolutely literal (as Premillennialists say we must), then it *only* includes those who were beheaded for the faith. Oh, you were crucified? Sorry, you can't live with Christ. Oh, you died a natural death? Sorry, you're out of luck.

In other words, taking this literally means almost every Premillennialist that has ever lived will have no part in living or reigning with Christ.

Christ is doomed to failure.

We referenced earlier that Jeremiah 22:28-30 says no descendant of Jeconiah would prosper sitting on the throne of David *and* ruling in Judea (note that if one does *both*, he will not prosper). They teach Christ will do both: sit on David's throne *and* rule from Jerusalem (which is in Judea)—thus their own doctrine requires Christ's so-called "thousand-year reign" be a horrible failure.

The fact is Jesus has been sitting on the throne of David, the throne of God, the throne of heaven (all ways of saying the same thing), but He is not reigning from Jerusalem—see Acts 2.

They have to add to the text.

In a book that closes with a curse on those who add to the prophecies of the book (22:18-19), you have to wonder about people who intentionally insert a word into the text that isn't there.

They use this verse to prove a literal, earthly reign in Jerusalem. The problem is that Jerusalem is not mentioned, nor hinted at, in the entire verse or the verses surrounding it. They have to insert the words "in Jerusalem" to the end of the verse to get it to teach a reign of Christ in Jerusalem.

They have to change the words of the text.

The text teaches a thousand-year reign of the dead saints. Premillennialists must change the word "they" to "He." They must change the subject of the verse from the dead saints to Jesus Christ. In short, they have to change the text to make it fit their theories.

WHAT DOES THIS MEAN FOR US TODAY?

Christ is NOW sitting at the right hand of God, on the throne in heaven (Acts 2:22-38).

Jesus said "all authority in heaven and on earth" was given to Him—and He's had that power now for nearing 2,000 years! (Matthew 28:18). Let me ask you a question: If Jesus already has *all* the authority in heaven and on earth, why would He need to come back and establish an earthly kingdom?

Since Christ is already the king over His kingdom (Colossians 1:13), we should be making sure we are living according to His laws.

STUDY FORTY-FIVE:
THE BINDING OF SATAN
(REVELATION 20:1-10)

Of all the sections of Revelation, chapter 20:1-10 is the most difficult to interpret. This is true regardless of which approach one takes to the book.

Premillennialists, as we saw last time, utterly destroy their own doctrine if they take this section literally. Post-millennialists can't really harmonize a powerful return of Satan at the end of the thousand-years with the idea Christ will come immediately after a thousand years of peace and a "golden age of evangelism." Even those who take the "thousand years" to be figuratively describing the entire Christian era have a problems with this passage—because at the end of it, Satan must rise again to power before the final judgment can take place.

I don't pretend to have all the answers—but as we go through this section of Scripture, we will look at what might be the answer, as well as what cannot be the answer.

Before we get into the text, it might be helpful to summarize the characters and events in the text.

- The angel with the key to the bottomless pit.
- Satan (the dragon/serpent/devil)
- A chain used to bind Satan and cast him into the pit.
- A seal on Satan [or the pit]
- A thousand years of captivity for Satan.
- A thousand years of reigning and victory for the dead saints with Christ.
- Another group of dead ones who didn't live until the thousand years were finished.
- The first resurrection, which protects from the second death.
- A thousand years of serving as priests while reigning.

- The end of the thousand years.
- Satan released to deceive the nations again and launch a massive war against the saints.
- God destroys Satan and his armies with fire, and casts Satan into the lake of fire to be tormented forever.

That's a lot of material to cover, and there are difficulties and questions we will probably still have when we finish. Even among those who agree that Revelation is dealing primarily with the period from AD 64-70, culminating in the destruction of Jerusalem, there is disagreement on how to deal with this passage…in fact, I've not found any two that agree at all!

Some believe this is a flashback, describing the ministry of Christ on earth (which was around a thousand days). This completely misses the context of martyred saints (killed under Nero's edict) living and reigning with Christ during those thousand years.

Others say it describes the time from Pentecost to the destruction of Jerusalem. Still others believe it is from the start of Jesus' ministry until the destruction of Jerusalem. Probably the biggest problem with either of these views is this: Satan was only supposed to have power for "a little while" after the thousand years—yet it is obvious to anyone with eyes to see that Satan is still active nearly 2,000 years since AD 70. That would hardly classify as "a little while."

Some believe it is the entire Christian age from Pentecost forward. Others believe it is the entire Christian age from AD 70 forward. And still others believe that it doesn't describe a time period at all, but instead just represents the complete victory of Christ and the Christians over Satan and Judaism.[1]

With all these different ideas swirling in the back of our minds, let's look at the text!

---

[1] The latter is the view of Foy. E. Wallace Jr..

THE ANGEL BINDS SATAN WITH A GREAT CHAIN FOR 1,000 YEARS (20:1-3)

And I saw an angel descend from heaven, having the key of the bottomless pit and a great chain in his hand. And he seized the dragon, that old serpent, who is the Devil and Satan, and bound him a thousand years, cast him into the bottomless pit, shut him up, and set a seal on him, so that he could no longer deceive the nations until the thousand years were fulfilled. And after that he must be loosed a short while.

An angel descends from heaven with the key to the bottomless pit.
If the bottomless pit (*abyss* in some translations) is the Hadean realm (see Romans 10:7, Luke 8:31), then this angel seems to represent Jesus Christ. Jesus clearly stated *He* was the one who possessed the keys of Hades (Revelation 1:18). Identifying this as Christ makes sense, because of what this messenger does to Satan.

He grabs Satan and chains him for a thousand years.
Who do Scriptures repeatedly picture as the one who defeats Satan? *Jesus Christ.*[2] Here, Satan is called by four names:

- **The dragon**—the power behind the beast (Nero) and the false prophet (Jerusalem).
- **That old serpent**—the one opposed to God's plans from the beginning (see Genesis 3).
- **The devil**—the accuser of God's people.
- **Satan**—literally, the slanderer.

The angel (Christ) binds him for a thousand years. If you remember at the end of chapter 19 (just three verses ago), the beast (Rome) and the false prophet (Israel) were cast into the lake of fire. But the

---

[2] See Study 29.

victory of Christ would not be complete without victory over the true enemy: Satan.

The angel (Christ) casts him into the abyss (the bottomless pit). He shuts Satan in the pit, and places a seal on him. Satan is now a prisoner.

After the thousand years, Satan will be loosed a short while.

As we will see in verses 7-9, this loosing again gave him the power to deceive the nations. We will discuss this more in that place.

In Christ's earthly ministry, He was in the process of limiting Satan's power.

He cast out demons, and then described it as "binding the strongman" (Matthew 12:29). When his disciples came back excited about being able to cast out demons, Jesus' response was "I beheld Satan, like lightning from heaven, fallen" (Luke 10:18). Jesus' death was to put a permanent defeat to Satan (John 12:31).

This binding was for a specific purpose: so Satan could not deceive the nations any more.

The Greek word translated *nations* is *ethnos* (from which we get the word *ethnic*). The same word is also translated *Gentiles* throughout the New Testament. When a Jewish audience saw the word *ethnos*, they usually understood it to mean *Gentiles*, non-Jews.

If you read through the Old Testament, you quickly get the idea there were very few Gentiles Satan hadn't completely corrupted. If you read through Romans 1, you get the same idea. The only people Satan hadn't completely corrupted were the Jews—and he was making good headway on them.

But beginning with John the Baptizer, then Jesus' ministry, and then Pentecost, God began binding Satan. The binding continued as the gospel began to be taken to the Gentiles. Satan fought back hard (using the Jews) against this and just about succeeded. But when Jerusalem was destroyed, the gospel exploded into the Gentile nations and Satan began to lose his power in large measure.

This is what I—and many other commentators in the church—believe this is talking about. It harmonizes perfectly with the rest of the Bible and with history. It also keeps this in context, because this significant binding by Christ takes place AFTER Nero and Jerusalem were destroyed (less than 10 verses before this).

The influence of Christianity has affected the entire world, severely limiting Satan's power. Don't get me wrong, Satan is still active, but he doesn't have *near* the universal power/influence he once did.

THE REIGNING OF THE SAINTS FOR A THOUSAND YEARS (20:4-6)

And I saw thrones, and they sat on them, and judgment was given to them. And I saw the souls of those who were beheaded for the witness of Jesus, and for the word of God, and who had not worshiped the beast, nor his image, neither had received his mark upon their foreheads or in their hands; and they lived and reigned with Christ a thousand years. But the rest of the dead did not live again until the thousand years were finished. This is the first resurrection. Blessed and holy is the one who has part in the first resurrection: the second death has no power on these, but they shall be priests of God and of Christ, and shall reign with him a thousand years.

Faithful saints sitting on thrones, living and reigning with Christ.
John specifically says:

- These were beheaded for the testimony of Christ.
- These were beheaded for the word of God.
- These refused to worship the beast, or his image, and did not receive his mark.

- This certainly includes the martyrs under the altar from chapter 6.
- This certainly includes the 144,000 and Great Multitude from chapter 14.
- This certainly includes Christians who overcame during the persecution of AD 64-70 (see Revelation 3:21).

From this passage, we can see a literal, physical reign is not under consideration. This is a spiritual reign—which includes the faithful from both the Old and New Testaments. Though these had died, they were raised to reign with Christ.

MOST commentaries say the living/reigning in verse 4 is "the first resurrection" in verse 5.

Those who have a part in the "first resurrection" are blessed and holy, and the "second death" (eternity in the lake of fire—see 20:14) has no power over them. The implication, then, is anyone who does NOT have a part in the first resurrection WILL be thrown into the lake of fire. The people involved in the first resurrection are priests of God and Christ, and reign with Him a thousand years.

Let's let the Scriptures explain what this means for us.

This section lists three things the saints *do* during the thousand-years: (1) live with Christ, (2) reign with Christ, and (3) are priests for God and Christ.

This seems to perfectly coincide with the apostle Paul's words:

> *"This is a faithful saying, For if we are **dead** with Him, we shall **live** with Him. If we suffer, we shall also **reign** with Him" (2 Timothy 2:11-12).*

This is a promise to all Christians, not just those who were murdered for their faith. But there is more meaning to this verse than you might realize…and we'll get to it in a moment.

Jesus Himself said:

> *"You who have followed me, in the regeneration*

*when the Son of man shall sit on the throne of His glory, you also shall **sit upon twelve thrones** judging the twelve tribes of Israel" (Matthew 19:28).*

Jesus has been sitting on His throne since at least Pentecost, AD 30 (Acts 2:33-36). Pay special attention to the word "regeneration," because we will come back to it momentarily.

Peter told Christians:

*"you are a chosen generation, a **royal priesthood**, a holy nation..." (1 Peter 2:9).*

Their service as priests of God was a present reality. The fact that they were a ROYAL priesthood shows that they were part of the family of the king—part of the ruling family.

All these things were promised *to all Christians*—not just those who were martyred.

Perhaps the most important question to ask right now is...

What does it mean to have part in the first resurrection?

Living and reigning with Christ is called "the first resurrection." It includes being priests for God and Christ.

Remember what Paul said in 2 Timothy 2:11?—If we are dead with Him, we shall also live with Him? Paul said the same thing in Romans 6:8. In that chapter, being "dead" with Christ is defined for us: dying to sin, buried with Him in baptism, and raised (resurrected) to walk in newness of life (6:3-4).

Jesus said the reward of sitting with Him and judging would take place "in the regeneration." The word "regeneration" only appears twice in the New Testament, and it literally means "rebirth" or "new birth." The only other time it is used, Paul says "according to His mercy He saved us by the washing of regeneration, and the renewing of a holy spirit" (Titus 3:5).[3]

---

[3] The "washing of regeneration" was universally agreed by scholars of all denominational backgrounds to refer to baptism until the last 150 or so years,

My friends, the "first resurrection"—wherein we are made to live and reign with Christ, and are made priests of Christ—is baptism! So we could faithfully interpret this passage to say:

> *Blessed are the baptized, because the second death has no power over them!*

SATAN'S RELEASE AND WAR ON THE SAINTS (20:7-9)

> *And when the thousand years have ended, Satan will be loosed out of his prison, and he will go out to deceive the nations which are in the four quarters of the land, Gog and Magog, to gather them together to battle: their number is like the sand of the sea. And they went up across the breadth of the earth, and surrounded the camp of the saints, and the beloved city: and fire came down from God out of heaven, and devoured them.*

After the thousand years end, Satan will be released.

What??? God will release him? How? Why?!?!?

This is the most difficult section of the entire chapter—perhaps the entire book—to explain. And we'll get back to it after we discuss what exactly the thousand years may be.

Satan's restrictions are removed.

He is again free to deceive the Gentiles (nations) which are in the four corners of the earth/land.

He gathers Gog and Magog—Gog is the ruler, Magog is the nation he leads. Gog is mentioned in Ezekiel 38, and represents the heathen. Some have seen in Gog a representation of national leaders (like Nero) who were opposed to God's people.

---

when a push began in earnest to minimize the connection of baptism and salvation.

The point of the verse is Satan gathers his army to persecute Christians. We need to remember this is a figurative book, and so while this persecution could be physical, it could also be a spiritual persecution. The key to understanding this is how we define the "thousand years."

This Satan-led and Satan-deceived army surrounded the camp of the saints, and the beloved city. Some have said this is the Roman armies led by Satan surrounding Jerusalem in AD 70. *Big Problem Here...* By that point, there were no saints in Jerusalem, because they had all left. But even bigger problem: it was *Christ* who directed the Romans in that war...not Satan.

The "beloved city" is *New* Jerusalem—the church—which is described in detail in the next chapter.

Fire came from heaven and devoured the enemies.

This statement MAY be the key to understanding this entire passage (it might not be, but I think it is).

There are only two other times in the Bible where *actual* fire from God devoured people—Leviticus 10:2 and Numbers 26:10. There are many times when it is used *figuratively* for destruction, and the vast majority has God promising destruction on the Jews who have become disobedient.

You might wonder, *Who were destroyed in the two literal accounts of fire coming from God?*

- Nadab and Abihu—chosen priests of God who had offered "strange fire" (Leviticus 10:1-3).
- 250 Israelite men who joined with Korah to fight against God's chosen leader, Moses.

Keep this in mind as we cover the part we've been skipping over:

THE THOUSAND YEARS

There are really only two prominent positions (and one not-so prominent) that merit our consideration (the others being too far-fetched to take seriously).

- The thousand years represents the entire Christian age until the final coming of Christ.
- The thousand years represents the complete victory of Christ and the Christians over their Jewish persecutors.
- We will mention the third option in a few moments

Most non-premillennialist commentaries take the position that it is speaking of the entire Christian age.

The general agreement is Satan is bound by the gospel message being preached. If indeed this is true, the following things must also be true:

- The thousand years is the entire length of time the gospel (which is binding Satan) is preached on earth.
- Therefore, there must come a time when the gospel will no longer be preached at all, because Satan is loosed; released from this prison and deceives the nations *en masse* to attack the Christians before he is finally judged.

This approach must logically conclude that the final coming of Christ *cannot* happen until such time as the gospel stops being preached, the last person who ever will obey the gospel has done so, and Satan gathers his forces for battle. Burton Coffman's commentary on this verse says:

> [W]e believe that the "little time" mentioned here means literally a brief period, beginning at the point after which God shall have finally achieved the full salvation of the total number of the redeemed, and lasting only a relatively very short while. Satan will

be "loosed" without any restraint whatever during that brief period. Due to all that is revealed of Satan's nature in the Bible, it cannot be supposed that the race of man, or the whole world, would continue very long after such an eventuality.

By this he means when the last person who will ever obey the gospel is converted, then Satan breaks loose and mounts his attack before God wipes out all the wicked and casts Satan into hell before the final judgment (which he sees described in the second half of chapter 20).

If indeed this is the correct view of the way things will end, <u>then we have no right to say Jesus could come at any moment</u>—because the gospel is still being preached, people are still being converted, and Satan hasn't mounted his all-out war against the saints. This, however, is the view of some of my professors, some favorite commentators, and many of my friends and fellow-preachers. And it may well be what is under consideration—but if it is, we have to give serious thought to whether we should ever say "Jesus could come at any moment."

The complete victory over the Jews and Nero position:

This view, advocated by Foy E. Wallace Jr., and others, is that the "thousand years" isn't a period of time, but instead is complete victory over the enemies of Christ (the Jews and Nero). Here's why this view makes sense:

The number 10 represents completeness (which is accepted by most Bible scholars). The number 1,000 represents absolute completeness (10x10x10). And so, it is thought, this is speaking of the absolutely complete victory of Christ and His people over Satan, the Jewish nation, and the Roman tyrant, Nero.

If this is indeed the case, it means some time after this victory, Satan would again work towards defeating the saints. This time, however, the bulk of the saints are Gentiles instead of Jews. This time, Satan goes out to deceive the Gentiles (who now make up the majority of the church).

If we follow this reasoning, it is *possible* Satan's release and war on the saints is to destroy the mostly-Gentile church from the inside (Wallace says this is through heathenism).

Fire from God *devours* these Gentiles. Fire from God *devoured* (same word) Nadab and Abihu—disobedient children of God. Fire from God *devoured* (same word) the 250 associates of Korah—who were all disobedient children of God. It is possible, then, that this phrase was used to show Satan's next attack was going to be from within—using disobedient Christians.

Historically, that is what happened with false doctrines creeping in and growing until the Catholic Church came into existence. And if this is the correct interpretation, then God is showing (like in the book of Jude) that those who become disobedient will be punished. Disobedient Christians have nothing to look forward to except for the *fiery* indignation of God which will *devour* His enemies (Hebrews 10:27).

While this interpretation fits with history, and it keeps the events within the time-frame of "shortly come to pass," it also has its difficulties.

- How could Satan's new war on the saints be called a "little season" when it has (1) lasted almost 1900 years, and (2) been an overwhelming success—just look at the number of corrupted churches and denominations in the world?
- And why exactly hasn't God destroyed those who have joined Satan's cause like it says He will do in verse 9?

This may be correct, but I'd need someone to explain those things to me.

A third interpretation: The Christian's victory through baptism.

The thousand years represents the complete victory of Christ over Satan at His death, burial and resurrection—but also the victory of every individual over Satan who is baptized into Christ (buried with Him, and raised to walk in newness of life) and lives and reigns with Him as His priests.

Christians join in Christ's victory over Satan (1 John 2:13-14). When they do so, they have died with Christ, and are given new life through Him (Romans 6:1-8). When they join in this victory through baptism, they become priests of Christ (1 Peter 2:9), and have been adopted into the family of God (Ephesians 1:3-5).

After someone is baptized, Satan (though limited because these are Christians clothed with Christ, wearing the whole armor of God) mounts his attacks against them. He is angry another person has defected from his side to the Kingdom of Jesus Christ, and uses those still under his influence (the nations/Gentiles—non-Christians) as some of his weapons. Unfortunately, some will fall, rejecting the King who saved them, and will make themselves enemies of God— destined to be destroyed by fire (Hebrews 10:26-31).

If this interpretation is correct, and the "thousand years" represents the victory over Satan that comes as each person is baptized into Christ, the lesson is: "Yes, you've won the victory, but keep on guard because the devil isn't going to give up."

This interpretation may be correct, but it is not without its difficulties. For one, the "thousand years" is clearly positioned *after* the "first resurrection," which is undeniably speaking of baptism. It is difficult to see how the "thousand years" could also refer to the same thing. .Second, if the "thousand years" is a single moment of great victory, we would have to have a reason to believe the actions during that period (living, reigning, serving as priests) extend *after* that "thousand years."

This commentator's position

This "thousand years" is not a literal period of a thousand years (as shown in the previous lesson). The "thousand years" figuratively describes *something*, which is tightly connected to *baptism* (the first resurrection). During this time, Christians live and serve as priests.

This could be a description of each Christian's life post-baptism. This could be a description of the church's existence free from Judaism since AD 70. Or it could represent something else.

Ultimately, I have to say, I know some of what it *can't* mean, but I don't know for certain what it *does* mean, because each proposed view has its difficulties. Sorry.

WHAT DOES THIS MEAN FOR US TODAY?

Hopefully you've noticed that we haven't said anything about verse 10 yet.

> *And the devil that deceived them was cast into the lake of fire and brimstone, where the beast and the false prophet are, and shall be tormented day and night forever and ever.*

Hell is the ultimate destiny of Satan and all who refuse to follow Jesus Christ.

This includes those who have never obeyed the gospel, as well as those who were once saved, but have since removed themselves from God's protective love (Hebrews 10:26-31).

The blessing of the first resurrection.

If there's only one thing you take from this lesson, let it be this: Blessed and holy are the ones who have truly been born again through baptism, because they are the ones who can avoid the second death—eternity in hell!

Have you?

STUDY FORTY-SIX:
THE JUDGMENT
(REVELATION 20:11-15)

The saints sit in stunned silence as they listen to the man in front of them, reading from a just-delivered scroll. It speaks about an impending deadly persecution.

The saints are scared. After all, things are difficult already, but they're about to get far worse? Some of them start to wonder if Christianity is really worth it.

As the reader continues, it becomes clear some of them—many of them—won't make it out alive. And again they wonder if Christianity is worth it.

But then they hear words that chill them to the bone. It reminds them of just how big the stakes are: *Whoever was not found written in the book of life was cast into the lake of fire...and shall be tormented day and night forever.*

Yes, what was about to happen would be worse than anything they'd ever experienced. But if they give up, they would face something far worse than anything humans can comprehend: eternity in the Lake of Fire.

The first Christians to hear Revelation read to them would have been overwhelmed with emotions when they heard the message.

- *Comfort*, knowing it was from God, and that the apostle John was—at least at this point—still alive.
- *Uncertainty* and *examination* as they take a spiritual inventory of their congregation to see if it matches up with Christ's ideal.
- *Awe* and *insignificance* as they hear about the throne of God.
- *Fear* and *dread* as they hear about the fast-approaching war.

- *Hopelessness* as they hear about Satan using the Roman Empire and Jewish nation in an effort to destroy them.
- *Relief* when they hear Christ will come to avenge His people and overthrow the persecutors.
- *Confidence* when they hear about their assured victory with Christ.
- *Rejoicing* when they hear about Satan's destruction.
- *Self-examination* when they hear about the judgment scene.

When we read Revelation today, *our* main emotion seems to be confusion, but that wasn't the case with them. To them Revelation was immediate, it was relevant, and their eternal lives hinged on what they did with the book! Let me suggest to you that we should feel the same way, because the principles and truths contained in it apply just as much to you as they did to those saints in the first century.

Keep that in mind as we look at some truths found in Revelation 20:11-15.

THERE IS A JUDGMENT DAY (20:11-12)

And I saw a great white throne, and the one who sat on it, from whose face the earth and the heaven fled away; and there was found no place for them. And I saw the dead, both small and great, standing before God; and the books were opened. And another book was opened, which is the book of life. And the dead were judged out of those things which were written in the books, according to their works.

This truth is taught throughout Scriptures.

Jesus taught it (Matthew 25:31-46). The apostles taught it (Acts 24:25). The apostles wrote it (1 Peter 4:17). It was as true for them as it is for us—there IS a judgment.

There is only ONE final judgment.

> *Hebrews 9:27—it is appointed unto men once to die,*
> *and after this, JUDGMENT (singular, not plural).*

Some groups teach a judgment for the righteous, followed a thousand years later by a judgment for the wicked. When Jesus described the one judgment in Matthew 25, it included all people: good and evil.

This truth is ignored by some religious groups. Jehovah's Witnesses teach there is no judgment—the wicked simply cease to exist when they die, and the righteous are made alive again when Christ returns. Universalists teach there is no judgment, because everyone (good and evil—including Satan) will be saved.

This is a judgment upon all the dead—righteous and wicked.
It includes the great and the small (20:12). It is a judgment upon the "dead ones" (20:12).

Some say this is only speaking of the wicked dead, but that contradicts clear teaching elsewhere in the New Testament. The judgment spoken of by Jesus includes the righteous and the wicked (Matthew 25). Christians were told, "we shall ALL stand before the judgment seat of Christ" (Romans 14:10). Paul expected to stand before Christ at the Judgment (2 Timothy 4:8).

To prove this point, look at Revelation 20:15—And whoever was not found in the book of life was cast into the lake of fire. This means that some of the dead ones *were* found in the book of life— thus, we have a judgment that involves righteous and wicked.

THE LORD IS THE JUDGE (20:11)

> *And I saw a great white throne, and the one who sat*
> *on it, from whose face the earth and the heaven fled*
> *away; and there was found no place for them.*

The one who sat on the great white throne was the judge.

It is the GREAT throne, because it shows the absolute highest authority—there is none higher. It is the great WHITE throne, because it is the throne of righteousness and purity—He doesn't make mistakes. It is the great white THRONE because it is the seat of the highest ruler—Christ is supreme!

Jesus Christ is the Judge.

We shall all appear before the judgment seat *of Christ* (2 Corinthians 5:10). All judgment and authority has been given *to Jesus* Christ (John 5:22, Matthew 28:18). Jesus is the *righteous judge* (2 Timothy 4:8).

The earth and the heaven fled away from the face of Christ.

Given the context of Revelation, as well as what takes place in chapter 21, this points to "heaven and earth" being a description of the Jewish system. Before you think me crazy, let me explain…

First, consider 2 Peter 3:5-7.

> *For they are willingly ignorant of this, that by the word of God the heavens existed of old, and the earth standing out of the water and in the water. And by it the world that then was, being overflowed with water, perished. But the heavens and the earth which now exist, are kept in store by the same word, reserved for fire at the day of judgment and perdition of ungodly men.*

Notice Peter uses the words "the heavens... and the earth" to refer to the way things were before the great flood of Genesis 6-9. Then Peter says there was a *different* "heavens and…earth" after the flood.

Peter, in describing judgment during Noah's day, said that "the heavens and the earth" *perished.* So why would we find it crazy to see John say something similar when judgment on the Jewish nation is carried out?

Consider also Matthew 5:18.

*For truly I say to you, Until heaven and earth pass
away, not one jot or one tittle shall in any way pass
from the law, until is it all fulfilled.*

The law of Moses (which Jesus is speaking of in this verse) fore-
told the rejection of the Jewish people (read the last few chapters of
Deuteronomy). It foretold of Jesus (the prophet like Moses, Deuter-
onomy 18:18-19). and when Jerusalem was surrounded by armies,
His followers would know that "all things written" were *fulfilled*
(Luke 21:20-22). This took place in AD 70.

Put those things together, and Jesus describes the destruction of
the Jewish system (including the temple, city, altar, and priesthood)
as "heaven and earth pass[ing] away." It was a figurative way of
saying their world was over. Jesus used the words "heaven and
earth" to describe the then-current order of things: Judaism.

The context of Revelation is the destruction of Jerusalem, so
when "heaven and earth fled away" from the face of Christ, it means
the Jewish system was obliterated by Christ.

Christ destroyed (judged) the Jewish persecutors, and is now
shown as the Supreme Judge of all. After seeing their misery (civil
war, lack of food), pain (mental, emotional, financial, and physical),
torment (demons, antagonistic gangs), and finally death—now you
find out that those issues were the least of their miseries. Now they
will spend eternity in the Lake of Fire—hell. Some believe this is
the *only* thing this judgment scene is portraying. But it does so using
language that elsewhere refers to a universal judgment when time is
no more (Matthew 25, 2 Corinthians 5:10, Acts 17:31).

The truths about judgment in this chapter, whether this passage
is specific to the defeated Jews or not, are universal in application.

YOU WILL BE THERE! (20:12)

And I saw the dead, both small and great, standing before God; and the books were opened. And another book was opened, which is the book of life. And the dead were judged out of those things which were written in the books, according to their works.

The dead ones, great and small, were there.

You in the group that includes the "small" and the "great." It is all-inclusive!

Those "dead ones" include you! You may say, "But I'm not dead!" But I say to you, "Remember the context!" Back in verse 4, the ones who were dead in Christ (baptized), lived with Him. If you are a Christian, you have died with Him, and are dead to sin (Romans 6:1-7).

Back in verse 5, it said "the rest of the dead." This group did *not* live, reign, and serve as priests for the "thousand years." These are the spiritually dead—the wicked. If you are not a Christian, this is the group you are in.

There's no getting around it—you are part of the group!

Look at how John describes it (verses 12-13):

- The "dead ones" are those who had either *died with Christ* via baptism, or were *spiritually dead* (they were called "the rest of the dead" in verse 5). Thus is includes the righteous and the wicked.
- The sea gave up her dead. *Sea* is figuratively used to describe Gentiles, so these are Gentiles who had already died. Thus it includes Jew and Gentile.
- Death and Hades gave up their dead. This describes those who had already died and were in Hades. Thus death is not the end of existence.

So, whether you are alive when the judgment comes or you've already died, you *will* be at that judgment (2 Thessalonians 4:16-17).

Since you *will* be at the judgment, it is important to know what the judgment is based on.

YOU WILL BE JUDGED BASED ON YOUR WORKS (20:12-15)

And I saw the dead, both small and great, standing before God; and the books were opened. And another book was opened, which is the book of life. And the dead were judged out of those things which were written in the books, according to their works. And the sea gave up the dead which were in it, and death and hades delivered up the dead which were in them. And they were judged, every person, according to their works. And death and hades were cast into the lake of fire. This is the second death. And whoever was not found written in the book of life was cast into the lake of fire.

The books were opened!

All people will be judged out of the things written in the books, according to their works. You will not be judged based on anyone else's actions—just your own. And yet some famous "pastors" proudly proclaim works have nothing to do with salvation. This passage alone obliterates that lying doctrine! And there's many other passages which do the same thing.

What books?

Some believe they are complete records of everything you've ever done, said, or thought—representing the omniscience of God (Matthew 12:36).

Others believe these are the books of the Bible, because we will be judged based on God's word.

The first option seems more likely, though both are biblically true. God knows everything you've ever done, and there is a record of it in heaven, waiting to be brought out at the judgment.

And then another book was opened.

This book is "the book of life." This is the book of those who died with Christ and were made alive with Him through the first resurrection—baptism! Some have said this is Jesus' family record-book—a listing of all those who are still "in Christ."

If your name is still found in this book, then it doesn't matter what things may have been recorded in your life (those other books). Because the blood of Christ washes those things away. It is like having a ledger book filled with sins, and across each one of them is a line of Jesus' blood covering it up—having cancelled the debt.

Death and hades cast into the lake of fire.

The lake of fire is hell, where the torment continues forever (Revelation 20:10; Mark 9:43-48). It also signifies destruction. At the judgment, there is no longer any physical death or hadean realm. There is simply heaven and hell.

This is the second death—and those not found in the book of life will experience it forever.

The second death only affects those outside of Christ (Revelation 20:6). It holds no power over ones involved in the "first resurrection" (baptism) whose names were not blotted out of the book of life.

The second death is eternal damnation in hell. This is where Nero is punished, where the Jewish leaders who killed Christ are punished, where Satan himself is punished (Revelation 20:10)—and it is the same place where *you* will be punished if you reject Christ's offer of salvation.

Satan is not in charge of hell. Hell is a place prepared by God to *punish* Satan. And if you don't do the works that show your allegiance to Jesus, you will experience the same punishment that God gives to Satan (Matthew 25:41-46).

WHAT DOES THIS MEAN FOR US TODAY?

It is completely UP TO YOU what the judgment will be.
It is according to *your own works* that you will be judged.

Are you a Christian? Are you living out your Christianity through your works? It is by works a man is justified, and not by faith only (James 2:24). Becoming a Christian is *not enough!* Afterwards, you must continue to live faithfully for Christ.

Simply becoming a Christian isn't enough.
Judgment *begins* at the house of God (the church), which means that some in the church will not be saved! Don't believe me, believe Peter—he is the one who said it (1 Peter 4:17).

Do not forget that some people will have their names blotted out of the book of life (Revelation 3:5, 22:19). That means someone who *was* listed there isn't anymore. You can *lose* your salvation (Galatians 5:4, Revelation chapters 2-3). Imagine coming to judgment, thinking all your sins are forgiven, only to discover your name had been removed! My friends, don't delay any longer! Take a spiritual inventory NOW and make sure that your name is there!

Study Forty-Seven:
The Glorious Church
(Revelation 21:1-22:5)

Back in Study three, we asked, "What on Earth is the Book of Revelation Talking About?" That study laid the groundwork for our whole journey, showing Revelation describes:

- The Roman-Jewish War and the persecution of Christians that came with it.
- The destruction of Jerusalem.
- And the revealing of the church in its glory.

The first two on that list have shown up in great detail throughout the first 20 chapters, but the last one not so much. There were the 144,000 and the Great Multitude—saints that endured through the Great Tribulation (the persecution under Nero which preceded the destruction of Jerusalem). This was a scene of victory, but also describes the church in its glory.

The glorious church was hinted at with the announcement of the marriage feast (19:7-10). But starting with chapter 21, the focus is completely on the glorious revealing of the church of Christ!

- Chapter 19 describes Jerusalem's destruction.
- The first part of chapter 20 describes the Christian's victory over Satan through baptism.
- The last part of chapter 20 describes judgment on the wicked (probably a quick look at the final judgment).
- Chapter 21 is a chapter of comfort and encouragement—because it describes us: the church.

THE "NEW HEAVEN AND NEW EARTH," "NEW JERUSALEM," AND THE "BRIDE OF THE LAMB" (21:1-2, 9-10)

Then I saw a new heaven and a new earth: for the first heaven and the first earth had passed away; and there was no more sea. And I, John, saw the holy city, new Jerusalem, coming from God down out of heaven, prepared like a bride adorned for her husband.

And one of the seven angels that had the seven bowls full of the seven final plagues came to me. and talked with me, saying, "Come here, I will show you the bride, the Lamb's wife. And he carried me away in the spirit to a great and tall mountain, and showed me that great city, the holy Jerusalem, descending from God out of heaven.

The "new heaven and new earth" is the same as the "new Jerusalem" (verse 2).

Jesus is the Lamb (Revelation 5), and His bride is the church. This is stated explicitly in Ephesians 5:25-32 and 2 Corinthians 11:2. The bride is called "the New Jerusalem."

So, the "new heaven and new earth," the "new Jerusalem," and the "Bride of the Lamb" *all refer to the same thing*.

This isn't a new idea.

The Old Testament connected The "new heavens and new earth" with the destruction of Jerusalem and the glorious revealing of the church *on earth*. Check out Isaiah 65:11-17:

But you are the ones who forsake Jehovah, that forget my holy mountain, that prepare a table for Gad

*[pagan god of fortune], and that furnish the drink of-
fering to Meni [pagan god of destiny]. Therefore I
say your destiny is death, and you will all bow down
to be slaughtered. Because when I called, you didn't
answer; when I spoke, you didn't listen; but instead
did evil before my eyes, and chose that which I did
not delight in. Therefore thus says the Lord Jehovah,
"Behold, my servants shall eat, but you will be hungry. Behold, my servants shall drink, but you will be
thirsty. Behold, my servants shall rejoice, but you
will be put to shame. Behold, my servants shall sing
from a heart of joy, but you will cry out from your
sorrow-filled heart, and will howl from you crushed
spirit. Your name will be a curse for my chosen people, because the Lord Jehovah will slaughter you,
and call His servants by another name. This is so that
whoever blesses in the land does so by the God of
truth; and he that swears in the land will do so by the
God of truth; because the former troubles are forgotten, and because they are hid from my eyes.*

*"For, behold, I create new heavens and a new earth:
the former will not be remembered, nor come into
mind."*

Here, God foretells the rejection/destruction of the Jews and the
establishment of the "new heavens and new earth." Note the con-
trasts: the Jews as a whole ("you who forsake Jehovah and forget
my holy mountain," verse 11) are *not* His true servants who will be
called by a new name (verse 15). They face destruction, the servants
receive blessings.

The new heavens and new earth, in Isaiah, is the church *on earth*.
The new name prophesied in Isaiah 65:15 was given *on earth*, and
that name is *Christian* (Acts 11:26).

Isaiah also calls the "new heavens and new earth" another name: "Jerusalem." See Isaiah 65:17-19.

> *See, I will create new heavens and a new earth. The former will not be remembered, nor will they come to mind. But be glad and rejoice forever in what I will create, for I will create Jerusalem to be a delight and its people a joy. I will rejoice over Jerusalem and take delight in my people; the sound of weeping and of crying will be heard in it no more."*

This new "Jerusalem" has rejoicing (verse 18), and no tears (verse 19). The inhabitants of New Jerusalem will call on the Lord, and He will hear and answer their call (verse 24).

Isaiah 66 continues the prophecy.

> *...Jehovah will come with fire, and with His chariots like a whirlwind, to execute his anger with fury, and his rebuke with flames of fire. For by fire and the sword Jehovah will plead with all flesh. Those slaughtered by Jehovah will be many (verses 15-16).*

This is the prophecy of Jerusalem's destruction. And it is shortly followed by another reference to the "new heavens and new earth." Verse 22 shows it will always remain before the Lord. During this time, people from all nations will come to the holy Jerusalem to worship God (verses 21, 23).

This describes the glorious church, still standing and blessed after the destruction of Jerusalem. Remember, until Jerusalem was destroyed, most people viewed Christianity as a sect of Judaism (Acts 24:5, 28:22). When Jerusalem was destroyed, it clearly revealed the church as God's only people, and it grew quickly, especially among the Gentiles.

2 Peter 3:13

Here Peter says he and other Christians were looking for (awaiting) the new heavens and new earth, where righteousness dwells. Some take this to mean they were waiting for the destruction of Jerusalem and the Jewish system so the church could be fully revealed as God's dwelling place. Others believe Peter is adapting the Old Testament imagery to describe heaven itself. Without getting into a lot of detail (which would require several pages), the context of Peter's words show it is something the then-living Christians would see.[1]

And now, one final passage before we get back into Revelation 21.

Hebrews 12:22-23.

> But you <u>have come</u> to Mt. Zion, and to the city of the living God, the <u>heavenly Jerusalem</u>, and to an innumerable company of angels, to the general assembly and <u>church of the firstborn ones which are written in heaven</u>..."

This "heavenly Jerusalem" is the "church." This was a *present reality* for first-century Christians. They were already part of it. Note the past-tense language: "you *have come*." The original readers of Hebrews were *already* in this heavenly Jerusalem when they received this letter.

Now look at Revelation 21, where a "new Jerusalem" comes "out of heaven" ("heavenly Jerusalem"). And this new Jerusalem is called the "bride of the Lamb."

---

[1] See Gerald Wright's *End of the World or the Jewish Age? Jewish Calamity or Universal Climax?* (Biblical Books Publications, 2018). This book is an exposition of 2 Peter 3. See also Bradley S. Cobb's *Don't Forget! A Commentary on the Second Letter of Peter* (Charleston, AR: Cobb Publishing, 2022).

WHERE IS THE NEW HEAVEN AND NEW EARTH/ NEW JERUSALEM? (21:1-5)

Then I saw a new heaven and a new earth: for the first heaven and the first earth had passed away; and there was no more sea. And I, John, saw the holy city, new Jerusalem, coming from God down out of heaven, prepared like a bride adorned for her husband.

And I heard a great voice out of heaven saying, "Behold, the tabernacle of God is with men, and He will dwell with them, and they will be his people, and God Himself shall be with them, and be their God. And God will wipe away all tears from their eyes; and there will be no more death, nor sorrow, nor crying, nor will there be any more pain: because the former things have passed away."

And He who sat on the throne said, "Behold, I make all things new." And he said to me, "Write. Because these words are true and faithful."

It is a new system of things (the first heaven and earth were passed away).

This is the language Peter used when describing the way things were before the flood vs. after the flood (2 Peter 3:6-7). Things after the flood were different, the world was different, the laws of God were different (animals were food for humans now, for example). But it wasn't a new location.

It came down <u>out of heaven</u> (21:2).

Wait! Isn't this talking about heaven? I was always told this was a chapter about heaven! But...it's repeated again in 10—the holy Jerusalem descended <u>out of heaven</u> from God. If it is something that came *out of* heaven, then how can anyone say it is describing heaven itself?

It is with humans

> *The tabernacle of God is **with men**, and He will dwell*
> *with them, they shall be His people, and God Himself*
> *will be with them, and be their God (21:3).*

The Greek word translated "men" is *anthropoi* (where we get the word *anthropology*), and it literally means *humans*. With that information in mind, let's ask some questions:

- Does God dwell with us? 1 John 4:12, 15-16 says He does.
- Are we God's people **now**? That is another *yes*.
- Is God **our** God **now**? And yet another *yes*.

This verse describes the wonderful blessing of being in the presence of God, being able to rely on Him and knowing He is on your side. It describes the blessings for the church here on earth—which is merely a foretaste of the blessings to come in heaven!

No Tears, no death, no pain.

"Wait!" I can hear it now. Someone is saying, "Look at verse 4! This describes a place of no tears—but we still cry; a place of no death—but we still die; no pain—but we still hurt! This can't be speaking of the church on earth!" And to this, I say: *Not so fast...*

What did Jesus say in John 11:26? Here, I'll look it up for you: Jesus said, "Whoever *lives* and believes in me *shall never die*. Do you believe this?" This sounds like Jesus promising then-living people they would never die. Of course they died *physically*, but Jesus was speaking of their *spiritual* life. They would never have to endure the second death (Revelation 20:6).

Secondly, God is the God of all comfort (2 Corinthians 1:3). God will wipe away all tears (Revelation 7:17). This is a reality for all faithful Christians here on earth. This is the "abundant life" Jesus promised His followers *in this world* (John 10:10).

In other words, these are *spiritual blessings*.

In the Old Testament, over and over again, God described blessings for His people in figurative language. For example: do you really think the Promised Land had rivers made of milk and honey? (Exodus 3:17). So it should be no surprise that He uses figurative language to describe blessings for His people in Revelation.

The former things are passed away…Behold I make all things new (21:4-5).

The system of the Law of Moses is the "former things" under consideration, because the writer of Hebrews wrote that it was "decaying and waxing old, and ready to vanish away" (Hebrews 8:13). Consider also 2 Corinthians 5:17:

> *If anyone is in Christ, He is a new creature. Old things have passed away, behold all things have become new.*

The Corinthian Christians were already experiencing this newness. It was something that had already happened ("have become" = past tense).

Regardless of whether the "former things" refers to Judaism or to our old lives of sin, the point is God is the one who brings us to a new life in Christ. And this takes place while we are living in Christ <u>here on earth</u>.

WHO RECEIVES THE BLESSINGS OF THE NEW JERUSALEM? (21:6-8)

> *And he said to me, "It is finished. I am Alpha and Omega, the beginning and the end. To him that is thirsty, I will give of the fountain of the water of life freely. The one who overcomes shall inherit all*

things; and I will be his God, and he shall be my son.
But the fearful, and unbelieving, and the abominable,
and murderers, and whoremongers, and sorcerers,
and idolaters, and all liars, shall have their part in
the lake which burns with fire and brimstone: which
is the second death.

It is finished—I am the Alpha and the Omega.

Christ said "it is finished" on the cross (John 19:30), showing
His earthly work was done. When Jerusalem was destroyed, the Old
Testament prophecies were completed (Luke 21:20-22). That work
was done, and now the church shines clearly as God's only people.

And God, by calling Himself the Alpha and the Omega, shows
He is the One behind it all.

The ones who thirst.

Jesus said, "Blessed are those who hunger and thirst after righteousness, for they shall be filled" (Matthew 5:6). Jesus promised the
water of life to those who come to Him (John 4:14).

The ones who overcome

Literally it is the ones who *are overcoming*—present tense.

They will inherit all things. Jesus said, "Blessed are the meek,
for they shall inherit the earth" (Matthew 5:5).

God says these overcomers will be His sons. This language
doesn't somehow mean women aren't allowed. Remember that in
the ancient cultures, the only ones who could receive an inheritance
were sons. This phrase means all His true followers will be acknowledged as His children, and all equally worthy to receive an inheritance from Him.

How does one become a "son" of God in order to receive this
inheritance? Galatians 3:26-27 answers this: "We are sons of God
by the faith, because as many of us as were baptized into Christ have
put on Christ." We overcome when we obey the gospel and are baptized (see also 1 John 2:13).

Who will <u>not</u> receive the blessings of the new heavens and new earth (the church)?

(1) The fearful

This is also translated "cowardly." It includes those too scared to act and become one of God's people, but also Christians who are too scared to live out their faith.

(2) The unbelieving

Those who don't believe in Christ, or do not hold onto the faith "once for all delivered to the saints" (Jude 3).

(3) The abominable

Those who intentionally sin. See Proverbs 6:16-19 for a list of some God calls abominable.

(4) Murderers

This is self-explanatory, but it could also include those who assassinate others' characters (as in James 4:2).

(5) Sorcerers

Those who seek mystical powers over others. This word comes from the Greek *pharmakeus*, from which we get the word *pharmacy* and *pharmaceuticals*. It would include, then, people who use drugs as a way to get power over others.

(6) Idolators

Those who put other things ahead of God. Paul said "covetousness, which is idolatry (Colossians 3:5).

(7) All liars

There is a misconception about lying. When the Bible describes liars, it refers to those who *knowingly* tell something false, with the *intention* of deceiving others, for the liar's own *benefit*.

It does not describe joking (telling something false, and immediately revealing it was said as humor). It does not describe *unknowingly* telling something false (being mistaken on a detail). It doesn't describe saying something false when you and the hearer both know it to be false (sarcasm often falls into this category). It does not describe saying something you *think* you will do, but end up not being able to fulfill (Peter didn't lie to Jesus when he said he would die for Him before he would deny Him. Peter meant it, but turned out he was wrong). It does not include telling an untruth in order to save someone's life (Rahab was praised for saving the spies—which she did by deceiving the Jericho soldiers. The midwives in Egypt were rewarded by God for telling Pharaoh false statements in order to save the newborn Hebrew boys).[2]

This is similar to the list of the "works of the flesh" which will keep people out of the kingdom (Galatians 5:19-21). These will all have their place in the lake of fire, the second death.

THE DESCRIPTION OF THE NEW (HEAVENLY) JERUSALEM (21:9-23)

And one of the seven angels who had the seven bowls full of the final seven plagues came and talked to me, saying, "Come here, I will show you the bride, the Lamb's wife." And he carried me away in the spirit to a great and tall mountain, and showed me that great city, the holy Jerusalem, descending out of heaven from God, having the glory of God. Her light was like a most precious stone, even like a jasper stone, clear as crystal. It had a great and tall wall, with twelve gates, and at the gates twelve angels, and names were written on them, the names of the twelve tribes of the children of Israel. On the east three gates; on the north three gates; on the south three gates; and on the west three gates. The wall of the city had twelve foundations, and in them were the

---

[2]This is a very brief overview. More examples could be given.

names of the twelve apostles of the Lamb.

And the one who talked with me had a golden measuring rod to measure the city, and its gates, and its wall. And the city was a square, the length as large as the breadth. He measured the city with the rod, it was 12,000 stadia. The length and the breadth and the height are the same. And he measured its wall, 144 cubits, according to the measure of a man, that is, of the angel.

And its wall was of jasper: and the city was purest gold, like clear glass. And the foundations of the wall of the city were decorated with all manner of precious stones. The first foundation was jasper; the second, sapphire; the third, an agate; the fourth, an emerald; the fifth, onyx; the sixth, sardius; the seventh, chrysolite; the eighth, beryl; the ninth, a topaz; the tenth, a chrysoprasus; the eleventh, a jacinth; the twelfth, an amethyst. And the twelve gates were twelve pearls; each gate was of one pearl: and the main street of the city was pure gold, like transparent glass.

And I saw no temple in it, because the Lord God Almighty and the Lamb are its temple. And the city had no need of the sun or the moon to shine in it, because the glory of God lighted it, and the Lamb is its light.

An angel showed John the bride of the Lamb.

The bride is the New Jerusalem (remember, the bride of Christ is the church). This angel is identified as one of the ones that had the seven bowls of the plagues—though why this is pointed out, I'm not sure.

Atop a great, tall mountain, John sees the New Jerusalem descending out of heaven.

This shows where the city originates—God. Ephesians 3:10-11 shows the church was in the eternal purpose of God.

And after we see how big the city is, you can understand why John had to be taken to an extremely tall mountain to see it.

It has the glory of God.

It has its own light (the glory of God provides the light, for the Lamb is the light—21:23). It is like a jasper stone, clear as crystal—it's beauty is as a sparkling diamond.

The wall is great and tall.

More on this momentarily.

There are twelve gates, and twelve angels at the gates.

The gates had the names of the twelve tribes of Israel. Since this is the heavenly Jerusalem, these names represent *spiritual* Israel. The Bible makes a distinction between *physical* Israel and *spiritual* Israel (Romans 9:6).

As far as the twelve angels/messengers at the gates, the only interpretation that makes sense to me is that in order to enter the gates, people must hear the message. "Those who call on the name of the Lord will be saved. But how can they call on Him in whom they have not believed? And How can they believe in Him when they haven't heard of Him? And how can they hear without a preacher?" (Romans 10:13-14).

The wall has twelve foundations, with the names of the apostles of Jesus Christ.

Don't get caught up in trying to figure out if Matthias or Paul made the list, because that's not what's under consideration. It isn't the individual apostles (what about Judas?), but their *teachings* (see Ephesians 2:20).

The city was measured.

It is a gigantic square. The length and width are the same: 12,000 furlongs/stadia. We will look at the modern-day equivalents momentarily, but *God chose this number for a reason*. The number 12 is the number of religion—there were twelve tribes, as well as twelve apostles. The number 1,000 often means something too large to count. This means the city is huge—large enough to house all who would come into it through obeying the apostles' teachings.

If you want actual measurements, this is the equivalent of 1377 miles long, 1377 miles wide.[3] This is roughly the area of the Roman Empire of that time. While I don't think this number has anything to do with the Roman Empire, it is noteworthy that in the decades after Jerusalem's destruction, Christianity spread like wildfire through the Empire.

It is also 12,000 furlongs/stadia in height. The walls are just as tall as the city is wide. To put this in perspective, airplanes fly at around 30,000 feet—that's around 6 miles. This city walls are more than 225 times higher than that! This is a perfect cube—a perfect city.

The walls are 144 cubits thick. 144 is 12 x 12. It is the perfect religion.

The city is composed of jewels.

The wall is jasper. The city is purest gold, like clear glass—no imperfections. This shows that there are no impurities in the church, for those who are truly in the church have been forgiven. Ephesians 5:5:25-26 says Jesus purifies all imperfections in His bride, the church.

The twelve foundations (the twelve apostles) are garnished with jasper, sapphire, agate, emerald, sardonyx, sardius, chrysolyte, beryl, topaz, chrysoprasus, jacinth, and amethyst. This shows the

---

[3] The NET Bible says "fourteen hundred miles."

preciousness of the gospel, the teachings of Christ through the apostles.

The twelve gates are twelve pearls. Each gate is of a single pearl (must be some big pearls!). Gates are how you enter the city. The entrance, then, is precious—baptism is how we enter the church (1 Corinthians 12:13).

The street of the city is pure gold.

The word "street" here means the broad street, or the main street in the city. The same word describes the main street of Jerusalem where the bodies of the two witnesses laid (Revelation 11:8)

This street is pure and precious, transparent. Most streets in the first century were dirty: people threw their garbage out on the street, animals did their bathroom business on the street. Some have said it was the filthiest part of a city. If so, then this shows that even the filthiest part of New Jerusalem (the church) is pure beyond comprehension. It was so clean and pure you could see through it.

There is no temple inside the city, because God and Christ ARE the temple.

We are the temple of God (2 Corinthians 6:16).

> *And what agreement does the temple of God have with idols? For you are the temple of the living God; as God has said, "I will dwell in them, and walk in them; and I will be their God, and they shall be my people."*

But if God dwells in us, we also dwell in God (I John 4:15-16).

> *Whoever shall confess that Jesus is the Son of God, God dwells in him, and he in God. And we have known and believed the love that God has toward us. God is love; and he that dwells in love dwells in God, and God in him.*

***There is no need for the sun or the moon, because the city is illu-
minated by the glory of God—the Lamb is the light of it.***

It is as though the city is self-illuminated (because the city has
the glory of God—verse 11).

THE PEOPLE IN THE CITY (21:24-27)

*And the Gentiles of those who are saved shall walk
in the light of it: and the kings of the land bring their
glory and honor into it. Its gates shall not be shut at
all by day: because there will be no night there. And
they shall bring the glory and honor of the Gentiles
into it. And nothing that defiles, nor anyone who
practices abomination, or makes a lie, shall in any
way enter the city—only those who are written in the
Lamb's book of life.*

The saved Gentles will walk in the light of the city.

The word "nations" (which appears in most Bible translations)
is the same word as "Gentiles."[4] The church was built on promises
to the Israelites, but is open to Gentiles as well. This includes you,
and me.

The kings of the earth/land bring their glory and honor into it (v.
24). The Gentiles will bring the glory and honor of the Gentiles into
it (v. 26). Thus, the bride is comprised of both Jew and Gentiles.

The gates will never be shut, because there is no night there (v. 25)

In physical Jerusalem (and any other ancient city with walls), the
gates were closed at night to keep out any intruders. But in heavenly
Jerusalem, the church, the gates are always open—the church welcomes all who will enter. Just as people are free to enter, they are

---

[4] The Greek word is *ethnos*, from which we get our words *ethnic* and *ethnicity*. The NET Bible has a note on this verse that points out "Gentiles" is an equally
valid translation.

also free to leave—it is possible to leave the new Jerusalem (some already had by this point—Galatians 5:4).

The wicked are unable to enter.

No defiled people can enter. None who practice abominations can enter. No liars can enter. Only those who are written in the book of life are allowed in.

Some think they have so many sins in their past that God couldn't possibly let them in, couldn't welcome them into His family. But what they miss is that Jesus' blood can cleanse them of all those sins—they can come into the family of God as a pure, clean, washed, sinless person whose past sins have been removed!

THE TREE OF LIFE (22:1-5)

> *And he showed me a pure river of water of life, clear as crystal, proceeding out of the throne of God and of the Lamb. In the midst of its street, and on both sides of the river, was the tree of life, which bore twelve kinds of fruits, and yielded its fruit every month: and the leaves of the tree were for the healing of the Gentiles. And there shall be no more curse: but the throne of God and of the Lamb shall be in it; and his servants shall serve him, and shall see his face; and his name shall be in their foreheads. And there shall be no night there; they need no candle, nor light of the sun; for the Lord God gives them light: and they shall reign forever and ever.*

A pure river of water came out from the throne of God.

It was clear as crystal. This is pure, perfect nourishment to quench the spiritual thirst of all who come to God through Jesus.

In the midst of the street, and on both sides of the river, was the tree of life.

This tree is huge, able to be accessed by everyone in the city.

That which was lost when Adam and Eve sinned is regained through Christ.

Adam and Eve were kicked out of the Garden of Eden to keep them from having access to the tree of life (Genesis 3:22-24). The tree of life would make them able to live forever. In the church, we have access to the tree of life so that we will never die (spiritually).

The tree gave twelve kinds of fruit.

This could represent the teaching of the apostles (12) as being the life-giving food for those in the New Jerusalem.

The tree gave fruit every month.

It is always in bloom, always ripe with fruit for the eating. This shows continual sustenance, continual blessings.

The curse that came through Adam (separation from God) is reversed in the church.

This is because the throne of God is there. The Lamb is there. They are present with mankind.

The servants of God will serve Him there.

It is the church who serves God. All *outside* of the church who claim to serve God are deceiving themselves.

They will see His face.

Jesus said, "Blessed are the pure in heart, for they shall see God" (Matthew 5:8). David asked God to "Make Your face to shine upon your servant: save me for your mercies' sake" (Psalm 31:16). This is a figurative description of God's approval.

His name will be in their foreheads.

They will be branded as God's (see the sealing of the 144,000 in chapter 7). Their thoughts are focused on Him.

They shall reign forever (22:5).

This reigning is promised to all who die with Christ in baptism (Revelation 20:4, Romans 6:3-4, 2 Timothy 2:11-12).

"Forever and ever" is the same as the "thousand years" of 20:4.

WHAT DOES THIS MEAN FOR US TODAY?

This describes the glories of the church here on earth.

The church was fully revealed to be God's only people at the destruction of Jerusalem—showing the church as the true bride of Christ. The next verse (22:6) makes this clear—"and he said unto me, These sayings are faithful and true: and the Lord God of the holy prophets sent his angel *to show to His servants the things which must* **shortly be done**."

With all the blessings described for the church in this chapter, why wouldn't you want to be a part of it?

Entrance into the New Jerusalem is free! You just gotta come to the gates and come in! The gate is baptism, the way you enter the church (Acts 2:14, 47). The blessings only come when you're inside the city!

Examine your life—have you unwittingly left the protection of God and the walls of His great city?

STUDY FORTY-EIGHT
THE CONCLUSION
(REVELATION 22:6-21)

If you've ever taken a speech class, you've heard the three rules for public speaking:

(1) Tell us what you're going to tell us
(2) Tell us
(3) Tell us what you told us.

That's the introduction, body, and conclusion of a basic speech.

The book of Revelation follows a similar pattern.

Chapter one tells what God was going to tell us:

- Things which must shortly come to pass.
- Jesus' coming in judgment against the "tribes of the earth," aka the Jews.
- Blessings on the ones who obey

Chapters 2-21 described those things.

- Things which must shortly come to pass.
- Jesus' coming in judgment against the Jews.
- Blessings on the ones who obey.

Chapter 22 (specifically verses 6-21) tells us what was told.

- Things which must shortly come to pass.
- Jesus coming in judgment against the tribes of the earth.
- Blessings on the ones who obey.

These are the main themes running through the final section of Revelation, and are our main thoughts for this, the final lesson.

THINGS WHICH MUST SHORTLY COME TO PASS

Five times in these 16 verses, God stresses the point that the things described in Revelation were about to take place.

Verse 6

> *And he [the angel] said to me, These sayings are faithful and true: and the Lord God of the holy prophets sent His angel to show to His servants **the things which must shortly be done**.*

In case anyone had any doubt as to whether or not these things were actually going to happen, the angel says three things:

1. These things are trustworthy (faithful) and true.
2. These things came directly from God.
3. These things **must** shortly be done

The word "must" means it is a moral necessity—a moral requirement. The sins of the Jews had stacked up to heaven and God's judgment demanded their punishment (18:5). And the word "shortly" means *it was about to take place*.

Verse 7

> **Behold I come quickly**: *Blessed is the one who keeps the sayings of the prophecy of this book.*

This is Jesus speaking *in present tense*. A literal translation of this is: "Look, I am coming quickly." The word "quickly" and the word "shortly" (verse 6) come from the same basic Greek word. This again stresses *these things are about to happen*.

Verse 10

> *And he says to me, "Do not seal up the sayings of the prophecy of this book: for **the time is at hand**."*

Notice first that this is a "prophecy"—it is of divine origin.

Then he says "the time is at hand," or "the time is near." During Christ's ministry, He said the kingdom of God was "at hand," or "near," and it arrived within just a few years (at Pentecost, Acts 2). So when the angel told John "the time is at hand," it means the time was very near—it would be during the lifetime of John's readers. The things prophesied in Revelation were fulfilled within a decade of its being written.

Verse 12

> **Behold I come quickly**; and my reward is with me, to give every man according as his work shall be.

This is the same as verse 7.

Verse 20

> He which testifies these things says, "**Surely I come quickly**." Amen. Even so, come Lord Jesus.

The word "surely" is the same word Jesus used on earth, usually translated "verily" (KJV) or "truly" (NIV). In other words, this is Jesus' final affirmation to the early Christians, "Yes. I am coming quickly."

But what kind of coming is under consideration?

A COMING IN JUDGMENT

Each time Jesus says he is "coming" quickly, He is speaking about a coming in judgment.

There are "plagues" written in this book. Plagues from God are a sign of judgment (as in the ten plagues). So plagues prove this is a coming in judgment.

And Jesus says this coming was (when John wrote) "near," "at hand," and "shortly come to pass." We must ask: *What coming in judgment took place soon after the book was written?* Assuming you've read *any* of this book, you know the answer. It was Jesus'

coming in judgment on the Jewish nation in AD 70. Jesus specifically called it the "coming of the Son of man" in Matthew 24:27, 30.

Verse 7—Behold I am coming quickly.

Verse 12—And behold I am coming quickly.

Verse 20—Surely I am coming quickly.

These three verses reiterate this coming of Christ was very near.
Christ was about to fulfill His mission. It was a coming in judgment
that would take place very soon after John wrote.

Verse 13

*I am Alpha and Omega, the beginning and the end,
the first and the last.*

This is Jesus' declaration of His *authority* to judge—He is deity.
This judgment, then, is deserved, just, and guaranteed.

Verse 16

*I, Jesus, have sent my angel to testify these things to
you in the churches. I am the root and the offspring
of David, and the bright and morning star.*

This verse gives two proofs of Jesus' authority to judge, and
show He is God.

1. Jesus sent **His** angel. Verse 6 says it was the **Lord God's**
   angel. This shows Jesus is God
2. Jesus calls Himself the root (the source) of David, as well
   as the offspring of David.

Jesus, as God, created all things (John 1:1-3, 14), which would
include all humans—including David. But Jesus, as a human, was
the royal descendant of David, and Messianic heir to the throne. In
picturesque language, Jesus here declares Himself the Creator (God)
and the Christ.

Interestingly, Jesus uses this same idea to confound the religious "scholars" of His day in Matthew 22:41-46.

Verse 20

> *Even so, come, Lord Jesus.*

John—though the message was bitter (10:10)—agreed it was necessary. He says, "come, Lord Jesus," or in other words, "Let it be so."

BLESSINGS ON THE OBEDIENT

Someone once said the entire book of Revelation boils down to one basic message: Jesus wins, and if we're on His side, we win too. A very condensed description, but true.

But the question everyone needs to ask is: *How do you make sure you're on His side?* The answer is simple: *by obeying Him.* This is the third focus of the last chapter.

Verse 7

> *Blessed is the one who keeps the sayings of the prophecy of this book.*

The word "keeps" here means "obeys." It is the same as when Jesus said, "If you love me, *keep* my commandments." He doesn't mean keep them in a scrapbook, or on your phone—he means *obey* them. The blessings come only from obedience.

You may remember some of the commands in Revelation:

- Remember where you have fallen from and repent (2:5).
- Be faithful to death (2:10).
- Worship God (22:8-9).

Verse 11

> *He that is unjust, let him remain unjust; and he who*

is filthy, let him remain filthy; and he who is right-
eous, let him remain righteous; and he who is holy,
let him remain holy.

There are different interpretations of this passage. Some believe it refers to the final judgment, and that whatever someone's state is at the final judgment, will be their eternal state. That reflects truth, but it can't be what is referred to here, because it doesn't jive with the "at hand" and "shortly" statements surrounding this verse.

Some have misapplied this passage to be a command for all time—and use it as an excuse to not evangelize. They'll say let people be who they are and don't try to change them—even if they are lost.

If we let the context be our guide (as we always should), the message to those first-century Christians is this: "Don't waste your time and risk your lives trying to convert any more of the Jews, because they won't repent. Instead, get out of Jerusalem so you can avoid the destruction coming on them and the city."

The second half of the verse is directed at the faithful Jewish Christians: stay righteous, stay holy, stay faithful.

Verse 12

I am coming quickly, and my reward is with me, to
give to every man according to his works.

This is another reminder: we are judged based on our works. The reward (or payment) we receive is based on how we live our lives. The faithful can expect to receive the crown of life (2:10). But the wicked will receive the lake of fire (21:8).

Verse 14

Blessed are those who do His commandments, so that
they may have right to the tree of life and may enter
in through the gates of the city.

This is a blessing on those already in the city (church) as well as those become Christians later. Please don't miss this very important point, though: access to the tree of life, and entrance into the heavenly city (New Jerusalem, the church) comes only by *doing* His commandments. In other words, there is no salvation without *doing* something. We might even say "Works are required for salvation," because that is exactly what this verse teaches. It doesn't mean we *earn* our salvation, but it *does* mean that Jesus requires obedience. Naaman the leper didn't *earn* his cleansing, but he was still required to *do something* to obtain it (2 Kings 5:1-ff).

Verse 15

> *Because outside the city are dogs [unclean beasts— a description of sinners] and sorcerers and whoremongers and murderers and idolators and those who love and make lies (verse 15).*

Besides access to the tree of life and entrance into the church, obedient followers of Jesus are blessed to not be among the lost! The people described in verse 15 cannot enter the kingdom.

Verses 18-19

> *I testify to everyone who hears the words of this prophecy of this book: If anyone adds to these things, God will add to him the plagues written in this book. And if anyone takes away from the words of the book of this prophecy, God will take away his part from the book of life, and from the holy city, and from the things written in this book.*

The blessings come to those who take the book for what it is. You can't add things to it (like an earthly reign of Christ from Jerusalem). You can't take things away from it (like ignoring the "at hand" statements). Either one ends with the same thing: destruction.

It is important to remember this was spoken *to Christians* as a warning. They could lose their part in the holy city (the church). They could lose access to the tree of life. They could lose the blessings.

In other words, "once saved, always saved" is a lie.

THE GREAT INVITATION, OR
WHAT DOES THIS MEAN FOR US TODAY?

The Spirit and the bride say," Come." And let the one who hears say, "Come." Let the thirsty come. And whoever will, can take the water of life freely (22:17).

The grace of our Lord Jesus Christ be with you all. Amen (22:21).

If you aren't a Christian, I want to personally invite you to become one. The Holy Spirit invites you, through His word, to come to Christ. The bride—that is, the church of Christ—invites you to come. All those who hear the gospel invite you to come. If you want to drink of the waters of life, then we invite you to come.

Come, believing in Jesus Christ. Come, leaving your sin behind. Come, confessing His name. Come and be baptized. And when you do, the grace of our Lord Jesus Christ will be with you.

Don't let anyone lead you away from following what the Bible says is the way to salvation in Christ.[1]

---

[1] Please take the time to read the Appendix, "Are You Saved?"

Appendix A:
External Evidence for the Early Date of Revelation

I've seen some very angry arguments over the date of Revelation. In the lesson, "When was Revelation Written?" I focused exclusively on biblical evidence—because that evidence is from God. But there is also *external* evidence (that is, evidence from *outside* the Bible) which points to Revelation being written before Jerusalem was destroyed.

Before we dig into the external evidence for an early date of Revelation, we need to address the star witness for the late-date view.

Examining Irenaeus

The prime piece of evidence used to try to prove Revelation was written *after* the destruction of Jerusalem, usually around AD 94-96, is a not-so clear quote from a guy named Irenaeus, born around AD 130. He wrote a book called *Against Heresies.* Though he wrote it in Greek, there are no known Greek manuscripts of this work. What we have are (1) partial Armenian translations (from the 500s), (2) partial Latin translations (from the 800s to 1500s), and (3) scattered quotations of it from other Greek writers, such as Eusebius (from around 325). Using these different sources, a complete copy has been cobbled together.

The quote (as given by those who use him as their witness) is an English translation of Eusebius' quotation of Irenaeus' Greek original. If that sounds confusing, don't worry, there's a reason I am pointing this out. Eusebius was not a fan of Revelation. In fact, he questioned whether the book was inspired at all, and suggested it could be "spurious," or fake,[1] and that it was not written by the apostle John.

Here is the star witness, Irenaeus' quotation, discussing the meaning of 666:

> *We will not, however, incur the risk of pronouncing positively as to the name of Antichrist; for if it were necessary that his name should be distinctly revealed in this present time, it would have been announced by him who beheld the apocalyptic vision. For that was seen no very long time since, but almost in our day, towards the end of Domitian's reign.*

If you take the quotation *as given in this English translation*, it seems iron-clad—Irenaeus places the date of Revelation at the end of Domitian's reign (approximately AD 95). But there are issues...

1. **"that was seen" may not be the best translation.** The Greek words can accurately be translated, "*he* was seen"—meaning *John* was seen near the end of Domitian's reign. The Greek is actually ambiguous here, and the translator is left to pick which of the two he thinks is what Irenaeus meant.

2. **"Domitian" may not be an accurate translation.** Dr. Robert Young, a well-respected expert in Hebrew, Greek, Latin, and other languages, translator of *Young's Literal Translation,* and creator of *Young's Analytical Concordance,* wrote the following in 1865:

"[Revelation] was written in Patmos about A.D. 68, whither John had been banished by Domitius Nero, as stated in the title of the Syriac version of the book; and with this concurs the express statement of Irenaeus in A.D. 175, who says it

---

[1] Eusebius, *Church History*, Book 3, chapter 25.

happened in the reign of *Domitianou*—i.e., Domitius (Nero). Sulpicius, Orosius, etc., <u>stupidly mistaking Dimitia*nou* for Domitia*nikos*, supposed Irenaeus to refer to Domitian</u>, A.D. 95, and most succeeding writers have fallen into the same blunder. The internal testimony is wholly in favor of the early date." [Underlining for emphasis][2]

I have found no writer who has tried to disprove Dr. Young's statement, even though they have had 157 years to do it. But I found several books and writers who agree with it. Take that for whatever it is worth, since I am not a scholar on Greek forms of Roman Emperor names.

Irenaeus himself also argues for an early date to Revelation. By the time he wrote around AD 180, there were some copies of Revelation that had 616 instead of 666 as the number of the beast. His response?

> *"Such, then, being the state of the case, and this number being found in all <u>the most approved and ancient copies</u> [of Revelation], and those men who saw John face to face bearing their testimony; while reason also leads us to conclude that the number of the name of the beast...will amount to six hundred and sixty and six."*

If we accept that Irenaeus was talking about Domitian (and not Nero) earlier, then he was saying AD 95 was (paraphrased) "not that long ago." But the copies of Revelation he discusses here are "ancient." Which would mean *before* Domitian's reign.

There are other issues with Irenaeus as a witness, but this should be enough to say the quotation from Irenaeus is (at the very least)

---

[2] Robert Young, *Concise Commentary on the Holy Bible* (Edinburgh: George Adam Young & Co. Bible Publishers, 1865), p. 179.

questionable as evidence—yet this is the #1 go-to exhibit for those who reject a pre-destruction-of-Jerusalem date.

So let's now consider the external evidence *for* the early date.

The Syriac Translations (late 1st/early 2nd century)

The Syriac (Aramaic) translations of the New Testament gives this title to the final book of the New Testament: "*The Revelation, which was made by God to John the Evangelist, in the island of Patmos, to which he was banished <u>by Nero the Emperor</u>.*" It was the opinion of the earliest translators of the New Testament that Revelation was written during the time of Nero (AD 58-64).

Clement of Alexandria (AD 150-215)

Regarding the completion of the ministry of Christ and His apostles, this second-century writer said, "For the teaching of our Lord at His advent, beginning with Augustus and Tiberius, was completed in the middle of the times of Tiberius. And that of the apostles, embracing the ministry of Paul, <u>end with Nero</u>" (Miscellanies 7:17). If their ministry ended with Nero, then Revelation couldn't have been written *after*.

The Muratorian Canon (c AD 170-210)

Contained in this listing of the books of the New Testament are these words: "Paul, following the order of his own predecessor John, writes to no more than seven churches by name." Paul died, by all accounts, in AD 68. If he was "following the order" of John's writing to seven churches (see Revelation 1:4), then Revelation was written before Paul finished writing his letters.

Fake Revelations (1st century)

Sir Isaac Newton (yes, *that* Isaac Newton) insisted the book of Revelation was written prior to the destruction of Jerusalem. One of his proofs was the amount of fake "Revelations" or "Apocalypses" that existed in imitation of the real thing. His commentary on Revelation includes this interesting information:

> "*Caius, who was contemporary with Tertullian, tells*

us that Cerinthus wrote his Revelations as [though he was] a great Apostle, and pretended the visions were shown him by Angels, asserting a millennium of carnal pleasures at Jerusalem after the resurrection; so that his Apocalypse was plainly written in imitation of John's: and yet he [Cerinthus] lived so early, that he resisted the Apostles at Jerusalem in or before the first year of Claudius, that is, 26 years before the death of Nero, and [he] died before John."

If fake "Revelations" were written in imitation of John's original, and these fake ones appeared before the death of Nero—then the original must have come before the death of Nero as well.

Jerome (342-420)

This respected writer said of John's later life:

"The blessed John the Evangelist lived in Ephesus until extreme old age. His disciples could barely carry him to church and he could not muster the voice to speak many words."

Most believe John died somewhere around AD 96 (not long after they think he wrote Revelation). If John was in such bad shape during his final years that he couldn't walk, and people could barely move him around—how could he possibly go on a multi-national preaching tour like Revelation says he would? (Revelation 10:11). The only way he would be able to go on this missionary journey is if he wrote it when he was much younger—meaning far earlier than the 90s AD.

Epiphanius (320-403)

This writer places John's exile to Patmos (where John wrote Revelation) very early:

"Later, therefore, though from caution and humility he had declined to be an evangelist, the Holy Spirit

compelled John to issue the Gospel in his old age when he was past ninety, after his return from Patmos under Claudius Caesar, and several years of his residence in Asia."[3]

Many writers assume he is not speaking of Claudius, but of Nero, who also took on the name Claudius. But either way, Epiphanius believed John was on Patmos (where he wrote Revelation) well before Jerusalem was destroyed.

Andreas of Cappadocia (563-637)

In his commentary on Revelation, he didn't take the early-date position. But he mentions there were people who did:

"There are not wanting [lacking] those who apply this passage to the siege and destruction of Jerusalem by Titus… These things are referred by some to those sufferings which were inflicted by the Romans upon the Jews."[4]

Arethas of Caesarea (c. 540)

Compiling his commentary on Revelation from earlier sources, Arethas said:

"Some refer this to the siege of Jerusalem by Vespasian…Here then, were manifestly shown to the Evangelist what things were to befall the Jews in their war against the Romans, in the way of avenging the sufferings inflicted upon Christ…When the Evangelist received these oracles, the destruction in which the Jews were involved was not yet inflicted by the Romans."[5]

---

[3] *The Panarion of Epiphanius*, Book I, Second Edition (Boston: Brill, 2009) p. 502.

[4] Notes on 6:12 and 7:1.

[5] Notes on 6:12, 7:1, and 7:4.

And he states plainly:

> *"For after [Mary's] death it is reported that [John] no longer chose to remain in Judaea, but passed over to Ephesus, where, as we have said, this present Apocalypse also was composed; which is a revelation of future things, inasmuch as forty years after the ascension of the Lord this tribulation came upon the Jews."*

Conclusion

As I said waaaaaaaay back in Study Two, it doesn't matter what uninspired men say. What matters is what God says.

But just in case you wanted to know whether early Christians thought Revelation was written early, and whether any of them applied it to the destruction of Jerusalem—the answer is *yes*.

APPENDIX B:
ARE YOU SAVED?

First of all, I want to thank you for picking up this book. It means a lot to me.

Secondly, I want to ask you the most important question that can be asked of you. *Are you saved?*

You may wonder, *why would he ask that? Of course I'm saved. Why else would I be looking at a Bible commentary?* I agree that you are likely very religious, and you love God's word. But that doesn't answer the question, *Are you saved?*

Here's the deal. I've picked up tons of books in my life, and I've been amazed at how many of them throw a section in at the end which claims to tell you how to pray a little prayer, and then congratulates you on being saved. Maybe you've seen those before.

They're promising a false hope.

I hate to say it, but in essence, they're *lying* to you. I don't say that with any sense of joy, but you need to know the truth. It is only the truth that will set you free (John 8:32). Salvation through prayer won't save you. Why do I say that? Plenty of reasons. If you'd like to know some of them, keep reading.

Not one single person in the entire Bible was ever told to pray in order to become a Christian.

Go ahead, read the gospel accounts, Acts, all the letters, and Revelation. You'll read a lot of things, but one thing you'll never read in the Bible is that someone was saved, made a child of God, by saying a prayer. If *not one* person in the entire New Testament became a Christian by praying, shouldn't that tell us something about how someone becomes saved?

But what about Saul of Tarsus (aka the apostle Paul)?

Let's talk about him for a moment. You can read just as well as I can. Look at Acts 9. There, Saul is blinded (he literally *saw the light*) on the road to Damascus. But Jesus told him to go into the city, and there it would be told to him what he **must do**. That's a very important point to remember.

Saul—now blinded—went into the city, with the aid of his friends, and spent the next three days fasting and praying. If *any* person in the history of Christianity could have been saved by praying, it was Saul. But he wasn't. You may ask, *How do you know he wasn't saved?* I know because the Bible says so.

In Acts 22, Saul (who now goes by the name of Paul) is standing up in front of some people, explaining his conversion to Christ. To put it in modern-day language, he was testifying about how he got saved. It was in this speech of Paul that he revealed the rest of the story. Here's what he said:

> *Since I could not see, because of the glory of that light, those with me led me by the hand into Damascus.*
>
> *Ananias, a devout man according to the law, of good reputation among all of the Jews living there, came to me, stood by me, and said, "Brother Saul, look up." In that instant I could see! Ananias continued, "The God of our fathers has chosen you to know his will, and to see the Righteous One, and to hear his voice, because you will be a witness for him to all people of the things you have seen and heard.*
>
> *"Now, why do you delay? Get up, call on his name, be immersed, and wash away your sins!" (Acts 22:11-16).*

Do you notice what I notice? It's there in the last paragraph. "Wash away your sins!" If he was saved on the road to Damascus, why weren't his sins washed away? The answer is: *He wasn't saved on the road to Damascus.* What about the three days he spent fasting and praying? If you're saved by saying a prayer, then shouldn't that have saved him? The fact is Saul wasn't saved through prayer either. If you don't believe me, look at that passage again. Saul was still guilty of his sins—he hadn't been forgiven yet. We know this because he was told to stop delaying and get up and wash away his sins!

No one—not even the apostle Paul—was ever told to say a prayer to be saved.

The idea of being saved from your sins by saying a prayer contradicts what the Bible says.

The gospel was preached in its fullness for the very first time in Acts 2. This was the Day of Pentecost, a celebration in Jerusalem when all the faithful Jews would come to worship God. It was there, in this big crowd of people, that the apostles of Jesus stood up and began to preach.

After explaining that they were speaking in foreign languages by the power of God, the very next thing that Peter said to them was:

> *"Men of Israel, hear these words." (Acts 2:22)*

Now make sure you understand this. Peter's entire mission in preaching was to save people. When he preached *this* sermon, his entire purpose was to save people. So, if we look at his sermon, it should give us a pretty good idea about what saves people. After all, he was given the words to speak directly from God.

The first thing Peter said they needed to do was to listen.

But what did they need to listen to? What was it that God wanted them to hear?

> *"Jesus of Nazareth, a man approved by God among*
> *you by the miracles, wonders, and signs that God did*
> *by him in your midst—and you know this! Him, being*

delivered by the determinate counsel and fore-knowledge of God, you have taken, and by wicked hands, you have crucified and killed Him.

"But God has raised Him up, having loosened the pains of death, because it was not possible that He should be held by it." (Acts 2:22-24)

They had to hear about Jesus, His death, and His resurrection.

But hearing about it wasn't enough. They had to **believe** it. That's why Peter went on to prove it. Peter and the apostles were working miracles, speaking in foreign languages that they didn't know before. Miracles were a sign that what the messenger was saying was truly from God (Mark 16:20). So, when Peter and the apostles were doing miracles, it proved what they were saying was the truth. Peter expected the people to believe what he was saying, because God was backing it up!

They had to believe in Jesus, His death, and His resurrection.

Perhaps you've heard a preacher for some big religious group say "all you have to do is believe, and you'll be saved!" It's also called "faith-only" salvation.

And it doesn't match with the Bible.

Remember what Peter's entire mission was: *to save people*. Now look back at Acts 2 again.

This group of religious, God-fearing, and God-believing men were listening to Peter preach this sermon. They heard about Jesus. They realized that He was the Christ, the Messiah, the one the Old Testament had told about, the one they had been waiting for. And the Bible says this:

And when they heard this, they were cut to the heart. And they said to Peter, and to the rest of the apostles, "Men, brethren! What shall we do?" (Acts 2:37)

If all you have to do is believe in order to be saved, then Peter's answer should have been, "Nothing! You're already saved because you believe!" After all, they wouldn't have asked the question if they didn't believe what Peter had been preaching. But that's not what Peter said. Peter—the man who was receiving his sermon directly from God—said this:

*"**Repent**, all of you." (Acts 2:38)*

The Jews had murdered Jesus less than two months earlier, and Peter stands in the midst of them and tells them all to repent. God was the one speaking through Peter, so God obviously thinks there more to being saved than just believing. But that's not all Peter said.

*"**Be baptized**, every one of you, for the forgiveness of sins." (Acts 2:38)*

God, the one with the power to save people, had Peter preach to *hear* about Jesus, *believe* in Jesus, *repent* of their sins, and *be baptized* to have their sins forgiven.

Do you remember what Saul was told?

"Now, why do you delay? Get up, call on his name, be immersed [baptized], and wash away your sins!" (Acts 22:16)

If Peter's job from God was to save people, and he commanded them to repent and be baptized, what do you think that means for us today?

So many people today are under the delusion that baptism is unimportant. They teach baptism has nothing to do with salvation.

The Bible says they're wrong.

You're a smart person. If the Bible says one thing, and a preacher says something else, who's right? Of course, the Bible is right. Well, take a look at what the Bible says about baptism.

"Therefore, go, and make disciples of all nations: baptizing them...and teaching them to observe all things that I have commanded you." (Matthew 28:19-20)

"The one having believed and having been baptized shall be saved. The one not believing will be damned." (Mark 16:16)

So many people say, *You're wrong. It doesn't say "he that is not baptized shall be damned!" Since baptism isn't mentioned in the last part of the verse, then baptism isn't important!* Let me ask you a really common-sense question. If someone doesn't believe in Jesus, are they ever going to be baptized?

Honestly, did Jesus have to spell it out?

If they didn't believe, they wouldn't be baptized. End of story. There wasn't any need to mention it in the second part of the verse. It's like saying, "He that gets in his car and drives 100 mph will be ticketed, he who doesn't get in his car won't be ticketed." There's no need to mention driving 100 mph in the second part of that statement, because it's already obvious that if you don't get in the car, you wouldn't drive 100 mph in the first place. It's already implied. But let's continue.

You are all the children of God by the faith, in Christ Jesus, because as many of you as were baptized into Christ have put on Christ. (Galatians 3:26-27)

Don't you know that as many of us as were baptized into Jesus Christ were baptized into His death? (Romans 6:3)

Can you be put into something if you're already in it? That may seem like an odd question, so let me ask it a different way. Can someone put you into a room if you are already in that room? Or how about this: can you put your straw into your cup if it is already in your cup? Think about that for a moment. Do you realize how dumb someone would sound if they told you to go into a building when you were already standing inside that building?

The Bible says plainly that when one is baptized, he is baptized *into* Christ. You can't be baptized *into* Christ if you were already *in* Christ. Just like you can't walk *into* a building if you're already inside the building.

In the entire Bible, there are only two verses that say something puts you *into* Christ. And both of them were just given for you: Galatians 3:26-27, and Romans 6:3. And if you'll look at those verses again, you'll see that both times the Bible says that it is *baptism* into Christ.

But let's assume that you're still not convinced. The words of Jesus in Matthew and Mark, and the words of Paul in Galatians and Romans aren't enough to convince you. You want something that comes right out and says "baptism saves you." Ask and ye shall receive.

> *...eight souls [Noah and his family] were saved by water. The antitype of this is **baptism which does also now save us**. It's not the putting off of the filth of the flesh [aka, taking a bath], but asking God for a clean conscience, through Jesus Christ. (1 Peter 3:20-21)*

By now, perhaps it's clear. God says baptism saves. The question is, have *you* been baptized in order to have your sins forgiven? In order to be saved?

The sinner's prayer is not in the Bible. The true plan of salvation, given by God, is in the Bible.

Hear the gospel of Jesus Christ (Acts 2:22, Romans 10:17)

Believe the gospel of Jesus Christ (John 8:24, Romans 10:9)

Repent of your sins (Acts 2:38, 2 Corinthians 7:10)

Confess Jesus Christ (Matthew 10:32-33, Romans 10:9)

Be baptized so that your sins will be forgiven (Acts 2:38, Mark 16:16, 1 Peter 3:21, Colossians 2:11-13, Romans 6:3-5, Galatians 3:26-27).

After doing these things, the Bible says *Be faithful unto death, and I will give you a crown of life* (Revelation 2:10).

If you've not done these things, I beg you to do so now. Don't delay. God's waiting for you. Contact the church of Christ nearest you, and tell them you need to obey the gospel.

www.ingramcontent.com/pod-product-compliance
Lightning Source LLC
Chambersburg PA
CBHW061129120626
46546CB00005B/1720